The Days of Rube,
Matty, Honus and Ty

The Days of Rube, Matty, Honus and Ty
Scenes from the Early Deadball Era, 1904–1907

CHUCK KIMBERLY

McFarland & Company, Inc., Publishers
Jefferson, North Carolina

LIBRARY OF CONGRESS CATALOGUING-IN-PUBLICATION DATA

Names: Kimberly, Chuck, 1940–, author.
Title: The days of Rube, Matty, Honus and Ty : scenes from the early deadball era, 1904–1907 / Chuck Kimberly.
Description: Jefferson : McFarland & Company, Inc., Publishers, 2019 | Includes bibliographical references and index.
Identifiers: LCCN 2018048540 | ISBN 9781476676104 (softcover : acid free paper) ∞
Subjects: LCSH: Baseball—United States—History—20th century. | Baseball players—United States—Biography.
Classification: LCC GV863.A1 K56 2019 | DDC 796.357/6409041—dc23
LC record available at https://lccn.loc.gov/2018048540

BRITISH LIBRARY CATALOGUING DATA ARE AVAILABLE

ISBN (print) 978-1-4766-7610-4
ISBN (ebook) 978-1-4766-3520-0

© 2019 Chuck Kimberly. All rights reserved

No part of this book may be reproduced or transmitted in any form or by any means, electronic or mechanical, including photocopying or recording, or by any information storage and retrieval system, without permission in writing from the publisher.

Front cover: Infielder Germany Schaefer playing with a photographer's camera (Library of Congress)

Printed in the United States of America

McFarland & Company, Inc., Publishers
  Box 611, Jefferson, North Carolina 28640
    www.mcfarlandpub.com

Table of Contents

PREFACE 1

INTRODUCTION: PEACE—EXCEPT IN MANHATTAN 3

One. 1904, National League 13
Surveying the Wartime Damage • M & M & Ms—A Tart Treat: New York • Built for Speed: Chicago • Overcoming Bad Luck: Cincinnati • Grit, Determination, Dissension: Pittsburgh • A Really Good Kid: St. Louis • Trying Too Hard: Brooklyn • When Your Team Is Hopelessly Behind, Again: Boston • A Miracle? Philadelphia • Hard Luck Ned Garvin • Irwin's Handy Invention

Two. 1904, American League 62
A Veritable Dogfight • Winning the Big Game: Boston • A Memorable, Painful, Finish: New York • Working on a Herculean Task: Chicago • Good at Everything but Staying Healthy: Cleveland • Yes, We Can; Yes, We Can. No, We Can't: Philadelphia • Say Goodbye to "The Crab": St. Louis • "A Hit, a Hit, My Franchise for a Hit!": Detroit • Royalty: Washington • Exhibition Series with a "Minor League"—No! • A Violent Year • The Odious Spitball

Three. 1905, National League 105
Make 'Em Throw the Ball • Muggsy's Favorite Team: New York • A Baseball Warrior: Pittsburgh • Zephyrs: Chicago • In the Afterglow—Still Winning: Philadelphia • Second Only to the Babe: Cincinnati • Jack Taylor II: St. Louis • Extreme Frugality: Boston • This Recipe Ain't So Good: Brooklyn

Four. 1905, American League 150
Spitballs! Spitball Pitchers Everywhere! • Aging Well—With an Injection of Youth: Philadelphia • Hitless? Not Quite; Wonders? Almost: Chicago • The Comedic Touch: Detroit • From Champions to "Roly-

v

Polys": Boston • The Answer Is Elmer Flick, .306 in 1905: Cleveland • Oh, What a Relief: New York • Mission Accomplished! Washington • The Man for the Job: St. Louis • "The Matty Show": 1905 World Series

Five. 1906, National League — 191

An Historic Season—116–36! Chicago • Bad Breaks: New York • Competing While Rebuilding: Pittsburgh • Don't Mess with the "Kid": Philadelphia • The Early Deadball Era's Dave Kingman: Brooklyn • Ned Hanlon's "Weeding Out"; Frank Chance's Revenge: Cincinnati • Like Fine Wine: St. Louis • Bright Spots in a Dreary Season: Boston

Six. 1906, American League — 232

Hitless Wonders: Chicago • Not Again! New York • A "Classic" Team: Cleveland • Lave's Absence and Rube's Thumb: Philadelphia • He Don't Look Like a Hitter: St. Louis • A Fighting Team: Detroit • But He Can Hit the Ball a Long Way: Washington • Thud! Boston • The "Slugging Wonders": 1906 World Series

Seven. 1907, National League — 268

Depth: Chicago • Improved Baserunning: Pittsburgh • Working at Their Craft: Philadelphia • Gee, That Sprint Took a Lot Out of Me: New York • Dan's Magical Elixir: Brooklyn • End of an Illustrious Career: Cincinnati • A Landing Zone for Ex-Pirates: Boston • A Potentially Great Player: St. Louis

Eight. 1907, American League — 300

Peace and Ginger Fizz: Detroit • Connie's Veterans Almost Pull It Off: Philadelphia • Baseball's Cinderella Team—The Year After: Chicago • Lajoie—Great Player, Yes; Great Manager, Not So Much: Cleveland • Unraveling: New York • As Red John's World Turns: St. Louis • A Tumultuous Season: Boston • Best Scouting Trip Ever! Washington • Cubs Kling to Victory: 1907 World Series

CHAPTER NOTES — 341
BIBLIOGRAPHY — 353
INDEX — 355

Preface

The years covered by this book, 1904 through 1907, featured some of baseball's most memorable seasons. John McGraw, who led the New York Giants to ten National League pennants, won his first flag in 1904. Following that season McGraw and the Giants' president, John T. Brush, refused to participate in a post-season matchup against the American League champions, the only time since 1903 that the two league champions failed to play each other in the World Series. The next season McGraw won his second pennant with the team he later named as the best he ever managed. The Giants agreed to play the Philadelphia Athletics that year, and were rewarded by one of the finest performances in World Series history, as Christy Mathewson threw three shutouts against the American League champions.

Meanwhile, in Chicago managers Frank Selee and Frank Chance were putting together the team that was arguably the best in Cubs history. In 1906 that team displaced the Giants as the dominant team in the National League, winning pennants in four of the next five years and setting the modern record for most wins and highest winning percentage.

In the American League, Jack Chesbro set a modern record for wins in 1904. He went 41–12 for the New York Highlanders, while demonstrating the effectiveness of a new pitch, the spitball. Adopted by other pitchers the next season, the "wet ball" helped to accelerate the decline in batting brought about by pitchers gradually adjusting to the longer pitching distance instituted in 1893 and the adoption of the modern foul-strike rule, in which the first two balls fouled off counted as strikes. As pitchers gained greater effectiveness, teams adjusted by placing greater emphasis on "scientific baseball," the term then used to describe the strategy now called "inside baseball." The 1906 Chicago White Sox gained a place in baseball lore through their effective use of such tactics, becoming known as the "Hitless Wonders."

This book's approach is intended to reflect the fact that every baseball season presents not one story or theme, but a multitude of them. Each chapter contains a section for each team in the league. For the top teams, the focus is on the club's leading players and its fate in the race for the championship. For second division teams, the discussion might cover notable players, a development affecting the club's position in the standings, or a weakness that led to a decline in performance. For each team a table is included summarizing that season's records for players who appeared in a substantial number of games. Position players are listed by the place they were most often assigned in the batting order during the season. Managers of the early Deadball Era seldom made dramatic changes in their lineups. Therefore, for most teams the tables present a reasonably accurate representation of the normal batting order. They are based on the lineups contained in the *Deadball Stars of the National League* and *Deadball Stars of the American League*, two excellent books by the Deadball Era Committee of the Society for American Baseball Research (SABR).

SABR is one of several organizations which have made baseball research much easier and more effective than it was just a few years ago. In addition to the descriptions of players' careers available in its Biography Project, SABR offers access to valuable information through internet sites such as Paper of Record, which has issues of *The Sporting News* and LA84 Foundation, which features issues of *Sporting Life* and *Baseball Magazine*. Newspaper coverage for the Deadball Era is available at several websites. Much useful statistical data can be found at the Baseball Reference and Retrosheet sites. The statistical tables included in this book are based on data provided by Retrosheet. All baseball researchers, including the author, owe a debt of gratitude to the people who have made this information available.

The author also wishes to express his thankfulness to his wife, Ana, and his son, Danny, for their patience and understanding regarding the amount of time required for researching and writing this book.

Introduction:
Peace—Except in Manhattan

For major league baseball, the winter of 1903–04 was a time for healing. During each of the previous five years the off-season had been marked by moves that shook the foundations of league stability.

From 1892 to 1899 the National League was an awkward conglomeration of the 12 teams that had survived a ruinous confrontation between the major league players and the owners of the two major leagues of the time, the National League and the American Association. Several franchises in the league struggled in the rough economic climate that existed in the late 90s. Following the 1898 season the owners of the tenth-place Brooklyn Bridegrooms and the second-place Baltimore Orioles decided to merge their holdings, with the players of the two teams coming under the control of a single group of owners. The Brooklyn team, re-christened the Superbas, was given the pick of the players, with the Orioles getting the leftovers. On the field the merger worked out pretty well. The Superbas, who featured several of the outstanding players of the pennant-winning Orioles of 1894–96, were a great team, winning the flag two years in a row. The Orioles were pretty good, too, finishing fourth in 1899, largely because two of their former Baltimore stars—John McGraw and Wilbert Robinson—refused to play in Brooklyn. McGraw served as the Orioles' manager, gaining praise for his team's scrappy style of play and condemnation for his continual umpire baiting.

That same off-season two other teams combined ownership. Frank DeHaas Robison and his brother Stanley, who owned the fifth-place Cleveland Spiders, obtained control of the last-place St. Louis Browns. The Spiders were a highly-regarded team that had seemed to underperform the preceding two years after finishing second to the Orioles in 1895 and 1896. The Browns were a terrible team, compiling a 39–111 record in 1898. The Cleveland-St. Louis merger was a complete failure. St. Louis got first call on the combined organization's players, but simply replaced Cleveland as a disappointing fifth-place team. The Spiders, left with a group of borderline major league players whose fans called them "The Misfits" by season's end, went 20–134. Their won-lost record was the worst in major league history and they finished 84 games behind the Superbas.[1]

The winter of 1899–1900 brought even more drastic changes. Barney Dreyfuss, the principal owner of the Louisville Colonels, became a minority owner of the Pittsburgh Pirates. He acquired 47 percent of the Pirates' stock and was named the team's President. Shortly afterwards a deal was completed in which Pittsburgh sent five players and $25,000 in cash to Louisville in exchange for Louisville's top 14 players. In retrospect, it is apparent this deal was made as a prelude to the big reorganization that was about to spring forth.[2]

In December, at the annual National League meeting, the owners of three teams—Dreyfuss' Louisville Colonels, the Cleveland Spiders, and the Washington Senators—agreed to sell their teams to the League. A circuit committee was formed to negotiate the terms of the sale with the representatives of these three teams and to deal with the Baltimore owners, who had turned down the price offered by the League. Pressured by threats to saddle their team with undesirable playing dates and high travel costs, the Baltimore owners eventually backed down. In March a settlement was reached by which the four franchises and their playing grounds were surrendered to the league. The Washington owners also agreed to transfer their players to the league.[3]

The reduction from 12 to eight teams resulted in a dramatic upgrading of the talent in the remaining National League franchises. Seven of the eight clubs added players from the four defunct organizations, eliminating weak spots in their 1899 lineups and adding depth to other parts of the team.[4] The other club, the Cincinnati Reds, took a different approach. The Reds owner, John T. Brush, had a disagreeable personality, but he was a shrewd operator. Aware that the minor leagues would be largely ignored in the rush to sign players freed up by the league reduction, Brush decided to go after the best young players available. In the spring of 1900, when asked which players he planned to sign, Brush told a reporter, "The Reds are a strong team. Last fall we purchased the players that were considered the cream of the minor leagues."[5] The Reds finished seventh in 1900, but the players Brush acquired for that season included a Hall of Fame outfielder (Sam Crawford), three others who became star players (Kid Elberfeld, Socks Seybold, and Jimmy Barrett) and a pitcher who later was recognized as one of the game's top left-handed pitchers (Casey Patten). Unfortunately for Brush and the Reds, because of future developments these stars and several of the Reds' other new players made their reputations with other teams.

The abandonment of four of the nation's largest cities, all having well-established associations with major league baseball, provided an opening for a group of ambitious baseball men. The owners of the principal minor league in the Midwest, the Western League, had reorganized in the fall of 1899, with a view of eventually challenging the National League's dominance of organized baseball. They moved one of their franchises from St. Paul to Chicago, put a team in Cleveland, and changed the organization's name to the American League. During the winter of 1900–01 they declared themselves a major league on a par with the National League. They placed teams in Washington and Baltimore and established rival clubs in Boston and Philadelphia. More importantly, they began to secretly recruit the older league's players, setting off a "baseball war."[6]

The American League quickly gained momentum in the confrontation. When the 1901 season opened its rosters included about 40 players who had jumped from the National League. About a dozen of these were men whose names routinely appeared in newspaper articles discussing hypothetical all-star teams. There were also about two dozen players who had dropped into the minors after the consolidation of 1900, but whose names would have been familiar to baseball fans. The American League of 1901 was still weaker than its opponent—a well-respected writer estimated in June that the National League was about 50 percent better[7]—but most fans seemed to feel it offered a high caliber of baseball. In Boston and Chicago the American League clubs outdrew their National League counterparts by wide margins, and in Philadelphia the Athletics attracted almost as many fans as the Phillies.

American League agents continued their raiding efforts during the 1901 season. In late July the Pirates released shortstop Fred Ely, accusing him of working for the rival league. In August reports surfaced that several Phillies players, including star slugger Ed Delahanty, had agreed to play for American League teams in 1902. The National League also had operatives working for its interests, reportedly offering high salaries to two Detroit players. The clandestine meetings became so frequent that in mid–September the Athletics' Lave Cross announced he had signed with the A's for 1902. Cross said he had asked owner Connie Mack to settle with him for 1902 so National League agents would stop annoying him.[8]

By Opening Day of 1902 it was apparent the American League had gained the upper hand. At least 33 players had left their 1901 National League teams to join the new league. Nine players jumped in the other direction, but seven of those nine were players who probably would have lost their starting jobs if they had remained with their previous teams. Tim Murnane, baseball editor of the *Boston Globe*, summarized the difference between the two leagues. He predicted a hot pennant race in the junior circuit. "The public are prepared to see the real thing in baseball this season when they visit an American League grounds," Murnane wrote. "The same is not true of the National League, for the reason that the old organization has not the goods to offer, and bluff teams will be discovered in short order by the baseball public who know a ballplayer when they see him perform."[9]

The situation was becoming so dire for their side that the National League owners finally decided to forget their long-standing intra-league hostilities and adopt a unified counter-strategy. They pledged to contribute to a $100,000 war fund to tempt players back to their side. On April 21, 1902, they received good news. A year earlier they had sought an injunction prohibiting Napoleon Lajoie and two other Phillies from jumping to the new league. The court had turned down the injunction, stating that the standard baseball contract was so lop-sided in binding the player to the club, but not the club to the player, that it lacked mutuality. The decision was appealed, and after pondering the issue for nearly 12 months the Pennsylvania State Supreme Court upheld the injunction. Citing the decision the owners demanded the return of all the players who had jumped from its teams into the new league. After taking a couple days to gather their wits, the American League responded with a legal opinion stating that, since the decision was issued by a state court, it applied only in the state of Pennsylvania. Therefore, only the ex-Phillies players were affected, and only when they were playing in Pennsylvania.

Only a few players changed teams as a result of the legal wrangling. Chick Fraser and Bill Duggleby, both pitchers who had left the Phillies to sign with the Athletics, jumped back to the Phillies. (Fraser was one of the three players named in the injunction.) Jimmy Sheckard, who had signed with Baltimore in 1901, but jumped back to the Superbas before the season started, had again signed with the Orioles for the 1902 season. After receiving news of the Pennsylvania Supreme Court's decision, he jumped back to the Superbas for the second year in a row. The other two players besides Fraser who were named in the injunction, Nap Lajoie and Bill Bernhard, were inactive for several weeks before signing with the Cleveland Blues. Elmer Flick, another former Phillie signed by Mack, also decided to play for Cleveland, arriving there about three weeks before Lajoie and Bernhard.

The National League struck again in July. This time the blow came from John McGraw, who had been a driving force in establishing the American League. McGraw was part owner and manager of the Baltimore Orioles. He and Ban Johnson, the league's autocratic president, had clashed on numerous occasions over McGraw's constant arguing with umpires. After receiving an indefinite suspension for cursing an umpire, McGraw lashed out in anger against Johnson. He claimed he was losing money in Baltimore because of Johnson's unfair treatment of him and his team. On July 7, he announced that after several weeks of discussions with Andrew Freedman, President of the New York Giants, he had come to an agreement to manage the Giants. The next day he arranged to sell all his shares in the Orioles and departed for New York. Shortly thereafter six of the Orioles' top players jumped to the National League, four of them going to New York and two to Cincinnati.

Johnson acted quickly to resolve the crisis. Acting under a league rule giving him authority to take control of any franchise unable to field a team, he issued a call for help from other American League teams, and cobbled together a team to finish the schedule. Ironically, McGraw's betrayal helped Johnson achieve one of his primary goals. He had been hoping to place a team in New York City, the nation's largest metropolis. Baltimore's troubles gave him a reason to shift McGraw's former franchise there in 1903, where it would compete with the ex-Oriole's new team.[10]

The two leagues continued to fight each other through the end of the year. By then the owners in both organizations had grown weary of the struggle and worried about the rapid escalation of player salaries. When the National League owners gathered for their annual meeting in December, St. Louis owner Frank DeHaas Robison suggested the formation of a committee to negotiate an end to the conflict. The dominant personality among the owners, John T. Brush, who had sold his interest in the Reds and replaced Freedman as the President of the Giants, was eager to continue the fight. But the majority supported Robison's motion. That evening a group of owners approached Ban Johnson, who was in New York at the time, to ask him if his colleagues were willing to enter into negotiations. Johnson told them his league would welcome such discussions.

The peace negotiations took place in January. The National League owners craved peace so much they were not only willing to concede territorial rights in the four cities already shared by the two organizations, but also recognized the new league's right to put a team in New York City. The negotiators reached agreement on these and several other matters fairly quickly on the first day. They had a more difficult time, however, when they began to discuss the 15 or more disputed players. The American League's Henry Killilea asserted that his league would never consent to the loss of Ed Delahanty or George Davis, denouncing the tactics used by McGraw and Brush when they enticed the two players to sign with the Giants. Killilea's self-righteous tone angered the National League negotiators, who gave examples of dirty tactics employed by Killilea's associates over the previous two years. At that point Cincinnati owner Garry Herrmann interrupted his colleagues. He said he had a social engagement he needed to attend, and suggested that the negotiators think the matter over and try to start over in calmer moods the next morning.

When they returned the next day, negotiators on both sides had concluded they had too much to lose if they let the peace agreement fall by the wayside because of a few players who sought to enrich themselves by playing the teams off against each other. Herrmann set an example for the other owners by announcing he would forego his claim on Sam Crawford, thereby letting him go to Detroit. "If we cannot parcel these rascally players among our teams in a way that will suit both leagues, it would be better to put them all on the ineligible list than to quarrel over them," he said. The negotiators then proceeded to "parcel" the remaining disputed players. They could not agree upon a system that would produce a result they could all live with, so they discussed each case individually. The general guideline that drove their decisions seemed to be that each league sought to protect its New York franchise without being too unfair to the other teams. Another unspoken assumption seemed to be that if the Brooklyn Superbas got hurt by a decision, that was all right.

About half of the disputed players were claimed by the New York Giants. Both during and after the 1902 season John McGraw had kept himself busy identifying potential jumpers and tempting them with fat contracts. He didn't seem to care whether they were covered by existing contractual commitments. Of course, McGraw was by no means the only baseball executive who displayed that attitude. The committee protected the Giants' interests by letting them keep Christy Mathewson and Frank Bowerman, who had signed with the St. Louis Browns in May before later agreeing to contracts with the Giants. They also awarded Sam Mertes to the Giants. (Mertes was also claimed by the Chicago White Stockings.) Three other players—George Davis (Chicago), Ed Delahanty (Washington), and Kid Elberfeld (Detroit)—all of whom were covered by two-year contracts extending through 1903 when McGraw signed them, were awarded to their original teams. Dave Fultz, who was a free agent, had listened to McGraw's entreaties and then signed a contract with the American League's new team, the New York Highlanders. McGraw claimed him, but Fultz denied having signed any agreement with the Giants. The peace negotiators awarded him to the Highlanders. McGraw also claimed Boston catcher John Warner. The negotiators didn't seem to know whether there was any substance to McGraw's claim, so they awarded him to the Giants on the condition that they produce an agreement dated prior to the peace agreement.[11]

Given the fact that most of these players were already committed to other teams when they signed with the Giants, most neutral observers would conclude that the peace negotiators had tried to deal fairly with the Giants, and possibly had favored them somewhat. But Giants President John T. Brush was enraged by the peace agreement. Upon hearing of the agreement's terms, Brush responded, "The report seems incomplete. There surely must be more than I have read. There should be some account of the National League Committee losing their pocketbooks to the Committee from the American League."[12]

Brush was, of course, upset by the territorial concession allowing an American League team in New York, as well as the allocation of players. Within a few days he obtained a preliminary court injunction prohibiting the league from enforcing the peace agreement.

Although Brush was used to having his way with his fellow owners, he found them unwilling to follow his lead when they met to consider ratifying the peace agreement. On the contrary, the owners seemed to have united in opposition to Brush. One of the first items of business was a letter from Philadelphia owner John I. Rogers protesting the New York club's claim to Delahanty. Rogers insisted Brush had violated an agreement of the previous September by signing Delahanty. He threatened to sue Brush over the matter. Later one of the Cincinnati owners offered a resolution requiring the New York club to put up a large bond to insure the National League against damage as a result of Brush's legal move. That resolution passed by a 6–1 vote, with Brooklyn opposing and New York abstaining. The owners ended the conference, which lasted two days, by ratifying the peace agreement, voting 6–2 on five articles of the agreement and 6–0 on the other three, with Brooklyn and New York either in opposition or abstaining.[13]

With the National League's ratification of the agreement, baseball followers voiced their satisfaction with the end of the baseball war. But the fighting had not quite ended. The agreement required players to return any advance payments they had received from teams whose contracts were not recognized in the peace agreement. Two players, George Davis and Ed Delahanty, had received large advances from the Giants. Neither player wanted to return the money, and both wanted to play for the Giants, who had offered much more money than they were to receive from the teams they played for in 1902. Delahanty, who had lost heavily betting on horse races during the off-season, eventually agreed to report to Washington, his debt to the Giants paid by the Senators on the understanding that it would be taken out of his pay over the next two years. Davis, however, refused to report to the White Stockings, as required in the peace agreement.

Davis's contract with the Giants allowed him to be paid even if he did not play any games for the team. He went to spring training with the Giants, but did not play for them when the season began. Upon the advice of his lawyer, he went to the Polo Grounds each day to fulfill the legal requirement of offering his services to the Giants. But, reportedly, he spent most of his afternoons at the race track. He had been advanced $2,750 of his $4,000 salary, but by early May his bankroll seemed to be getting thin. He contacted Charlie Comiskey, who sent him some money and arranged for transportation to Chicago. Davis changed his mind, however, probably at the behest of Brush or McGraw. He remained in New York.

In June the Detroit Tigers suspended shortstop Kid Elberfeld for lackadaisical playing. They announced that Elberfeld would never again play for the team, and then traded him to the New York Highlanders. The Elberfeld trade was the excuse Brush had been looking for, both to activate Davis and to rekindle the war between the two major leagues. Brush claimed the Elberfeld deal violated the peace agreement. He talked the National League's President, Harry Pulliam, into allowing him to activate Davis.

Upon learning of Brush's move Ban Johnson exploded in a rage. He reminded Pulliam that several National League clubs, including the Giants, had sent players to Philadelphia in an effort to strengthen the Phillies, even though the American League also had a franchise in that city.[14] When it seemed as if a majority of the other league's owners were willing to support Brush, Johnson issued a stern warning. "If the American League is forced into another war," he declared, "I am here to say that there will be no peace until the National League has been completely annihilated."[15]

Baseball's followers groaned with disappointment at the prospect that the baseball war would be reignited. It seemed that the national pastime was in the hands of men who were not responsible. Tim Murnane of the *Boston Globe* lamented, "Just when everything looked peaceful in baseball along comes the irresistible John T. Brush and starts more trouble.

New York Giants owner John T. Brush disliked the 1903 peace agreement between the American and National leagues and tried to sabotage it (Library of Congress).

Strange that it should be this individual that has started every good-sized trouble in major league ball for the last 14 years, and is now in a position to keep the thing going as long as he lives."[16]

The National League scheduled a meeting for July 20 to take an official stand on the issue. Newspaper reporters did not know what to expect from the meeting, but many thought Brush would carry the day. Behind the scenes, however, Brush was beginning to lose support among his colleagues. When the National League owners came together Brush found himself standing alone in his desire to repudiate the peace agreement. The owners voted 7–1 to prohibit the Giants from playing Davis in any more games. Six weeks later the two major leagues concluded their negotiations with the minor leagues, establishing a new National Agreement.[17]

Peace once again descended upon the baseball world, except perhaps on the small part of Manhattan occupied by the offices of the New York National League baseball club.

One

1904, National League

Surveying the Wartime Damage

Although all the National League teams had been weakened by the American League raids, the damage had not been spread evenly. Three franchises had emerged from the struggle well-equipped to compete at the somewhat watered-down performance level of 16 teams dividing up major league talent, rather than the eight or 12 competitors that existed before the baseball war.

The Pittsburgh Pirates had finished second in the high-quality competition of 1900. They were only marginally affected by player defections in 1901 and 1902, winning the pennant both years. The 1902 Pirates were far superior to the other National League teams that season, going 103–36 and finishing 27½ games ahead of the second place Brooklyn Superbas. However, the last American League raid, in 1902, took away five Pirates. The biggest losses were Jack Chesbro and Jesse Tannehill, half of the starting pitchers who had been one of the team's strengths. Chesbro had posted a 28–6 record in 1902, while Tannehill went 20–6, with a 1.95 ERA. The other three defectors were shortstop Wid Conroy, outfielder Lefty Davis, and catcher Jack O'Connor. O'Connor's departure, combined with the retirement of Chief Zimmer, left the Pirates with a comparably inexperienced catching staff. Nevertheless, the Pirates had been so much better than the rest of the league that were still able to grab their third straight pennant in 1903.

The New York Giants finished last in 1900 and 1902, rising as high as seventh place in 1901. They were a weak team over most of those three years. But in July of 1902 John McGraw began a quick and effective overhaul. He brought four good players with him from Baltimore, including star pitcher Joe McGinnity. During the summer and fall he devoted considerable energy to signing players for 1903, landing three more solid players. Had the peace negotiators allowed New York to keep outfielder Dave Fultz and future Hall of Famers Ed Delahanty and George Davis, the Giants might have been able to nose out the Pirates in the 1903 pennant race. Even without those stars, the Giants finished second. They were a good defensive team and finished third in batting average. But their strength was in their two star pitchers, Joe McGinnity and Christy Mathewson, who hurled about two-thirds of the staff's total innings pitched and were credited with 61 of the team's 81 wins.

The Chicago club, which had just acquired the new nickname "Cubs" in 1902, finished fifth, sixth, and fifth from 1900 to 1902. The 1901 team, dubbed the "Remnants" by a *Chicago Tribune* writer because it was composed of the leftovers after the more sought-after players went elsewhere,[1] ended up 37 games behind the first-place Pirates, one game ahead of the last-place Reds. It earned sixth place by posting a won-lost percentage that was .001 ahead of the seventh place Giants, who also finished 37 games out of first. The Cubs hired a new manager in 1902, bringing in Frank Selee, who had won five pennants with the Boston Beaneaters during the 1890s.

Selee followed a rebuilding plan centered around a policy of acquiring a few journeyman major leaguers from other teams to provide a measure of stability and filtering through a steady stream of young minor leaguers. He awarded a starting job to catcher Johnny Kling, a holdover from the 1901 team, and tried to find a new position for Frank Chance. Chance was a good hitter and a decent catcher, but kept getting hurt. The Cubs' 1901 manager had tried him in the outfield, but without much success. Selee let Chance do some catching, but gave him a trial at first base after a minor league recruit had proved insufficient. The experiment was successful enough in 1902 for Selee to make the change permanent the following year. Among the minor leaguers tried out in 1902 there were two pretty good infielders—shortstop Joe Tinker and second baseman Johnny Evers—and an effective pitcher, Carl Lundgren. In 1903 the Cubs added two more talented pitchers, Jake Weimer and Bob Wicker. That year the Cubs' three top pitchers, Weimer, Wicker and veteran Jack Taylor, won 20, 20, and 21 games, respectively, matching the win total of the two Giants stars, McGinnity and Mathewson.[2]

These three teams—the Pirates, Giants, and Cubs—had built, or in the Pirates' case retained, a solid core of above-average players. All three remained strong for years. They won all the National League pennants over the next ten years and usually monopolized the first three positions in the standings. The remaining five faced serious rebuilding needs. Nearly a decade passed before any of them mounted a serious challenge for the National League pennant. Twice during the next decade one of the five managed to edge out one of the big three for third place, and once—in 1913—one of them climbed all the way up to second place.

At the end of the 1903 season, it appeared that there would be five strong teams, rather than three.[3] The fourth-place Cincinnati Reds and the fifth-place Brooklyn Superbas both had finished several games over .500

in 1903. The Reds finished 8½ games out of third and the Superbas trailed the third-place Cubs by 11 games. But there was a bigger gap separating the Superbas from the bottom three teams.

The Reds had benefited from the implosion of the Baltimore Orioles in 1902. Joe Kelley and Cy Seymour, both outstanding players, came from Baltimore as part of McGraw's rebellion against Ban Johnson. Mike Donlin, who possessed elite baseball talent, came indirectly from Baltimore by way of a Maryland prison after serving time for a drunken assault on an actress friend during the off-season.[4] This trio combined with veteran first baseman Jake Beckley and young third baseman Harry Steinfeldt to form one of the most potent offenses in the league in 1903.

By 1903 the Superbas had lost most of the players from their great teams of 1899 and 1900. Manager Ned Hanlon had acquired a conglomeration of veterans who played well enough to keep the club competitive. The team got a boost from two pitchers imported from the independent California League. One of them, Henry Schmidt, threw a variety of curves that puzzled National League batters throughout the 1903 season. Schmidt went 22–13 and ended the season with a nine-game winning streak. But he missed his wife, who had remained in California, and decided to sign with a West Coast team again in 1904.[5] He left behind a fine major league career record—1903 was his only major league season—and a team that badly needed his services in 1904.

The bottom three teams of 1903—Boston, St. Louis, and Philadelphia—had at least a couple of features in common. One was that they all shared their cities with American League teams. Another was that by 1903 almost all of their 1900 stars were playing in the rival league. The Beaneaters were the most successful of the three because they had held on to Fred Tenney and Vic Willis, two top-notch players from their pennant winning years, and Togie Pittinger, a talented pitcher who had come to the team in 1900. The Cardinals and Phillies were still trying to recover from the American League raids preceding the 1902 season. During that off-season the Cardinals lost three-fourths of their infield, two-thirds of their outfield and three-fourths of their starting rotation. The Phillies lost nine players at that time, but two returned as a result of the court decision in the Lajoie case, and a third returned in mid-season because he was unhappy with his new team.[6]

1904 National League Standings

Team	W	L	Pct.	GB
New York	106	47	.693	—
Chicago	93	60	.608	13
Cincinnati	88	65	.575	18
Pittsburgh	87	66	.569	19

Team	W	L	Pct.	GB
St. Louis	75	79	.487	31.5
Brooklyn	56	97	.366	50
Boston	55	98	.359	51
Philadelphia	52	100	.342	53.5

M & M & Ms—A Tart Treat: New York

In the early sixties the great New York Yankee teams featured the "M & M Boys," Mickey Mantle and Roger Maris. In 1904 the champion New York Giants team was led by the "M & M & M Boys," John McGraw, Joe McGinnity, and Christy Mathewson

McGraw put the team together and set the tone on the field. Although he no longer played very often (he appeared in five games in 1904), he was a very active presence on the field. He often coached third base, and constantly jawed at the umpires. McGraw was widely criticized for his rowdy behavior on the field and his team earned a reputation as the rowdiest team in baseball. "New York is not a popular team around the circuit, nor is it composed of parlor babies. There's no mamma's darling business about the New Yorks," said a Chicago writer. "They are more like the Baltimore rowdies, in whose school McGraw, [Frank] Bowerman, [Dan] McGann, and McGinnity were educated. They play ball, they chew at the umpire, and they raise old Ned generally."[7]

In most games McGraw's men were just loud, tough competitors. However, they were constantly pushing the limits of what could be considered acceptable behavior. McGraw was 31 years old, but at times he acted like a bad-mannered teenager. In Philadelphia, for instance, he spit at catcher Red Dooin. When Dooin approached him after the game for a man-to-man confrontation over the act, McGraw ran away. In a Brooklyn game he called Oscar Jones several "vile" names. After that game he hid behind his players so Jones could not confront him over the name-calling. In Cincinnati it was the umpire who had to withstand a steady flow of cursing from the Giants' manager and his players.[8]

New York (106–47)

Regular Lineup	AVG	OBP	SLG	R	RBI	SB
Roger Bresnahan, cf	.284	.381	.410	81	33	13
George Browne, rf	.284	.332	.347	99	39	24
Art Devlin, 3b	.281	.371	.354	81	66	33
Dan McGann, 1b	.286	.354	.387	81	71	42

Regular Lineup	AVG	OBP	SLG	R	RBI	SB
Sam Mertes, lf	.276	.346	.393	83	78	47
or Moose McCormick, cf	.266	.323	.374	28	26	13
Bill Dahlen, ss	.268	.326	.337	70	80	47
or Jack Dunn, ut	.309	.356	.414	27	19	11
Billy Gilbert, 2b	.253	.340	.299	57	54	33
John Warner, c	.199	.253	.233	29	15	7
or Frank Bowerman, c	.232	.288	.318	38	27	7

Leading Pitchers	W	L	PCT.	IP	H	ERA
Joe McGinnity	35	8	.814	408	307	1.61
Christy Mathewson	33	12	.733	367.7	306	2.03
Dummy Taylor	21	15	.583	296.3	231	2.34
Hooks Wiltse	13	3	.813	164.7	150	2.84
Red Ames	4	6	.400	115	94	2.27

In July the Giants exchanged obscene insults with Cincinnati fans throughout a game. After the game McGraw continued the quarrel by shouting at people passing by in streetcars, threatening to punch out a few of them. On their next trip to Cincinnati the Giants resumed their quarrel with the Cincinnati fans. This time obscenities seemed insufficient, so Frank Bowerman went into the stands and slugged a fan. He was arrested and taken to a police station, but released without being charged.

In St. Louis the Giants trailed the Cardinals 1–0 going into the ninth inning. With one out Jack Warner singled. McGraw put himself into the game as a pinch-runner for Warner. The next batter, Roger Bresnahan, drove a pitch into left field, the ball bouncing past the fielder. McGraw scored from first base on the hit. As Bresnahan rounded first base he was joined in his trip around the bases by Billy Gilbert, who was coaching first base. When Bresnahan and Gilbert approached third base, other Giant players gathered there. Bresnahan stopped at third, but one of the Giants in the group around third broke for home, drawing a throw from Jake Beckley, the Cardinals first baseman. In the confusion, the Cardinals' catcher had left the plate uncovered, so the throw went wild and Bresnahan sprinted home with what proved to be the winning run. Although the Cardinals lodged a protest, neither the umpires nor National League President Pulliam saw fit to overturn the play.[9]

During the 1904 season National League umpires threw McGraw out of seven games. Dan McGann and Bill Dahlen were ejected four times each. Only two Giant regulars—rookie Art Devlin and right fielder George Browne—failed to be dismissed. McGinnity and utilityman Jack Dunn were each thrown out once. Doc Marshall, a catcher who was with the team briefly, evidently felt he had to be sent packing by an umpire in order to be one of the boys. Although he played in only ten games he managed to get thrown out of one of them. Altogether, McGraw and his players totaled a combined 28 ejections in 1904. By comparison, the Reds were second with 15 ejections, six of those by Manager Joe Kelley, McGraw's former teammate with the Baltimore Orioles. Among the other contenders, the Cubs had five players ejected and Pirates three. One of the Pirates thrown out of a game was Honus Wagner, who became furious when McGraw, coaching at third base for the Giants, called out for Wagner to throw the ball to third on a play. In fielding the ball Wagner had gotten into a position where he could not see third base. He made the play believing the instruction had come from third baseman Tommy Leach. After the play Wagner protested so vigorously the umpire sent him to the bench.[10]

McGraw was widely condemned for his pugnacious behavior. On the other hand, he was highly praised for his managerial accomplishments. A typical comment came from a St. Louis writer who lauded McGraw for his success with the Giants. "McGraw has used his team with splendid judgment," the writer said. "There are few who realize the great amount of baseball knowledge possessed by the New York manager regarding baseball, its players, and the men who are connected with the game."[11]

John McGraw was criticized for his team's rowdy behavior, but praised for his knowledge of the game (Library of Congress).

McGraw's knowledge of the game was shown by the improvement he made in the Giants in less than two years. He took over a last place team in July of 1902 and built it into a second-place team in 1903, largely through raids on American League teams. Entering the 1904 season, McGraw knew his team still had some holes that needed to be filled despite their high ranking in the standings the previous year. Billy Lauder, the third baseman, had suffered a career-ending eye injury. Center fielder George Van Haltren was 37 in 1903 and had begun to show his age. Van Haltren batted only .257 that year, and lost his job to Roger Bresnahan in midseason. Bresnahan had begun the 1903 season as McGraw's super-utilityman before replacing Van

Haltren, and McGraw apparently intended to use him in a utility role again in 1904. Shortstop Charlie Babb was at best a journeyman major leaguer. He was somewhat stiff in the field and was only an average hitter. Two starting pitchers McGraw had brought over from the American League in 1902, Roscoe Miller and Jack Cronin, had pitched poorly with the Giants and were relegated to backup roles before the 1903 season was very old.

McGraw, characteristically, was as aggressive in addressing these shortcomings as he had been in raiding the American League earlier. As the manager of the dominant team in baseball's biggest city, he operated from a position of great strength. In his most important move, he took advantage of the financial weakness of the other National League team in the greater New York area, the Brooklyn Superbas. He traded Babb and Cronin, two players he no longer held in high regard, for Bill Dahlen, one of the top shortstops in baseball. Throughout baseball the trade was generally considered a salary dump by the Superbas, who could no longer afford Dahlen's high salary.[12]

To replace Lauder and Van Haltren, McGraw purchased two of the best prospects in the minor leagues, Art Devlin and Harry "Moose" McCormick. Devlin had a fine rookie season, and remained the Giants' starting third baseman through the 1911 season. McCormick played well for the Giants, but his most valuable contribution to the team on a long-term basis may have come in the manner in which he left the team. He was part of a three-way trade in August that brought Mike Donlin to the Giants. Donlin was a difficult man to manage, but he possessed baseball talent on a level with the best Deadball Era players.

To strengthen his pitching staff, McGraw added Red Ames and Hooks Wiltse. Ames had joined the team at the end of the 1903 season. In his debut he pitched a five-inning no-hitter against St. Louis. Not one Cardinal batter managed to get the ball out of the infield against Ames and seven struck out. He made one more start in 1903, beating Pittsburgh 7–2. He struck out seven Pirate batters, including Honus Wagner twice in succession. Ames' stuff was so good it began to be mentioned in awed tones before he pitched a major league inning. Frank Bowerman caught the young pitcher when he was auditioning for the Giants. Bowerman said that after he caught a few fastballs, Ames shook off his signal for another fastball. Bowerman prepared to receive a breaking pitch. "The ball he sent me had speed," Bowerman said, "and I kept waiting for it to break. When within about two feet it shot in and down so suddenly that I could not get my glove in front. Although it hit on the leg I almost lost consciousness, so terrible was the pain." McGraw said he had never seen anything to compare with Ames' speed, and insisted Ames had the sharpest curves he had ever seen.[13] During spring training of 1904 Ames came down with a sore arm. McGraw rarely used him during the first half of the season, and spotted him as the fifth starter during the second half. Ames won 22 games for the Giants in 1905 and remained with them until 1913, when he was traded to St. Louis. Except for the 1905 season he did not live up to his potential while with the Giants. He later had several good seasons with Cincinnati and St. Louis, retiring after the 1919 season with a career won-lost record of 183–167.

Hooks Wiltse, a left-hander with a sharp breaking ball, pitched for the Giants for a decade, twice winning over 20 games. His role in 1904 was secondary. The Giants already had an effective third starter. Dummy Taylor had been an able pitcher for the Giants since 1900. Wiltse was nominally the Giants' fourth starter, but given the way McGraw handled the Giants' pitching staff, that was the equivalent of being an extra pitcher on most other teams.

In preseason predictions, the Giants were generally viewed as a potential contender, with big questions remaining to be answered. The Giants had depended heavily upon McGinnity and Mathewson for their 1903 success, and it was by no means certain the two stars would pitch as well in 1904. The trade for Dahlen had strengthened the infield, but third base remained a question, as did center field. Even McGraw was considered an uncertainty. He had been a great asset to the team in 1903, but his track record as a manager was by no means one of unbroken success. He had been a managerial prodigy in 1899 as the leader of the Baltimore end of the Brooklyn-Baltimore syndicate. But with the American League Orioles he hurt the team more than he helped it with his constant umpire baiting. And he had not been able to lift the 1902 Giants out of the basement. Ira "Sy" Sanborn of the *Chicago Tribune* probably voiced a widespread view when he wrote that the Giants had "several uncertainties" in its lineup. In assessing the team's chances in 1904, Sanborn concluded, "I look for McGraw's team to be awful good this year or awful bad."[14]

The Giants, of course, turned out to be "awful good." It didn't hurt at all that they opened the season against the league's three weakest teams, Brooklyn, Boston, and Philadelphia. They were 12–3 before they played a game against the Western Division, where the other league powers were located. They stumbled a bit on their first western trip, winning eight and losing seven, dropping a few games behind Cincinnati and Chicago. Through the middle of June the Giants, Cubs, and Reds battled for the lead in what seemed to be the beginning of a close, exciting race. At that point, however, the Giants took advantage of a soft spot in their schedule to blow the race wide open. They won 18 games in a row, 17 against the Eastern Division bottom feeders and one against fifth-place St. Louis. By the time the streak ended they had built up a 10½-game lead over the Reds and Cubs. They maintained a sizeable lead through the rest of the season, at one point moving 19 games ahead of the second-place Cubs.

Chief Zimmer, the veteran catcher who had turned to umpiring in 1904, rated the 1904 Giants as one of the best teams he had ever seen. "No National League team has played as good baseball in years as the New Yorks are putting up," Zimmer told a reporter. "In the first place they have good material on their team; and then they play the game for all there is in it.... No opportunities are overlooked and the least weakness shown by their opponents is taken full advantage of by the New Yorks. They are in all points of the game, and they play them for all they are worth."[15]

No matter how good their teamwork or how spirited their play, the Giants would not have run away from the other National League teams without the other two members of the M & M & M combination, McGinnity and Mathewson. Although McGraw worked hard to strengthen his pitching staff going into the 1904 season, and seemed to have been successful in doing so, when the season started he was unwilling to trust his young pitchers. He used a three-man rotation of McGinnity, Mathewson, and Taylor until the Giants built a sizable lead, using his other pitchers sparingly, for the most part bringing them into games only after either the Giants or their opponents had a game under control.

Entering the 1904 season, McGinnity had completed five seasons in the major leagues. As a 28-year old rookie with McGraw's fourth-place Baltimore team in 1899 he had led the National League in wins, going 28–16. The next year, playing with the pennant-winning Brooklyn Superbas, he led the league with a 28–8 record. Continuing to move around the baseball map, he won 26 games with the American League Orioles in 1901 and had a combined 21–18 record in 1902 with the Orioles and Giants. In 1903 he went 31–20, giving him an average of 26.8 wins per season at that point in his career.

When he arrived at Baltimore in 1899, McGinnity was at times referred to as the "Indian Territory" man, because for a number of years his family had lived in the area that is now Oklahoma but was then known by that name. By the end of his second season, however, he was being called the "Iron Man," ostensibly because he owned and worked in an iron foundry.[16] Some other ballplayers at the time were also identified in newspaper articles by their youthful non-baseball occupations, but such nicknames seldom gained widespread currency. "Iron Man" became a big part of McGinnity's identity because it described one of his foremost traits as a pitcher. At a time when pitchers logged a lot of innings, McGinnity pitched more than anyone else, appearing as a reliever when a game had to be saved as well as starting nearly 40 games almost every season. He led the league in innings pitched in four of his first six years and was in the top six in nine of his ten major league campaigns. Over his career he averaged over 344 innings pitched per season.

The "Iron Man" often frustrated batters with an underhand raise ball he fondly called "Old Sal." He bent his knee as he released the ball, starting the pitch down near the ground and angling it upward as it approached the plate. He could make the pitch curve both to the left and right. Batters tended to swing under it, resulting in pop flies. In his later years McGinnity told a reporter, "You know, if you take a flat rock and throw it underhand, it will sail and curve. Well, a baseball will do the same thing if thrown just right.... The batter thinks he can hit it a mile, but he can't. If he hits it, it just pops up in the air." McGinnity also threw overhand and sidearm pitches, the variety of motions lessening the strain on his arm.[17]

McGinnity got off to a great start in 1904. For the first several weeks of the season his pitching kept the Giants in the race. The Giants started the season by going 12–3 against the weak Eastern teams, but both Mathewson and Taylor were roughed up on the team's first Western trip, while McGinnity won all four games he started. At that point in the season the Giants' record was 18–10. McGinnity had started and won eight of the Giants' 18 wins and had finished two others as a reliever. He had not yet lost a game. The Iron Man kept winning when the team returned home. He won 12 straight starts without a loss before hooking up in a pitchers' duel on June 11 with the Cubs' Bob Wicker. McGinnity pitched a fine game, shutting the Cubs out for 11 innings. Wicker pitched better. He allowed a scratch hit in the first inning, then held the Giants hitless for the next eight innings, before allowing a single in the tenth. McGinnity lost when the Cubs pushed a run home in the twelfth on two singles and a fielder's choice.

McGinnity lost again in his next start, then won five in a row during the Giants' 18-game winning streak. He started the game that broke the streak but left for a pinch hitter with the game tied in the top of the ninth inning. Dummy Taylor relieved him and took the loss when he gave up a run in the tenth inning. McGinnity's next two appearances came in relief. In the first game of a doubleheader in St. Louis on July 9, he replaced Mathewson in the eighth inning, with the Giants leading 2–1. He gave up the tying run but the Giants rallied for three runs in the ninth for the win. In the second game he relieved Hooks Wiltse in the bottom of the ninth, with the Giants leading 5–3. He pitched one inning for the save. The Giants ended the day with a 51–17 record. At that stage of the season, with less than half the schedule completed McGinnity already had racked up at least

18 wins, and possibly one or two more, depending upon the official scorer's rulings in a couple of games the Iron Man finished as a reliever.

The day after his relief appearances in both games of the doubleheader, McGinnity started the first game of another doubleheader against the Cardinals. He allowed only six hits, but was uncharacteristically wild, walking six men in a 3–2 loss. Another loss followed, this time to Cincinnati by a 4–3 score. Over the succeeding two months the Iron Man notched winning streaks of three, four, and nine games, as the Giants pulled away from the rest of the league. On September 26 his record stood at 35–6. He lost his last two starts, as the Giants staggered through the last ten games of the season, winning two and losing eight.

The 1904 season was statistically the best of McGinnity's career. He led the league in wins (35), winning percentage (.814), saves (5), earned run average (.161), shutouts (9), games pitched (51), and innings pitched (408). He also led the National League in a more modern statistic, his WHIP (walks plus hits per inning pitched) of 0.963 being the league's best.

The third of the M & M & M Boys, Christy Mathewson, may have had the least celebrated great season in baseball history. His won-lost record was 33–12, for a .733 winning percentage. He shouldered a heavy workload, starting a league-leading 41 games and pitching 368 innings. Despite the large number of innings pitched he had a low earned run average (2.03) and gave up relatively few hits. (He allowed 7.49 hits per nine innings, the sixth lowest in the league.) He led the league in strikeouts (212) and finished second in strikeouts per game (5.19).

Despite the great numbers, praise for Matty's accomplishments was somewhat muted at the time. The reason for the lack of attention is obvious, of course, when viewed in the context of the 1904 season. Matty's record wasn't even the best on his own team. McGinnity had an even better season. Moreover, in 1904 he was only the third-best pitcher in his home city. Jack Chesbro of the rival New York Highlanders won 41 games that year.

Matty was somewhat inconsistent early in the year. He won five of his first six games, but two of the wins were by 7–6 and 10–5 scores. On the Giants' first Western trip he lost all four of his decisions to even his record at 5–5 on May 20. From then until the end of the season, however, he was outstanding. On June 10, he threw a one-hit shutout against the Cubs. In late September, after the Giants recorded win number 104, beating the Pirates' previous record for wins in a season, the team went into a sort of malaise. McGraw allowed his focus to stray from the Polo Grounds to the nearby race tracks. He spent the early part of most afternoons betting on the ponies, barely making it to the park in time for his team's games.[18] The Giants lost six games in a row and fans began grumbling that they were not getting a fair effort from their team. Matty, ever the real-life Frank Merriwell eager to come to the rescue, turned in an exceptional performance in his last start, thereby salvaging a modicum of respect for his team. On October 3, he fanned 16 Cardinals while holding them to six hits in a 3–1 victory. Although McGinnity was beaten the next day, the Giants beat the Superbas 5–0 in their final game, finishing the season at 106–47. Their victory total was the highest in National League history up to that time, though the record would be short-lived. Two years later the Cubs would beat it by ten games.

Built for Speed: Chicago

As the Cubs gathered for spring training in 1904 a Chicago writer noted one the team's strengths. "The speed of the Chicago National League team ought to be one of the biggest features of its play this season," he wrote. "Kling and O'Neill can garner as many sacks as the average catcher. [He very generously estimated that as 25 steals combined for the two men.] Frank Chance is the best baserunner in the business, and will purloin 70 cushions or more. Evers is speedy. Tinker can do his share in the thievery. Casey is a foxy and clever kleptomaniac. McCarthy is good for steal ever and anon. Slagle is one of the fastest in the game, and Jones contributes a sack occasionally." The writer figured the Cubs would total 300 stolen bases. "Any club that can get away with 300 steals during the season is going to stay up in the first division just on the resulting runs," he concluded.

Near the end of spring training the Cubs' manager, Frank Selee, sounded an even more optimistic note. "This year we will deliver the goods. We have a championship team—one that is all enthusiasm and spirit.... Our infield is especially strong. In fact, it is almost a stone wall. Our outfield is doing beautiful work, and we have a pitching corps second to none in the big league." Selee said his men had put in a lot of time practicing the hit-and-run. "If we can perfect ourselves in this," he asserted, "there is no doubt about our standing when the percentages are figured out."[19]

Chicago (93–60)

Regular Lineup	AVG	OBP	SLG	R	RBI	SB
Jimmy Slagle, lf	.260	.322	.333	73	31	28
Doc Casey, 3b	.268	.300	.325	71	43	21
Frank Chance, 1b	.310	.382	.430	89	49	42
Jack McCarthy, cf	.264	.307	.306	36	51	14
Davy Jones, rf	.244	.330	.333	44	39	14

Regular Lineup	AVG	OBP	SLG	R	RBI	SB
or Shad Barry, ut*	.244	.300	.286	44	29	14
Johnny Evers, 2b	.265	.307	.318	49	47	26
Johnny Kling, c	.243	.271	.296	41	46	7
Joe Tinker, ss	.221	.268	.318	55	41	41
or Otto Williams, ut	.200	.256	.232	21	8	9
or Jack O'Neill, c	.214	.258	.262	8	19	1

Leading Pitchers	W	L	PCT.	IP	H	ERA
Jake Weimer	20	14	.588	307	229	1.91
Buttons Briggs	19	11	.633	277	252	2.05
Carl Lundgren	17	9	.654	242	203	2.60
Bob Wicker	17	9	.654	229	201	2.67
Three Finger Brown	15	10	.600	212.3	155	1.86

*Includes record with Philadelphia

Both the writer and Selee were too optimistic. The Cubs stole 227 bases in 1904, a good record but a distant second to the Giants' 283. The team won 93 games, also a fine record, but 13 less than the Giants won. Early in the season it looked as if his team would fulfill Selee's rosy prediction. After posting a 10–9 record through May 11—good for fourth place, five games behind the first-place Giants—the Cubs won eight games in a row. The streak put them in a tie for first place in a three-way race with New York and Cincinnati. The three teams battled each other on nearly equal terms until mid–June, when New York launched its 18-game winning streak. When it ended the Cubs and Reds each trailed the Giants by ten games.

Through the remainder of the season the Cubs battled the Reds, and later also the Pirates, for second place. The closest they could get to New York was seven games behind in late July, and the Giants' lead grew as high as 19 games by mid–September.

By 1904 Selee had gathered together a solid core group of players, although clearly his team was not yet the equal of McGraw's. In preparation for the season he had added Mordecai "Three-Finger" Brown, a future great who came from St. Louis in exchange for Jack Taylor, one of the Cubs' three 20-game winners in 1903. Buttons Briggs, a minor league veteran who had pitched for Chicago in the late 1890s, was also added to the pitching staff, joining holdovers Carl Lundgren and Bob Wicker.

Although Brown would have by far the most distinguished career of the team's pitchers, the staff ace in 1904 was Jake Weimer. Already a seasoned minor league pitcher at age 29 when he joined the Cubs in 1903, Weimer won 20 games in three of his first four major league seasons and was 18–12 in the other one. Weimer possessed an outstanding fastball. After watching him pitch during his rookie season, Cincinnati writers gave him the nickname "Tornado," likely as an alternate to "Cyclone," the name usually shortened to "Cy" and attached to hurlers, such as Cy Young, who had outstanding fastballs.[20]

Possibly because he was relatively old for a newcomer and had been bouncing around the minor leagues since 1895, Weimer wasn't the typical rookie, who would ordinarily be expected to "know his place" and defer to more experienced players. In one of his first games, a victory over Cincinnati, the Reds' veteran player-manager, Joe Kelley, tried to intimidate him. As they passed each other at the end of the game Kelley snarled "You were lucky to win that game." Weimer stared coldly at the older player and remarked, "Some people are lucky to be playing ball at all," bringing the exchange to an abrupt end.[21]

While Selee made full use of his pitching staff in 1904, he juggled their starts so Weimer started 37 times, seven more than any other pitcher. Weimer could be a bit wild at times—he had three games in which he walked seven batters and 14 with four or more walks—but he was tough to hit. In the National League only Mordecai Brown gave up fewer hits per game. Weimer and Christy Mathewson virtually tied for second place in the league in strikeouts per game with 5.19 per game. (Matty beat him out by fanning 5.190 batters to Weimer's 5.189.) Weimer pitched in tough luck in 1904. He threw five three-hitters, but had only a 3–2 record in them. He had 16 games in which he allowed five or fewer hits. His record in those games was 10–6.

The 1904 season didn't go too smoothly for Weimer. In July he was jerked from a game against Boston after giving up runs in each of the first two innings, supposedly because of a sore pitching arm. Selee evidently didn't believe Weimer's discomfort was of the kind that should excuse him from pitching. He suspended Weimer for three days without pay. In late August, Weimer and Joe McGinnity took a pitchers' duel into extra innings with the score tied at one run each. After the first two Giant batters in the tenth reached base, Weimer began yelling at the umpire. He ignored his teammates' efforts to calm him down and was ejected from the game. Bob Wicker had to be rushed into the game to replace him. Wicker was wild, giving up three bases on balls and hitting a batter, as the Giants scored three times for the win. The Cubs trailed the Giants by ten games at the time, but the rivalry with the Giants had already become a bitter one. After the game the other Cub players let Weimer know they weren't happy that he lost control of himself and possibly cost them the game. Tempers flared, leading to a fight between Weimer and Joe Tinker in which Weimer suffered a black eye.[22]

Mordecai Brown pitched about as well as Weimer in 1904, but logged far fewer innings. When Brown was traded by St. Louis in December of 1903, *The Sporting News* reported that his former Cardinal teammates were predicting he would be the Cubs' best pitcher in 1904.[23] They might have been right if Mordecai had not missed three weeks early in the season for unspecified reasons and sat out the last three weeks of September with a shoulder injury. He appeared in only 26 games, 23 of them as starter. When he pitched, he was usually very effective. In 11 games—almost half of his starts—he allowed five or fewer hits. For the season he averaged only 6.57 hits per nine innings, the lowest in the league. He was second only to McGinnity in WHIP (walks plus hits per nine innings), at 0.965, and was third in earned run average (1.86).

Brown did not possess overwhelming speed. He was effective because he made a baseball asset out of the childhood tragedy that left him with a deformed hand. Brown lost most of his index finger while helping his brother run a feed chopper. His other fingers were severely cut, but were sewn up and bandaged by a local doctor. A couple weeks later Brown fell while playing and broke his remaining fingers in several places. Brown and his sister re-bandaged the fingers themselves. When Brown's hand healed he was left with the stump of his index finger, a crooked middle finger and a little finger that had little sense of touch and could not be completely straightened out.

Every pitch Mordecai threw had movement. He had an outstanding curve ball, which he could throw in much the same way as other pitchers. His fastball dipped as it reached the plate, somewhat like the modern split finger fastball. He used the stump of his index finger to throw a pitch that acted somewhat like a knuckleball, with a tendency to break down and in toward a righthanded batter.[24]

The Cubs' pitchers all benefited from an outstanding defense. Johnny Kling was widely recognized as the best catcher in the National League. Left fielder Jimmy Slagle and right fielder Davy Jones were both very good fielders and center fielder Jack McCarthy was above average. Doc Casey at third base was solid and Frank Chance had worked hard to become a very good defensive first baseman. The heart of the defense, for the Cubs as for most Deadball Era teams, was the keystone combination—shortstop Joe Tinker and second baseman Johnny Evers. In an analysis of the Cubs' lineup at the start of the 1904 season, Chicago writer W. A. Phelon said that Tinker, who had been a third baseman in the minors, "has mastered the angles of the shortstop's position till he is a star in every way." Evers likewise was recognized as one of the game's stars. Near the end of the 1903 season, another Chicago writer had claimed, "Outside of Lajoie, Johnny Evers is the most valuable second baseman now in the game." A year later a Boston writer called Evers "one of the few really clever players who have broken into the game of late."[25]

While the Cubs were a strong team, they were not impressive in one of the most important elements of the game. When it came to hitting the ball, they were, at best, a mediocre team. In retrospect it is difficult to imagine how they could have been anywhere near as successful as they were in 1904 without Frank Chance. The Cubs' first baseman outhit the next-best Cub by over 40 points. His slugging average was nearly 100 points higher than that of any other regular player on the team. He led the Cubs in stolen bases and seemed to be in the middle of every batting rally.

Chance sparked the Cubs to victory with his bat, his baserunning, and, occasionally, with his glove. Some examples:

> May 15: Chance capped a 3-run rally by doubling against the right field fence, driving in the tying and lead runs in a victory over Philadelphia.
>
> May 18: Chance beat the Superbas with a home run drive in the eighth inning. He scored three of the Cubs' five runs in the game and, according to Brooklyn reporter Abe Yager, "made a number of remarkable plays at first that cut off several hits."
>
> June 11: He scored the run that ended Joe McGinnity's 12-game winning streak. He opened the twelfth inning with a single. He reached second by beating Art Devlin's throw to second base, as Johnny Kling grounded out on a 5-4-3 putout at first base. He moved to third on another groundout and scored on Johnny Evers' single.
>
> June 13: Chance got three of the Cubs' four hits off the Giants' other ace, Christy Mathewson, rapping out a double, triple, and homerun in the Cubs' 3-2 victory. In the first inning of that game Chance doubled home Jimmy Slagle for the Cubs first run. He forced a play at third base on Johnny Kling's chopper in front of the plate, sliding in safely at third as Art Devlin dropped the throw. Then, with the Giants' infield playing in, Chance raced home on a grounder to shortstop, scoring on a high throw to the plate. He scored the eventual winning run in his next at-bat, smashing a low line drive past the center fielder and legging out an inside-the-park homerun.[26]

A few days later, when the Cubs reached Cincinnati, a reporter remarked, "When they talk about great ballplayers the name of Frank Chance should never be omitted. Chance is a great ballplayer. He is not only a good batsman and fielder, but there is not another player in the business who is his size and possesses his speed. With Chance off the team the Chicago aggregation would be decidedly weakened."[27]

Frank Selee, who had chosen Kling over Chance as the Cubs catcher, was full of praise for Frank Chance, the first baseman. On a visit to the press box while the Cubs were in Pittsburgh he told a group of reporters, "They may all talk about their great players, but I think the Chicago club has in Frank Chance the greatest all around player in the world today." Having caught the reporters' full attention with that remark, Selee explained, "In my judgment he is without a peer as a first baseman, fielding ground balls better than any other man playing the position. In addition to this he is a reliable batsman and an exceptionally fast baserunner." When a reporter reminded Selee that lots of people thought Fred Tenney was the top first baseman, Selee replied that he thought Chance was a better first baseman, but he could easily find a place for Tenney on the Chicago team.[28] Danny Shay, the Cardinals second baseman, had a similarly high opinion of Chance. In November of 1904, while visiting Seattle, Shay told a local reporter, "You hear a lot about Lajoie and Wagner being wonderful ball players, but there is one you don't hear so very much about, and yet I think he is in their class. This fellow is Husk Chance. Chance is one great artist, and to my mind ranks with Lajoie and Wagner. He is everything they are— a great hitter, splendid fielder, fast baserunner and has a head full of brains."[29]

Looking back more than a century later, one could envision a scenario in which a fast talker from Pittsburgh or Cleveland might be able to persuade Selee to trade Chance for either Wagner or Lajoie. But, still, Chance was a very good player. From 1903 through 1907 no regular National League first baseman had a higher OPS (on-base plus slugging percentage) than Chance. And in 1908 his OPS was exceeded only by Kitty Bransfield, who by then was a Phillie playing half his games in hitter-friendly Baker Field.

Overcoming Bad Luck: Cincinnati

In early May, after the Reds finished a road trip, Harry Steinfeldt came back to his hotel room in the Walnut Hills section of Cincinnati. Somehow, as Harry started to doze off during the night, the flame in the gas furnace heating his room went off. The natural gas, however, continued to flow, filling the room. Aroused by the presence of the gas, Steinfeldt got up in the middle of the night, and fumbled unsuccessfully with the furnace, while shouting for help. The hotel owner came to his aid, and managed to turn off the gas. Although a reporter wrote that Steiny had come close to being asphyxiated, he seemed to emerge from the scare without any ill effects. That was one of the few things that went right for him or, for that matter, for the Reds in 1904. Shortly after the gas scare, Steiny went into the hospital for an operation on his leg. He missed several weeks due to the operation. In July his arm was injured when he was hit by a pitch. A month or so later, he came down with a case of malaria and missed more time. When Steiny got into the lineup afterwards he couldn't run normally. He hit poorly and didn't play well in the field. He told a Cincinnati writer he was feeling fine, but his legs didn't seem to work right.[30]

Cincinnati (88–65)

Regular Lineup	AVG	OBP	SLG	R	RBI	SB
Miller Huggins, 2b	.263	.377	.328	96	30	13
Cy Seymour, cf	.313	.352	.439	71	58	11
or Mike Donlin, lf*	.329	.383	.457	59	52	22
Joe Kelley, 1b	.281	.359	.385	75	63	15
Cozy Dolan, rf-1b	.284	.342	.383	88	51	19
Fred Odwell, lf	.284	.333	.380	75	58	30
Harry Steinfeldt, 3b	.244	.313	.318	35	52	17
or Sam Woodruff, 3b	.190	.244	.255	20	20	9
Tommy Corcoran, ss	.230	.257	.301	55	74	19
Admiral Schlei, c	.237	.297	.285	25	32	7
or Heinie Peitz, c	.243	.282	.316	32	30	1
Leading Pitchers	W	L	PCT.	IP	H	ERA
Noodles Hahn	16	18	.471	297.7	258	2.06
Jack Harper	23	9	.719	293.7	262	2.30
Win Kellum	15	10	.600	224.7	206	2.60
Tom Walker	15	8	.652	217	196	2.24
Bob Ewing, Cin	11	13	.458	212	198	2.46

*Includes record with New York

Steinfeldt's poor year was symptomatic of the way the 1904 season went for the Reds. Things seemed to go haywire all season long. Mike Donlin, the team's wayward potential superstar, went on his first debilitating drinking spree in April and essentially drank his way off the team by July 4. Cozy Dolan, who did a good job in battling the sun in right field in 1903, couldn't deal with it in 1904. Catcher Heinie Peitz couldn't play at the beginning of the season because of a sore arm. When he did play he threw "rainbows" to second base trying to nab baserunners. A new balk rule so confounded pitcher Bob Ewing he couldn't focus on the strike zone. It took most of the season for him to figure out how to pitch within the new rule and still get the ball over the plate.[31]

A couple of the Reds' veterans, Cy Seymour and Jack Harper, made it through the season without injury and turned in very good seasons. Seymour was one of the better hitters in the league for several years, and 1904 was one of them. Harper was an erratic pitcher who had three good seasons, including the 1904 campaign. Mike Donlin performed well when his nighttime activities didn't put him out of commission. But the Reds would almost certainly have finished much lower in the standings had they not been successful in adding players from the minor leagues. Miller Huggins, who won the second base job in spring training, outfielder Fred Odwell, catcher Admiral Schlei, infielder Sam Woodruff, and pitchers Win Kellum and Tom Walker all played key roles in 1904. Except for Walker, who was 22 in 1904, none of these ex-minor leaguers was very young. Huggins and Schlei were 26, Woodruff 27, Kellum 28, and Odwell 31. They were well-seasoned players who were already about as good as they were ever going to be. Even Walker had been around for a while. Despite his tender age, he was beginning his sixth professional season in 1904. He had gone 26–7 for Louisville in the class A American Association in 1903.

The best of the Reds' rookies was Miller Huggins. He had hit .309 for the St. Paul Saints in 1903, leading them to the American Association pennant. He was considered one of the top players in the minor leagues, and several other major league teams had tried to obtain him from the Saints after the 1903 season. Huggins hit for a decent average, showed the ability to battle his way on base by coaxing lots of walks, and played excellent defense. His 88 bases on balls in 1904 were second highest in the National League, and he led the league in walks four times during his career. Huggins remained in the league as a player until 1916. He became manager of the St. Louis Cardinals in 1913 and moved to the Yankees in 1918. He was, of course, later inducted into the Hall of Fame as a manager.

Fred Odwell began the season as a fourth outfielder. He filled in for Cy Seymour early in the season when Seymour was sidelined with a leg injury, and played a few games in right field in place of Dolan. He became a regular after Donlin self-destructed. Odwell was far less talented than Donlin, but far more attentive to the subtleties of the game. Odwell's strong point was his fielding. Both Kelley and Brooklyn manager Ned Hanlon said he was one of the greatest defensive outfielders they had ever seen. "He is making catches in left field every day that other fielders would not get near," Kelley said. "As a thrower he has few if any equals, and it is all because he practices throwing. Watch him during practice and you will see him throw to all the bases. In this way he not only keeps his arm in good trim, but he gets a good line on distance and becomes accurate." Odwell hit fairly well in 1904, but his average fell off after that. He played for the Reds through the 1907 season before returning to the minors, where he played until 1912 when he was 39 years old.

Schlei became the Reds' number one catcher because of Peitz' sore arm. After Peitz recovered, Schlei remained the team's top catcher because of his defensive ability. In his first series against St. Louis the Cardinals tested his throwing arm. After he threw four baserunners out in one game, they decided he had passed the test and stopped running against him. He was agile for a catcher. By mid-season some writers were saying the Reds had never had a catcher who was as good at fielding bunts as Schlei. Although Schlei hit over .250 only once in during his major league career—his lifetime batting average equaled his 1904 average of .237—his batting numbers usually placed him in the middle of the pack for catchers in his era.

Sam Woodruff was the man who filled in for Steinfeldt during his long absences. Woodruff was another graduate of the American Association. With Indianapolis the preceding two seasons he had been a good-field, fair-hit infielder. With the Reds he was good-field, no-hit. His fielding average at third base was 45 points higher than Steinfeldt's. But when a player bats under .200 he can figure his time with a team will probably be pretty short. Before the season ended Woodruff was traded back into the American Association.[32]

Win Kellum was one of those pitchers we now refer to as "a soft-tossing lefty," often in a context implying Lefty isn't up to the standard of those hard-throwing right-handers who can bring it on at 90-plus mph. In Kellum's day that kind of pitcher would more often be called "brainy," or "foxy," as Joe Kelley did when he told reporters he might use Kellum as the Reds' opening-day starter. "I am inclined to look upon Kellum as the Foxy Grandpa of our staff," said Kelley. "He knows what he is there for, and is as hard to rattle as an ice man." Sportswriter Ed Grillo made a similar comment after seeing Kellum pitch his first game for the Reds. "Kellum showed that he is not a green hand at the game, but a finished pitcher," Grillo said. "Kellum belongs to that class of pitchers who have a reason for pitching every ball. It is not a case of just slamming the ball toward the plate and trusting to luck with Kellum."

Kellum didn't start the opening game for the Reds, but he helped the team get off to a good start by winning his first six decisions. In addition to being one of the Reds' most reliable starters, he became Kelley's "bullpen ace," of sorts. Kelley relieved his starting pitcher only 15 times in 1904. Kellum was the relief pitcher in seven of those games, winning two, losing two and saving two. In his other relief effort he got a non-baseball save of Jack Harper's health when he pitched the last three innings of a 10–2 blowout in the intense heat and humidity of a game in St. Louis.

Despite Kellum's good pitching for the Reds in 1904, Manager Kelley didn't seem to consider him an important part of the team's future. In December, the Reds announced a deal in which Kellum was to be transferred to Philadelphia, evidently as a good-will gesture by Garry Herrmann to build up a poor team located in a key National League city. That deal was later canceled, and in January Kellum was sold to St. Louis. When the 1904 season was only halfway over, he was sold to Toledo of the American Association.[33]

Tom Walker was, like Kellum, a finesse pitcher. During the season he was compared with Clark Griffith and Old Hoss Radbourne, both great pitchers who lacked outstanding fastballs. The Reds' business manager, Frank Bancroft, made the comparison to Radbourne because Old Hoss was adept at pitching his way out of jams. Walker managed to hang on with the Reds for two years while constantly flirting with danger on the mound. After going 9–7 with a relatively high 3.24 earned run average in 1905, he jumped to Williamsport in the Tri-State League, which was an "outlaw league"—that is, it was outside the business trust that called itself organized baseball. He pitched for Williamsport again in 1907. He sat out the 1908 season and made his last appearance in 1909 with Reading of the independent Atlantic League.[34]

Grit, Determination, Dissension: Pittsburgh

Grit, determination, internal strife. These were part of the disappointing season that ended the Pirates' three-year run as National League champions.

Gritty—that was Sam Leever. In the spring of 1904 Leever was still suffering from the sore arm that had ended his 1903 season. "It was in the second game of the last series with the Boston Nationals, in September, that I last pitched as a well man," Leever told reporters just before the season opened. After the Boston game, Leever had worn his uniform, still wet with perspiration, back to the hotel. His arm stiffened in the cold New England autumn air. A series of hot baths failed to help. His arm remained sore. Two appearances in the World Series, one lasting only an inning because of the soreness in his arm, and the other a complete game, were "a big mistake," Leever said. "Last winter my rheumatism was so bad that I could not shut a door." Leever had taken treatments at Mt. Clemens, a mineral water spa, before spring training. The treatments seemed to have provided some relief. "My movement is as free as ever," he told reporters, "but when I throw hard I can feel soreness in my shoulder."

Leever's first start, which came in the Pirates' tenth game, ended quickly, but not because of his tender shoulder. Sam's idea of what was permissible under the new balk rule differed from the umpire's. In the second inning, after being called for his second balk, Sam confronted the umpire, pushed him around and was ejected from the game. His next start came two weeks later. He held the Phillies to four hits in ten innings, but lost 2–0. He started regularly after that, and pitched well, even after taking a line drive off his pitching wrist. He won seven of his first ten decisions. On June 23, however, before his scheduled start against St. Louis, he told Clarke his arm wasn't feeling very good. He pitched two innings, giving up four hits and two runs on pitches that had little speed or movement. When his next turn to start came up, Sam took the mound again, despite the discomfort, and beat the Cubs 5–4, holding them down to five hits, only two of which left the infield.

On June 29, when the Pirates were in Youngstown, Ohio for an exhibition game, Leever visited Bonesetter Reese, a therapist noted for his success in curing muscular problems. Reese manipulated Sam's arm and assured him it would be as good as new within a week. Reese said Sam's arm must have caused tremendous pain whenever he delivered the ball. "It did hurt like all get out," Sam said, "but I did not want to complain, because I knew the club needed me in the game." A couple days later Sam told reporters his pitching elbow was entirely free from pain and his shoulder felt much better. "Last night was the first time in more than eight months that I was able to sleep without keeping my arm above my head," he said.

Unfortunately for Sam, Reese's treatment had not resulted in a cure. His next appearance came in relief on July 8. He allowed four runs in five innings. A few days later he pitched a complete game, beating the Beaneaters 10–4, but according to a Pittsburgh writer he had "about as much speed as a blind mule attached to an ash wagon." Sam continued to take the mound about every five days. On August 1, he told a reporter his "pitching wing" was still full of rheumatism, but he was going to demonstrate on the upcoming Eastern trip that he was not a dead one. Sam won his first two games on the trip, and got credit for winning the third game, though he pitched to only one batter. In the bottom of the first, Boston's leadoff batter lined a ball through the box that Sam tried to stop, splitting his pitching hand. The scoring rules of the day gave Sam the win because the Pirates had a lead when he left the game. He lasted only two innings in his next start and skipped the turn after that, pitching four innings of relief instead. The light duty for a two-week period evidently helped. Sam finished out the season, taking the mound each time his turn came around and pitching effectively. Despite the pain in his arm, Sam led the Pirates in 1904 in games started and innings pitched. Although he probably never again pitched without some pain, Sam continued to pitch for the Pirates through the 1910 season, when he was 38 years old.[35]

Pittsburgh (87–66)

Regular Lineup	AVG	OBP	SLG	R	RBI	SB
Tommy Leach, 3b	.257	.316	.335	92	56	23
Ginger Beaumont, cf	.301	.338	.374	97	54	28
Fred Clarke, lf	.306	.367	.410	51	25	11
or Moose McCormick, rf-lf*	.279	.328	.392	53	49	19
Honus Wagner, ss	.349	.423	.520	97	75	53

Regular Lineup	AVG	OBP	SLG	R	RBI	SB
Kitty Bransfield, 1b	.223	.259	.290	47	60	11
Jimmy Sebring, rf**	.250	.292	.323	50	56	16
or Otto Krueger, ut	.194	.282	.243	34	26	8
Claude Ritchey, 2b	.263	.338	.347	79	51	12
Ed Phelps, c	.242	.289	.278	29	28	2
or Harry Smith, c	.248	.346	.284	17	18	5
or Fred Carisch, c	.248	.299	.288	9	8	3

Leading Pitchers	W	L	PCT.	IP	H	ERA
Sam Leever	18	11	.621	253.3	224	2.17
Patsy Flaherty	19	9	.679	242	210	2.05
Mike Lynch	15	11	.577	222.7	200	2.71
Deacon Phillippe	10	10	.500	166.7	183	3.24
Charlie Case	10	5	.667	141	129	2.94
Roscoe Miller	7	7	.500	134.3	133	3.35

*Includes record with New York
**Includes record with Cincinnati

One reason Leever pushed himself as hard as he did in 1904 was that the Pirates' pitching staff was a mess. Sam and Deacon Phillippe were the only holdovers from the already depleted 1903 staff, and Phillippe missed almost half the season because of arm miseries. Ed Doheny, who won 16 games in 1903, was gone because of illness and Roaring Bill Kennedy, the only other reliable starter on the 1903 staff, had been released. Manager Fred Clarke was forced to rebuild his pitching staff while defending the championship. The team got off to a bad start. In early May the Pirates were 5–12, and facing a "must-win" game against the Phillies to avoid falling into the National League cellar. The Pirates rallied, but as late as June 26 they were only one game over .500. By then the Giants were well into the 18-game winning streak that virtually clinched the pennant by July 4.

The frustration of seeing their pennant hopes vanish almost at the outset of the season led to internal turmoil among the players. During spring training Tommy Leach, the Pirates' diminutive third baseman, and Bucky Veil, a reserve pitcher, had gotten into a fight at the team's hotel. It was an incident that might have been forgotten had the season gone well. Veil was released after pitching in one regular-season game, reportedly because he was weak from an illness he couldn't shake. Veil's close friend on the team, Jimmy Sebring, became upset over Veil's release, believing Veil had not been treated well by the Pirates. Sebring evidently harbored his resentment for some time afterward. In late June the Pirates lost an exhibition game to a semi-professional team. During the contest Honus Wagner, who was in charge of the team that day, accused Sebring of loafing after a ball hit into right field. A short while later Wagner again criticized Sebring for the way he handled ground balls in a game. Sebring grew angry and challenged Wagner to a fight. The other players intervened to prevent any further trouble, but the next day team owner Barney Dreyfuss criticized the young outfielder for his behavior.

On July 31 Sebring injured his ankle sliding into third while running out a triple. The next evening the Pirates were scheduled to leave on an Eastern trip. The Pirates' team physician had told Sebring he would not be able to play for a week or ten days, so the injured player asked Dreyfuss for permission to spend the recovery time at home with his wife and newborn baby. Dreyfuss refused. When Sebring arrived at the train station he again told the Pirates' owner it made no sense for him to go with the team to New York. Dreyfuss replied, "Well, I want you to go and you'll go." This upset Sebring, who replied that he wasn't going. Dreyfuss informed his young player that he could quit the team. Sebring then handed his traveling bag to a teammate and walked away. Within a week Sebring was sent packing to Cincinnati.[36]

Kitty Bransfield's situation was different. Sebring's troubles were like a fire that smoldered out of sight for a while then burst into flames in full public view. With Bransfield there was a lot of smoke but no flames. Bransfield had a miserable season in 1904. He started the season in a slump. By mid-June his average had dropped below .200. As the season progressed he struggled back into the .220s, but he never got much higher than the .223 average he had at the end of the season. His fielding was sensational in some games, but terrible in others.

All season long, rumors of management's discontent over Bransfield's play swirled around Exposition Field. In late May Clarke took him out of the lineup. Pittsburgh papers reported Bransfield was being rested so he could recover from an attack of malaria. A Cincinnati paper said he was benched because of poor playing. In mid-June Clarke proposed a trade that would send Bransfield to Boston for Fred Tenney. When Boston turned down the deal, Clarke told reporters that was OK, because when "Kit" was right he was the best in the business. He had just gotten into a bad rut, Clarke said, and would soon return to his old form. About the same time a Pittsburgh paper attributed Bransfield's problems to his being "too sensitive" to criticism from a group of gamblers who occupied the seats just back of first base. A couple weeks later a note appeared in *Sporting Life* asserting the Pirates were negotiating for the contract of a minor league first baseman. In the insensitive language sometimes used in newspapers of the era, the noted added: "Bransfield is completely out of favor for stupid play at critical points." Trade rumors persisted throughout the season, ending only in mid-winter when Bransfield was sent to the Phillies in a multi-player trade.[37]

A Really Good Kid: St. Louis

The Cardinals didn't exactly rebuild in 1904, but they did reload. Their attempts to recover from the devastating American League raid of 1901–02 yielded teams that struggled to win 40 percent of their games in 1902 and 1903. In preparation for the 1904 season the Cardinals tried a different approach. They signed and traded for several pretty good veterans who were nearing the end of their careers, but were still able to perform at a fairly high level.

St. Louis (75–79)

Regular Lineup	AVG	OBP	SLG	R	RBI	SB
John Farrell, 2b	.255	.320	.312	72	20	16
Spike Shannon, rf	.280	.349	.318	84	26	34
Jake Beckley, 1b	.325	.375	.403	72	67	17
Homer Smoot, cf	.281	.331	.365	58	66	23
George Barclay, lf*	.205	.241	.254	46	38	17
or Dave Brain, ss-3b-of	.266	.291	.408	57	72	18
or Jack Dunleavy, rf	.233	.305	.326	23	14	8
Jimmy Burke, 3b	.227	.271	.266	37	37	17
Danny Shay, ss-3b	.256	.338	.303	45	18	36
Mike Grady, c	.313	.376	.474	44	43	6

Leading Pitchers	W	L	PCT.	IP	H	ERA
Jack Taylor	20	19	.513	352	297	2.22
Kid Nichols	21	13	.618	317	268	2.02
Chappie McFarland	14	18	.438	269.3	266	3.21
Mike O'Neill	10	14	.417	220	229	2.09
Joe Corbett	5	8	.385	108.7	110	4.39

*Includes record with Boston

Jake Beckley, 36 years old and starting his 17th major league season, came over from Cincinnati. Jake had one good season and one fair one left. Mike Grady, a comparative youngster of 34 years, had first surfaced in the National League in 1894. He came to St. Louis from Kansas City of the American Association, where he had spent the previous two seasons playing for Dale Gear, his teammate with the 1901 Washington Senators. Grady was a good utility player. He was adequate defensively as a catcher or first baseman, and could fill in at other positions in an emergency. He wasn't good at any position. But he could hit. His career average over 11 seasons was .294, and not many players who wore catching gear for a significant amount of time in the Deadball Era could say that. Another player who strengthened the team was Danny Shay, a minor league veteran who was 27 in 1904. Not much of hitter, Shay gave the team solid defense at shortstop in the 97 games he played there. The shortstop position had been a glaring weakness for the 1903 Cardinals.

The Cardinals' greatest improvement was in their pitching. They had two of the top pitchers in the league. Jack Taylor had been obtained from the Cubs in a trade for Mordecai Brown. Brown was by far the better of the two over the course of their careers, but in 1904 Taylor was probably a bit more valuable because of his durability. The Cardinals' other standout pitcher was Charlie "Kid" Nichols, who was also the team's new manager.

Like Grady, Nichols was 34. The leading pitcher for the great Boston Beaneaters teams of the 1890s, he had dropped out of the major leagues after the 1901 season to try his hand as player-manager and part-owner of the Kansas City Blue Stockings of the Western League. Near the end of spring training in preparation for the 1902 season, Ernest Lanigan, a highly respected writer and baseball statistician, lamented Nichols' departure from the National League. "The appearance of a Boston team without the 'Kid' will for some time to come resemble a production of 'Hamlet' with Hamlet omitted," Lanigan moaned. "Here in Philadelphia we have ever considered Nichols as one of the really great pitchers in the history of the National Game."

Lanigan took a nostalgic look back at Nichols' National League career. In 12 seasons, beginning with his rookie year in 1890, Nichols had recorded 30 or more victories seven times, and had pitched his team to five pennants. His won-lost percentage had been better than his team's in ten of the 12 seasons, the exceptions being 1899 and 1900. He had won almost a third of the games played by the Beaneaters during his career and had always been the man the team looked to in tough games. Lanigan calculated Nichols' career record through the 1901 season as 331–180 (modern records show it as 329–183). Over the same dozen years, only one other pitcher came close to matching it. Cy Young had gone 319–174, by Lanigan's calculations (modern records put Young's record at 319–180). No other pitcher had come close to this pair. Clark Griffith (189–109); Roaring Bill Kennedy (176–153) and George Cuppy (159–102) came the closest, all three of them pitching in ten seasons since 1890.[38]

At about the same time, a *Sporting News* correspondent from Atlanta, who had just attended a Beaneaters spring training game, wrote, "It was a great disappointment to the 'old-timers' hereabouts not to see the quiet, gentlemanly and certainly most wonderful pitcher, Kid Nichols, with the Boston aggregation." The correspondent compared Nichols to Pud Galvin, the durable pitcher who, according to modern records, won more games than any other 19th century pitcher. (Galvin went 361–308 in the major leagues from 1879 to 1892 and had a 4–2 record in 1875 in the old National Association.) "To my mind there was little in common between them except the marvelous stamina possessed by both, which enabled them to pitch good ball for years and years," he said. "But Nichols was the superior man and better pitcher."

By the time Nichols went to Kansas City, testimonials to his high standing in baseball history had been forthcoming for several years. Henry Chadwick, whose coverage of baseball games pre-dated the National League, had written in 1898 that Nichols' achievements amounted to "the best record known to baseball pitching history." *The Sporting News* had called him "the greatest pitcher ever identified with baseball from the standpoint of continuous and consistent effectiveness." Therefore, Nichols' decision to pursue a career as a baseball executive was widely perceived as the end of a baseball era, the passing of one of the sport's greatest players.[39]

For Nichols, the move to Kansas City was a business decision, on a par with decisions made by men such as Clark Griffith, Jimmy Collins, and John McGraw to cast their lot with the new American League. The three men who owned the Beaneaters—known in baseball as The Triumvirate—were tight-fisted businessmen. As long as Nichols was winning 30 games a year they reluctantly agreed to pay him $3,000 each season, the top salary allowable under the strict pay structure enforced by National League owners. By 1902, with Nichols starting to lose a little off his great fastball and the Beaneaters no longer being a contending team, the Triumvirate made clear their intention to cut his pay. To maintain his income at its previous level, Nichols had a choice. He could sign with Detroit, which had offered him $5,000 for three years, or he could become part of the ownership group connected with a new Western League franchise in Kansas City. Nichols chose the latter.[40]

The Kansas City venture didn't go as well as Nichols had hoped. He was successful on the field. In 1902 he pitched his team to the Western League pennant. He posted a 26–7 record, with a 1.82 ERA—evidence that he was still a fine pitcher. He also developed two pitchers—Jake Weimer and Norwood Gibson—who won over 20 games with Kansas City in 1902 and pitched well in the major leagues in 1903 and afterwards. In 1903 Nichols had another good season personally, going 21–12 with a 2.51 ERA. His team performed well again on the field, finishing in third place, but lost a more important battle at the box office. A rival league, the American

Association, had also placed a team—the Cowboys—in Kansas City. The Cowboys outdrew Nichols' Blue Stockings. Having lost as much money as they could withstand, Nichols' ownership group sold out to their competitors, leaving him without a position for 1904. Nichols wasn't out of a job for long. The Cardinals had already decided to fire player-manager Patsy Donovan. Nichols fit their needs exactly—a top-flight player who also had some managerial experience. They hired him as soon as he became available.[41]

While the Kid Nichols of 1904 wasn't quite as speedy or as durable as he had been during the 90s, he was still a very good pitcher. At the height of his career he relied primarily upon superb control and an excellent fastball, which many observers said had a "jump" to it. The "jump" was an illusion created by his pitching pattern. Nichols pitched high in the strike zone, and batters would often swing under a pitch, fouling it back. Charlie Bennett, who caught him in the early 90s, said Nichols threw his fastball and changeup with nearly identical motions. "Only a man who catches him right along or watches him constantly can tell what he is going to throw," Bennett said. "What fools many of the batters is the way he throws a straight ball. He will give it just a little upward movement or outward shoot of not more than a few inches, but it takes a very quick eye to gauge it." According to Cincinnati manager Joe Kelley, who had faced Nichols since the early 90s, the only change from before was that in 1904 Nichols mixed in more curve balls and relied more on the change of pace than he did when he was younger.[42]

Nichols was a steadying force on his own pitching staff. When the Cardinals were struggling to get over .500 early in the season, Nichols five times won games that brought the team back to that level. His record stood at 18–6 on August 26. He lost several well-pitched games in September enroute to a 21–13 finish. His season was marked by two noteworthy pitching feats. On August 11 he pitched a 17-inning victory over the Brooklyn Superbas. He gave up only one run through the first 14 innings, before tiring somewhat. He and rival pitcher Oscar Jones both allowed a run in the 15th. The Cardinals scored two in the top of the 17th to go ahead 4–2. The Superbas responded with one run in the bottom of the inning, but Nichols held on for the win. He struck out 14 batters during the game, while walking only one and allowing ten hits.

That game gave Nichols an opportunity to validate an opinion he had offered the previous week when a reporter asked him if he thought Bill Dinneen might have hurt his pitching arm by pitching a 15-inning game. "There is very little chance of that," Nichols said. "After a pitcher is hardened up the longest game should do no more than to make him tired. A day or two rest is enough to bring him around in as good condition as ever. Personally I do not think a long game is an exceptional hardship on a pitcher. There is very little hitting as a rule in a long game, and the pitcher is much less exhausted than he would be in a game where there was lots of hitting and baserunning." Nichols followed up on his 17-inning marathon game by winning his next three starts and continuing to pitch well after that.

A month later, when his pitching staff was suffering from injuries, Nichols decided to pitch both games of a doubleheader against Cincinnati. He was superb in the opener, holding the Reds to three hits in a 4–2 win. Both runs scored as the result of errors. The second game was a different story. He was hit hard throughout the game, giving up 14 hits in an 8–5 loss.

The 1904 season was Nichols' best since 1898. He had the fifth-best earned run average in the National League (2.02) and was tied for second with McGinnity in opponents' on-base percentage (.256). It was his last good year. Nichols became sick during spring training in 1905 and was unable to get into proper condition at the beginning of the season. In his only appearance during the first six weeks of the season he was knocked out of the box after two innings. In his role as the Cardinals' manager he incurred the displeasure of Stanley Robison, who had taken over as the chief executive of the team during the illness of his brother, Frank Robison. Stanley Robison blamed Nichols for losing the pre-season intra-city series with the Browns. When the Cardinals got off to a slow start during the regular season, Robison replaced Nichols as the manager, although he kept him on the roster as a pitcher. Nichols didn't pitch again until the end of May, and even then he pitched poorly. He had a 1–5 record in seven games when the Cardinals sold him to the Phillies in mid–July. He seemed to have recovered fully after he joined the Phillies. He went 10–6 with a 2.27 ERA over the remainder of the season. His troubles returned the next spring, however. He struggled badly in four games with the Phillies in 1906, allowing a run for each inning pitched and losing his only decision in the four games he pitched before deciding to retire.

When Nichols left the National League for the second time, four years after Lanigan described him as one of the game's greatest pitchers, his career record was 361–208. Because he had decided to return to the minors while he was still relatively young, he had added little to the stellar record he had compiled through the age of 31. Still, the 32 wins he recorded in 1904 and 1905 raised his career total to a level reached by only the very best pitchers in baseball history. There are five pitchers in baseball history who have won more games than Nichols: Cy Young (511), Walter Johnson (417), Christy Mathewson (373), Grover Cleveland Alexander (373), and Warren Spahn

(363). Pud Galvin matched Nichols' win total. Considering Nichols' record at Kansas City in 1902 and 1903, when he went 47–19 at the highest minor league level and his steady performance in 1904, when he ranked among the National League's best pitchers, it is quite possible Nichols could have won 39 more games if he had pitched for a major league team during those two Kansas City years. That would have given him 400 career wins and put him in a class with Young and Johnson as the only pitchers with 400 or more major league victories. Barring injury, he would at the very least have picked up the 13 victories needed to move him past Spahn, Mathewson and Alexander into third place on the all-time list.

Given his record and the fact that reporters of his time commonly recognized his great accomplishments, it is somewhat mystifying why Nichols received very few votes in the early Hall of Fame voting. His high-water mark was a measly seven votes in the 1939 balloting. Part of the explanation for his poor showing would seem to lie in the confusion over how to deal with players like Nichols whose careers spanned both the 19th century and the early years of the 20th. Few players of Nichols' generation fared well in the voting. Nichols gained admission to the Hall of Fame in 1949 when he was selected by the Veterans Committee.[43]

Trying Too Hard: Brooklyn

For the Superbas each season after 1900 was a downward step in competitiveness. The 1899–1900 Superbas were, in a word, superb—one of the great teams of the era. Their star players began leaving in 1901, but the team still finished 22 games over .500. In 1902 more stars left and they fell to nine games over the break-even mark. The 1903 Superbas dropped to fifth place, but won four more than they lost. By 1904 almost all of the championship team's players had left. The collection of minor league hopefuls and major league retreads now representing the team needed all the help they could get. The one star remaining from the champion Superba teams, Jimmy Sheckard, was naturally seen as the man the team could depend upon in clutch situations.

Brooklyn (56–97)

Regular Lineup	AVG	OBP	SLG	R	RBI	SB
John Dobbs, cf	.248	.304	.303	36	30	11
or Doc Gessler, cf	.290	.355	.384	41	28	13
Pop Dillon, 1b	.258	.313	.317	60	31	13
Harry Lumley, rf	.279	.331	.428	79	78	30

Regular Lineup	AVG	OBP	SLG	R	RBI	SB
Jimmy Sheckard, lf	.239	.317	.314	70	46	21
Sammy Strang, 2b	.192	.316	.244	28	9	16
Charlie Babb, ss	.265	.345	.311	49	53	34
Mike McCormick, 3b	.184	.278	.222	28	27	22
or Dutch Jordan, 2b	.179	.225	.234	21	19	7
Bill Bergen, c	.182	.204	.207	17	12	3
or Lew Ritter, c	.248	.318	.276	23	19	17

Leading Pitchers	W	L	PCT.	IP	H	ERA
Oscar Jones	17	25	.405	377	387	2.75
Jack Cronin	12	23	.343	307	284	2.70
Ned Garvin	5	15	.250	181.7	141	1.68
Ed Poole	8	14	.364	178	178	3.39
Doc Scanlan*	7	9	.438	126	115	2.64

*Includes record with Pittsburgh

Sheckard had been recognized as one of the game's top players for several years. Brooklyn purchased his contract from a minor league team in 1897, when Jimmy was only 18 years old. He became a regular the next season, at an age when most players were still in amateur ball or just beginning their minor league careers. At 20, playing for John McGraw in Baltimore, he led the National League with 77 stolen bases. Two years later he led the league in triples–the mark of a long-ball hitter in the Deadball Era—and in slugging percentage. In 1903 he led the league in home runs and stolen bases.

In 1900, the Superbas' last championship season, Sheckard was an eager 21-year-old surrounded by a group of seasoned veterans—men such as Hughie Jennings, Willie Keeler, and Joe Kelley, all members of the great Orioles teams, and Bill Dahlen, Duke Farrell, Tom Daly, and Deacon McGuire, all standout players who had long before mastered the techniques of "scientific baseball"—the use of aggressive baserunning, bunting, and hit-and-run tactics. The veterans set the tone for the team. Jimmy's role was to utilize his natural talent and learn the methods of scientific baseball from the older players.

Over the next three seasons almost all of those veterans moved on to other teams. As they left, Jimmy's role changed from that of a young player still learning the fine points of the game to being one of the team's stars, an outstanding player in all aspects of the game. Always, however, there were other players who assumed the role of team leaders. Even in 1903, when many of the Superbas were new to the team and the National League, leadership was provided by Bill Dahlen and Jack Doyle, two old-timers whose careers dated back to the early 90s. Jimmy was still free to focus on his own game.

In 1904 that changed. Dahlen was traded to New York over the winter and Doyle was released two weeks into the season. The formal team captain was Pop Dillon, who had spent the previous two seasons in the Pacific Coast League. Dillon was 30 years old in 1904. He knew baseball, but had never played more than 74 games in one season at the major league level. He was a borderline big league player, and as such was not in a position to exercise strong leadership. There was no player on the team who came close to matching Sheckard's experience or stature as a player. It was apparent the team needed his on-field leadership. Jimmy tried. But he didn't have the personality for the role.

Although he was entering his seventh National League season in 1904, Sheckard was still only 25—a young, relatively immature 25. He wasn't the kind of person who could take over the helm of a ship floundering in storm-tossed seas and steer it to safety. He was more like the guy you wanted to keep away from the pilot house, even in calm seas. He was the person who needed steadying advice, not the one who could assist others.

As a rookie with Brooklyn in 1898 Jimmy began complaining of stomach pains shortly after he joined the team. When asked what might have caused the problem, Jimmy said he didn't know, but he thought he had caught a cold. A short time later, team captain Mike Griffin happened to observe Jimmy in the hotel dining room. According to Griffin, who undoubtedly exaggerated for effect as he told the story, at one setting he watched the youngster put down a meal of frogs' legs, oyster patties, filet of beef, corn beef and cabbage, calves' liver and bacon, pie, pudding, orange marmalade, chocolate ice cream, cheese, coffee, nuts, and fruit. Griffin watched in amazement, which only increased when he saw Sheckard pick up a menu to see if he had missed anything. Approaching Jimmy's table, Griffin smiled and asked, "What's the matter, Sheck, have you lost your appetite?" Jimmy responded that he thought he might be able to hold a little more. "Well," Griffin said, "you take the cake, where do you expect to put it?" Griffin then told Sheckard his eating habits were the cause of his stomach pains. He advised Jimmy to confine himself to a little soup, fish, and steak for a few days. Reportedly Sheckard took the advice, but a year later, after the 1899 season ended, he told a reporter he was going to Mt. Clemens to treat a stomach problem of long standing. A year after that he was swallowing a glass of hot water with a pinch of salt before breakfast each morning, recommending the drink to anyone troubled with dyspepsia.[44]

Jimmy had a great season in 1901, batting .354 and, as noted above, leading the National League in triples and slugging percentage. His talent was obvious, but so, too, was tendency toward youthful lapses in judgment. One such lapse provoked a comment from *Brooklyn Daily Eagle* reporter Abe

Yager: "Sheckard is a daring baserunner and the crowd likes to see him reach first, expecting to see some sensational sprinting," Yager wrote. "But sometimes Sheck gets reckless and tries to do the impossible. This happened in the seventh when he tried to race from first to third on a little fumble by Cross, who had no trouble in nailing the speedy Jim."

In another game Sheckard came to bat in the middle of a rally with runners on first and third. The Superbas had just lined out three straight hits to score a run and tie the score. Sheckard surprised everyone on the field by laying down a bunt, on which the runner on third was thrown out at the plate. The next batter lined into a double play to end the rally. When Sheckard returned to the bench manager Ned Hanlon asked him why he had bunted in that situation. "Why, that was one of those [un]expected plays we talk so much about," replied Jimmy. "You bet it was not expected," said Hanlon. "It was so unexpected that no one knew anything about it, not even our own players. It isn't your own team that you want to surprise, but the other fellows. The next time you work that game just tip off the man at third."[45]

Already a seasoned veteran at 25, Jimmy Sheckard felt great pressure to provide team leadership for the Superbas in 1904, his performance suffering as a result (Library of Congress).

In 1902, after he jumped to Baltimore for the second year in a row, then back to Brooklyn after playing four games with the Orioles, Sheckard had a poor season. Early in the season he took a lot of heat from the fans for his "double jump," but he may have been more distracted by a law suit brought against him by John McGraw.[46] Whatever the reason or reasons, he seemed to be distracted. His batting average dropped 89 points from the previous season. Sheckard bounced back to have a fine season in 1903, batting .332 and leading the league in home runs and stolen bases. In 1904, placed in a position where his performance was essential to his team's success, he collapsed.

Modern fans have seen a number of recent versions of Sheckard's 1904 season. In our time Sheckard's role is usually occupied by a high-priced free agent who has just signed a new contract. Feeling great pressure to justify his salary, the player gets away from the natural flow of his game and performs way below par. Similarly, Sheckard put great pressure on himself to carry his team, which had mediocre talent, and failed to play up to even that mediocre level.

Jimmy opened the season in a batting slump that lasted until roughly mid–September. In mid–May, after 25 games, his average stood at .175. He managed to get it into the low .200s by mid–June, but it stayed at pretty much that level until deep into September. When he was going well in previous years, Jimmy was capable of not only playing the hit-and-run game but also of driving the ball against the fences. In 1904 a St. Louis writer described a much different hitter. "Sheckard is a fiend for placing the ball and seldom made a swing," he wrote. Later, after Jimmy drove in the winning run in a game, the *Eagle's* Yager noted that the hit was "a sharp drive past [second baseman] Farrell in lieu of the weak infield grounders that had become his norm."[47]

The pressure affected Jimmy's fielding, as well as his hitting. Early in the season he tried to make some difficult catches in clutch situations, only to have his attempts backfire and cost his team a couple games. As a result he became tentative in his play. In a May article Yager said Sheckard contributed to a loss to Cincinnati by taking a conservative approach on a line drive. After the leadoff hitter in the second inning walked, "Odwell followed with a liner toward left that Sheckard ordinarily would have smothered," Yager wrote, "but, remembering his play of the previous day, he hesitated when almost within reaching distance and lost the catch." In June after Sheckard passed up a chance to throw out a slow runner at the plate, Yager said, "Things are altogether at sixes and sevens with our crack left fielder and he is not taking the chances he used to when things were going right. In other words, whatever good play Jimmy has attempted this season has gone wrong, and he played a safe game, fearing that a throw to the plate might send Hulswitt to second and give the Phillies another run. That is not winning ball, but the discretionary article that falls far short of the brilliant."[48]

Eventually, Sheckard made the necessary mental adjustments. His play picked up in September. During the winter, on a holiday visit to Brooklyn, he was asked what caused his poor season. With a painful look, Jimmy responded, "Why wring a harrowing confession out of a man when his heart is bleeding for his batting average." There wasn't any special problem, he said. The problem was general. It was one of those off years every player runs into. "It isn't necessary to say that I had it bad," he said. "I know it. I used to wake up nights and think of it, but I don't get any such attacks again. I'm taking things to prevent it. I'll be stinging the ball next year instead of popping it up."

Jimmy rebounded from his nightmare season to hit .292 in 1905 and play his usual well-rounded game. Hanlon applied his own bit of psychological therapy on his young veteran by naming him team captain in 1905. Near the end of spring training Hanlon told a reporter the move seemed to help Sheckard. "He has reached that point where he thinks it up to him to show others that he is a capable ball player," Hanlon said. "I'd rather have him with that disposition than to have him as he was last year, when he quickly became discouraged, and not only lost confidence in the team but lost confidence in himself."[49]

When Your Team Is Hopelessly Behind, Again: Boston

Fans of tail-end teams know the sensation of trying to maintain interest in a game in which your team, a chronic loser, has fallen so far behind in the early innings that it is a stretch of the imagination to believe they have any chance at all of winning that day's game. Attendees at the Beaneaters' games probably had that feeling all too often in 1904. The team still had some good players. Fred Tenney was the best fielding first baseman in the game, Vic Willis and Togie Pittinger were among the league's best pitchers, and several regulars were solid major leaguers. But the parts didn't fit together very well. The team lost almost two-thirds of their games. They struggled to win two games in a row. Losing streaks, on the other hand, were common. The Beaneaters lost two straight games six times, three straight four times, four straight seven times, five straight three times, seven straight once and eight straight once. The atmosphere at their games had to be a lot different than in the 1890s, when they won five pennants. There must have been many times when a Beaneaters fan would have let his attention stray from the play on the field.

Boston (55–98)

Regular Lineup	*AVG*	*OBP*	*SLG*	*R*	*RBI*	*SB*
Phil Geier, cf	.243	.314	.284	70	27	18
Fred Tenney, 1b	.270	.351	.341	76	37	17
Ed Abbaticchio, ss	.256	.309	.337	76	54	24
Duff Cooley, lf	.272	.312	.373	41	70	14

Regular Lineup	AVG	OBP	SLG	R	RBI	SB
Jim Delahanty, 3b	.285	.333	.389	56	60	16
Fred Raymer, 2b	.210	.236	.260	28	27	17
Rip Cannell, rf	.234	.286	.254	32	18	10
or Pat Carney, rf	.204	.240	.237	24	11	6
Tom Needham, c	.260	.292	.372	18	19	3
or Pat Moran, c	.226	.267	.299	26	34	10

Leading Pitchers	W	L	PCT.	IP	H	ERA
Vic Willis	18	25	.419	350	357	2.85
Togie Pittinger	15	21	.417	335.3	298	2.66
Kaiser Wilhelm	14	20	.412	288	316	3.69
Tom Fisher	6	16	.273	214	257	4.25
Ed McNichol	2	12	.143	122	120	4.28

Suppose you're a fan at one of the Beaneaters' 1904 games. Action has slowed down, possibly because Ed McNichol is having one of those long innings when he just can't get a pitch over the plate. So you and a friend start throwing some trivia questions at each other. Some possible questions involving Beaneaters players:

Question: Which Beaneater was considered about as good a prospect as Nap Lajoie when the Phillies purchased both of them from Fall River in 1896? (Some sources say he was the player the Phillies valued most highly. Lajoie, the Cleveland star, was considered by many experts in 1904 to be the game's best active player and by some to be the best ever up to that time.)

Answer: Phil Geier. When Phillies Manager Billy Nash scouted the Fall River team, Geier was the player he came to see. During negotiations with Fall River, Geier and Lajoie became part of a package offered for $1,500, a pretty high price at the time for New England League players. Geier turned out to be the equivalent of a modern day Four-A player—one who excels at the highest minor league level, but can't quite cut it in the major leagues. The Phillies gave him a thorough trial in 1896 and 1897 before returning him to the minors. He was given chances with Cincinnati in 1900, the Philadelphia Athletics and Milwaukee Brewers in 1901, and the Beaneaters in 1904, but couldn't stick with any of those teams. From 1902 through 1906, Geier hit .324, .361, .332, and .304 with St. Paul of the Class A American Association. His .361 average in 1903 led the league. The one year he had a poor batting average during that five-year span was 1904, when he hit .243 for the Beaneaters.[50]

Question: Beaneaters outfielder Pat Carney received his medical degree from Georgetown University in 1904,[51] thus automatically qualifying for the baseball nickname "Doc." Name three other baseball "Docs" active in 1904.

Answer: This should have been fairly easy for an avid baseball fan of

1904. "Doc" Casey (Chicago Cubs) had been around for a while, "Doc" White (Chicago White Sox) was one of the best pitchers in baseball, and Mike "Doc" Powers was a well established catcher for the Philadelphia Athletics. "Doc" Marshall bounced around the National League that year, catching for the Phillies, and Giants. He also came to Boston on loan from the Giants when injuries depleted the Beaneaters' catching staff. Brooklyn players could be assured of reliable first aid when injured, since the team roster included "Doc" Gessler, "Doc" Reisling and "Doc" Scanlan. Cincinnati pitcher "Noodles" Hahn was a veterinarian. Normally, newspaper reporters would have bestowed the nickname "Doc" on Hahn when he got his degree, but evidently they were sensible enough to appreciate the better, more exclusive, nickname he had carried from childhood. Jimmy Sheckard might have been in line for the nickname, since he enrolled in the Baltimore School of Dentistry in 1900. But Jimmy only associated himself with the dental school because he wanted to play on its football team. He didn't attend any classes. Had he made it to at least a few classes he would have qualified as a "Doc" under the relaxed attitude among newspaper writers of the time. That would have given the Superbas four "Docs" on their team, which surely must be an all-time record.[52]

Associated Question: For a bonus on this question, who won the National League's "Battle of the Doctors" in 1897?

Answer: Arlie "Doc" Pond beat "Doc" McJames. There were actually two battles between the esteemed medical practitioners. Pond won them both. Pitching for the Baltimore Orioles, Pond beat McJames and the Washington Senators 6–3 on July 1 and 14–2 on July 28. The two doctors were teammates for a brief time with the Orioles in 1898.

Question: Boston first baseman Fred Tenney, a left-handed thrower, is considered the top-fielding first baseman in the game. He played a different position when he first came to Boston. What was that?

Answer: Although he was left-handed, Tenney was a catcher when he first appeared with the Beaneaters in 1894. He caught 71 games for Boston during his career.

Associated Question: Tenney is not the only player active in 1904 who caught in the major leagues despite being a left-handed thrower. Who else had that distinction?

Answer: Jiggs Donahue, the Chicago White Sox' first baseman, was also a catcher when he debuted in the major leagues. He caught a total of three games for Pittsburgh in 1900–01, and went behind the plate 42 times for the Milwaukee/St. Louis franchise in 1901–02, before returning to the minors and switching to first base.

Question: How many players on the 1904 Beaneaters team refused to play baseball on Sundays?

Answer: Three. First baseman and captain Fred Tenney, pitcher Kaiser Wilhelm and pitcher Togie Pittinger had provisions in their contracts allowing them to sit out on Sundays. Since, normally, only western teams scheduled games on Sundays, the effect on the Beaneaters was much less than it would be in modern times. The Beaneaters played eight Sunday games in 1904. Two of them were in Brooklyn, as the Superbas searched for a loophole in the local law that would allow them to play on Sundays.[53]

A Miracle? Philadelphia

It must have been a miracle. It happened on August 21. Maybe about three o'clock in the afternoon. That's when the Phillies were suddenly transformed from an abject loser—on a level with the 1962 Mets—into a solid, competitive team, one that would finish just behind the National League's perennial pennant contenders (Chicago, New York, and Pittsburgh) for the rest of the decade.

We're just kidding about the miracle. But for most of the season the Phillies were a terrible team. For them a winning streak was to win two games in a row, which they managed to do seven times before August 21. They didn't win more than two straight over that period. After the first game of a doubleheader on August 21—which, naturally, they lost—the Phillies' record stood at 27–79, giving them a won-lost percentage of .255. They won the second game and went on to finish the season with a 25–21 record. And it wasn't a temporary change. They finished fourth in 1905 and stayed pretty much at that level until 1913, when they finished second.

Philadelphia (52-100)

Regular Lineup	AVG	OBP	SLG	R	RBI	SB
Roy Thomas, cf	.290	.416	.345	92	29	28
Kid Gleason, 2b	.274	.319	.334	61	42	17
Harry Wolverton, 3b	.266	.321	.329	43	49	18
or Bob Hall, 3b	.160	.226	.184	11	17	5
Sherry Magee, rf	.277	.308	.409	51	57	11
Jack Doyle, 1b*	.221	.295	.298	22	24	5
or Johnny Lush, 1b-of-p	.276	.336	.369	39	42	12
John Titus, lf	.294	.362	.387	60	55	15
Rudy Hulswitt, ss	.244	.276	.298	36	36	8
or She Donahue, ss-3b**	.219	.229	.237	22	16	10
Red Dooin, c	.242	.261	.346	41	36	15
or Frank Roth, c	.258	.298	.314	28	20	8

Leading Pitchers	W	L	PCT.	IP	H	ERA
Chick Fraser	14	24	.368	302	287	3.25
Jack Sutthoff***	11	19	.367	253.7	255	3.19
Bill Duggleby	12	13	.480	223.7	265	3.78
Tully Sparks	7	16	.304	200.7	208	2.65
Frank Corridon****	11	10	.524	194.7	176	2.64
Fred Mitchell*	6	12	.333	174.7	206	3.56
John McPherson	1	12	.077	128	130	3.66

*Includes record with Brooklyn
**Includes record with St. Louis
***Includes record with Cincinnati
****Includes record with Chicago

Two major weaknesses emerged early in the Phillies' season. They weren't real good at catching and throwing the ball, and they only had two pitchers who were able to overcome the poor fielding support. Fielding errors were common in this era, but with the Phillies they came as steadily as rain in a tropical forest. Some Phillies games featured a veritable storm of errors. In ten April games the Phillies made six errors twice, four errors once, and three errors four times. In May they had three seven-error games and two more six-error games. In 33 games played through May 31, they managed to avoid making an error in only two games. In league averages compiled through May 26, they were fielding .930 as a team. The next worst mark in the league was .941.[54] By the end of the season the Phillies had raised their team fielding average to .937, but that was still eight points behind the Beaneaters and Superbas, who tied for second-worst with .945 averages.

The Phillies didn't win many games while they were so busy kicking the ball around the diamond. The few games they did win came when either Chick Fraser or Bill Duggleby was pitching. On June 17 Fred Mitchell beat the Beaneaters 12–7 in the second game of a doubleheader. Before that game, Duggleby had a 4–5 won-lost record, Fraser was 5–7, and the rest of the Phillies staff was 0–23.[55] Even after Mitchell's breakthrough victory, the Phillies' 10–35 record put them solidly in last place. They trailed the first-place Giants by 20½ games and the seventh-place Beaneaters by seven games. The Phillies got a little better in June and July, but through the third week in August they were still losing about three games for each victory.

Why the sudden change of fortune beginning on August 21? Well, there were no reports of lightning bolts striking the visitor's clubhouse in Cincinnati (where they were playing), so it was almost certainly the cumulative result of several changes made during the summer. Early in the season Manager Hugh Duffy had picked up veteran Jack Doyle to fill a hole at first base and had made room in the lineup for Bob Hall, who came from Class A Milwaukee with Duffy. Both of those moves failed badly. Doyle could no longer perform up to his former standards. He hit only .212 and was no longer an asset in the field or on the bases. Hall, it turned out, could neither hit nor field at the major league level. He hit .160 and had fielding averages of .800 at shortstop and .853 at third base. Duffy replaced Doyle with Johnny Lush, a talented 18-year-old, who started the season as a pitcher, moved to the outfield after going 0-6 on the mound, and settled in at first base in August. Before his release in early August, Hall had already been benched in favor of shortstop Rudy Hulswitt and third baseman Harry Wolverton, the 1903 regulars at those positions.[56]

As the losses mounted, Duffy became frustrated over his inability to do anything about the team's plight. "Managing a tail-end team is about the hardest proposition that I can imagine," Duffy complained. "People seem to think that when you have a loser all you have to do is to snap your fingers and get star ballplayers by the dozen." He had made all sorts of offers, Duffy said, but no one wanted to make a deal. "The clubs which have good men, whether they be major or minor league clubs, want to keep them just as badly as we want them."[57]

Near the end of June Duffy signed a 19-year-old outfielder named Sherry Magee, who had been playing with a semi-pro team in Carlisle, Pennsylvania. Magee misjudged two fly balls in his first game, but still looked good enough to be rated "a likely looking youngster" in the game summary. Magee was substituting for John Titus, who was out with an injury. He continued to play regularly, even after Titus returned to the lineup. In his first season of professional baseball Magee hit .277 in 95 games, with 15 doubles, 12 triples and three home runs. Playing only two-thirds of a season he finished sixth in the National League in triples. Near the end of the season Honus Wagner predicted Magee would become a star. Wagner was right. Magee's career statistics were good enough to merit serious consideration for the Hall of Fame.[58]

The Phillies' pitching staff was fortified with help from other National League teams. Cincinnati more or less gave the Phillies Jack Sutthoff. Chicago agreed to give up Frank Corridon for Shad Barry, an outfielder who rarely played under Duffy. In addition, Tully Sparks, who had been shelled in his appearances early in the season, figured out a way to get batters out. These pitchers gave the Phillies a decent chance to win whenever they took the mound. In the final 46 games, when the Phillies won more often than they lost, Corridon was 5-1, Sparks was 4-4, and Sutthoff 4-6. The big winner over that span was Bill Duggleby, who finished the season by winning his last seven decisions.

Hard Luck Ned Garvin

Bill James called Virgil "Ned" Garvin "the tough-luck pitcher of the decade, if not the hard-luck pitcher of all time." Garvin had a good earned run average every year, and a losing record every year but one. That season he went 11–11 with a 2.09 ERA. His career ERA was a good 2.72, but his career won-lost record was a terrible 58–97. Garvin would have agreed with James' assessment—in fact, he said much the same thing eight decades before James wrote it. "Ill luck pursues me," Garvin complained after losing several games due to his teammates' errors. "They used to say that about me when I was a boy, but somehow or other I still believe I will break this hoodoo. The great batters of the league say I am hard to hit and I am bound some day to get proper club support."[59]

One of the league's better hitters, Lave Cross, told a reporter, "It is a good thing there ain't many Garvins in this league, or we would not reach the .200 mark.... He can curve them underhand and overhand. He has got benders on his speed that break right at the plate, and no matter how hard you try you will miss them a mile. He is one of the best pitchers I ever stacked up against." Garvin's fingers were extraordinarily long, which helped him master an assortment of curves. He had a "fadeaway" pitch before Christy Mathewson made that pitch famous. His best pitch was an overhand curve that Atlantic League batters had called a "break-off ball." And his breaking pitches were supplemented by one of the better fastballs in the league.[60]

A colorful personality who earned the nicknames "Bullet Proof Ned" and "The Navasota Tarantula," Garvin clearly had the makings of a winning pitcher. Still, he pitched in the major leagues for six years, and luck usually evens out over that period of time. Tough luck might have contributed somewhat to Garvin's losing record, but surely other factors also contributed. Garvin seems to have lacked the stamina demanded of pitchers in the Deadball Era. "Garvin is a tall, angular fellow standing 6 feet 3¾ inches in height and he looked like a bean pole when standing still in the center of the diamond," wrote one reporter. "In fact, there was considerable similarity between his form and the pole that supports the championship pennant in center field. His appearance was fairly well described by a lot of rooters in the fifty cent stand, who kept up a continued shout of: 'Garvin, Garvin, you must be starvin.'" Early in his career Garvin acquired a reputation as a "seven-inning pitcher"—at a time when seven innings was considered a failed pitching effort rather than a quality start. He eventually overcame that reputation, but he never overcame a related weakness, the tendency to give up big-run innings.[61]

Garvin undoubtedly lost some games because of his weakness in the field and at bat. Although his fielding averages were about normal for the era, he seems to have been a poor fielder, one writer saying, "Of the really good pitchers in the league who are handicapped by poor fielding ability, there is no more shining example than Virgil Garvin." He was a weak batter, with a career batting average of .122, including a scintillating .075 mark in 1903. After one game in which Garvin was taken out for a pinch-hitter, a reporter commented, "It looks as if the Brooklyns will have to do some tall slugging before Virgil Garvin pitches a full nine-inning game. His appearance at the bat has become a joke and besides he almost invariably looms up with an error that loses a close game. A knowledge of curves is not the only requisite of a twirler and Garvin ought to brush up on batting and fielding."[62]

To a great extent a pitcher's won-lost percentage is, of course, a product of the quality of the teams he plays for. Garvin's teams finished near the middle of the standings every season except one, the 1901 Milwaukee Brewers coming in last with a 48–89 record. Excluding token appearances with three clubs, in which Garvin went 1–3, other pitchers on his teams posted a combined 331–366 record, for a .475 won-lost percentage. With Garvin on the mound, those clubs went 57–94 for a .377 percentage.

If Garvin was pursued by "ill luck" on the diamond, he was plagued by an even worse demon off the field. While his normal manner was gentlemanly and congenial, when he drank he became just plain nasty. His career was marked by violent escapades and undoubtedly was shortened by them. In 1901, while playing for Milwaukee, he entered a barber shop after having become intoxicated. He approached an African American man, named James Harrison, who was busy shining shoes, and asked him if he knew what they did to people of his race in Texas. Harrison told Garvin he didn't care what they did in Texas. "He got into the chair next to the one where I was at work," Harrison said later, "and when I had my head down he struck me. He pulled a gun. I went through the door into the washroom and on down into the basement. Just as I was going through the door Garvin shot twice. One bullet lodged in the door, but the other we never found." After the incident, Garvin was arrested and charged with attempted murder. Before his trial the charge was lowered to assault and battery. He was found guilty and fined $50 and court costs.[63]

Roughly a year later, again while drunk, "Bullet-Proof Ned" began brandishing a revolver in a Chicago saloon. One of the patrons fled the saloon and called a policeman. The policeman tried to pacify Garvin, who knocked him down with his pistol and began to take aim at the fallen officer. At that point the bartender intervened, struggling with Garvin for the pistol. Garvin shot the bartender in the shoulder and fled from the scene. The next day, after sobering up, Garvin turned himself in. When a reporter asked him about the incident, Garvin said, "I don't care to talk about it— just let it rest where it is. I shot at somebody, I guess. I was drunk at the time." Once again Garvin got off with a fine.[64]

With Brooklyn in 1904, Garvin marked the beginning and end of his season by getting involved in fights. In early May, while in Philadelphia, he was cut up and robbed while out on a binge. In August he became drunk, along with several teammates, on the train that was taking the Superbas to Pittsburgh. Although the team tried to cover up the incident, evidently Garvin punched the team's financial secretary, an elderly gentleman. This time Garvin was given a choice of an indefinite suspension or his release. Confident that his pitching ability would always enable him to land a job with another team, Garvin chose the release.[65] He was immediately signed by the New York Highlanders.

Garvin pitched two games with the Highlanders during September before again drawing his release. No major league team would touch him after that. He pitched in the Pacific Coast League in 1905and 1906 and in the Northwestern League in 1907.

The next year Dame Fortune dealt him the ultimate blow. Somewhere during his travels Garvin contracted "galloping consumption"—a deadly form of tuberculosis. He passed away on June 16, 1908, at the age of 34.[66]

Irwin's Handy Invention

Arthur Irwin liked to tell how he came to invent the fielder's glove:

It was quite by accident that I introduced it. I was hit on the hand by a pitched ball. My finger was so badly bruised that I could not handle a grounder without suffering excruciating pain. It was in 1883. I was with the Providence team. We were right up in the championship swim. It was very important that I should stay in my place. I finally thought of a glove, and I called on a glove maker in Boston. He made me a glove, the finger for the little and next finger to it being in one. I wore it and it was so comfortable that I had another one made with all the fingers in it. Then Johnny Ward, who had been pitching, was just starting out as an infielder. He saw my glove and asked me to have one made for him. I telegraphed to the maker and forwarded one immediately.

Three weeks later I got a telegram from Ward from Cleveland. It read: "Some one stole my glove today. Must have another one; can't get along without it." I at once secured him another glove. I believe it was the glove that kept Ward in the business as an infielder. Without the glove he would have had trouble. It helped him to become one of the best in the business. It was not long until other infielders fell into the glove idea. In less than two years every fielder in the business, with rare exceptions, like McPhee and Dunlap, were wearing gloves.[67]

In the great tradition of old ex-ballplayers, Irwin told this story often, the details varying with each telling but the main storyline holding firm (more or less). Most modern historians are content to give Irwin credit for "inventing" the fielder's glove, without trying to nail down the details surrounding the event.[68]

By the early 1900s there were basically three types of gloves being used by major league ballplayers: the infielder's glove Irwin devised, a catcher's mitt, and a "baseman's mitt." Catchers were the first ballplayers to wear gloves. At first they wore two leather gloves with the fingers cut out. In the late 1880s and early 1890s they began wearing a heavily padded mitt. By 1900 the catcher's mitt looked somewhat like a big leather donut—it was circular, with thick padding all around the glove. The center of the glove—the donut hole—was a deep pocket. The thumb was separated from the rest of the mitt, connected only by a leather lace.

First basemen wore a mitt clearly modeled on the catcher's mitt but smaller and oblong, with much less padding (envision a glove shaped like a small child's mitten). The thumb of the first baseman's mitt was connected to the longer portion by a one or two laces, much like the catcher's mitt. The mitt might have a ridge at the base that helped to form a pocket of sorts.

Irwin's infielder's glove had changed only a little over the 20-some years since he first wore it. His glove was a leather glove with extra padding. By 1904 the fielder's glove had gotten somewhat bigger and a little more sturdy, but still looked somewhat like a stuffed, oversized version of a normal leather glove. The back side of the glove was cut away, except for a strap to hold the glove on, much as more modern gloves have been for many decades. The size of the glove varied somewhat. Some players' gloves might be only about an inch larger than their hands, while others might wear gloves with padded fingers extending as much as a couple inches beyond the player's fingers. In 1904 the fielder's glove worn by most players had no laces connecting the thumb with the fingers, though by 1905 the Spalding Company was offering gloves with a very small web connecting the base of the thumb with the base of the first finger.[69]

The glove not only offered protection for the fielder's hands; it also aided the fielder in catching the ball. An example of the glove's impact can be seen in the experience of Cincinnati second baseman Bid McPhee.

By 1892 the only National League fielders who continued to play barehanded were McPhee and third baseman Jerry Denny, both considered among the best at their positions. (However, there were still a number of pitchers who, possibly not considering fielding a big part of their job, continued to play barehanded.) Denny's last major league season was 1894, leaving McPhee as the last barehanded infielder.

Early in the 1895 season, Bid injured the little finger of his left hand. He decided to use a glove temporarily while the finger healed. When a reporter talked to him about it, McPhee remarked, "It feels strange to play with a glove. During the fourteen years in which I have been with the Cincinnati team, I have never had any protection for the hands, except perhaps in a few practice games that were played in cold weather and before my hands were toughened. I find it very awkward playing with a glove, and never feel safe on a hit or a thrown ball." Asked if he would continue to wear the glove after the finger healed, Bid responded, "No I will not continue to use a glove, though I may grow accustomed to it. As soon as my finger is again in shape I shall fire the pad and go back to the old style with which I am more familiar."[70]

Once he got used to the glove, however, McPhee couldn't give it up. In 1896, the season after he first tried the glove, he posted a .978 fielding average, an extraordinarily high mark for the time. After the season ended, McPhee said, "I have become thoroughly accustomed to wearing a glove while playing second base, and don't ever expect to play without one again. I find a glove of great help to me in playing second base, and that certainly is a sufficient reason for not desiring to go back to bare hands."[71]

Although they were definitely a help to the fielder, the small gloves of the early 1900s could not come close to providing the fielding assistance furnished by the well-designed, elaborate gloves of our time. The gloves of the early Deadball Era offered protection for the fielder's hand and might have padding at the bottom forming a shallow pocket that helped a fielder hold onto the ball. But to catch a baseball the fielder still had to grab and hold the ball in the palm of his hand, and the accepted method of catching the ball was with two hands, the glove cushioning the impact of the ball and the non-gloved hand helping to secure the ball.

While the fielders of the early 1900s were much more proficient than their predecessors of the previous two or three decades, they still made a lot of errors. From 1900 through 1903 league-wide fielding averages ranged from .938 to .953. In 1904 the American League fielding average climbed to .959, and for the next ten years the two leagues averaged in the high .950s. By contrast, in our own time, the leagues average in the low to mid .980s and the top fielding teams make only a couple dozen more errors than the average shortstop made in the early 1900s.

The fact is that fielding required considerable skill in the early 1900s, given the small gloves and playing fields that were much rougher than they are now. Fans of all sports view games with expectations about the level of play. Fans at major league games applaud plays that clearly exceed expectations for players performing at the sport's highest level (and boo plays that don't meet the minimum expectations). Game summaries and the special comments that accompanied them in almost all newspapers of the day tell us much about the level of fielding skill fans expected to see in the early 1900s.

One thing that stands out about the newspaper coverage is how much it focused on fielding. That is not to say that fielding was considered more important than hitting—after all, the game is about scoring runs, and fans liked to see and read about hitting. Game summaries devoted most of the available space to describing how the runs were scored, then as now. But in a description of the day's game, it seemed almost obligatory for a writer to give credit for good fielding plays. Even a one-paragraph description of an out-of-town game could well include a sentence mentioning a catch as "a feature of the game." A Detroit writer summed up the fans' feelings: "Another thing that may be stated as a fact is that there isn't the clamor for heavy hitting and big scores that there is generally asserted to be. The public likes to see the ball hit, but it prefers a game in which a lot of hit balls are turned into outs by brilliant fielding to a game in which about a dozen safe hits are made on each side, for a 10 to 7 score. Assuredly the series here between Detroit and Cleveland was a light hitting one, but the fans seemed to be pretty well pleased with most of the games. Because of the fact that the small scores were due to brilliant fielding behind fine pitching. They like to see the ball hit, and they like to see it fielded also."[72]

Recognition of the day's outstanding fielding plays often appeared as an item or two in the subsections of game summaries that usually carried distinctive regularly-used sub-titles, such as "Notes of the Game" or "Diamond Gems." A phrase that appeared very frequently in descriptions of noteworthy plays was "one-handed catch." The phrase was at times used without any further description of the play, suggesting that making a catch with one hand was considered difficult enough in itself to constitute an exceptional play. Some examples:

> "There were no features except a one-hand pickup by Corcoran and good hitting by Wagner, Seymour and Peitz."[73]
>
> "Baseball Notes and Comments. Fred Tenney is still one of the greatest first basemen the game has ever known. He made two or three good catches yesterday, one of them, the one-hand capture of a high throw, being particularly brilliant."[74]
>
> "In the sixth inning Wagner made one of those marvelous one-hand stops for which he is famous, but was unable to get the ball to first in time to retire the runner. The crowd cheered the play for fully five minutes."[75]
>
> "Notes of the Colts' Game. Gleason speared Chance's liner in the sixth with one hand. Wicker was retired in the fifth on a one-handed catch by Donahue."[76]
>
> "Notes of the Game. No game seems to be complete without Flick making a spectacular one-handed catch. Yesterday he took one down that fell only a few inches outside the house behind the scoreboard."[77]

> "Notes of the Game. Captain [Lave] Cross and Harry Davis made star one-hand plays on Holmes in the ninth. Monte Cross made a lightning scoop and play on Isbell in the tenth."[78]
>
> "Nearly every man on both teams at some time or another did a circus stunt which prolonged the battle. Perhaps the most sensational were Davis's one handed catch of a line drive from Stovall's bat in the tenth, after a high jump, Jackson's one handed stab of a drive from Tannehill after a long run, Jones's capture of another stinging liner from Stovall, which was going straight over his head when he turned and gave chase successfully, and the work of Tannehill and Donahue on a bunt by Bradley. Lee scooped the ball up with one hand on the dead run and threw wild in his haste, but Jiggs stuck out his mitt and speared the ball close to the ground as far away as he could stretch."[79]

While all major league players attempted one-handed catches when a catch could not be made with two hands, in the early 1900s the ability to consistently make one-handed catches was the mark of a good fielder. In one of the comments cited above the writer noted that Honus Wagner had made "one of those marvelous one-hand stops for which he is famous." This writer encountered almost identical wording used to describe plays by Bill Bradley, Jimmy Collins, Nap Lajoie, Claude Ritchey and Johnny Evers. A more thorough search might find the phrase applied to a dozen or so other players.[80]

The difficulty of making catches using the small gloves of the day is also shown by the fact that a fielder could be credited with a fine play even if he did not manage to hold on to the ball. In such cases the fielder would be praised for having "beat down," "knocked down," "blocked," or "batted down" the ball. Often on such a play the fielder would pick up the ball and throw the runner out, but the play would be described as remarkable even if no out resulted:

> "Pittsburgh's hitting was led by Hans [sic] Wagner, who cracked out three two-baggers and a single. On one of the doubles Dick Cooley made a wonderful try for the ball against the fence, barely missing it after a pretty block."[81]
>
> "Notes of the Third Nationals' Game. Casey blocked Dooin's hot grounder in the sixth, had time to turn around twice, looking for the ball, and then threw Dooin out."[82]
>
> "Notes of the Nationals' Game. Devlin made two corking stops of fierce bounders in the sixth and seventh that saved Mathewson. In each instance the ball, after being blocked down, rolled straight in front of him, enabling him to get his man."[83]

One descriptive phrase that is not often seen in the descriptions of good fielding plays is "backhand catch." In 1904 the *Cincinnati Commercial Tribune* ran a picture of Fred Tenney with the caption, "From a snapshot taken by Commercial Tribune photographer, showing Tenney making his famous back-hand catch." The picture, which may have been posed, depicts Tenney (a left-handed thrower) reaching out to his left with the ball nestled in his mitt's small pocket, in the area secured by the thumb and first two or three fingers. (The glove is so small that the ball takes up most of the pocket.) The caption implies that Tenney was making a catch that few other fielders could make, and on at least one occasion Tenney was criticized for attempting backhand catches. After one game Boston writer Tim Murnane wrote, "Tenney, at first, was away off. When a ball was thrown to his left he tried to swing his gloved hand around while hugging the base, in each instance allowing the ball to pull him, when he should have stepped out and played the throw with his left hand, even if bare." Murnane, who played first base for Boston in the 1870s and 1880s, explained: "For years men played with bare hands and never complained, when the throwing was just as hot and perhaps a shade wilder than at the present time."[84]

It is likely that other smooth-fielding first basemen, such as Jiggs Donahue and Dan McGann, also attempted backhand catches with some frequency. The first baseman's mitt of the early 1900s had a leather lace or two holding the top of the thumb to the rest of the glove, which would have been of some assistance in making a backhand catch. It would have been much harder, however, for a player to make a backhand catch using the fielder's glove of the day.

Three different pictures carried in the newspapers of 1903–04 show infielders Miller Huggins, Ed Greminger, and Hunter Hill preparing to make catches. In all three pictures the glove is held with the thumb and fingers splayed outward, with the non-glove hand extended ready to secure the ball.[85] With such an approach the catch would be made with the palm, which could be moved with a natural motion on balls to the gloved side or front of a fielder. On a ball to the throwing-hand side, however, as the ball goes further away from the body it becomes increasingly more difficult to keep the palm in a good position to catch the ball. With only a single lace or even a very small web at the base of the thumb to hold the hand together against the impact, the force of a well-hit ball would tend to drive the thumb and fingers apart, causing the ball to be dropped if a backhand catch were attempted. Therefore it is likely that on balls hit to the bare-hand side, fielders would try to catch the ball using both the gloved and ungloved hands to form a pocket in a manner similar to the approach used by old-timers before gloves were used—cupping both hands together to make a pocket.

While game summaries almost never refer to backhand catches—even by first basemen—descriptions of barehand catches appear with some regularity. Except for third basemen scooping up a bunt with the bare hand and throwing to first in the same motion, such catches were not frequent. But neither were they rare. They were common enough so that once in a while a baseball reporter might note in a game summary that a player made a great fielding play, but fail to mention that the play was made with the bare hand, rather than the gloved hand.[86] The following are a small sample of the descriptions of barehanded catches noted by the author:

> "Prettiest play in the game was [third baseman] Coughlin's barehand stop of Lajoie's wicked drive, in the second. It was bound down the line, tagged for two."[87]
>
> "[Shortstop] Mike Doolin stirred up the enthusiasm of those present by a pretty stop with his ungloved hand of Delahanty's hard-hit grounder, which he fielded in short left field and got the ball to Bransfield ahead of the runner. He had to throw the ball without steadying himself, but it bounded nicely to Bransfield."[88]
>
> "Notes of the Game. It is a very unusual thing to see a great play duplicated on the next man to bat, but that is what happened in the second inning. Oom Paul Krueger poked a red-hot one over second base that [second baseman] Miller Huggins made one of his celebrated impossible plays on. The midget ran over back of the bag, just did reach the ball with his bare hand, and threw to first while off his balance, getting his man. Charley Dooin didn't think he could do it again, so he put one in exactly the same place, and Huggins treated him in exactly the same manner. The two plays were as nearly similar as any two plays in baseball can be, and both were extremely difficult."[89]
>
> [Kip Selbach hit a screaming rocket in the sixth inning.] "Not at any time until he caught it did it seem possible for [leftfielder George] Stone to break down or stop the ball, not to speak of catching it. It seemed a certain double, a possible triple. Stone cut across at top speed. He seized the ball with his bare left hand and held it. The remarkable part of it was that when Stone did reach the ball there was no stabbing, or wild grasping, or luck about it. he reached for, seized and held the ball with as perfect composure, design and certainty as if he was plucking a flower off its stem."[90]

The following description of a play made by Brooklyn outfielder Billy Maloney offers some idea of what might have been the pecking order for a player in making a catch of a ball hit to his bare-hand side: "One play stood out more prominently than all the rest during the game, Maloney pulling it off in the first inning on Tenney. The Boston manager slammed out a long liner between left and center and Billy went after it at almost right angles. He could not face around to take the ball with two hands, and it was impossible to use his bare hand. He did the only thing left to him, and that was to turn his mitt backhanded around his side and make the catch. It was the most remarkable play of the season on the local grounds and has seldom, if ever been seen anywhere else. As somebody remarked, the only thing left for Maloney is to catch a fly behind his back."[91]

While Arthur Irwin's invention had made the fielder's lot in life somewhat easier, game summaries from the early 1900s and related comments show that the fielding side of the game still required considerable skill. Aspects of the game that today are taken for granted—one-handed catches, backhand catches, hanging on to hard-hit line drives—were deemed difficult plays in the early 1900s.

Two

1904, American League

A Veritable Dogfight

The competitive balance in the American League was far different than in the National League. A different team had won the pennant in each of the young league's first three seasons. The Chicago White Stockings, who by 1904 were known as the "White Sox," a trendier version of the same nickname, had won the first league championship. The Philadelphia Athletics took the flag in 1902 and the Boston Americans the following season. Four teams—Boston, Philadelphia, Cleveland, and New York—were considered solid contenders for the 1904 pennant, and three others—Chicago, Detroit, and St. Louis—were considered solid teams who would fight for fifth place, and possibly a first division berth. Only Washington was considered a truly weak team.

Boston, which still had no widely accepted nickname, generally being called simply the "Boston Americans," had a core of players who had been strong contenders for the first two league championships and had won in 1903 and then beat Pittsburgh in the first World Series. Player-manager Jimmy Collins was considered the game's best third baseman by most baseball observers. Collins, center fielder Chick Stahl, and first-baseman/outfielder Buck Freeman were among the league's top sluggers. Cy Young was the premier pitcher in all of baseball at this time. Lou Criger, his favorite catcher, was great defensively. Like almost all catchers of this era, Criger didn't do much with a bat in his hands. Shortstop Fred Parent and second baseman Hobe Ferris were outstanding in the field. Pitcher Bill Dinneen came from the Beaneaters in 1902, teaming with Young to give the team two dominant starters. That same year outfielder Patsy Dougherty joined the team. Dougherty was not a great fielder, but he excelled as a leadoff hitter.

Philadelphia's lineup featured speed at the top of the batting order and solid hitting in the next few spots. Leadoff man Topsy Hartsel was adept at coaxing bases on balls and usually was at or near the top of the league in on-base percentage and runs scored. First baseman Harry Davis and outfielder Socks Seybold were among the league's leading sluggers. They were also adept at the hit-and-run game, as was third baseman Lave Cross. Pitcher Rube Waddell had overpowering stuff. He led the team to the 1902 pennant. Left-hander Eddie Plank used a fine cross-fire pitch to advantage, winning over 20 games in both 1902 and 1903. Charles "Chief" Bender joined the team in 1903, making three future Hall-of-Famers on the A's pitching staff.

The Cleveland Naps had the league's best player in second baseman Nap Lajoie, who hit .426 in the American League's first season and had the top batting average in each of its next two campaigns. Third baseman Bill Bradley was often mentioned as being in Collins' class as a fielder, and he was one of the league's top hitters. Outfielder Elmer Flick excelled in all aspects of the game. Pitchers Addie Joss, Earl Moore and Bill Bernhard were tough to beat, but tended to be sidelined when the pennant races heated up.

The New York Highlanders were put together in 1903 as the successor to the Baltimore franchise after John McGraw and John Brush broke up the team. American League President Ban Johnson did all he could to ensure that the new team was competitive. He gave the team five players who had defected from the Pittsburgh Pirates' great 1902 team, including Jack Chesbro and Jesse Tannehill—half of the great Pirates starting rotation. Clark Griffith, who managed the pennant-winning Chicago White Stockings in 1901, moved to New York as the team's player-manager. Willie Keeler, considered the master of "scientific batting," jumped from the Brooklyn Superbas.

The White Sox had fallen to seventh place in 1903 largely because the defection of shortstop George Davis had thrown their infield into complete disarray and the loss of Sam Mertes had taken away one of the team's best hitters. Davis' return in 1904 plus player acquisitions by owner Charlie Comiskey were expected to make the team competitive once again. Disappointed with his team's inability to keep pace with the league's top teams in 1903, the St. Louis Browns' manager, Jimmy McAleer, had decided in mid-season to clear the decks for a renewed effort. He made a couple of trades that didn't work out well and unwittingly greased the skids for a downturn in the franchise's fortunes that led to a last-place finish a couple years later.

The Tigers, like the Browns, were in the middle of a re-make that led downward for a couple of years before eventually resulting in a swift rise to the top. By 1903 the Tigers had acquired outfielder Sam Crawford, one of the elite hitters of the era; shortstop Charley O'Leary, a top-notch defender; and three above-average pitchers—Bill Donovan, George Mullin, and Ed Killian.

The Senators had a few good players, notably pitchers Casey Patten and Al Orth, and third baseman Bill Coughlin, but they were busy living up (or down) to the mocking characterization: "Washington: first in war, first in peace, and last in the American League."

1904 American League Standings

Team	W	L	Pct.	GB
Boston	95	59	.617	—
New York	92	59	.609	1.5
Chicago	89	65	.578	6
Cleveland	86	65	.570	7.5
Philadelphia	81	70	.536	12.5
St. Louis	65	87	.428	29
Detroit	62	90	.408	32
Washington	38	113	.252	55.5

Winning the Big Game: Boston

A team that wins the pennant by 14½ games doesn't usually look to make sweeping changes in the off-season. Thus the Boston Americans made only minor changes to their 1903 world championship team. Manager Jimmy Collins became unhappy with pitcher Tom Hughes when Hughes "broke training" during the World Series. He arranged a trade with the New York Highlanders for Jesse Tannehill, who had found a spot in Manager Clark Griffith's doghouse. On paper the trade was a swap of two pitchers of about equal ability. Both men were fine pitchers. Both had personal traits that eventually grated on teammates and managers. Hughes drank too much and didn't seem to take the game seriously enough for Collins' tastes. Tannehill had a prickly personality that clashed with Griffith's "Do what I say" attitude.[1] The only other change of consequence made by the Americans was to release Jack O'Brien, who had hit a robust .210 as their reserve outfielder, and bring in Bill O'Neill, a promising youngster.

By mid–June Boston's baseball reporters began echoing a refrain that would be heard all season long: "the boys aren't hitting." Only Jimmy Collins and Freddy Parent hit well in the early going and three regulars—Lou Criger, Hobe Ferris and Candy Lachance—were still under .200 in mid–June. The Americans were in first place largely because they had excellent pitching and a rock-solid defense. So Boston fans were shocked on June 17 when they learned their team had traded Patsy Dougherty to the New York Highlanders. Dougherty, the Americans' leadoff batter, was the team's catalyst on offense. In 1903 he had led the team in batting and the entire league in runs scored. Thus far in 1904 he was batting .272 and was leading the team with 33 runs scored. Making the trade even more puzzling was the player the Americans got in return: Bob Unglaub, a rookie reserve infielder who was sick and might not be able to play for weeks.

For many Boston fans (and lots of writers and fans in other cities) there could be only one explanation. Ban Johnson wanted his pet New York team to win. He was moving Dougherty to New York both to strengthen the Highlanders and weaken the Americans. Boston owner John I. Taylor and Manager Jimmy Collins both quickly issued statements denying the rumors and insisting the trade had been made in the best interests of the Boston team. Dougherty was a poor fielder, they said, and was not hitting like he did in the past. He had hit only .110 on the recent Western trip, Taylor pointed out. Bill O'Neill, who would replace Dougherty, was a good fielder. They were confident he would become a good hitter.[2]

Boston (95–59)

Regular Lineup	AVG	OBP	SLG	R	RBI	SB
Kip Selbach, lf*	.264	.351	.356	65	44	19
Jimmy Collins, 3b	.271	.306	.379	85	67	19
Chick Stahl, cf	.290	.366	.416	83	67	11
Buck Freeman, rf	.280	.329	.412	64	84	7
Freddy Parent, ss	.291	.330	.389	85	77	20
Candy LaChance, 1b	.227	.265	.283	55	47	7
Hobe Ferris, 2b	.213	.245	.306	50	63	7
Lou Criger, c	.211	.283	.298	34	34	1
or Duke Farrell, c	.212	.281	.278	11	15	1
Leading Pitchers	W	L	PCT.	IP	H	ERA
Cy Young	26	16	.619	380	327	1.97
Bill Dinneen	23	14	.622	335.7	283	2.20
Jesse Tannehill	21	11	.656	281.7	256	2.04
Norwood Gibson	17	14	.548	273	216	2.21
George Winter	8	4	.667	135.7	126	2.32

*Includes record with Washington

Poor Bill O'Neill. The rookie had been set up for failure. Before the trade he had played a total of six games all season and had gotten four hits in 17 times up. He had to be a little rusty from riding the bench so much. In his first game after the trade, which mercifully was on the road, he dropped one fly ball and misjudged another. He was thrown out twice on the basepaths. He settled down in the field after that, but wasn't able to do much with the bat. When the Americans returned to Boston, the team's first series was against the Highlanders. Boston fans cheered young O'Neill to show their support for him, but cheered just as loudly for Dougherty, their old favorite. O'Neill managed a hit in the opening game of the series; Dougherty went four-for-five. In the remaining two games of the series, which went to New York two games to one, Dougherty added four more hits while O'Neill got one more. By then O'Neill's batting average had dropped to .196 and Boston's management had decided to look elsewhere for Dougherty's replacement. They shipped O'Neill to Washington for Kip Selbach, in a deal that was essentially the Dougherty-Unglaub deal in reverse.

Selbach was available because he was a high-salaried player on a last-place team that was finding it difficult to meet its payroll. The Senators had arranged to trade him to New York in May, before the Highlanders picked up Dougherty, but the Senators' new manager, Patsy Donovan, who had just joined the team, canceled the deal. Selbach had greased the skids for his exit from Washington by making five errors in one game in late June. (This was not Kip's first five-error game. He also made five errors in a game with the Orioles in 1902.) Selbach's bungling performance had earned him a league suspension for "indifferent play." In Boston Selbach was elated to be able to play for a contender and after a few games the Boston fans were quite happy to have him. He had six putouts in his first game with the Americans and scored the winning run. The Americans won the first eight games he played, and he contributed to the victories by going 10-for-27 with three doubles, two triples and two stolen bases. More important, perhaps, was the fact that his strong performance quieted the complaints about the Dougherty trade. His teammates were glad to have him on the team. In September a Boston player was quoted as saying, "But for Selbach we would have been out of the race long ago."[3]

Despite the occasional five-error game, Selbach was a good defensive player. His solid play in left field added to the team's already strong defense and indirectly magnified the team's greatest strength, the league's best and deepest pitching staff. The Americans carried only five pitchers, but they had all pitched on pennant-winning teams before 1904 and three of them (Cy Young, Bill Dinneen, and Jesse Tannehill) were among the best pitchers of the era. All of them, including the fourth and fifth starters (Norwood Gibson and George Winter), came through with big wins at some point in the season.

The leader of the staff was still Cy Young, who turned 37 just before the season opened. For the first time in the American League's four-year history, Young didn't lead the league in wins. Jack Chesbro outpaced everybody in his fabulous 41–12 season. But Old Cy finished high in all the most important categories. He was second in wins (26), sixth in won-lost percentage (.619) and sixth in ERA (1.97). He was still a workhorse, starting 41 games and completing 40 of them while pitching 380 innings. He led the league in shutouts with ten, and tied Chesbro for the lead in WHIP (Walks plus Hits per Inning Pitched) with 0.937.

Young started the season by giving up eight runs on opening day. He gave up two runs in each of his next two starts, one of them a loss. Then he ran off a streak of 45 straight scoreless innings, including 22 consecutive no-hit innings. On May 5, Old Cy pitched a perfect game against the Philadelphia Athletics. He had held the Senators hitless in seven innings of relief work in his previous appearance and he threw six more no-hit innings against Detroit in his next start, on the way to a 15-inning 1–0 victory. His scoreless streak ended in the eighth inning of a 3–1 loss to Cleveland on May 17. Oddly, in the games constituting the 45-inning scoreless streak Cy's record was only two wins, one loss and one save. His season's record following the Cleveland game was a modest 4–4.[4]

Through June Dinneen and Tannehill were the Americans' big winners. On June 28, Dinneen's record was 11–3, Tannehill's 9–5. Young was just behind them at 8–6. Dinneen hurt his ankle in practice that day. Tannehill was pitching with a sore finger and soon afterward came down with a tender shoulder. With their lead already down to a half-game over New York and one game over Chicago, the Americans would have to rely on a starting rotation of the veteran Young; Gibson, who was 4–6 at the time; and Winter, who had not yet fully recovered from a serious illness of the previous season. It looked like the team was in big trouble. But instead of falling back in the race, the Americans went on a winning spurt. They won 10 of their next 11 games, and after Tannehill returned to the mound ran the streak to 13 of 15. Young won five straight games during the streak, Gibson went 3–0, and Winter 3–1. Tannehill appeared in three games, splitting two starts and winning another in relief of Winter.

The spurt brought a lead of five games for the Americans, but that proved to be short-lived. A six-game losing streak cut the lead back to one-half game by July 30. Both Young and Dinneen hit rough spots in late July and August, Dinneen losing six of his first eight decisions after he returned from his injury and Young losing six out of his next eight decisions after August 1. The Americans lost their lead on August 4, falling behind the White Sox by a half game. They trailed the White Sox, and at times also the Highlanders through most of August, but never fell more than two games off the lead. The team's pitching depth once again paid off. While Young and Dinneen were slumping, Tannehill got hot. He went 7–0 in August. One of his victories was a no-hitter over the White Sox. In that game he put two runners on base in the first inning by walking one and hitting the other. Then he set the White Sox down in order over the next eight innings.[5]

The Americans regained first place on August 29, moving a game ahead of the Highlanders, who had replaced the White Sox as the leaders. Boston and New York traded the lead eight times in September. The Americans grabbed a half-game lead on October 2 and still held on to it when the two teams began a season-ending series of five games on October 7. The games were to be played over four days, a single game in New York on a Friday followed by a doubleheader in Boston on Saturday and another doubleheader in New York on Monday. Both teams were somewhat battered entering the series. Boston was without the services of Tannehill, who suffered a groin injury in mid–September.[6] Jimmy Collins was also below par. He played the last two months of the season with an injured leg. New York had lost pitcher Al Orth due to a sore arm. Like Collins, Willie Keeler was playing through an injury. He had injured a finger a week earlier. Orth's injury was especially important, since the Highlanders had relied on a three-man rotation all season long to compensate for a relatively thin pitching staff.

The first game of the series pitted Gibson against Chesbro, who was 40–10 entering the game. Both Gibson and Chesbro pitched well, Gibson allowing only five hits and Chesbro four. The Highlanders prevailed, 3–2, with the help of two errors committed by first baseman Candy Lachance. The victory put the Highlanders in first place, leading by a half-game.

In Boston the next day, the Americans struck back. Chesbro started the first game of the doubleheader. He was pitching for the second day in a row after having rested only two days before starting the opening game of the series. As might be expected, the burden proved too much for him. After shutting out the Americans for three innings he imploded, allowing six runs in the fourth inning. Chesbro was taken out after that inning, but the Americans continued to hit, scoring seven more runs in a 13–2 rout. The second game of the doubleheader was entirely different. Cy Young, who had pitched shutouts in his previous two starts was matched against Jack Powell, the Highlanders' other star pitcher. Both pitchers were effective. In a game called after seven innings because of darkness, Young shut out the Highlanders on six hits, walking none and striking out five batters. Powell allowed only four hits, but one of them brought defeat. In the fifth inning Hobe Ferris reached first on an infield hit. He moved to second base on a sacrifice. The next batter, Young, hit a fly ball to right field, deep enough to allow Ferris to go to third. When the right fielder's throw bounced away from the third baseman, Ferris scampered home with the game's only run. The Americans now led by one and one-half games with two left to play.

With their season on the line the Highlanders started Chesbro once again in the first game of the Monday doubleheader. Boston started Bill Dinneen, who had beaten Chesbro on Saturday. Chesbro was pitching for the fourth time in a week, but he seemed to be as good as ever. Both teams were held scoreless until the bottom of the fifth inning, when the Highlanders broke through against Dinneen, sending six men to the plate after two were out. Despite all the action only two runs scored, the last out coming on a grounder to Dinneen with the bases full. Boston tied the score in the seventh. Candy Lachance reached first on an infield single. Ferris hit a grounder to second baseman Jimmy Williams, who bobbled the ball, both runners reaching base safely. They moved up on a sacrifice. Dinneen then hit an easy grounder to Williams, who threw home trying to get Lachance. The throw was in the dirt, bouncing away from the catcher and allowing both Lachance and Ferris to score, tying the game.

In the top of the ninth, Lou Criger beat out an infield hit to deep short. Dinneen sacrificed him to second. Selbach bounced a grounder to short, moving Criger to third. Chesbro got two strikes on the next batter, Freddy Parent. Then he tried to finish him off with one of his famous spitballs. The pitch sailed over the catcher's head, going to the backstop as Criger ran home with the lead run. Parent singled on the next pitch, a hit that would have scored Criger had the wild pitch not occurred. In the bottom of the ninth Dinneen was wild. He fanned the first batter, but it took seven pitches to do it. The next batter walked. Catcher Red Kleinow, who had two hits earlier in the game, popped up to second. Veteran Jim McGuire, pinch-hitting for Chesbro, coaxed another walk from Dinneen, moving the tying run to second with Patsy Dougherty, the ex-Boston outfielder, coming to bat. Dougherty had hit well whenever he faced his old team. He worked the count to two-and-two. Dinneen fired the next pitch low and over the inside corner of the plate. Patsy swung and missed, ending the game and the pennant race. New York won the meaningless second game, 1–0 in ten innings.[7]

A Memorable, Painful, Finish: New York

The Highlanders had ended the 1903 season on a high note, going 19–10 in September. They were aggressive in the off-season, making several moves that appeared to considerably improve the team. The 1903 team was weak in two positions—left field, where Lefty Davis had played poorly, and catcher, where Monte Beville and Jack O'Connor had failed to meet expectations. To replace Davis, who was released, the Highlanders acquired John Anderson from the Browns. Anderson had exhausted his manager's patience in St. Louis by making too many baserunning blunders. But he was one of the league's better long-ball hitters and he was adequate in the outfield, which was an improvement over the way Davis played in New York. The Highlanders signed veteran Deacon McGuire to serve as their primary catcher and purchased Red Kleinow, a minor league standout, as the alternate catcher.

New York (92–59)

Regular Lineup	AVG	OBP	SLG	R	RBI	SB
Patsy Dougherty, lf*	.280	.329	.379	113	26	21
Willie Keeler, rf	.343	.390	.409	78	40	21
Kid Elberfeld, ss	.263	.337	.328	55	46	18
John Anderson, cf-lf-1b	.278	.313	.385	62	82	20
Jimmy Williams, 2b	.263	.314	.354	62	74	14
John Ganzel, 1b	.260	.309	.376	50	48	13
or Dave Fultz, cf	.274	.324	.366	39	32	17
Wid Conroy, 3b	.243	.314	.335	58	52	30
or Jack Thoney, 3b-of**	.227	.264	.283	23	18	11
Deacon McGuire, c	.208	.276	.258	17	20	2
or Red Kleinow, c	.206	.259	.282	12	16	4

Leading Pitchers	W	L	PCT.	IP	H	ERA
Jack Chesbro	41	12	.774	454.7	338	1.82
Jack Powell	23	19	.548	390.3	340	2.44
Al Orth**	14	10	.583	211.3	210	3.41
Clark Griffith	7	5	.583	100.3	91	2.87

*Includes record with Boston
**Includes record with Washington

The biggest improvement on paper was in the team's pitching. While the trade of Jesse Tannehill for Tom Hughes was seen as pretty much a wash—both men being good pitchers and clubhouse liabilities—the exchange of Harry Howell for Jack Powell was seen as a steal. Howell had never been more than an extra pitcher. Powell, on the other hand, had been the Browns' ace. He was available only because of a salary dispute. *The Sporting News* cited the Highlanders' pitching staff—Chesbro, Powell, Hughes, Clark Griffith, and young Barney Wolfe—as one of the principal reasons the team was expected to finish near the top of the standings.[8]

Two. 1904, American League

The Highlanders continued to make aggressive moves to strengthen the team after the season started. When it became apparent that center fielder Dave Fultz would miss a significant amount of playing time because of chronic leg injuries, they arranged a trade with the Senators for Kip Selbach and catcher Malachi Kittridge. When that trade fell through, they obtained Patsy Dougherty in the controversial trade with Boston. Tom Hughes started the season well, but pitched poorly in June and July, possibly because of arm trouble. On July 17 the Highlanders traded Long Tom and Barney Wolfe to Washington, getting Al Orth in return.

The Highlanders got solid, but not great, seasons from almost every player in their lineup. Dougherty hit .280, normally only a modest average but in 1904 the 11th best in the league. He led the league in runs scored with 113, which was 16 more than anyone else. Big John Anderson hit .278, with 27 doubles, 12 triples and three home runs. He had 82 RBIs, the fourth-highest total in the league. Jimmy Williams hit only .263, but ranked fourth in doubles with 31 and seventh in RBIs with 74. The other regulars put up batting marks that put them about in the middle of the rankings for their positions.

The only Highlander who truly excelled at bat was Willie Keeler, who had a great season. Willie's season would have been recognized as even more outstanding if it were not for Nap Lajoie, who had another year like his 1901 season when he hit as if he belonged in a league of his own. Willie was second to Lajoie in batting average and on-base percentage, but he ranked far above anyone else in those categories. His .343 batting average was 34 points better than that of Harry Davis, who finished third. Willie's on-base percentage was 19 points better than the next guy's. And, although Willie had only 24 extra-base hits, he managed to beat out enough infield chops to finish ninth in the league with a .409 slugging percentage.

Early in the season Willie was the Highlanders' leadoff batter. One of the reasons Griffith wanted Dougherty was so he could return Keeler to the number two spot, where his talents were best utilized. With Willie at bat a runner at first base was seldom forced out, and even if that occurred, Willie was so fast he was rarely doubled up at first base.[9] Like any good number two man, he made the batters immediately in front of him and just behind him more effective than they might otherwise have been. Dougherty, for instance, led the league in runs scored by a wide margin even though his on-base percentage was only the 18th best in the league. Anderson probably also benefited from Willie's work. His batting marks were significantly lower than the men who drove in a similar number of runs.

The Highlanders' pitching staff was both the team's biggest disappointment and the reason the team almost won the pennant. Griffith was injured before he got into his first game. He sustained the injury while throwing, but he wasn't throwing a pitch. It was a punch. At a photographer who refused to take no for an answer when Griffith told him he couldn't take a team picture.[10] The injury sidelined Griffith for five weeks. When he returned he pitched infrequently, starting only 11 games all year and relieving five times.

Rather than taking a chance on one of his younger pitchers to fill the void he left, Griffith chose to go with a three-man rotation. His New York managerial rival, John McGraw, got away with a similar approach, but it didn't really work out too well for Griffith. Tom Hughes lost effectiveness as the season progressed, losing eight of his last 11 starts before he was traded. Hughes' replacement, Al Orth, injured his arm the last week of the season and was unavailable for the crucial showdown series with Boston. Jack Powell, always a willing worker, gave his best whenever Griffith sent him to the mound. There were times when Powell's best wasn't all that good. He had a stretch in May when he gave up 30 runs in four games and had a handful of other games in which he was hit hard throughout the game. But, overall, Powell held up well under the heavy workload, better than his 23–19 record might suggest. That record doesn't reflect the clutch pitching he did in three high-pressure games in September. The games all ended in 1–1 ties — two against Boston and one against Cleveland, hard-hitting teams the Highlanders had to beat to remain in contention.

Despite only limited success on the part of most of their hurlers, pitching was a strong point for the Highlanders because one member of the staff excelled at a historic level. Jack Chesbro won the most games any pitcher has ever won in a season pitching at the 60'6" distance. His 41–12 record gave him the highest won-lost percentage in the league (.774) and he was the hardest pitcher to hit, allowing 6.69 hits per nine innings. He finished second to Cy Young in on-base percentage, .252 to .251. His earned run average (1.82) was the fourth-lowest in the league. Chesbro combined his stingy on-base efficiency with one of the heaviest workloads of any pitcher working at the 60'6" distance. He appeared in 55 games, starting 51 of them and completing 48. He pitched 454⅔ innings, more than any pitcher since Amos Rusie threw 482 innings in 1893. Only Ed Walsh, who pitched 464 innings in 1908, has pitched more since then.

The key to Chesbro's success in 1904 was his mastery of the spitball. He got the idea for the pitch from Elmer Stricklett while on an exhibition trip to California in the fall of 1902, and worked on it throughout the 1903 season and the spring of 1904.[11] Chesbro later told a writer that after he saw Stricklett throw the pitch he said to himself, "There is something, Mr. Chesbro, that you must learn." According to Chesbro, the thumb "did all the work" in the spitball delivery. "The saliva is put on the ball for the sole purpose of making the fingers slip off the ball first," he said. "In throwing curves the fingers do the work. By wetting the ball it leaves the fingers first and the thumb last and the spitball could be rightly called a thumb ball. It is not necessary to thoroughly wet the ball. All you need to do is to moisten it so as to remove the friction from the part of the ball the fingers cover and which slides off the fingers." Chesbro claimed he could make the ball drop two inches or a foot and a half, and he could make it drop straight down or to the outside to a right-handed batter.[12]

Using a devastating new pitch, the spitball, Jack Chesbro won 41 games for the New York Highlanders in 1904 (Library of Congress).

Chesbro didn't use the new pitch in the first few games of the season. Griffith had told him he shouldn't fool around with "that trick stuff," saying Chesbro was already a great pitcher with what he had and he shouldn't take a chance on hurting his arm. When the team went to Cleveland on its first Western trip, however, Chesbro was hit hard in the early innings of a game. He told Griffith he didn't have a thing on the ball and that he was going to use the spitball the next inning. He used it regularly after that.[13]

Chesbro pitched two games in Cleveland on the trip. He lost the first game on May 12 by a 7–0 score. The loss dropped his won-lost record to 4–3. He pitched again two days later, beating the Naps 10–1. That was the first of 14 straight wins. During the streak Chesbro threw three shutouts, had eight games of two or fewer runs, and never allowed more than three runs in a game.

The streak spotlighted the fact that Chesbro had come up with a mysterious new pitch. In early July an umpire remarked, "The greatest event of the season, so far as the game itself is concerned, is the invention of a new delivery, or 'ball,' as the players call it, by Jack Chesbro." Although he had been umpiring for a good many years, the umpire said, he had never seen anything like it. "It comes floating up so slowly that you can see the seams. It doesn't appear to be revolving at all and it seems as if it would never get to the plate. It generally goes over the outside corner for a strike, but it's the hardest ball for an umpire to judge that I have ever seen pitched. If it bothers the umpire, it is easy to see how troublesome it must be to a batter."[14]

The umpire's remark came about the time Chesbro's 14-game streak ended with a 4–1 loss to Boston. Two days later the Americans beat him again, 2–1. After that Chesbro strung together a series of winning streaks between each loss: three in a row, three again, four, then nine. The last win of the nine-game streak came on September 20. Chesbro's record that day stood at 37–8. He had won his last nine games in only 21 days. Most people would agree that pitching nine games in 21 days constitutes a pretty heavy workload, but for Chesbro the *really* heavy workload was still in the future.

After a rest of five days—made possible largely by three off-days during that time—Chesbro pitched the opening day of a doubleheader in Cleveland, losing 4–3. The next day he pitched 11 innings, beating Detroit 4–1. Two days of rest brought another start, but this time Chesbro lasted only three innings and gave up all four runs in a 4–0 loss to Chicago. For Chesbro a three-inning outing was almost like a day off. So he started again the next day, beating the White Sox 7–2. His last start before the crucial Boston series came with another two days of rest. He shut out St. Louis 6–0.

The Highlanders finished the St. Louis series on October 5. After their last game they boarded a train headed for New York. Their trip was delayed by a wreck. Griffith had to book a special train to get to the metropolis in time for the opening game. The team arrived at 12:30, three hours before game time. They played the game in their road uniforms. Chesbro, of course pitched that game, recording his 41st and last win of the season.[15] With the Highlanders' season on the line, Chesbro pitched that game on a Friday, and went back to the mound again on Saturday and Monday. His last game was his eighth start in 14 days. Given his workload, to pitch as well as he did in that game was a remarkable feat. Sadly, the lasting memory of the game was not his extraordinary pitching effort, but the wild pitch that lost the game.

Working on a Herculean Task: Chicago

Late in the 1903 season, after the White Sox had dropped to seventh place, Ira Sanborn of the *Chicago Tribune* noted that Charlie Comiskey had "made a start toward getting a new team" for the 1904 season. "It will be a herculean task in the present condition of the baseball market," Sanborn said, "when tried players of value are not to be had at any price and the minor leagues are being searched with fine-tooth combs for possible talent."[16] A year later, almost to the day, the White Sox slipped past the Boston Americans into first place. Comiskey was able to complete the "herculean task" of rebuilding his team almost overnight. More accurately, it was more a "reassembling" than a "rebuilding."

Comiskey was able to remake his team into a contender in near-record time partly due to the decisions by his fellow owners that returned George Davis and Fielder Jones to Chicago. Davis, of course had been the center of a controversy that almost reignited the baseball war. Jones, on the other hand, had quietly signed a contract that let him stay with Chicago in 1903, but bound him to the Giants in 1904. That contract was nullified by the magnates in a conference aimed primarily at settling the issues raised by Davis's holdout. The return of Davis to the Chicago infield had a big impact—three positions were improved as a result. Davis was one of the best shortstops in baseball. His 1903 replacement, Lee Tannehill, had been inconsistent. He made some sensational plays, but committed too many errors and wasn't Davis's equal in playing the mind games associated with scientific baseball. When the White Sox moved Tannehill to third base in spring training, however, they discovered he was a great fielder at third, a vast improvement over Jimmy Callahan. Callahan shifted over to second base, where he was a slight improvement over the 1903 second baseman, largely because of his bat. When left fielder Ducky Holmes went down with a knee injury, Callahan move there, where he was better defensively. The new second baseman, Gus Dundon, was mediocre with the bat, but was outstanding defensively. Jiggs Donahue, who took over at first base was good defensively and was a big improvement over Frank Isbell with the bat. The changes transformed a White Sox vulnerability—infield defense—from a weakness to a strength.

The White Sox outfield wasn't anywhere near the league's best, but it provided much of the team's offense. The retention of Jones gave the team outstanding defense in center field to somewhat offset relative fielding weakness in the two corner spots. The team's catching was improved by Billy Sullivan's return to health. Sullivan had played only 32 games in 1903, missing three months due to an appendicitis operation. His two backups, Jack Slattery and Ed McFarland, had played poorly. Slattery lacked the skills to play well at the major league level; McFarland lacked the ability to lay off alcohol. Comiskey had suspended McFarland before the 1903 season ended and vowed to never play him again. He relented in April of 1904, however, partially because McFarland seemed to have reformed and partially because he needed McFarland's bat.[17]

Chicago (89–65)

Regular Lineup	AVG	OBP	SLG	R	RBI	SB
Danny Green, rf	.265	.352	.343	83	62	28
or Ducky Holmes, lf	.311	.354	.438	42	19	13
Fielder Jones, cf	.243	.316	.303	72	42	25
Jimmy Callahan, lf-2b	.261	.318	.317	66	54	29
George Davis, ss	.252	.311	.359	75	69	32
Jiggs Donahue, 1b	.248	.298	.319	46	48	18
or Frank Isbell, 1b-2b	.210	.255	.271	27	34	19
or Gus Dundon, 2b	.228	.292	.268	40	36	19
Lee Tannehill, 3b	.229	.260	.303	50	61	14
Billy Sullivan, c	.229	.255	.307	29	44	11
or Ed McFarland, c	.275	.348	.381	22	20	2

Leading Pitchers	W	L	PCT.	IP	H	ERA
Frank Owen	21	15	.583	315	243	1.94
Nick Altrock	19	14	.576	307	274	2.96
Doc White	16	12	.571	228	201	1.78
Frank Smith	16	9	.640	203.3	157	2.08
Roy Patterson	9	9	.500	165	148	2.29
Ed Walsh	6	3	.667	110.7	90	2.60

The greatest improvement in the team was in the pitching staff. Frank Owen was a project left over from 1903. He had long been identified as a possible star. George Stallings kept him with the Detroit Tigers throughout the 1901 season, even though Owen was not quite ready for major league action. Comiskey purchased him from Omaha of the Class A Western League after the 1902 season. Owen was still somewhat raw around the edges in 1903. He was used as an extra pitcher, starting 20 games and relieving in six. His record was a mediocre 8–12. *Tribune* writer Sanborn blamed McFarland for Owen's troubles, saying he had led the youngster astray.[18] In 1904 Owen started the White Sox' opening game and pitched more innings than any other Sox pitcher. He won 21 games and finished the season with the fifth-best ERA in the American League (1.94).

Nick Altrock was another holdover from 1903, having been picked up early in the season after the Boston Americans released him. Altrock wasn't used much in 1903. He pitched in 12 games, four of those in relief. He went 4–3, with a good 2.15 ERA. In 1904 Altrock pitched regularly. Because he was a left-hander, he was at times spotted against teams considered vulnerable to southpaws, and he was sometimes given extra rest, possibly avoiding teams with strong right-handed hitters. Unfortunately for Altrock, one of the teams considered weak against lefthanders was Boston. Ten of his starts—over a fourth of his season's total—came against the Americans.

He shut them out in his first two outings, but finished the season with only a 5–5 record against them.

Frank Smith was a rookie in 1904. He didn't start his first game for the White Sox until May 2, and didn't get a second start until June 3. Like Joe McGinnity, Smith threw a variety of pitches and threw them from different arm slots. After Smith beat Cleveland 2–1 in one of his first starts, Sanborn wrote, "Smith is a hard man to catch, with a wealth of speed and some tricky curves."[19] Smith didn't find a spot in the White Sox' crowded rotation until well into July, and even then he frequently went a week or so between starts. But he was effective when given the chance to pitch. He had the best won-lost percentage of the White Sox starters. He gave up the third-fewest hits per game in the league and had the eighth-best ERA.

Another White Sox rookie was Ed Walsh, whose pitching skills were still very unpolished in 1904. Big Ed had dominated hitters in the Connecticut State League and the Eastern League with an overpowering fastball, but didn't have much else. Manager Jimmy Callahan didn't think Walsh could get by with just his fastball in the American League, but kept him on the team anyway, hoping he could develop a better off-speed pitch. Walsh appeared in only 18 games in 1904, ten of them in relief. He won six games and lost three, with a pretty good 2.60 ERA. His record was somewhat deceptive, however. Half his appearances and four of his six wins came against the Washington Senators, who in 1904 basically defined the word "inept." Walsh had not yet mastered the spitball. When he did, he became a great pitcher, compiling a career ERA of 1.82 and winning 40 games in 1908.[20]

The White Sox' young pitchers pushed two of the 1903 pitchers to the back of the bullpen. Patsy Flaherty, who pitched in 40 games for the White Sox in 1903, started only five games before being sold to the Pittsburgh Pirates in June. Patsy was only 1–2 for the White Sox, but went 19–9 for the Pirates. Roy Patterson, a regular starter since the team's minor league days of 1900, found a seat at the end of the bench in April and stayed there most of the season. Between opening day and the last week of August, he moved off his spot on the bench often enough to make seven starts and five relief appearances. His record in those games was 2–6. Then, with the double-headers piling up, Manager Fielder Jones decided to see what Patterson could do. He sent Patterson to Brockton, Massachusetts to tune up his arm by pitching in a semi-pro game. Then he started Patterson against Philadelphia. Patterson shut out the A's, holding them to four hits. Three days later Patterson beat Washington, 5–2, allowing six hits. Then came another shutout, a seven-hitter against Detroit. "Patterson pitched a strong, heady game all the way," Sanborn remarked after that game. "The Chicago twirler is showing all the old-time form that once gained him the appellation of "Boy Wonder," and it is hard to see how Manager Jones has overlooked him so long and let him warm the bench all season." Over the last six weeks of the season Patterson started ten games and relieved in one. He threw four shutouts while compiling a 7–3 record. It was a good streak, but it didn't change anything for Patterson. He spent three more seasons with the White Sox, all of them as a part-time starter.[21]

The team Comiskey had reassembled was one built along the lines he preferred—strong pitching, solid defense, and batters who could manufacture runs from only a few hits. "The Sox are light batters and are compelled to make up for it by speed and by grasping every opportunity both in the attack and the defense. They are obliged to score more runs for the same number of hits than any other of their near rivals in order to win," Sanborn said.[22] It was a formula Comiskey had used successfully in the past and it worked for the White Sox in 1904. They battled for every game. During the first ten weeks of the season they bounced between third place and fifth place, along with New York, Philadelphia and Cleveland, always remaining only a few games out of first. In late July they began challenging Boston and New York for the lead, which they finally gained on August 4. They remained in the lead or within a half-game of it for three weeks before fading somewhat at the end of August. They continued to play well in September, staying close to the two leaders until the season ended.

Good at Everything but Staying Healthy: Cleveland

The Naps were a very good team. They had good hitting. They had a strong and deep pitching staff. In 1904 they had the third-best fielding average in the league. What they lacked was good health. Injuries are a part of the game. But the Naps had more than their share of those, plus—in the case of two key players—diseases serious enough to require hospitalization.

Cleveland (86–65)

Regular Lineup	AVG	OBP	SLG	R	RBI	SB
Harry Bay, cf	.241	.307	.318	69	36	38
Billy Lush, lf	.258	.359	.325	76	50	12
Bill Bradley, 3b	.300	.334	.409	94	83	23
Nap Lajoie, 2b	.376	.413	.546	92	102	29
Elmer Flick, rf	.306	.371	.449	97	56	38
Charlie Hickman, 1b*	.274	.312	.437	52	67	12

Regular Lineup	AVG	OBP	SLG	R	RBI	SB
or George Stovall, 1b	.298	.317	.381	18	31	3
Terry Turner, ss	.235	.255	.295	41	45	5
Harry Bemis, c	.226	.259	.295	35	25	6
or Fred Abbott, c	.169	.206	.231	14	12	2
or Fritz Buelow, c*	.141	.204	.176	17	10	4

Leading Pitchers	W	L	PCT.	IP	H	ERA
Bill Bernhard	23	13	.639	320.7	323	2.13
Red Donahue	19	14	.576	277	281	2.40
Earl Moore	12	11	.522	227.7	186	2.25
Addie Joss	14	10	.583	192.3	160	1.59
Bob Rhoads	10	9	.526	175.3	175	2.87
Otto Hess	8	7	.533	151.3	134	1.67

*Includes record with Detroit

Their troubles started in the spring. The team's training site in San Antonio, Texas had no dressing facilities. When they finished practice the players rode back to their hotel in open streetcars, cooling off in the brisk spring breeze. To players sweating from a good workout, the breeze undoubtedly felt good. The pleasant feeling, however, faded away when many of them came down with sore arms that lingered through the training period. When the season started, three of the team's stars were still hampered. Nap Lajoie played despite the soreness, but cost the team a number of double plays in the first few weeks of the season because he could not put much steam behind his throws. Earl Moore started the season at Mt. Clemens, a mineral spa in southern Michigan, hoping the water's curative powers would relieve the soreness in his arm.

Addie Joss stayed with the team but didn't pitch for ten days. He appeared in three games over the next two weeks before being hospitalized with a high fever. Doctors at first feared he had typhoid fever. That turned out not to be the case, but the fever lingered, keeping Joss out of the lineup for five weeks. He returned to the mound in mid-June, but still suffered the after-effects of his illness. He required more rest than previously between his starts and at times had nothing on the ball when he took the mound. It was mid-July before he fully regained his strength. From August 25 through the end of the season Joss demonstrated what he could do when completely healthy. In his last ten games he threw three shutouts and held the opposition to one run six times. He allowed three runs in the other game. His record in those ten games was 7–3. The three losses were all by 1–0 scores. Although his record at the end of the season was only 14–10 Joss had the lowest ERA in the league (1.59).[23]

The Naps also lost rookie shortstop Terry Turner to illness. Turner got off to a fine start, batting .299 in his first 23 games and playing splendid defense. While the Naps were on an Eastern trip in May, Turner had to be hospitalized with an illness later diagnosed as typhoid fever. He was so sick he was unable to return to his home in Cleveland for several weeks and was unable to play again until late July. When he rejoined the team he played more like his predecessor John Gochnaur, who hit .185 in both of his seasons with Cleveland, than like the Terry Turner of that spring. Fortunately, Turner recovered sufficiently over the winter to fashion a long major league career, playing with the Naps until 1918 and becoming one of the team's most popular players.[24]

Other injuries in 1904 included sore arms by pitcher Bill Bernhard and catcher Harry Bemis, injuries to both knees by catcher Fred Abbott, and a split finger on his glove hand suffered by pitcher Red Donahue when he attempted to catch a line drive through the box. All of these players tried to play through their injuries. Bernhard, in fact, seemed to have a great year. He went 23–13 with the ninth-best ERA in the league (2.13). A deeper look, however, suggests those numbers were the result of a big smile from Lady Luck, as well as a generous application of veteran pitching skill. Bernhard allowed 9.1 hits per game, almost a hit above the league average. He had great control, walking only 1.5 batters a game, and thus was able to hold down opposition scoring. Even so, he would have won several fewer games had the Naps not supported him with generous run support. They scored an average of 6.89 runs per game in his 23 wins.

The multiple injuries and Turner's long illness exposed the Naps' thin bench. To replace Turner, Lajoie was moved to shortstop, Charlie Hickman replaced him at second, and rookie Bill Schwartz tried his hand at first base. Lajoie was adequate as a shortstop but did not have Turner's range. At second, Hickman fielded like ... well, like Charlie Hickman, a good hitter who lasted only a short while in any position before his manager moved him elsewhere hoping to find a place he could handle. Schwartz hit only .155 and was soon followed by a procession of would-be replacements. The impact on the team was what might be expected. Although the infielders didn't make too many physical errors, the mental errors added up. At one point the fans started booing the team. "Cleveland has always been loyal to the local team," a reporter explained, "but the rooters grew tired of seeing dumb plays and the knocking was the result."[25]

The "dumb" plays that upset the fans occurred on offense as well as defense. The Naps were widely criticized for being just a bunch of "sluggers" who weren't adept at scientific baseball. After one game a Detroit writer said, "The Cleveland crowd bunts badly. Two men struck out trying to sacrifice, and two more were caught out on puny popups. Stand and slug is their game." Another time a Cleveland writer complained, "It would not hurt the locals if they would go out and do a little work in practicing bunting. Most of them are arrant failures at bunting in the pinch."[26] Given a lack of detailed information, it's difficult to determine how accurate these judgments were. Without a doubt, the Naps bunted poorly in some games and had some baserunning misadventures—all Deadball Era teams did. But at the end of the season the Naps ranked second in the league in sacrifices and in stolen bases, both indicators that a team relied heavily on the tactics of scientific baseball. They led the league in runs scored, beating out the second-place Boston Americans by 39 runs. Interestingly, the Americans were also criticized for their failure to play scientific baseball.

One reason the Naps put up such good offensive numbers was that Lajoie had another exceptional season. American League batting averages suffered in 1904, the league average dropping 11 points from the preceding year, from .255 to .244. Lajoie's average went up 32 points, from .344 to .376. He hit .450 in the Nap's first 25 games. He didn't fall below .400 until early June when his average dipped into the .390s. After 79 games he was batting .401, a lead of .079 over second-place Jimmy Callahan's .322. He was within a few hits of .400 as late as August 29, when his average stood at .392. A comparative slump in September reduced his final average to .376. As mentioned above, Willie Keeler trailed him by 33 points at .343. Harry Davis came in third at .309. Although the raw numbers were not as impressive as those of his 1901 season—when he hit .426 and led the league in virtually every important batting category—Lajoie outclassed the league almost as much in 1904 as he had in the American League's inaugural season. He led in batting average, on-base percentage (.413), slugging percentage (.546), hits (208), doubles (49) and RBIs (102). While Lajoie wasn't noted for his baserunning, in 1904 he tied for sixth in stolen bases with 29.[27]

Despite the injuries and illnesses, the Naps remained in the five-team mix of contenders throughout the season. They rose to second place in late May and stayed there for a couple of weeks. After that they bounced between third and fifth places, never dropping very far off the lead, their pennant chances disappearing when they ran out of games left on the schedule.

Yes, We Can; Yes, We Can. No, We Can't: Philadelphia

For A's fans the 1904 season was one long tease. Until deep into September the A's were close enough to the lead that a pennant seemed quite possible. But almost always there were a couple other teams between them and the leaders, so a fan's normal optimism had to be restrained somewhat. On offense, half the team's batters were having good seasons, while the other half were having a miserable time. On the mound, Rube Waddell was behaving himself—relatively speaking—and Eddie Plank was winning steadily. Chief Bender, on the other hand, was in poor health. In these circumstances a fan's inner voice is always saying something like "All we need is for Hartsel or Pickering to be himself and for Bender to recover and we're a shoo-in for first." Of course, those things didn't happen. The tease ended in mid-September. Harry Davis, who was having a fine season, broke a bone in his hand. A week later Rube hurt his shoulder. With a couple weeks left in the race the A's faded to fifth place and their fans were free to give most of their attention to college football.

Philadelphia (81-70)

Regular Lineup	AVG	OBP	SLG	R	RBI	SB
Topsy Hartsel, lf	.253	.347	.341	79	25	19
Ollie Pickering, cf	.226	.299	.262	56	30	17
Harry Davis, 1b	.309	.350	.490	54	62	12
Lave Cross, 3b	.290	.310	.379	73	71	10
Socks Seybold, rf	.292	.351	.396	56	64	12
or Danny Hoffman, of	.299	.329	.426	31	24	9
Danny Murphy, 2b	.287	.320	.440	78	77	22
Monte Cross, ss	.189	.266	.256	33	38	19
Ossee Schrecongost, c	.186	.199	.232	23	21	3
or Doc Powers, c	.190	.220	.207	11	11	3
or Pete Noonan, c	.202	.209	.298	13	13	1

Leading Pitchers	W	L	PCT.	IP	H	ERA
Rube Waddell	25	19	.568	383	307	1.62
Eddie Plank	26	17	.605	357.3	311	2.17
Weldon Henley	15	17	.469	295.7	245	2.53
Chief Bender	10	11	.476	203.7	167	2.87

As the season unfolded, A's fans were able to see Waddell put together one of baseball's greatest seasons in terms of strikeouts. Rube set a strikeout record that was not surpassed for six decades. In a way Rube's strikeout total lived up to the zany left-hander who set it. The total was initially listed as 343. In 1946 Bob Feller, openly pursuing Rube's record, struck out 348 batters. Feller was briefly credited with a new record until a recheck of Rube's 1904 stats resulted in a revised total of 349, returning Rube to the throne as the reigning strikeout king. Two decades later, in 1966, Sandy Koufax dethroned Rube for good when he fanned 382 batters. Nolan Ryan raised the record to 383 a few years later.[28] Rube's highest single-game strikeout total in 1904 was 16, coming in a 12-inning game against New York. He struck out 15 Cleveland batters in an 11-inning game. His highest total in nine innings was 14 New York Highlanders in a 5–2 loss.

Aside from his strikeout feats, the best game Rube pitched in 1904 came against Boston on May 2. Rube shut out the Americans, allowing only one hit, a bunt by Patsy Dougherty. Rube came close to getting a no-hitter. Dougherty's bunt was not particularly good, but Rube fell down fielding the ball, which otherwise would have been an out.[29]

In the all-important deportment category, Rube had a good year—or maybe, from a Philadelphia reporter's perspective, an off-year. He was still Rube, however, so there were a few screwball incidents. When the A's visited Chicago on their first Western trip Rube decided to don the hero's cape. He announced he was going to pitch all four games of a series against the White Sox. He was so adamant—much like a demanding two-year-old—that Connie Mack gave in and let him try the feat.[30] Unfortunately for Rube, he was more the goat than the hero. He was hit hard in the series opener, allowing six hits and three runs in the first three innings of what became a 14–2 blowout. The second game went smoother. Rube won the game 6–3 and punctuated the performance by turning a cartwheel after he retired the last Chicago batter. Game three was disappointing to the would-be hero. Rube could get no speed behind his fastball and was hit hard. He lost 6–3, allowing ten hits and striking out only one batter. The next day Mack gave Rube permission to go on a fishing trip, being careful of course to extract a promise that Rube would return in time to catch the team's train out of Chicago.[31]

On two or three occasions Rube failed to appear at the park on the day he was scheduled to pitch. For any other player those would have been significant contract violations, met with fines and suspensions. With Rube, though, such days were understood to be part of the package and brought no significant punishment.

One of the A's young players possessed a great deal of natural talent. Mack considered Danny Hoffman to be a possible future star. Over the first half of the year Hoffman appeared to be on the way to fulfilling Mack's expectations. He was a fast runner and an excellent defensive outfielder. Through July 2 he had appeared in 46 games and was batting .317, the seventh-highest average in the league. A couple of his long hits had caught the attention of baseball humorist Charley Dryden, who called the hits Hoffman's "horse-slaying swats." According to Dryden, while playing for Bridgeport a few years earlier, Hoffman had driven a ball to deep center field, where a group of spectators were watching the game from their carriages.

Hoffman's powerful drive had struck a horse on the temple, Dryden said, killing him instantly.[32]

On July 1 Hoffman was hit over the right eye by a pitch. He dropped to the ground, unconscious. He was initially diagnosed as suffering a concussion. It was believed he would be out of the lineup for only a week or so. The injury, however, turned out to be much more serious. Hoffman's cheekbone was fractured and his eye damaged. He lost all vision in the center of one eye. "If Danny was looking at you he couldn't see you with his right eye," Mack later explained. "His field of vision was OK around the edges. He could see the second story of the building behind you and he could see your feet, but your face, at which his eye was pointed, would not register at all. Naturally he couldn't see a baseball approaching."[33]

Hoffman recovered in time to play a few games at the end of the season. He remained in the major leagues until 1911, playing with the Athletics, Highlanders and Browns. He never again played as well as he had the first half of the 1904 season, posting a career .256 batting average. Evidence of his vision problem appears in his strikeout totals, which were relatively high every season. He led the league in strikeouts twice, fanning 106 times in 1905 and 99 times in 1907, both high totals for the Deadball Era.

Say Goodbye to "The Crab": St. Louis

The Browns were in transition in 1904. There had been high hopes for the group of players who jumped from the St. Louis Cardinals to the city's new American League team, the Browns, in 1902. They seemed on the way to fulfilling those expectations that first season when they finished in second place with a 78–58 record, only five games behind the Athletics. They got off to a decent start in 1903. On June 5 they were in second place with a 21–14 record, just one game behind first-place Boston. Then the wheels on their pennant wagon began wobbling. They lost seven games in a row, followed by a quick adjustment that brought a five-game winning streak. That spurt proved to be an anomaly. The Browns lost their next 11 games to fall to 26–32. As the team stumbled around, manager Jimmy McAleer and owner Robert Hedges came to the conclusion that the team did not have the makings of a championship team. McAleer decided upon a drastic reconstruction of the team. With two months remaining in the season he began trading away players who met his displeasure, both run-of-the-mill guys like infielder Barry McCormick, who was versatile and dependable in the field, but not much of a hitter, and stars like Red Donahue, a three-time

20-game winner when McAleer sent him packing to Cleveland in August of 1903. During the 1904 season about half of the regulars from the previous two years were still in St. Louis, but all of the remaining ex–Cardinals except Bobby Wallace were gone by the time the team gathered for spring training in 1905.

Browns fans would have had little to get excited about in 1904 other than individual players' accomplishments. The team settled into sixth place by early May and remained there for the rest of the season, except for a few weeks in August and early September when they sank down to seventh.

St. Louis (65–87)

Regular Lineup	AVG	OBP	SLG	R	RBI	SB
Jesse Burkett, lf	.271	.363	.343	72	27	12
Emmet Heidrick, cf	.273	.294	.342	66	36	35
Bobby Wallace, ss	.275	.330	.355	57	69	20
Charlie Hemphill, rf	.256	.311	.308	47	45	23
or Pat Hynes, rf	.236	.248	.287	23	15	3
Tom Jones, 1b	.243	.270	.309	53	68	16
Dick Padden, 2b	.238	.325	.298	42	36	23
Charles Moran, 3b*	.196	.265	.225	42	21	9
or Harry Gleason, 3b-ss	.213	.247	.271	10	6	1
Joe Sugden, c	.267	.331	.302	25	30	6
or Mike Kahoe, c	.216	.242	.250	9	12	4

Leading Pitchers	W	L	PCT.	IP	H	ERA
Barney Pelty	15	18	.455	301	270	2.84
Harry Howell	13	21	.382	299.7	254	2.19
Fred Glade	18	15	.545	289	248	2.27
Willie Sudhoff	8	15	.348	222.3	232	3.76
Ed Siever	10	15	.400	217	235	2.65

*Includes record with Washington

Perhaps the most accomplished of the players swept away by McAleer's housecleaning broom was Jesse Burkett. The Browns' leadoff batter and left fielder was a slightly larger, slightly more powerful, and much more volatile version of Wee Willie Keeler. His batting style and skills were similar to Willie's. He choked up on the bat, hugged the plate, and snapped the bat at the ball. He sprayed most of his hits into left field, but pulled the ball when it appeared advantageous. Like Keeler, he picked up a lot of hits on bunts. Willie usually chopped at the ball on his bunts, often producing a high bounce that he could beat out. Burkett, on the other hand, was noted for his ability to deaden the ball and place it between the fielders. "No one excels him in laying the ball down and beating it out," a reporter said after one game. "Jess don't care a continental who the third baseman and pitcher are when he bunts. He knows that none of them can get him when he is right."[34]

As a "scientific batter," Jesse was not considered quite as adept as Keeler, but he was frequently mentioned as one of the best. As with Willie, fans loved it when Jesse sprayed hits past frustrated opposing infields. In the mid-1890s a writer described with relish a game in which Jesse toyed with the Louisville infield. "The first time up he smashed a pretty hit between the second baseman and the first baseman," the account began. "When he went to bat in the second inning the fielders moved over to the right to play for him. Burkett grinned and planted one directly over the second base bag, where neither the second baseman nor the shortstop could reach it. Then the Louisville fielders were miserable and moved back towards left. In the fourth inning Burkett varied things by making as pretty a bunt as ever was seen and easily reached first. This time the Louisville fielders thought they had him and played close in on him for another bunt. But instead of bunting the great hitter waited until he got a ball to his liking and then he sent it just over the heads of the infielders. He certainly is a great one."[35]

Many of the top hitters in the mid and late 1890s were little men—Keeler, McGraw, Billy Hamilton, Hughie Jennings, and Burkett. Their game was to battle the pitcher by fouling off pitches until they walked or got a pitch they could bunt or punch for a base hit. Burkett excelled at that tactic, but his offensive game was the most balanced of this group of stars. Burkett walked often, but he could also drive the ball for extra base hits. His slugging average was usually quite respectable.

Burkett set high standards for himself. After his team's disappointing sixth place finish in 1900, Burkett remarked that he had not done well enough. "But just watch my smoke next season," he said. "I'll make any of them hustle to beat me out. It ain't the least trouble for me to hit .300. Why, I ought to bunt better than that and never knock a ball out of the diamond [infield]."[36]

Among contemporaries Burkett was noted almost as much for his personality as for his hitting. His nickname, "The Crab," came not only from his frequent complaints to umpires, but also from his conduct on the field. The interaction between players and the fans attending the games was much greater when Burkett played than it is today. It was not uncommon for a player to trade remarks with a fan. Burkett liked to carry on a constant banter with the fans in the stands. A typical incident occurred in a game against Boston. After Burkett failed in a bunt attempt, a fan yelled out, "Hit 'er out." Burkett turned in the fan's direction and shouted sarcastically, "Come down and put on a uniform. There's big money to be made."[37]

In 1899, after he had been transferred to St. Louis along with Cleveland's other top players, Burkett mangled a liner hit at him and, in a fit of petty anger, refused to retrieve it while the opposing baserunners circled the bases. When St. Louis fans showered him with boos and hisses, he responded by tipping his hat. Later in the game, still being jeered for his petulance, he made an exaggerated bow towards the grandstand and shouted out a few wisecracks at the fans.[38]

One of his teammates tried to explain his conduct. "A better fellow than Burkett never lived," said Joe Quinn. "He would go through fire for a friend and never in his career has he injured a player during a game. It is his anxiety to win that makes him disagreeable in a game. He does not know his friends from his foes after the bell rings. He is always chewing and fighting, but it is all because he wants to win."[39]

Burkett was one of several future greats who first came to the major leagues in 1890. That was the year the players rebelled against the existing major leagues, setting up their own league. Many of the best players went to the new league, leaving the two older leagues, the National League and the American Association, searching for warm bodies to fill their roster spots. Burkett was one of those warm bodies. He had been a good pitcher in lower-level minor leagues the two previous years, winning 27 games for Scranton in 1888 and over 30 for Worcester in 1889. He came to New York in 1890 and found out he was not yet ready for prime time. "I was too wild," Burkett later said, explaining his 3–10 record. But, given the scarcity of talent in 1890, the Giants held on to him. "As they saw I could hit, they used me in the field," he said.[40] He could hit. He had a .309 batting average and the fifth highest slugging percentage in the league. He couldn't field. Out of 18 outfielders who played at least 50 games in 1890, Burkett ranked last, with a fielding average of .824. The next worst fielder had an .871 fielding average.

In 1891, after the Players' League collapsed and many of the top players returned to the National League, New York released Burkett. He signed with Lincoln in the Western Association. That year Jesse still thought his future lay on the mound, but older baseball men thought otherwise. Patsy Tebeau, the Cleveland Spiders' manager, heard about Burkett from his brother, George Tebeau. "He wrote me," Patsy said, "telling me how good a sticker and runner Burkett was, but how 'punk' he was as a pitcher." When the Lincoln club failed to pay him for several weeks, Burkett left the team. He was immediately signed by Cleveland as an outfielder.[41]

Burkett continued to have fielding problems for several years after he returned to the National League. While he no longer was absolutely the worst outfielder in the league, he was not close to being the best. He had decent range, but made lots of errors. To some extent his troubles were attributable to the park in which he played. Left field was the sun field in Cleveland, and it was widely recognized as the worst in the league. Games typically started at 3:30 and lasted around two hours. Late in the day, especially during spring and late summer games, the sun could be brutal. Burkett claimed the sun shone in his eyes on every fly ball and was affecting his sight. Players on other teams also complained about the sun field in Cleveland. They said it was difficult for the left fielder to pick up the ball when it left the pitcher's hand, turning many fly balls into hits or errors.[42]

By 1896 Burkett had raised his fielding average to a respectable level. Newspaper reporters, who had previously complained constantly about his fielding, started giving him compliments. One wrote, "When Jesse Burkett was first introduced to the outfield after his career as a twirler was wound up, he was as awkward as the bovine in the china shop on any kind of a ball. But constant practice and familiarity with the position eradicated the weakness and Burkett, while no means a star, is today one of the most consistent outfielders in the major league."[43]

Throughout his career Jesse's fielding deficiencies could be overlooked because of his impressive batting skills. In 1892, his first full year, he scored 119 runs, to rank sixth in the league. That year the National League played a split schedule, with the winners of each half facing each other in a playoff to determine the pennant winner. Burkett's bat and speed on the bases helped Cleveland win the second half, although the Spiders lost to Boston in the playoff. The next year, the first at the 60 feet, 6 inches pitching distance, he hit .348 and scored 145 runs, third highest in the league. Jesse scored at least 100 runs in nine of the ten years between 1892 and 1901. The exception was 1900, when he was dropped from his normal leadoff spot in the batting order to make way for John McGraw.

Led by Burkett and such other stars as pitchers Cy Young and George Cuppy, shortstop Ed McKean, and second baseman Cupid Childs, the Spiders remained one of the top teams of the 1890s. They were usually viewed as possible pennant winners, coming in second to the Baltimore Orioles in 1895 and 1896 and finishing well over .500 in other years. The Spiders vied with the Orioles for the distinction of being the rowdiest team in baseball. They were constantly giving the umpire a hard time, disputing every call that looked close and some that weren't. Burkett was, of course, often in the middle of the team's outbursts.

The mid–1890s saw an offensive surge similar to that of the 1920s. Burkett, who reached his prime then, was at the top of that surge. He led the league in 1895 and 1896 with batting averages of .405 and .410. In 1897 he dropped to .383, but that still left him with a three-year average of .401. In 1899 he finished second in batting with an average calculated at .402 at the time, his third season with a batting average over .400. Since then his 1899 average has been revised downward to .396. Even after his 1899 average was downgraded, there were still only three men with more .400 seasons than Burkett—Ty Cobb, Rogers Hornsby, and Ed Delahanty.

Beginning with the 1902 season the years began to weigh on Burkett, though Jesse wasn't sure just how many years were pressing down on him. He had no birth certificate, and didn't know for certain what his birth date was. His best guess was either in December of 1868 or February of 1870.[44] Playing his first year for the Browns in 1902, his batting average dropped to .306, a good average but not quite up to his previous standards. In 1903 he dropped to .293, the first time he had hit under .300 since 1892. In 1904 his average dropped another 22 points.

As Burkett grew older he had put on weight and lost speed. The bunts that had padded his batting average at the peak of his career now just added to his frustration level, since now he seldom beat them out. In August of 1904, a correspondent for *The Sporting News* remarked that Jesse "was no longer a star." At one time opposing teams became concerned when Jesse came to bat, the correspondent said. "The pitcher and third baseman were most concerned, for he kept them on a tension by his exasperating bunts or terrific line drives." But that had changed. "He attracts no more attention and creates no more anxiety now than the average batsman. The third baseman does not give him uncommon consideration and the pitcher proceeds to put the ball over the plate without trepidation."[45]

In May McAleer took Jesse out of the leadoff spot. It was "an event of more than passing interest," according to a St. Louis reporter. "As long as the fans can remember, Jesse has led off for the teams he has played with, and switching him from that position must have reminded Jesse that he is not as young as he used to be, and that his days as a king with the stick are about over."[46] A few days later Burkett was again batting leadoff. While he might not have been "a king with the stick" any longer, he was a better leadoff man than any other Browns player. In fact, in 1904 he posted the fifth-best on-base percentage in the league (.363). Jesse still had considerable trade value. After the season ended McAleer sent him to Boston. In exchange the Browns received George Stone, a highly regarded young outfielder who had led the American Association in batting with a .406 average. Two years later Stone had a great season for the Browns, leading the American League with a .358 batting average.

Like many other ballplayers of his time, Burkett continued playing baseball in the minor leagues after leaving the major leagues. He bought the Worcester team of the New England League in 1906. He was the team's owner-manager for the next ten years and played the outfield through the 1913 season, winning the pennant his first four years. He sold the team before the 1916 season. Jesse later was a coach for the Giants under his old nemesis, John McGraw.[47]

Burkett's career batting numbers are very close to Keeler's. Burkett batted .338 and scored 1720 runs, Keeler batted .341 and scored 1719 runs. Jesse's career on-base percentage and slugging percentage are both higher than Keeler's. Most contemporaries didn't consider Burkett to be quite as good as Keeler, but they rated him quite high. When voting was taken for the first members of the Hall of Fame, Burkett was one of three outfielders listed as possible candidates for election as a "pre–1900 immortal." (The other two were Fred Clarke and Hugh Duffy. Keeler was on the list of post–1900 players, but got the third-highest total in the voting for pre–1900 players. Needless to say, the polling was somewhat disorganized.) Burkett got one vote in an election where support was so widely distributed that no one was elected. He received a token vote or two in the Hall of Fame elections that followed until 1946, when a special old-timers committee voted him in, along with ten others.[48]

"A Hit, a Hit, My Franchise for a Hit!": Detroit

Ed Barrow, who later played a major role in building the New York Yankee powerhouses of the 20s, 30s, and 40s, was the Detroit manager in 1904. In his memoirs, which include interesting comments on baseball luminaries he met during his 50 years in baseball, as well as descriptions of several fistfights he engaged in during those years, he takes credit for laying the foundations for the pennant-winning Tiger teams of 1907–09. Barrow pointed out that he acquired three-quarters of those teams' infield. He acquired shortstop Charley O'Leary from a minor league team before the 1904 season started, traded for third baseman Bill Coughlin in July, and purchased the contract of second baseman Herman Schaefer near the end of the season.

Barrow should rightly get credit for adding those three players. He also was responsible for contributing to the turmoil of a dissension-riddled team that played well below its talent level while he was its manager. The team Barrow inherited in 1903 was adept at "scientific baseball." The Detroit players had become used to employing aggressive baserunning and hit-

and-run tactics. Barrow's preferred strategy was much more conservative, with an emphasis on using the sacrifice to advance runners and then hitting away. Kid Elberfeld and Kid Gleason, two of the players who clashed with Barrow in 1903, didn't particularly like that style of play. Both were gone before the 1904 season started. Another dissatisfied player, Jimmy Barrett, told the manager, "Mr. Barrow, your methods take all the individuality away from a ballplayer."[49]

Barrow resigned near the end of July, partly because of the friction with a few players and partially because his team was not playing well. Relying on the sacrifice and straightaway hitting only work if a team can hit. The 1904 Tigers didn't do that very well.

Detroit (62–90)

Regular Lineup	AVG	OBP	SLG	R	RBI	SB
Jimmy Barrett, cf	.268	.353	.300	83	31	15
Matty McIntyre, lf	.253	.310	.317	74	46	11
Charlie Carr, 1b*	217	.246	.271	38	47	6
Sam Crawford, rf	.254	.309	.361	49	73	20
Ed Gremminger, 3b	.214	.257	.285	18	28	3
or Rabbit Robinson, ss-2b	.241	.314	.319	30	37	14
Bobby Lowe, 2b	.208	.236	.259	47	40	15
Lew Drill, c**	.255	.359	.328	24	24	5
or Bob Wood, c	.246	.271	.320	15	17	1
or Monte Beville, c***	.214	.260	.260	16	15	2
Charley O'Leary, ss	.213	.254	.254	39	16	9
Leading Pitchers	W	L	PCT.	IP	H	ERA
George Mullin	17	23	.425	382.3	345	2.40
Ed Killian	15	20	.429	331.7	293	2.44
Wild Bill Donovan	16	16	.500	293	251	2.46
Frank Kitson	9	13	.409	199.7	211	3.07
Jesse Stovall	2	13	.133	146.7	170	4.42

*Includes record with Cleveland
**Includes record with Washington
***Includes record with New York

Sam Crawford was the team's star. From 1901 to 1903 Sam had hit .330, .333 and .335. He had led the National League in home runs in 1901 with 16, and in triples the next season with 22. In 1903, his first season in Detroit, He had led the American League in triples with 25. His batting average in 1904 was a meager .254, the worst of his career except for 1917, his last year, when he served primarily as a pinch-hitter. Years later Crawford insisted he hit the ball as well in 1904 as in other years. "Throughout that entire season I seemed to be dogged by the misfortune of batting directly at fielders or in some way having my best efforts nullified by circumstances," he said.[50]

While Crawford's memory might have been accurate, it is likely that his relatively poor batting marks in 1904 were to some extent the result of opposing pitchers refusing to give him any good pitches to hit. They had little reason to take chances with Crawford, since the men who hit just before and after him were having terrible seasons, as were most of the Detroit players. During the first half of the season Charlie Carr preceded Crawford in the Detroit lineup. Carr had hit .303 in 1903, but in a spring training game he was hit in the face by a pitch. He suffered a broken nose and afterwards became somewhat gunshy in the batter's box. He hit only .214 with Detroit in 1904, with few walks and little power. Either Ed Gremminger of Bobby Lowe followed Crawford. Gremminger's numbers were very close to Carr's, to the degree of having an identical .214 batting average. Lowe hit a robust .208. Over the last two months several other players came before and after Crawford in the batting order. Only one—Charlie Hickman—hit very well, and Hickman slumped badly after a good start with the Tigers.

The Tigers finished seventh in the league in batting average, on-base percentage, and slugging percentage. They were spared last place in those categories by the presence of the Senators, who fielded one of the worst teams in major league history. Among the Detroit regulars, only Jimmy Barrett, the leadoff batter, had a higher batting average than Crawford, and none of the regulars had a higher On-Base-plus-Slugging Percentage. The weakness of the Tiger batters is highlighted by the fact that the two highest batting averages on the team belonged to pitchers George Mullin (.290) and Bill Donovan (.271).

Royalty: Washington

The 1904 Senators weren't the worst team in American League history. They were only the second-worst. Their 38–113 record gave them a won-lost percentage of .252. The 1916 Philadelphia Athletics went 36–117, for a percentage of .235. In the National League, the 1935 Boston Braves (38–115, .248) and the 1962 New York Mets (40–120, .250) had marginally poorer records. But, during the modern era, the 1904 Senators had a worse record than all the other teams in the major leagues. Therefore, while the 1904 Senators can't be considered the Kings of Bad, they certainly deserve membership in the Royal Family of Bad.

Washington (38–113)

Regular Lineup	AVG	OBP	SLG	R	RBI	SB
Bill O'Neill, cf*	.238	.286	.276	40	21	22
or Bill Coughlin, 3b**	.255	.285	.316	50	34	11
Hunter Hill, 3b***	.204	.236	.226	37	31	14
Jake Stahl, 1b	.262	.309	.381	54	50	25
Frank Huelsman, lf****	.245	.311	.343	28	35	7
Barry McCormick, 2b	.218	.274	.250	36	39	9
or Jim Mullin*****	.203	.252	.250	19	13	7
Joe Cassidy, ss	.241	.265	.332	63	33	17
Patsy Donovan, rf	.229	.271	.243	30	19	17
Malachi Kittridge, c	.242	.266	.268	11	24	2
or Boileryard Clarke, c-1b	.211	.269	.247	23	17	5

Leading Pitchers	W	L	PCT.	IP	H	ERA
Casey Patten	14	23	.378	357.7	367	3.07
Jack Townsend	5	26	.161	291.3	319	3.58
Long Tom Hughes******	10	23	.303	260.7	274	3.59
Beany Jacobson	5	23	.179	253.7	276	3.55
Barney Wolfe******	6	13	.316	160.3	162	3.26
Dunkle, Davey	2	9	.182	74.3	95	4.96

*Includes record with Boston
**Includes record with Detroit
***Includes record with St. Louis
****Includes record with St. Louis, Chicago and Detroit
*****Includes record with Philadelphia
******Includes record with New York

Such an exalted status cannot be reached without the combined efforts of ownership, management and players. The Senators' bad season started, as awful performance often does, with missteps by those at the top of the organization. The ownership group that took over from Jimmy Manning, the 1901 owner, had proven unsatisfactory and the team had passed into a sort of receivership under the control of the American League. While the league was searching for new owners Ban Johnson oversaw the club from Chicago. He wanted to avoid unnecessary expenditures, so the Senators saved some money by avoiding the expenses associated with traveling to a more southern climate for spring training. Instead, the team conducted workouts in Washington. Unfortunately, it rained frequently in Washington that spring. Most of the Senators' workouts were held inside the National Guard Armory. The team was able to play only a couple of practice games against the local Georgetown College team before the season started.[51]

Johnson succeeded in finding a new ownership group in late March. The new owners decided to bring in a new manager to replace Tom Loftus.

The man they wanted—Patsy Donovan—was unable to commit to the position because of an on-going dispute with his previous team, the St. Louis Cardinals. Loftus, who remained in Washington after the sale, continued to be nominally in charge of the team, when he could spare the time. The situation prompted Washington's *Sporting News* correspondent to remark, "The Senators are without a head virtually, for Loftus is giving his attention to other business of the club." Loftus left town about a week before the season opened. Veteran catcher Malachi Kittridge was named interim manager until Donovan could free himself to come to Washington.[52]

Partly because of the unsettled conditions, when the season opened on April 14 there were still some minor details that needed to be addressed. Two of those details were called center field and right field. The Senators had no outfielders to put there. A quick SOS to other teams brought Harry Hoffman and Jack Thoney from Detroit and New York, respectively. Both were loaned to the Senators for an indefinite period.[53] Hoffman batted .100 in ten games with the Senators. Thoney hit well, batting .300 in 17 games before Clark Griffith recalled him to the major league team in New York. In his 17 games in the Senators' outfield, however, Thoney made six errors, compiling a fielding average of .860. After Hoffman and Thoney departed, the Senators muddled along for a while with catcher Lew Drill and infielder Joe Cassidy doing their best to fill the two outfield spots.

As one might expect, the lack of proper conditioning in the spring took a toll on the throwing arms of the Senators' pitchers. Highball Wilson, who pitched the opening game, made it through two more games before incurring a career-ending injury. Dave Dunkle pitched with a tender arm, while Del Mason pitched ineffectively, thereby earning a trip to the Eastern League after five appearances. Al Orth missed several weeks because of an illness.[54] The one Senators pitcher who was effective in the early going—Casey Patten—worked so often he was showing signs of overwork by mid-May.

Having been set up for a losing season, on April 14 the Senators roared out of the starting gate at full speed—in reverse gear, of course. They went through their first four series with a record marred only by a tie. That is, they were 0–10 over that time, including a game against Philadelphia in which Patten struggled to a 10-inning 6–6 tie. They lost three more contests before the Highlanders, in a charitable mood, contributed eight errors to a 9–4 Washington victory, thereby bringing the Senators' losing streak to an end at 13 in a row. Patten pitched the last 4⅔ innings of that game. Three more losses followed before Patten again put a brake on the Senators' skid, beating St. Louis 7–3 in a game he pitched on one day's rest after a nine-inning relief outing. Over the next six weeks the losses continued to come, interrupted by an occasional win. On June 27 the Senators' record stood at 9–45. In the 54 games played at that point of the season, the Senators had managed to win two in a row exactly one time.

After his arrival on May 10, Patsy Donovan worked diligently to teach the tactics of "scientific baseball" to his young players. Washington's press corps was convinced those tactics would eventually result in more competitive play.[55] Donovan's task was made more difficult, however, by ownership policies. In a pattern quite familiar to the fans of current small market teams, the new owners sought to limit their losses by getting rid of their high-priced players. Kip Selbach quickly became a target. Selbach was receiving a salary of $4,000, a carryover from the baseball war. As we mentioned above, it took two tries to unload Selbach, Donovan objecting to the first attempt. Dunkle, who pitched in two of the Senators first four wins, went next. Dunkle was a veteran pitcher who had been quite successful at the minor league level but mediocre as a major leaguer. The Senators sold him to Louisville of the American Association. Catcher Lew Drill and third baseman Bill Coughlin went to Detroit in separate cash deals. Coughlin, who missed several weeks at the beginning of the season because of illness, brought a reported $8,000, a handsome sum in 1904.[56]

The owners took other steps that were bound to demoralize their team. Selbach and Kittridge were each fined $100 for "drinking in public" because they had a glass of beer with their evening meal. After the Senators played an exhibition game in Saginaw, the players were given a choice between waiting around until 1:30 a.m. the next morning for a cheaply-priced excursion train or paying their own way back to their Detroit hotel.[57]

Buoyed by Patten's good pitching and solid performances from first baseman Jake Stahl and shortstop Joe Cassidy, the Senators improved somewhat as the season progressed. They had four more two-game winning "streaks" and even managed to win three games in a row once. On October 10, during the first game of a season-ending doubleheader against the Athletics, Donovan was interrupted as he approached the plate to take his turn at bat. Rube Waddell came up to him holding a package. Donovan looked at it suspiciously as Rube unwrapped the package and unfolded a tattered American flag. Rube presented the Senators' manager with the explanation that it was emblematic of the cellar championship.[58]

Exhibition Series with a "Minor League?"—No!

The matchup between the Boston Americans and the Pittsburgh Pirates following the 1903 season—the games now memorialized as the "First

World Series"—had been very popular with the nations' fans. Before the 1904 season was very old, people began to talk about a rematch between the champions of the two major leagues. There was no provision in the National Agreement, baseball's governing document, requiring such a series. It had been arranged by Barney Dreyfuss and Henry Killilea, the owners of the two teams. The Pittsburgh-Boston series was just one of several played after the 1903 season. The major league teams located in Chicago, Philadelphia and St. Louis had played each other for local bragging rights, while Cincinnati and Cleveland had squared off for the "Ohio Championship." The four teams representing St. Louis and Ohio also faced each other in a brief series pitting the two National League teams against the two American League teams. It is not clear what title was in contention in this last series—perhaps the winner was to be crowned "Champion of Major League Inland Cities Located Near Large Bodies of Water." Conspicuously absent from this burst of intra-city, intra-state and inter-aqua playoffs was a playoff series between the two New York teams. The Highlanders were quite willing to play the Giants, but neither Brush nor McGraw wanted any part of such a series.[59]

By late July of 1904 the Giants had built up a sizeable lead in the National League pennant race. While the Giants were playing in Chicago a local writer asked McGraw if the Giants would agree to a playoff against the American League champion, which at that time could have been any one of five or six teams, including the Highlanders. McGraw was unequivocal in his response. "The Giants will not play a post-season series with the American League champions, regardless of what team it may be," he said. "This is final and absolute, so far as I am concerned. I never talked with Mr. Brush or any stockholders in our club about the matter, and I do not care what the owners say, or intend to do. I am the manager of the club, and I guess I have something to say."[60]

Although American League President Ban Johnson strongly supported a postseason series between the two league champions, and most fans and baseball writers agreed with him, McGraw's statements on the subject didn't change. McGraw didn't have to fear any disagreement coming from the Giants' president, John T. Brush, regarding this matter. Brush's opposition was just as strong as McGraw's. Brush let McGraw do most of the talking on the subject until the season was nearly over. But he took steps to mollify the Giants players, who all wanted to play against the American League champions and collect their portion of the gate proceeds. The players threatened to organize their own series against the American League champions, with the games to take place in late October, when their 1904 National League contracts expired. In response to that threat, Brush paid star pitchers

Joe McGinnity and Christy Mathewson $3,000 each to "go home after the season ended," figuring that no player-organized series would be successful without the two star pitchers. For the other Giants players Brush organized a benefit dinner, with all of the proceeds going to the players.[61]

On September 27, after the Giants clinched the National League pennant, Brush issued a statement praising McGraw and the Giants players. The National League, Brush said, was the premier baseball league in the nation. One of the purposes of the league was to "establish and regulate the professional baseball championship of the United States." Each year after the league had completed its schedule, Brush said, the victorious club has rested with its laurels unquestioned. "There is nothing in the constitution or playing rules of the National League which requires its victorious club to submit its championship honors to a contest with a victorious club in a minor league." Therefore, Brush said, when the National League season ended, the Giants would be content to rest on their laurels and would be ready to defend their title when the 1905 season opened.[62]

Brush's statement provoked a strong reaction throughout baseball, especially his reference to the American League as a "minor league." The reaction was so strong even Brush eventually backed down from his opposition to a post-season playoff with the American League champion. That winter the owners of the two leagues formalized an agreement establishing the World Series as an annual event.

A Violent Year

In 1920 Ray Chapman died after being hit on the head by a pitch, the only instance of a major league player dying as a result of an errant pitch. It is a wonder that the 1904 season did not produce a tragedy such as that which befell Chapman.

As the 1904 season drew to a close, a note in *Sporting Life* stated that the year had been "remarkably prolific in the matter of player accidents and fatalities." Nationwide nine players had been killed and about 50 seriously injured. The nine fatalities came from lightning strikes, sunstroke and fatal beanings. The note ended by naming eight major league players who "have been severely injured by being hit on head or face by pitched balls."[63] If the author of the piece had possessed the internet, computers and other resources now available for research he undoubtedly would have named a few more major league players who were hit in the head by pitches. We found mention of 16 instances of a batter being hit in the head or face by a pitch during the 1904 season.

Spring Training—Detroit first baseman Charley Carr was hit in the face during an exhibition game in Nashville. The pitch broke his nose and blackened his left eye. After a local physician treated him, Carr returned to Detroit "with his nose anchored to his face with several strips of court plaster." After Carr complained of discomfort and an inability to smell anything, a Detroit doctor had to break his nose again and reset it. During the season Carr couldn't seem to get the spring training beanball out of his mind. His batting average dropped 64 points from the preceding year.[64]

May 30—Cubs first baseman Frank Chance was hit in the head by a pitch thrown by Cincinnati's Jack Harper. According to the game summary, Chance "was out for several minutes. The Chicago captain recovered, and continued in the game with nothing worse than a blackened eye, but it was a narrow escape, for if the blow had been an inch farther back it would have killed him." This was a rough day for Chance. He was hit by a pitch four times, three times by Harper in the opening game of a doubleheader and once by Win Kellem in the second game.[65]

June 13—Otto Krueger, Pittsburgh's primary utility player, "took a terrific blow to the side of the head and was down and out for several minutes." Krueger suffered a severe concussion. He returned to his hotel after the game, but became delerious. He was out of action for several weeks before returning to the lineup. This was the second year in a row that Krueger suffered serious consequences as a result of being hit in the head by a pitch. In 1903 he also missed several weeks after being beaned by a pitch.[66]

June 17—Pitcher Chappie McFarland of the St. Louis Cardinals was hit behind the ear with a pitch. He was unconscious for two hours. McFarland missed two weeks before starting his next game.[67]

July 1—Outfielder Danny Hoffman of the Philadelphia Athletics was hit over the right eye with a pitch. He "fell like a log." Hoffman's cheekbone was broken and he suffered permanent damage to his vision.[68]

July 11—Pittsburgh catcher Ed Phelps was hit on the left side of the head. He "fell to the ground with a groan…. It could be plainly seen that Phelps was badly hurt, and when he was picked up limp and apparently lifeless many of those in the grandstand turned their heads, and expressions of sorrow could be heard on all sides. Mrs. Phelps was in the stand and many eyes were turned in her direction. She calmly left her seat and went to the club office, where she requested permission to go to the club house, but this was denied her by Dr. Berg."

Phelps was out of the lineup for six weeks. After the season, when the Pirates played the Cleveland Naps in an exhibition series, a Pittsburgh reporter praised the Naps two catchers, but said a comparison with the Pittsburgh catcher would not be fair. "Phelps was Pittsburgh's catcher," the reporter said, "but he has been, as he asserts himself, 'dead for three months.'"[69]

July 15—Outfielder Frank Huelsman had just been traded from the St. Louis Browns to the Washington Senators. In his second time at-bat against his former teammates, "One of [Fred] Glade's nasty wild curves hit Huelsman a crack on the side of the head and put him into dreamland a few moments." The next day Huelsman came to the clubhouse "wearing a large knob on his damaged head," and complaining of dizziness. He was out of the lineup for only a couple of days. In the same game that Huelsman was hit, Glade also hit Bill O'Neill on the head, but in O'Neill's case "it was more like a bird shot than the one that hit Huelsman."[70]

July 22—Nineteen-year-old Johnny Lush, a pitcher-outfielder-first baseman for the Philadelphia Phillies, was unable to avoid "a swift in-shoot, which struck him on the side of the head and stretched him out at the plate insensible." Lush was taken to the hospital and treated for a concussion. He did not return to the lineup until mid–August.[71]

July 28—Cincinnati second baseman Miller Huggins was hit in the head by a pitch. "He was unconscious for a minute, but was subsequently able to walk to the Reds' bench. He tried to duck but only succeeded in stopping the pitch with the back of his head." Huggins was back in the lineup the next day.[72]

July 29—In the fifth inning of the second game of a doubleheader Washington pitcher Barney Wolfe hit Elmer Flick and George Stovall in consecutive at-bats. Stovall was hit in the back of the head. He was removed for a pinch-runner. Bill Bradley scored both baserunners with a triple. Wolfe then hit Nap Lajoie with a pitch, his third hit batter of the inning. Stovall was not seriously injured.[73]

July 30—In the first inning of a game, St. Louis Cardinals outfielder Spike Shannon "walked into one of Roscoe [Miller's] fast ones with his head and it was thought that the Knoxville boy was down for the count, but he came to after a few minutes' doctoring and limped to first, from where he tore to second on the first pitched ball."[74]

August 2—St. Louis utility infielder Harry Gleason—Kid Gleason's younger brother—couldn't get out of the way of a Rube Waddell pitch. It hit him in the head. He never lost consciousness, but had to be carried to the clubhouse, vomiting and bleeding from the nose, ears and mouth. He was taken to the hospital. That evening Rube came to visit him, staying most of the night, as well as the next evening. Two weeks after the incident Gleason said the left side of his head was in a continual state of numbness, and his right arm and shoulder were almost useless. The right side of his body seemed partially paralyzed. "I think my time on the diamond is over,"

Gleason told a reporter. "I intend to have a final examination made by a physician, but I don't expect he will give any favorable answer. He has already told me that I ought never to put on a uniform again."

Six weeks later Gleason reported that he was feeling fine and would continue to play baseball. He played 150 games for the Browns in 1905, his last major league season. He continued to play professionally until 1911, when he was 36.[75]

August 4—Detroit third baseman Bill Coughlin was hit by "a wild and swift pitch by [New York pitcher Al] Orth, the ball banging Coughlin on the side of his head and dropping him like a dead man. He was carried away, and the game proceeded with [Clyde] Robinson on third." Coughlin was out of the lineup for a week.[76]

August 11—In a game against Detroit, Washington outfielder-first baseman Jake Stahl "was laid out in the eighth with a hard thunk on the head. His football experience stood him in good stead, however, and he was resuscitated, and continued in the game."[77]

September 14—In the second game of a doubleheader between Chicago and Cleveland, "one of [Roy] Patterson's benders struck [Fritz] Buelow in the side of the head and it looked for a minute like a fatality, for the backstop dropped like a log, and had to be carried from the plate to the bench. But he did not lose consciousness and soon left the park without assistance, although he had a nasty looking lump on the side of his head." Buelow was back behind the plate two days later.[78]

The Odious Spitball

During the off-season of 1904–05 no baseball topic was discussed more often than the Spitball. Every aspect of the pitch was examined. What were the mechanics of the pitch? Who gets the credit (or blame) for discovering it? What would be the effect on batting averages and run scoring? What, if anything, should be done about it? Practically speaking, what could be done about it?

The pitch. The spitball was thrust into the center of the baseball spotlight, of course, because Jack Chesbro was spectacularly successful using it. By the last six or eight weeks of the season several pitchers had added it to their repertoires and many others were experimenting with it. Two nascent spitballers, Harry Howell of the St. Louis Browns and Bob Ewing of the Cincinnati Reds, described the grip and delivery of the ball in pretty much the same words as Chesbro. The ball was held the same as a curve ball, with the first and second fingers placed between the seams and the ball clasped between the thumb and third finger. Chesbro described applying saliva directly on the ball, while both Howell and Ewing said they applied it to the first two fingers. The key to the delivery was to release the ball with little or no friction between the ball and the first two fingers, so the ball would not rotate as it traveled to the plate. When the ball reached the plate it broke sharply downward.

The spitball was not easy to master. According to Howell, Chesbro practiced the pitch intermittently for over a year before using it in a game. Howell, who was a teammate of Chesbro's with New York in 1903, began working on it in mid-season of 1904 when he saw the success Chesbro had with it. "When I first started to experiment I had no control over the ball," Howell said, "for it would slip off my fingers at the wrong time and perhaps go a dozen feet over the batter's head." After a while Howell gained mastery of the pitch. "I finally acquired the knack of releasing the ball at the proper moment," he said, "and as I have always been able to throw very wide curves, I was soon able to get very sharp breaks."

While Chesbro claimed he could control the amount of break on the ball and the direction of the break, neither Howell nor Ewing made such a claim. "Unlike an ordinary curved ball, the pitcher cannot be certain of the side direction the ball will take as it breaks downward," Howell said. "The side breaks are determined by the manner in which the ball leaves the pitcher's hand. If the hand is turned with the arm facing down and to one side the break at the plate will be different than if the ball left the hand with the palm not turned over so far." Ewing simply said, "There seems to be no way to control the spitball at present. All a pitcher can do is to throw and take his chances of having it go in the right direction to fool the batsman."[79]

Who was using the pitch in 1904? By the last month or two of the season baseball writers were on the lookout for pitchers who had adopted Chesbro's prize pitch, but it's anybody's guess as to how many spitball sightings were actually spitballs. The major league pitchers who were using the pitch by the end of the season probably included: American League–Chesbro and Jack Powell (New York), Bill Dinneen and Norwood Gibson (Boston), Dusty Rhoads (Cleveland), Howell (St. Louis), Wild Bill Donovan and George Mullin (Detroit), Jack Townsend and Casey Patten (Washington); National League—Frank Corridon (Chicago-Philadelphia) and Ewell and Tom Walker (Cincinnati). Among the higher minor leagues, the Pacific Coast League seemed to have the most spitball pitchers. In the American Association, St. Paul had three pitchers who used the pitch frequently. The Eastern League didn't seem to have any spitballers until the last month of the season, when a couple pitchers apparently mastered it.[80]

Who first threw the pitch? Chesbro was not the first pitcher to use the spitball. He said he learned it from Elmer Stricklett, who in turn said he got the idea from Frank Corridon. In 1902, when he was with Newark in the Eastern League, Stricklett had watched Corridon, an opposing pitcher, throw a pitch that broke so sharply his catcher couldn't handle it. He noticed that Corridon spit on the ball before delivering it. For the remainder of the game he studied Corridon's method of throwing the pitch. Shortly afterwards Stricklett jumped to Sacramento of the Pacific Coast League. There he tried to imitate Corridon's delivery. He gradually learned to control the pitch, which Corridon had been unable to do while with Providence.[81]

Several ex-players of the time insisted the pitch had been used years before Chesbro learned to throw it. Bill Hart, an umpire who had pitched for several teams in the American Association and National League in the 1880s and 1890s, said he threw a spitball many times. (Since Hart had a career record of 66–120, there wasn't a real rush among his contemporaries to imitate his stuff.) Hart claimed Bobby Mathews had as good a spitball as any pitcher he ever saw. Mathews' career predated the National League. He pitched from 1871 to 1887, beginning his career in the National Association and ending it in the American Association. Charlie Bennett, a star catcher who played at the same time as Hart, also cited Mathews as an early spitball pitcher. Bennett told a reporter, "I don't believe that even the spitball is new. Bobby Mathews had a big drop and a curve which broke sharply. He never told how it was done, but I noticed that when he pitched, a little white streak appeared on a dirty ball. I think he was using the spit ball before Jack Chesbro was ever heard of."[82]

Elmer Stricklett was credited by *The Sporting News* **as being the pitcher who first developed the spitball (Library of Congress).**

The possible impact. Since nobody, not even Chesbro, had used the pitch for an entire season, the spitball's impact upon the game was still mostly a matter of imagination entering the 1905 season. Not everyone was convinced the spitball would be widely used. Nick Altrock, a White Sox pitcher, said, "The spitball is an effective delivery, but too dangerous to fool with unless you have to." Altrock pointed to the fact that the wet ball caused wild throws by infielders and catchers. It was also a difficult pitch for catchers to handle and caused injuries to the catchers' hands and bodies. When veteran Cleveland pitcher Red Donahue was asked about the pitch he replied, "The spitball is all right for any pitcher foolish enough to monkey with it. But none of it for me. I think I have been in the game long enough to know better than to fool with that ball." Donahue said the pitch was thrown much like a slow straight ball. "The slow straight, which is the same as the spitball, knocks spots out of your arm and will put any pitcher using it a great deal out of the business in short order," he said.

Despite views such as those expressed by Altrock and Donahue, the prevailing assumption was that nearly every pitcher in organized baseball would at the very least experiment with the pitch in 1905, and lots of them would be using it in games. For some people that was a foreboding prospect. Patsy Donovan, Washington's manager, told the editor of *Sporting Life* he had read with great interest an article the paper presented about the spitball. "Do you know it has changed the game more than anything for years?" Donovan said. "Unhittable? Well, almost so. Some pitchers got the hang of the ball so that you could not do anything with the delivery." Donovan then described a game in which Jack Townsend had baffled the Cleveland Naps for seven innings using the spitter. Not a Cleveland batter had been able to get the ball out of the infield and even when they hit the ball the resulting grounders were "puny affairs, not one hit on the nose."

Chicago's player-manager, Fielder Jones, wanted the rules changed to lessen the spitball's impact. "If baseball legislators want to do any legislating this winter let them pass a rule against the spitball," Jones said. "There's no way a batter can get at that ball, and the pitcher is already too strong for him," he claimed. "The trouble with that spitball is that no one can judge in the least which way it is going to break," he said. "If it is breast high, it shoots downward and to either side, but which slant it is going to take is absolutely impossible to pick. The ball comes floating up to the plate exactly the same every time. It is faster than a slow ball, but slower than a curve. It looks big as a house then drops out of sight."[83]

Proposed changes. The two major baseball publications of the day, *The Sporting News* and *Sporting Life*, both responded to the introduction of the spitball by calling for changes in baseball's official rules. The editor of *Sporting Life* wanted the pitch banned. He wrote, "It seems to us that the present rule against discoloring the ball could cover the case, but as umpires will not enforce that rule newer and more explicit regulation is necessary. The *Sporting News* editor took the position that direct legislation against the spitball would not work. "If the twirler is forbidden to spit upon his fingers, or the ball, he will conceal a wet sponge in his shirt or pants pocket, or find some other way to evade the law," he said. Instead of trying to outlaw the pitch, *The Sporting News* recommended a rule change that would limit its effectiveness: reducing the strike zone to the area between the batter's hip and his shoulder. Other suggestions included changing the ball-strike ratio to either three balls and three strikes or four balls and four strikes.[84] Inevitably, the spitball controversy became mixed in with the continuing opposition to the modern foul-strike rule. A vocal minority still wanted to revert to the old rule, and used the spitball as an additional argument for that change.

Despite the calls for action, the spitball remained legal in 1905 and for 14 more years after that. It was outlawed in 1920.

Three

1905, National League

Make 'Em Throw the Ball

In May of 1900 Cincinnati pitcher Ed Scott decided he had suffered enough from Roy Thomas' antics. Thomas, known for his ability to rap out foul balls at will, had just fouled off about a dozen pitches while trying to work Scott for a base on balls. Scott had complained to the umpire that Thomas was intentionally fouling off pitches, which was against the rules. But the umpire had refused to take any action, which was the normal response to such complaints. So Scott reared back and fired his best fastball, hitting Thomas "in the fleshy part of his anatomy."[1]

Later in the season, while Cincinnati was in Philadelphia on a hot, humid August day, Thomas again began fouling off pitch after pitch. In the eighth inning, after Thomas had flicked away four pitches during an at-bat, pitcher Bill Phillips walked off the mound toward the plate. There wasn't much of an exchange between Phillips and Thomas. All the umpire heard was Phillips saying, "What, do you mean to say I'm a liar?" Then Phillips staggered Thomas with a right to the jaw. Phillips was immediately ejected from the game, but evidently was intent on ensuring that Thomas got the message. In the next series between the two teams he greeted Thomas with a fastball to the ribs on Thomas' first plate appearance.[2]

That winter Scott and Phillips secured revenge against Thomas and other National League batters in a broader and more far-reaching manner than they ever could have achieved on the field. Organized baseball's Rules Committee amended the rules to state that the first two fouls in an at-bat would be scored as strikes. (Since 1894 foul bunts were already counted as strikes.) The rationale behind the change was that the intentional fouls were unpopular with the fans and needlessly extended the amount of time required to complete a game.[3]

The "foul-strike rule," as it was called, seemed to have an immediate effect upon players' batting averages. The league batting average in the

National League fell from .279 in 1900 to .267 in 1901. In the American League, adoption of the rule resulted in a decline from .275 in 1902, when the league played under the previous rule, to .255 in 1903, after the new foul-strike rule was enforced as part of the peace agreement ending the baseball war. Major league batting averages fell even further over the next few years, reaching a low of .239 in both leagues in 1908.

While the foul-strike rule played a key part in the decline of hitting during the Deadball Era, it was only one of several factors dragging down batting averages. When the pitching distance was moved back to 60 feet, six inches in 1893, the result was an explosion of batting numbers. In 1892 National League batters were able to bat out the ball at a meager .245 clip. The next year, with pitchers trying to adjust to the longer distance, they rapped out a league-wide average of .280, and boosted that number up to .309 in 1894. As time passed, however, the pitchers adjusted to the new distance and added a few wrinkles, such as scuffing the ball or cutting it with their spikes (illegal but largely ignored by the umpires) and applying foreign substances such as saliva. Baseball's rules-makers also contributed to the decline. In 1900 they redesigned home plate, changing it from a 12-inch square to a five-sided object, with a width of 17 inches. The next year the catcher was required to move closer to the plate, These changes gave the pitcher a better target and made it easier for the umpire to call strikes.

The decline in hitting—and the lower scores that resulted from it—led to a greater reliance on the tactics of "scientific baseball." The rule of thumb was that with a lead less than three or four runs a team had to use "science" rather than just swinging away at the ball. Modern fans are familiar with the tactics employed—the sacrifice bunt, hit-and-run and stolen base. The difference between now and the early Deadball Era is that the tactics were not reserved for the late innings of close games; they were seen as the means for building up a lead or overcoming a couple of runs at any point in the game.

The unwritten "book" on the proper way to play the game started with the employment of the bunt. With a man on first base and no outs, fans expected the batter to bunt. Some managers, Boston's Jimmy Collins being one of them, preferred to let the hitters pick out a pitch and swing away. If Boston won the game, no criticism was usually heard. After a loss, the game summary might note that Collins was not playing "up-to-date baseball."[4] With a man on first and one out, the sacrifice was not considered a good option, but a steal or hit-and-run would frequently be attempted if the manager felt the game situation justified the gamble. When there was a man at second and no outs, the sacrifice was again considered a good option. With men on first and second and no outs, a sacrifice became almost mandatory. Even great hitters such as Ed Delahanty, Honus Wagner and Napoleon Lajoie quite often sacrificed in that situation.

Two of the most successful managers of the era, John McGraw and Connie Mack, were known to favor the hit-and-run.[5] Because that tactic was not recorded on official score sheets, it is difficult to determine how frequently it was tried or which game situations called for its use. Baseball reporters would sometimes note that a batter had punched the ball through a hole vacated by the shortstop or second baseman who left his position because the baserunner had started for second. At other times the summary would state that a man went from first base to third base on an infield grounder, suggesting a hit-and-run play, but not ruling out other possibilities.

A high stolen base total was often (but not always) an indication that a team was proficient in playing "scientific baseball." The stolen base was a feature of play during all of baseball's history before 1920. All Deadball Era teams had stolen base totals that would be considered high by today's standards.

By the middle of the Deadball Era's first decade a slight revision was made to the unwritten book of strategy, emphasizing the effectiveness of aggressive baserunning. In *Touching Second*, a book ghost-written for Johnny Evers, Hugh Fullerton summarized the reasoning behind the strategy: "In the old days the motto of every manager was 'run and keep running, make the other fellow throw.' It was a baseball adage in those times that any team that could keep the opposing team throwing the ball around would win. As a matter of fact, the modern manager recognizes the same thing. He knows that if he can make the other team throw, it is only a question of time until they throw away the game."[6]

Fifty years after Fullerton made that comment Ty Cobb, who made his debut with Detroit in 1905 and became possibly the foremost practitioner of scientific baseball, echoed the writer's observation in his autobiography. In discussing his success in stealing bases and his ability to escape being tagged out when trapped on the basepaths, Cobb said, "Nine out of ten times I'd get out of the jam and advance a base for a most simple reason. All I had to do was make the opposition keep on throwing the ball. Sooner or later, somebody would make a wild throw. 'Make 'em throw the ball' should be Rule One in every baserunner's primer."[7]

The rationale behind aggressive baserunning in the Deadball Era is apparent when the focus is turned to the small, almost primitive gloves used by the fielders of the era. It wasn't easy to make fast, clean plays with those gloves. Almost all infielders used two hands in completing tag plays, which would increase by a fraction of a second the time required to put the ball on a runner—certainly not a lot of time, but often enough to make the difference between a runner being out or safe. The practice of using two hands to make a catch would also reduce a fielder's ability to reach out for a hit ball or a throw, forcing him at times to move his entire body for a throw that today's players would simply snag in the webbing of their gloves. In addition—and perhaps most importantly—the anticipation that a play had to be completed quickly to catch a runner would cause fielders to hurry and increase the likelihood of a misplay.

The emphasis on drawing throws applied to all facets of baserunning. It was most apparent in the number of times a baserunner went from first base to third base on a bunt or an infield out, or tried to score from second base on an infield hit or even an infield out. Such plays were rarely seen before the Deadball Era, when they became notable plays but not rare ones. Double steals, in which runners on first and second would both attempt to steal also became more common. The delayed steal was another play that was tried with increasing frequency. The tactic was used when runners were at first and third, usually with two outs. The runner on first would start for second as soon as the pitcher released the ball, hoping to draw a throw from the catcher. The runner on third would hold his base until he saw that the ball was headed for second. Then he would race home. The objective of the play, of course, was to manufacture a run without having to rely on the batter's ability to get a base hit.

In 1905 New York Highlanders manager Clark Griffith gained renown as the "inventor" of the squeeze play. In fact, the play had been seen before as an unplanned, off-the-cuff decision by a batter to bunt, rather than hit away, with a runner on third. In spring training of 1905 Griffith decided to add the play to his team's playbook, He drilled his players in pulling off the play, and employed it often during the season, as did other managers, who quickly saw its effectiveness. Griffith's version of the play was what we would now recognize as the "suicide squeeze." In response to a question from a reader, a *Washington Post* reporter described the play as follows: "The "squeeze play is executed by a runner on third and a batter, when one man is out. Both men must know just when it is to be pulled off, usually by the batter signaling to the baserunner to dash home when a certain ball is pitched. The batter bunts this ball, and there is no way for the runner to be caught coming home, unless the batter misses the ball."[8]

When a batter drove the ball for an extra-base hit, he was more likely to challenge the outfielder's arm by trying to stretch a hit. An instance occurred in 1905 when Jimmy Sebring was thrown out at the plate trying to stretch a triple into a home run on a wet field. Cincinnati *Enquirer* reporter Jack Ryder defended Sebring's decision. "There were two out at the time and one run was needed to tie the score. The hit was to right field and on a perfectly dry field would easily have been good for the circuit.... Sebring did the right thing in trying to score. It was only fast handling by Josh Clarke and a perfect relay by Grady that cut him down. The slightest inaccuracy would have saved him."[9] Most of the time such plays were simply noted without comment, but the prevailing attitude seemed to be that displayed by Ryder: aggressive baserunning wins games, and the outs that might result were just an acceptable part of the strategy.

A player's ability to get around the bases fast was, of course, important in pulling off these plays. Speed was widely recognized as a key factor in a player's makeup. In 1900, at the dawn of the Deadball Era, Cincinnati writer Ren Mulford had noted the fact that the top teams all had several speedy runners. "I venture to say that baseball will never again see a championship team with less than three or four fast men on it—men who can get down to first and around the circuit like a flash," Mulford said. "There is nothing so demoralizing to the opposing team as fast work on the bases. When a fast man is at the bat the infield becomes alert, and sometimes nervous. They realize that it will require the fastest kind of work to retire the batsman should he hit to either of them. Fleet-footed players can turn what is ordinarily an easy out into a base hit. A fast man on his feet has every advantage, and the team that has the most fast men will be sure to cut a large figure in the race."[10]

In 1903 Cincinnati manager Joe Kelley voiced a similar opinion. "Speed is everything," he said. "I dare say that more games are won through speed than through batting. What good is a bunt if the batter can't get a start from the plate, let them be able to get on their toes and fly to first and the opposing infield is on the nervous seat all the time and wild throws and fumbles result. Many a grounder is turned into a base hit by fast running."[11]

The ability to make quick judgments both as a baserunner and as a fielder was considered about as important as speed afoot. Sam Crane, a highly respected ex-ballplayer who stayed up with the game as a reporter for a couple New York newspapers, stated a widely held viewpoint: "In these days of speedy, fast baseball," said Crane, "players' minds got to be working overtime looking for advantages and if they don't the other fellows will—that's all. Any diminution of speed with either mind or feet causes havoc. There is no excuse for a player nowadays not to sprint with his mind as well as his feet, and they both have got to work in unison. There is as much necessity for team work between a player and himself as between a player and his fellows."[12]

Decades after they retired two of the old-timers interviewed by

Lawrence Ritter for his wonderful book *The Glory of Their Times* expressed the opinion that the biggest difference between the game they played and the game of later days was in the mental demands on the players. Sam Crawford remarked, "You know, ballplayers were tough in those days, but they were real smart, too. Plenty smart. There's no doubt at all in my mind that the old-time ballplayer was smarter than the modern player. No doubt at all. That's what baseball was all about then, a game of strategy and tactics, and if you played in the Big Leagues you had to know how to think, and think quick, or you'd be back in the minors before you knew what in the world hit you."

Fred Snodgrass expressed the same opinion, in very similar words. "I will tell you something about those players, though, that I think is usually overlooked. They were rough and tough, all right, but they were good thinkers, too. Players in my day played baseball with their brains as much as with their brawn. They were intelligent, smart ballplayers. Why you *had* to be! You didn't stay in the Big Leagues very long in those days unless you used your head every second of every game…. There was a premium on intelligence in those days, on the ability to outwit and outthink the other team."[13]

1905 National League Standings

Team	W	L	Pct.	GB
New York	105	48	.686	—
Pittsburgh	96	57	.627	9
Chicago	92	61	.601	13
Philadelphia	83	69	.546	21.5
Cincinnati	79	74	.516	26
St. Louis	58	96	.377	47.5
Boston	51	103	.331	54.5
Brooklyn	48	104	.316	56.5

Muggsy's Favorite Team: New York

"I regard the Giants of 1905 as the greatest ball club that I have managed. I look upon it as one of the greatest ball teams of the last thirty years…. I say this, too, in due regard for the fact that I have handled other clubs that were greater hitters and greater baserunners. I hand the laurels to the 1905 team for its smartness. We did not have a really slow-thinking player on the club."[14] John McGraw wrote this as part of a series of newspaper articles published in the fall of 1922. They were put together in book form the next year under the title *My Thirty Years in Baseball*.

New York (105–48)

Regular Lineup	AVG	OBP	SLG	R	RBI	SB
George Browne, rf	.293	.321	.397	95	43	26
or Moonlight Graham, rf	.000	.000	.000	0	0	0
Mike Donlin, cf	.356	.413	.495	124	80	33
Dan McGann, 1b	.299	.391	.434	88	75	22
Sam Mertes, lf	.279	.351	.417	81	108	52
Bill Dahlen, ss	.242	.337	.337	67	81	37
Art Devlin, 3b	.246	.344	.310	74	61	59
Billy Gilbert, 2b	.247	.331	.293	45	24	11
or Sammy Strang, ut	.259	.389	.347	51	29	23
Roger Bresnahan, c	.302	.411	.375	58	46	11
or Frank Bowerman, c	.269	.322	.333	37	41	6

Leading Pitchers	W	L	Pct	IP	H	ERA
Christy Mathewson	31	9	.775	338.7	252	1.28
Joe McGinnity	21	15	.583	320.3	289	2.87
Red Ames	22	8	.733	262.7	220	2.74
Dummy Taylor	16	9	.640	213.3	200	2.66
Hooks Wiltse	15	6	.714	197	158	2.47
Claude Elliott	0	1	.000	38	41	4.03

The 1905 Giants didn't differ greatly from the 1904 team. Since that team had won 106 games no smart baseball man would have made major changes to it, and McGraw possessed great baseball intelligence. Nevertheless, he made some seemingly small changes which almost certainly made it a better team. The most important change had been made the preceding August, when Mike Donlin was acquired from Cincinnati. Donlin ranked with the best players of the early Deadball Era. He hit at a level exceeded only by players who were later voted into the Hall of Fame. He was a fast runner. He had started his baseball career as a pitcher, and accordingly possessed a strong, if sometimes erratic, arm. In his book *The New Bill James Baseball Historical Abstract*, Bill James selected the long-forgotten Donlin as the left fielder in his all-star team for the 1900–09 decade, alongside Ty Cobb and Sam Crawford, the Tigers' Hall of Fame outfielders.[15]

Donlin came to the Giants in a three-way trade involving two young players who had short major league careers. He was batting .356 for the Reds at the time of the trade, about 90 points better than the two other players involved in the trade. These circumstances might cause a casual observer to conclude that factors other than baseball skills led to the deal. That would be correct. Donlin, in effect, drank his way off the team. He had repeatedly gotten intoxicated and had shown up at a couple of games unable to perform adequately. Reds manager Joe Kelley had tried to get

Mike to change his habits but had reached the end of his patience. In early July Kelley announced that Donlin was being fined and given a 30-day suspension. As soon as the suspension ended, the Reds completed the deal, giving the Giants a great player and a potentially king-sized headache.[16]

McGraw already had considerable first-hand knowledge of Donlin's on-field virtues and off-field vices. They had been teammates in St. Louis in 1900. McGraw was then winding down his very accomplished career as a player, while Donlin was playing his first full season in the major leagues. Mike had an impressive year with the bat. He finished third in the league in home runs and would have finished among the leaders in batting average, on-base percentage and slugging percentage if he had accumulated enough at-bats to qualify. One reason he didn't get enough at-bats was because of his off-field activities, which included one night in which he barely survived a barroom brawl, receiving a knife slash to the throat that came close to puncturing his jugular vein.

Donlin followed McGraw to Baltimore when the American League was formed in 1901. Again he excelled with the bat, finishing second in batting average, third in on-base percentage, and eighth in slugging percentage. Mike made it all the way through the 1901 season without any serious mishaps, but during the off-season he became involved in a drunken fight that led to a six-month jail sentence. After his release in August, Mike signed with Cincinnati. He promised the team and himself that he would curtail his drinking, a pledge he followed pretty well until tumbling off the wagon in the spring of 1904.[17]

Over the course of his career, McGraw took on several reclamation projects, with only middling success. For a while the Donlin experiment looked like a big success. Mike batted only .280 in his two months with the Giants in 1904—good for an ordinary player, but one of the worst averages of his career. Because left field at the Polo Grounds was the sun field, and Mike didn't field well when having to battle the sun, in 1905 McGraw put him in center field. This allowed Roger Bresnahan, the Giants center fielder in 1904, to become the number one catcher, giving the team a top-notch hitter at a position normally filled by a weak hitter. Donlin had one of his normal years—that is, playing at a Hall-of-Fame level—at bat. He finished third in the league in batting average, fifth in on-base percentage, and third in slugging percentage. He led the league with 124 runs scored and finished eighth in runs batted in, despite batting either leadoff or the second most of the season.

Another notable addition to the 1905 team was Sammy Strang, who became a valuable utility player and effective pinch-hitter for the Giants. Strang was versatile in the field. He could play any position except pitcher or catcher, though he wasn't a great fielder in any of them. McGraw used him primarily at second base and in the outfield. Sammy didn't put up great batting averages, but he excelled at getting on base and scoring runs. He had scored 108 runs for the Chicago White Sox in 1902 and 101 for Brooklyn in 1903. He was injured part of the season in 1904, when his batting average dropped to .192, and the Superbas decided to let him go. With the Giants Strang returned to his previous run-producing ways.

Strang fit well with the New York team. McGraw built his teams around speed and the characteristic he called "smartness." The Giants looked for an edge wherever they could find one. They led the league in batting average, but also worked the pitchers for bases on balls and knew how to lean into an inside pitch for a free pass to first base, also ranking number one in those categories. They had the most stolen bases and, though no statistics reflected it, undoubtedly ranked high in taking extra bases on hits and getting thrown out trying for extra bases. While giving away outs on the bases is frowned upon in modern times, in the Deadball Era, when gloves were minuscule compared to the current models, the pressure of knowing the Giants were always going to press for an extra base almost certainly led to an increase in fielding miscues by their opponents. The batters in the middle of the team's lineup—Dan McGann, Sam Mertes, and Bill Dahlen—were adept at the hit-and-run, one of McGraw's favorite tactics for applying pressure and moving runners along the bases. Art Devlin led the National League in stolen bases with 59, Mertes was fourth (52), Dahlen finished seventh (37) and Donlin eighth (33).

The Giants started the 1905 season with an emphatic statement, routing the Beaneaters 10–1 in their opening game and following that with a 15–0 pounding in the next game. They won 13 of their first 16 games. By May 23 they were 25–6, with a 7½-game lead over the second place Pirates. They maintained a lead of about that amount for the rest of the season. In mid–September the Pirates pulled to within five games of the Giants by winning 19 of 21 games. When the two teams began a three-game series on September 25, the lead was six games. The Giants responded by smacking down their challenger with three straight victories.

McGraw's men opened the series by scoring five runs in the first inning. They did it in typical Giant style. Three men reached first after being hit by a pitch, a specialty of McGraw's teams. In 1905 Deacon Phillippe pitched 279 innings and hit ten batters with pitches, 30 percent of them in this one inning. Roger Bresnahan led off the game by leaning into a pitch and getting first on it. He was sacrificed to second and scored on Mike Donlin's single. Dan McGann and Sam Mertes were then hit by pitches, loading the bases. Bill Dahlen grounded to short, but Honus Wagner's throw went over the first baseman's head, all three Giants scoring. Dahlen took third on the error and scored on a fly ball to left field. Phillippe held the Giants scoreless for the next six innings, while the Pirates chipped away at the lead, scoring four runs off Christy Mathewson to pull within a run at 5–4.

But in the eighth and ninth the Giants scored five more runs to put the game on ice. This time they showed their batting muscle. McGann and Mertes led off the eighth with back-to-back triples. Dahlen scored Mertes with a single. Devlin bunted and reached first on an error. The two baserunners moved up on a sacrifice and Dahlen was brought home by Mathewson's single. Two singles and a double brought in two more runs in the top of the ninth.

The next day the Giants coaxed eight walks from Mike Lynch, who had a tendency to be wild, and mixed in seven hits, including four doubles and a home run, while again pounding the Pirates, 9–5. Mathewson pitched the last three innings of this game in relief of Ames. Wiltse won the final game, 5–3, the victory mathematically clinching the pennant for the Giants.[18]

It was fitting that Mathewson played a key role in wrapping up the pennant for the Giants. He had an outstanding season. For almost any other pitcher it would stand out as the highlight of his career, but for Matty it was just one of several magnificent seasons. His 31 wins was the twelfth highest single-season total for the period after 1900. A fine achievement, but Matty won more in two other seasons. His 1.28 ERA ranks 13th lowest in the major leagues since 1900. Matty did better in 1909 (1.14). He led the league in 1905 with eight shutouts. Again, a notable achievement, but Matty had eight in two other seasons and notched 11 in 1908. On June 13, in one of his classic duels with the Cubs' Three-Finger Brown, Matty pitched the second no-hitter of his career. He came close to pitching a perfect game. He didn't walk a batter, but two Cubs reached first on errors, both on infield grounders. Matty also threw a two-hitter and six three-hitters.[19]

For Joe McGinnity, the Giants' other superstar pitcher, 1905 was a year in which he appeared to be something less than an Iron Man. On June 9, he failed to get an out in a start against the Pirates, giving up five runs in the first inning. The next day a New York newspaper reported, "McGraw is a little worried about the condition of Joe McGinnity, as his arm has been out of shape in the last two games pitched. The famous 'Iron Man' was given a week's rest, but yesterday he was pounded all over the lot."[20] Two days later McGinnity started again and lasted seven innings in a 4–0 loss to the Cubs. He started on a regular basis throughout the remainder of the season and was used eight times in relief, saving three games. But he had several games in which he was ineffective, and both his won-lost percentage and his earned run average were inferior to other Giants starters.

Given the fact that they won 105 games, it should not be surprising to see that the Giants led the league in most of the important team statistical categories. They were first in batting average, on-base percentage, slugging percentage, stolen bases and—as a natural result of all that—scored 44 more runs than any other team. New York pitchers were second to the Cubs in runs allowed and earned runs. As always the team led the league by far in men thrown out of games and riotous conduct both on and off the field.

It didn't take the team long to have its first intemperate outburst on the field. On April 22, in the fifth game of the season, against Philadelphia, McGann tried to score from second base on a single to right field. The outfielder made a good throw, the ball beating McGann to the plate by about ten feet. Frustrated, McGann punched catcher Fred Abbott, who threw the ball at his attacker, hitting him "upon the fleshy part of his rear development." The two men then squared up opposite each other ready to fight. The umpire intervened in time to prevent any more blows, but McGraw ran out to get into the action and other Giants began milling around the scene. In the confusion that followed Christy Mathewson, the squeaky clean, all-American idol of the fans, punched out a teen-age lemonade seller. After the game a large crowd of fans gathered around the Giants' team carriages. At first the crowd just hooted at the despised visiting team, but then a few of them began throwing stones. One of them threw a brick, which struck a Giants player. The ballplayers responded by trying to pull down the hoods of their carriages. One of the players hit a rioter with a bat. Eventually the carriage drivers managed to get their teams moving down the street, driving through a hail of stones and other objects.[21]

A month later, in a series against second-place Pittsburgh at the Polo Grounds, McGraw fired a steady stream of criticisms and insults at the umpires and Pirate players. In the first game of the series, as McGraw was walking back to the bench from an encounter with the umpire, he yelled to the crowd, "I'd as soon let [Pirates owner] Barney Dreyfuss umpire; it would be all the same thing." In the second game, his umpire-baiting was so excessive that the New York crowd eventually turned against him and hooted at him. In game three McGraw's abuse of Pirate pitcher Mike Lynch became so nasty umpire Johnstone told him to stop. When McGraw ignored the admonishment, Johnstone threw him out of the game.[22]

Before the third Pittsburgh game Dreyfuss was standing at an entrance to the Polo Grounds. McGraw came over to where Dreyfuss was standing and shouted a series of insults at the Pirates' president. According to Dreyfuss, McGraw charged him with being crooked and controlling the National League umpires. Dreyfuss appealed to National League President Harry Pulliam, who brought the matter before the league board of directors. When

McGraw learned of Pulliam's action, he telephoned Pulliam and objected in typical McGraw language. Pulliam responded by fining McGraw $150 and suspending him for 15 days.

The league board was composed of Dreyfuss (the accuser), John T. Brush (the Giants' president), Boston owner Arthur H. Soden (who was also a part-owner of the Giants), and Chicago owner James Hart. When the matter was taken up, Brush brought half a dozen witnesses who testified that McGraw had said nothing offensive. The board ruled in McGraw's favor and formally rebuked Dreyfuss for acting in an "undignified manner" in engaging in the encounter at a ballpark. But in a second vote, the board upheld Pulliam's punishment of McGraw. Brush and McGraw reacted to the second vote by securing an injunction prohibiting Pulliam from carrying out the punishment. When the case came to trial, the judge ruled in McGraw's favor.[23]

On the field the wrangling with umpires continued unabated. In August the Giants forfeited a game to Pittsburgh that was tied 5–5 going into the ninth inning. Claude Ritchey led off the bottom of the ninth with a double. He advanced to third on a sacrifice attempt, beating Mathewson's throw to the base. Several Giants players surrounded the umpire, protesting the call. "Then out came the great Muggsy," wrote a Pittsburgh reporter, using a nickname McGraw detested, "jumping like a kangaroo, taking five feet at a time, as if he was particularly worked up. He burst through the crowd of excited Giants, shook his head, tapped [umpire] Bausewine on the breast in a not friendly manner, and pointed at Ritchey." After berating Bausewine for a moment, McGraw turned to Bob Emslie, the other umpire, and tapped him on the chest also. At that point Bausewine pulled his watch, gave the Giants a brief moment to calm down, and declared the game forfeited to Pittsburgh.[24]

Two weeks later, McGraw managed to irritate umpire Jim Johnstone, a favorite target for his barbs, so much that Johnstone threw the Giants manager out of the game when his team held a 9–2 lead.[25]

The Giants' reputation for rowdy behavior contributed to the aura of conflict that seemed to follow the team around the league. They had altercations with fans in the street outside the ball parks in both Philadelphia and Pittsburgh. After a game in St. Louis McGraw was hit by an umbrella and fans threw stones at the team as they left the field. "The Giants have come to be marked men in the baseball world," remarked a St. Louis reporter. "They cannot resort to the same tricks which are generally considered legitimate and fair without bringing down on their heads the wrath of a frenzied mob like that of yesterday. Unless McGraw and his men conduct themselves meekly they will surely be roughly handled. Certain it is that were the Giants to play away from home, depending on the foreign games to win another pennant, they would never succeed, for the crowds would not permit the tactics which win games for the Giants.[26]

When McGraw's "Muggsy" side was not busy aggravating umpires and opposing players, his baseball strategist side—nicknamed "the Little Napoleon"–was developing a new approach to handling a pitching staff. Along with five very solid starters, the Giant pitching staff included a young man named Claude Elliott who, in McGraw's opinion, possessed great potential. Elliott was acquired from Cincinnati in late August of 1904. "The young pitcher has great speed and many curves, but is crude in their use," a reporter commented. "He is being coached constantly by McGraw and [catcher Frank] Bowerman, both of whom think he is a sure comer and predict that he will develop into a National League star. He has a peculiar drop ball to which he puts an outcurve, and with the terrific speed he uses with it, McGraw thinks [it] will puzzle the best batter in the league."[27]

A quick glance at the leadership tables for 1905 would indicate that Elliott was well on his way to becoming a star reliever. He topped the National League in saves that year, albeit with a relatively modest total of six. When it is noted that he appeared in only eight games as a reliever, his league-leading total of six saves appears more imposing, especially considering that no other pitcher had more than three. So far, so good for young Mr. Elliott. Unfortunately, a closer look at the record indicates that, while McGraw used Elliott as a closer and to obtain saves, the Little Napoleon was not using him the way a modern closer is used. McGraw actually wasn't using young Claude to save games—he was using him to save the arms of his more experienced pitchers. Elliott's saves came in games the Giants led by wide margins. Twice he came on when the Giants had a six-run lead; his other four saves came when his team was eight runs ahead.

A few years later McGraw developed the first successful relief specialist. Doc Crandall earned that distinction, his first year performing in that role coming in 1909.

An interesting footnote to the 1905 season involved a speedy young outfielder named Archie Graham. Graham reported to the Giants in late May, after finishing his course work at Baltimore Medical College. He was given the nickname "Moonlight" as a minor league player because "he was supposed to be fast as a flash." He made his first and only appearance on the field on June 29, in an 11–1 blow-out victory over Brooklyn, coming in as a defensive replacement for right fielder George Browne long after the game had been decided. He had no official at-bats or fielding chances. He was sent to the minor leagues by the Giants a few days later. Graham retired from baseball following the 1908 season. He eventually settled down in

Chisholm, Minnesota, practicing medicine there until his death in 1965. Author W. P. Kinsella noticed Dr. Graham's statistical line while writing a book, *Shoeless* Joe, about White Sox outfielder, Shoeless Joe Jackson. He used it and the outlines of Dr. Graham's career in Chisholm as the basis for one of the characters. When the book became the basis for a movie titled *Field of Dreams*, Dr. Graham's character was played by Burt Lancaster.[28]

A Baseball Warrior: Pittsburgh

Fred Clarke was on second base. Still a lad of only 21 years, he had been playing for the Louisville Colonels less than two weeks and was learning the rough and tumble ways of the National League. The Louisville batter smashed a single into center field. Clarke rounded third and headed home as the throw came in from the outfield. Brooklyn catcher Con Daily moved to the third base side of the plate, blocking it from Clarke, who had to come in standing up. Clarke, who weighed around 150 pounds, rammed into the sturdy, 200-pound Daily, knocking him over. Daily got up and ran over to Clarke. He touched him on the back with the ball, then landed a roundhouse right on his cheek, followed by a left cross. "Clarke was declared out," said a writer who described the incident.[29]

A ball player less determined than Fred Clarke might have been intimidated by Daily's reaction to his hard-nosed play at the plate. For Clarke, the play and, to some extent Daily's response, were just part of the game. A few years later Clarke suffered a bruised rib when Chicago third baseman Fred Raymer "accidentally" collided with him as Clarke was rounding third base. Some of the Pirates accused Raymer of using a dirty tactic when he shoved his shoulder into Clarke. Clarke made no such criticism. "The boss Pirate has his own idea of baseball," explained a Pittsburgh writer. "In his opinion you cannot make a parlor game out of it, and when he once gets on the bases he goes ahead without taking much account of the human obstacles, but if a collision occurs and he gets the worst of it, he never complains."[30]

Pittsburgh (96–57)

Regular Lineup	AVG	OBP	SLG	R	RBI	SB
Otis Clymer, rf	.296	.332	.353	74	23	23
Fred Clarke, lf	.299	.368	.402	95	51	24
Ginger Beaumont, cf	.328	.365	.424	60	40	21
or Tommy Leach, 3b-cf	.257	.309	.345	71	53	17
Honus Wagner, ss	.363	.427	.505	114	101	57

Regular Lineup	AVG	OBP	SLG	R	RBI	SB
Del Howard, 1b	.292	.345	.370	56	63	19
or Bill Clancy, 1b	.229	.246	.330	23	34	3
or Homer Hillebrand, ut	.236	.282	.300	9	7	1
Dave Brain, 3b	.257	.296	.381	31	46	8
Claude Ritchey, 2b	.255	.324	.332	54	52	12
Heinie Peitz, c	.223	.289	.259	18	27	2
or George Gibson, c	.178	.270	.267	14	14	2

Leading Pitchers	W	L	Pct	IP	H	ERA
Deacon Phillippe	20	13	.606	279	235	2.19
Sam Leever	20	5	.800	229.7	199	2.70
Charlie Case	11	11	.500	217	202	2.57
Mike Lynch	17	8	.680	206.3	191	3.79
Patsy Flaherty	10	10	.500	187.7	197	3.50
Chick Robertaille	8	5	.615	120.3	126	2.92
Homer Hillebrand	5	2	.714	60.7	43	2.82
Lefty Leifield	5	2	.714	56	52	2.89

Indeed, basepath collisions occurred with some regularity during Clarke's career, and he had several fights with opposing players because of them. In 1897 Clarke and George Davis of the New York Giants clashed in a home-and-home confrontation. The first match took place in Louisville in July. Davis and Clarke "fought a one-round draw" near second base during the afternoon. That evening Davis and his manager, Bill "Scrappy" Joyce, met Clarke at his hotel lobby and challenged him to a fight. Clarke responded that he wasn't looking for trouble and didn't think a fight was proper. But if nothing else but trouble would satisfy them, he said, then he would accommodate them. The two Giants left the hotel without a fight, but warned Clarke, "Wait till you come to New York, and we will take your scalp." A month later Clarke and Davis squared off again, this time near second base at the Polo Grounds. The umpire quickly broke up the match, ordering both fighters off the field.[31]

Other fights involving Clarke broke out over the next several years. In 1900 he and Cupid Childs argued during a game in Chicago. Childs was angry over two rolling blocks he received from Clarke while trying to turn double plays. After the game the two men encountered each other while waiting to board a train. While Clarke was talking to a Pirates player Childs came up behind him, cussed him and punched him. Clarke turned and punched back. The two men fought for several minutes. According to a Pittsburgh writer, during the fight, "Clarke tore Childs' linen almost off and left marks which the fat infielder will carry for some moons. Childs did just as much damage and Clarke's face was in a jelly-like condition when a policeman stopped proceedings."[32]

Pittsburgh writers generally defended Clarke when he got into a fight. But outside Pittsburgh most people placed the blame on his shoulders. After the Childs fight, Boston writer Tim Murnane commented, "Cupid Childs has the sympathy of nearly all the league players in his trouble with Fred Clarke. Clarke has a reputation of often trying to go out of his way to injure his fellow players." In *The Sporting News* a writer claimed, "No player in the profession has a worse reputation as a spiker than Pittsburgh's manager Clarke."[33]

It was a spiking incident that led to a run-in with Fred Tenney in 1902. In the seventh inning of a game Clarke hit a ground ball that the Boston shortstop just managed to stop. The throw to first was a little wide, but Tenney managed to grab it "by one of his famous stretches." When the umpire called Clarke safe, Tenney pointed to his foot, indicating that Clarke had run over it with his spikes. Play resumed without further incident until the end of the eighth inning when Clarke trotted in toward the bench, passing Tenney as the first baseman was about to take his position. Tenney growled at Clarke, "You dirty yeller dog." Clarke stopped and yelled something back at Tenney, who walked up to Clarke, cursed him and shoved his hand into Clarke's face. Clarke kicked at Tenney and hit him in the jaw. The two went at it briefly before their fellow players could separate them.

After the Tenney fight, Clarke found some defenders outside of his own circle. The consensus among the Brooklyn players was that Tenney should have tried to settle the matter off the playing field. They said Clarke had previously been "a dangerous man going down to first," but agreed that he had mended his ways.[34]

Clarke's aggressive, maybe even bellicose, ways should be viewed in the context of the era when he played. In the 1890s baseball was a rougher, more wide-open game. Baserunners had to contend with fielders who grabbed at them, shoved them, and blocked their paths as they were going around the bases. Fist fights erupted with some frequency, and involved umpires, as well as players. The game was somewhat like modern hockey with respect to its tolerance for rough play. Clarke undoubtedly felt he was standing up for his rights when he battled the opposition by using his fists as well as his bat and glove.

Clarke's teammates, who for most of his career were under his management, seemed for the most part to take inspiration from his aggressive attitude. To them Clarke was fighting for the team's success. They were exposed to the entirety of Clarke's character, which was, everything considered, quite admirable. Most of them would probably agree with Bobby Lowe, the Boston second baseman who came to admire Clarke after years of opposing him on the field. "People who have seen Clarke only during a game imagine that he is a rough, uncouth fellow," Lowe said. "But they are

Pittsburgh player-manager Fred Clarke did not shy away from collisions on the basepaths (Library of Congress).

wrong. Off the field he is one of the most polished gentlemen imaginable. He is a worker in the game and the most sarcastic individual I ever heard on the coaching line. But that's in the game. Any man that works as hard as Clarke does deserves success and I hope he will have it with the Pittsburgh club this year."[35]

Hard work and self-discipline were key to Clarke's success and central to his personality. Clarke's first job in professional baseball came in 1892, when he answered an advertisement to try out for the Hastings team in the Nebraska State League. Clarke made the team and was placed in the outfield, a new position for him. He was terrible. "I was lucky to catch half of the drives hit to me," Clarke said many years later. Characteristically, Clarke worked hard to learn the new position. "An old-timer told me I could improve by practice," he said, "so I went out to the field at 8 o'clock in the morning and practiced until game time in the afternoon. After a while I got so I could catch fly balls pretty well."[36]

When Clarke joined the Colonels he was given a hard time by the team's veterans. They didn't view him as a young player who might help the team, but rather as a kid who was taking a job away from one of their friends. During practice one of the veterans made fun of Clarke's bat, which was smaller than most, telling Clarke National League pitchers would knock that toothpick out of his hands. Clarke had a great response to the remark. He went five-for-five in his first game, including a double. "I waved that bat in the face of the guy who had wisecracked about it," Clarke later said, "told him off and became a member of the hard-bitten crew."[37]

Clarke batted only .274 in his rookie year, not a great average in a season when the league batting average was .309. He raised his average to .347 in 1895, however, and hit .325 in 1896. He enjoyed a terrific year in 1897, when he hit .390, the second best average in the league. He became recognized as one of the finest players in the league. A Cincinnati team official revealed that before the 1897 season Cincinnati had offered Louisville $10,000 for Clarke. At that time $10,000 was a largely symbolic figure a baseball owner might offer for a true star, knowing his offer would not be accepted. But it stamped Clarke as one of baseball's superstars.[38]

Although Clarke ranked among the better hitters in the National League almost every year until 1911, his last as a regular player, his strongest suit was his fielding. He was a fast runner and he fielded with the almost reckless intensity he displayed when he ran the bases. For many years he used an acrobatic approach to catching low fly balls that seemed just out of his reach. Here are two views of the same catch made on September 2, 1901, against Boston:

> *Pittsburgh Dispatch*: Clarke made a catch of a fly ball from DeMontreville's bat in the ninth inning that was a wonder. The ball was good for two bases if Clarke had not started for it right away. The manager-captain saw that he was not likely to reach it and he made a running dive, just barely getting it and being compelled to turn a somersault.
>
> *Boston Globe*: Demont hit a low liner 10 yards inside the left line that looked like

a 50 to 1 shot. Clarke started with the crack of the bat and after a short sprint threw himself out like a flying fish, just reaching the ball, which was within a few inches of the ground. He rolled over and over, but held the leather, while the crowd cheered him with a will. This was fast work by the greatest left fielder in the business.

Game summaries contain some other references to Clarke turning somersaults after catching a low fly ball. On July 4, 1903, he injured his shoulder making such a catch. Indicative of Clarke's competitive drive, he got to his feet and threw to second in time to double up a runner on the play in which he was injured. After another diving catch in 1906 aggravated a back injury, Pirates own Barney Dreyfuss declared, "Fred must quit making that kind of play. I have told him often that I would prefer that he never go after such a difficult kind of ball, but Fred forgets everything but the play in front of him when in a game and never stops to think that he may be seriously injured in making those diving catches."[39]

During most of his career Clarke was not only responsible for his own play, but also for that of his team. He was only 24 years old when he became manager of the Colonels. Possibly because of his age, it took a while for him to gain respect. It seemed that when the Colonels lost it was Clarke's fault, when they played well it was because he took the advice of a veteran player. The opinion expressed by J. Ed Grillo at the beginning of the 1900 season was widely held. "I have always doubted Clarke's ability to manage a team," Grillo said, "and I have not yet had occasion to change my mind. The [Pittsburgh] team has a lot of good ballplayers in it and they can all hit, but the head is lacking. [Catcher Chief] Zimmer, of course, knows the game and plays it for every point and Clarke would do well to consult him as much as possible."[40]

As one might expect, the critics' estimate of Clarke's managerial ability went up greatly after the Pirates came close to beating Ned Hanlon's Superbas in 1900, and even more when they began winning pennants in 1901. Even then, however, the critics saw flaws in Clarke's managing. "Clarke is not a good bench manager yet," one reporter said in June of 1901. "In the game he is fearless and plucky and his men follow him willingly and confidently. On the bench Freddy seems helpless, and is so nervous that he worries the other players and torments himself." By 1904, after his teams won three straight pennants, most baseball men agreed that Clarke was among the game's best managers. Even Grillo, who had expressed his doubts earlier, had changed his mind. In the spring of 1904 he wrote, "The youngsters on the Pittsburgh team regard Fred Clarke as the greatest general in the business—and they are not far wrong."[41]

Any remaining doubts about Clarke's ability as a manager should have been erased by the Pirates' performance in 1905. He basically rebuilt a fading team on the fly, while relentlessly chasing McGraw's high-flying Giants. After the 1904 season ended he made two trades that were criticized in the local press, but which paid good dividends over the course of the 1905 season. Kitty Bransfield had fallen into disfavor because of a tendency to sulk when things didn't go his way. He had slumped at bat and played inconsistently in the field. In December Clarke arranged a trade that sent Bransfield, utility player Otto Krueger, and outfielder Harry McCormick to Philadelphia for an untried youngster, Del Howard, who could play either the outfield or first base. Shortly thereafter he sent catcher Ed Phelps to Cincinnati for Heinie Peitz, a good catcher whose best days were believed to be behind him.[42]

Howard justified the trade by putting up good numbers in 1905, which turned out to be his only season with the Pirates. He started the season in the outfield, splitting time with rookie Otis Clymer, and switched to first base when Bill Clancy, another rookie, was injured. Howard batted .292, adding a solid bat to the middle of the Pirate batting order, and fielded adequately in both right field and first base. Peitz began the season playing well, but seemed to melt in the hot summer sun. In the spring, "his throwing to the bases was simply phenomenal and he was a terror to would-be base stealers.... He was hitting the ball like a league leader and was away up about the .300 clouters," remarked Ralph Davis, the Pittsburgh columnist for *The Sporting News*. But "things went their natural course," Davis continued. "The Old Baron has again slowed up, at least, to his 1904 gait, his throwing to bases recently has been decidedly on the lurid order and his batting average is slowly but surely shrinking."[43] Peitz remained of value to the Pirates, however, by virtue of his peppery personality, which added vinegar to the team's field presence, and because he was able to impart his deep knowledge of the game to several young pitchers Clarke had added to reinvigorate the pitching staff.

In May Clarke acquired third baseman Dave Brain from the St. Louis Cardinals. Brain was one of those players whose talent would have been better appreciated in one of the lively-ball eras. He was a power-hitting infielder, who was at best only adequate in the field. His addition to the team enabled Tommy Leach to begin a transition from third base to the outfield.

On the mound the Pirates were once again led by Deacon Phillippe and Sam Leever, both of whom won 20 games. Leever led the National League in won-lost percentage (20–5 .800), thanks to run support of almost six runs a game. Behind the two venerable veterans the pitching staff was in flux. Patsy Flaherty, who won 20 games in 1904, was inconsistent, possibly because he spent much of the spring trying to master the spitball without fully gaining control of it.[44] The team's top young pitcher, Mike Lynch, posted a fine won-lost record (17–8), but a poor earned run average for the Deadball Era (3.79) and walked 107 batters in 206 innings—not a good thing in any baseball era, but especially bad for the Deadball Era. Clarke gave ample opportunities to Charlie Case, Chick Robitaille, and Homer Hillebrand, but none of the three showed enough potential to stick with the Pirates for more than a few games beyond the 1905 season. A fourth youngster, Lefty Leifield, was acquired when the minor league seasons ended. He turned out to be the real thing, becoming a leading starter for the Pirates through the 1911 season and remaining in the major leagues until 1920.

Zephyrs: Chicago

Chicago Tribune sportswriter Ira Sanborn was fond of creating his own nickname for his city's National League baseball club. In 1901, after most of the team's stars had jumped to the American League, Sanborn dubbed those who remained behind the "Remnants." When the team turned to young players as part of its rebuilding program, he brought back the previously discarded nickname of "Colts." Other writers preferred "Cubs," which has of course been used for over a century. Sanborn continued to use his preferred term until the spring of 1905, when he switched again, this time referring to Chicago's National Leaguers as the "Zephyrs."

According to Webster's dictionary, a zephyr is a gentle, westerly wind. Sanborn didn't explain clearly what, exactly, he meant by the term, but it is likely he was implying that the team's players could "run like the wind." In his first *Sporting News* article after he began using the term, Sanborn began his coverage by stating, "Manager Selee's fast Windy City bunch, dubbed Zephyrs for short, have been doing well indeed."[45] Certainly Chicago's manager would have been happy with that characterization. At about that same time, the *Boston Globe's* Tim Murnane commented, "Frank Selee is dead anxious to have it known that he has the speed players of the trade, the fastest team that he ever managed, even with some of his stars out."[46]

Chicago (92–61)

Regular Lineup	AVG	OBP	SLG	R	RBI	SB
Jimmy Slagle, cf	.269	.379	.317	96	37	27
Wildfire Schulte, lf	.274	.326	.367	67	47	16
Billy Maloney, rf	.260	.325	.351	78	56	59
or Jack McCarthy, of	.276	.320	.335	16	14	8
Frank Chance, 1b	.316	.450	.434	92	70	38
Joe Tinker, ss	.247	.292	.320	70	66	31

Regular Lineup	AVG	OBP	SLG	R	RBI	SB
Johnny Evers, 2b	.276	.333	.329	44	37	19
or Solly Hofman, ut	.237	.289	.324	43	38	15
Doc Casey, 3b	.232	.295	.316	66	56	22
Johnny Kling, c	.218	.272	.279	26	52	13
or Jack O'Neill, c	.198	.277	.244	16	12	6

Leading Pitchers	W	L	Pct	IP	H	ERA
Ed Reulbach	18	14	.563	291.7	208	1.42
Jake Weimer	18	12	.600	250.3	212	2.26
Mordecai Brown	18	12	.600	249	219	2.17
Bob Wicker	13	6	.684	178	139	2.02
Carl Lundgren	13	5	.722	169.3	132	2.23
Buttons Briggs	8	8	.500	168	141	2.14

Selee had built his team to maximize the preferred strategies of the day—relying on speed and aggressive baserunning to manufacture runs. The 1905 Cubs were not potent batters—their team batting average ranked seventh in the league—but they excelled at scratching out runs. Jack Ryder of the *Cincinnati Enquirer* marveled that the Cubs had twice scored from second base with two outs on grounders to second base. Both times the baserunner had rounded third and headed for home even though the inning seemed over. On one occasion the batter beat the throw to first and on the other the throw was wide. "The Seleeites take every chance, no matter how slight," Ryder said. "That's the way Frank Selee teaches his men to play.... Selee tolerates no loafing, and is a deadly foe to mechanical, go-easy playing. Every man on his team must run out every play at top speed. More than that, he must be looking for a chance to run out a play. So the Cubs are always dangerous at every stage of every game, and they are sure of a good position in the race all the time."[47] A St. Louis reporter echoed the sentiment: "That Chicago club is about the fastest thing on foot seen here in some moons. They run bases and cover ground like fiends. In [Billy] Maloney they have about the fastest baserunner in harness. The lad went from first to third on stolen bases the only time he got to first by hitting, the second steal being a double affair with little Evers in his wake."

The Cubs' captain and star first baseman, Frank Chance, set the tone for the team with his own aggressive baserunning, as a look at his high stolen base totals would indicate. In *Touching Second*, Hugh Fullerton described Chance as "always a baserunner of rare judgment, coupled with great daring." Game summaries indicate that Chance, like Cobb, was willing to risk being thrown out to gain an extra base, especially third base, or to score a run. Fullerton stated that, shortly after taking charge of the team, Chance taught his players to use a false start tactic to fool the middle infielders on a steal attempt. The runner on first would take a couple of quick steps toward second and then stop. Then, after the catcher had relaxed from his throwing position and the second baseman and shortstop had started back to their positions, the runner would dash for second base. Chance pulled off the play himself at least twice in 1905. Chance was always looking for an opening. He won a game against Brooklyn in July by scoring from third on a ground ball when the Superba infield was drawn in to head off a run at the plate. The batter hit the ball to second baseman Charlie Malay. Chance advanced about 20 feet on the grounder, enough to draw a throw. When Malay threw to third baseman Emil Batch, Chance raced toward the plate. Batch's throw to the catcher was high and Chance slid in safely, scoring the only run of a 1–0 Cub victory. A similar play against the Giants, however, backfired. That time Chance was at third base and Joe Tinker was on second. Tinker led off far enough to draw a throw from catcher Roger Bresnahan. As soon as the throw left Bresnahan's hand, Chance dashed for the plate. However, the return throw to Bresnahan was in time for the put out.[48]

The Cubs' alertness to the game situation and all-out effort applied when they were in the field, as well as at bat. Over the course of the season every Cub regular, as well as utilityman Solly Hofman, was described in newspaper coverage as being an excellent fielder. One fielding accomplishment, however, stands out, even a century later. On April 26 the Cubs edged out the Pirates in a close game, 2–1, thanks greatly to a most unusual feat pulled off by center fielder Jack McCarthy. In the bottom of the sixth inning, the Cubs led 1–0 with one out. Ginger Beaumont lashed out a triple. The next batter popped a short fly into center. Beaumont decided to take a

The Cubs' Frank Chance set the tone for his team with his aggressive baserunning (Library of Congress).

chance on the play, and McCarthy nailed him at home plate. Two innings later the Pirates scored their only run on a single and Patsy Flaherty's triple. The next batter beat out an infield hit, but Flaherty held third, where he remained as the next batter popped up to the infield. When Beaumont rapped a fly to center field, Flaherty tried to score. McCarthy again fired the ball to the plate for the out. In the ninth, with one out, Bill Clancy smashed out another triple. Tommy Leach followed with a fly to McCarthy. Clancy tagged and again challenged McCarthy's arm. The Cub outfielder responded with another fine throw, flagging Clancy at the plate, for his third double play assist of the game, and the third time he had ended an inning by throwing out a runner at the plate.[49]

On the mound the Cubs had the deepest and best pitching staff in the league. The team earned run average was a meager 2.04, almost a run less than the league average of 2.99. Due to injuries and FrankSelee's philosophy of using his entire pitching staff, six Cub pitchers started at least 19 games in 1905 and Jake Weimer topped the staff with 30 starts. Although the 1904 team had included five effective pitchers, a new starter was added. Ed Reulbach made his debut on May 16. He lost that game to the Giants, 4–0, but gave an indication of what was to come by allowing the league leaders only five hits. He went on to tie Weimer and Mordecai Brown for the most wins by a Cub pitcher with 18, and he led the team with an ERA of 1.42. Reulbach showed his mettle by grinding his way through two marathon contests. On June 24, he hooked up with the Cardinals' veteran ace, Jack Taylor, in an 18-inning duel, coming out on top, 2–1. The victory was his eighth straight, after losing his first two major league starts. Two months later he went 20 innings against the Phillies' Tully Sparks, again winning by a 2–1 score. The game tied the National League record for the most innings up to that time.[50]

Mordecai "Three-Finger" Brown had a relatively rough season in 1905. He had a losing record for a good part of the season. His arm became sore in late July, putting him out of action for about five weeks.[51] When he came back from his injury, however, he was the dominating pitcher he had been the previous year and would be for the remainder of the decade. It is a measure of Brown's greatness that his 2.31 ERA in 1905 was highest he would have over a seven-year period from 1904 through 1910, and was almost a third of a run per game higher than his next worst ERA during that time. On June 13, Mordecai allowed only 6 hits and one run in a matchup with his soon-to-be arch-rival, Christy Mathewson. Unfortunately for Brown, that was the game in which Matty threw his no-hitter. A month later Mordecai got even, holding the Giants to two hits in an 8–1 victory over Mathewson.

The Cubs got off to a sluggish start in 1905. They were beset by injuries to several of their key players. They were below .500 as late as June 7, when their record stood at 23–24. After that they went 69–37, a .651 pace, but by that time the Giants had already built up an insurmountable lead.

Frank Selee, the man who put together the 1905 Cubs, was in poor health when the season began. He had become ill during the previous winter, losing 15 pounds by the time spring training started. His health continued to be a problem during the first three months of the season. Before the season was very old he stopped taking road trips with the team, leaving team Captain Frank Chance in charge. By the end of June Selee's condition had deteriorated to the point that he left the team in hopes of recuperating at home. Shortly thereafter he learned he had tuberculosis. On July 30 he resigned as the team's manager, with Frank Chance succeeding him. The team Sanborn dubbed the "Zephyrs" had become the team of the man whose style of play had inspired the nickname. The team was now Chance's Zephyrs.[52]

In the Afterglow—Still Winning: Philadelphia

It wasn't a worst-to-first shocker, but when a team goes from 52–100 to 83–69 in one season, that's a pretty nice improvement. We've already suggested above that it bordered on being a miracle. The turnaround that came on August 21, 1904, continued throughout the 1905 season. The miserable Phillies of 1904 became a rock-solid team in 1905. The new version of the Phillies was a mixture of dependable veterans and good-looking youngsters. They weren't on a level with the Giants or the Pirates in 1905, but they almost beat out the Cubs—who were on the verge of becoming the National League's next super team. The Phillies reached a high-water mark in mid-June, when they edged ahead of Pittsburgh into second place. A short while later they dropped a few games behind the Pirates, dueling Chicago for third until the last week of August, when a seven-game losing streak put them in fourth place, seven games behind the Cubs. They remained in that position for the rest of the campaign.

Philadelphia (83–69)

Regular Lineup	AVG	OBP	SLG	R	RBI	SB
Roy Thomas, cf	.317	.417	.358	118	31	23
Kid Gleason, 2b	.247	.302	.303	95	50	16
Ernie Courtney, 3b	.275	.334	.331	77	77	17
John Titus, rf	.308	.397	.436	99	89	11
Sherry Magee, lf	.299	.354	.420	100	98	48

Regular Lineup	AVG	OBP	SLG	R	RBI	SB
Kitty Bransfield, 1b	.259	.294	.345	55	76	27
Mickey Doolin, ss	.254	.292	.360	53	48	17
or Otto Krueger, ut	.184	.273	.211	10	12	1
Red Dooin, c	.250	.269	.311	45	36	12
or Fred Abbott, c	.195	.248	.258	9	12	4

Leading Pitchers	W	L	Pct	IP	H	ERA
Togie Pittinger	23	14	.622	337.3	311	3.09
Bill Duggleby	18	17	.514	289.3	270	2.46
Tully Sparks	14	11	.560	259.7	217	2.18
Frank Corridon	10	12	.455	212	203	3.48
Kid Nichols*	11	11	.500	190.3	193	3.12
Jack Sutthoff	3	4	.429	77.7	82	3.82

*Includes record with St. Louis

Manager Hugh Duffy had upgraded the team over the winter by swinging several deals that brought in a half-dozen new players–a major retooling when you consider that teams carried about 16 or 17 players in 1905. The infield, a major weakness in 1904, featured three new regulars. Kitty Bransfield, obtained from the Pirates in a multi-player deal, added a good bat to the lineup and steady fielding at first base. Third baseman Ernie Courtney came from Buffalo of the Eastern League. He had already spent a couple of years in the majors. Courtney possessed borderline major league ability, but he enjoyed the best season of his career, making a substantial contribution to the Phillies' success by playing adequately in a key position and batting well above the league average. Mickey Doolin hit like almost every Deadball Era shortstop–poorly–but he gave the Phillies excellent defense, which was their greatest need. In addition, Doolin had one of his best years at bat in 1905.

Duffy traded a good pitcher, Chick Fraser, to Boston for another good pitcher, Togie Pittinger, who happened to have a very good year in 1905. In July the Phillies manager brought in one of his old teammates with the Boston Beaneaters, Kid Nichols. The 35-year-old "Kid" had his last good year, going 10–6 for the Phillies after losing five out of six decisions with the Cardinals.

The main strength of the team was in its outfield. In early August a St. Louis reporter remarked, "The Phillies are going to be a very hard club to beat from now on. Duffy has what is probably the best outfield in the country, all points considered. Magee, Thomas and Titus cover a world of ground, and their returns to the diamond are swift and accurate."[53]

All three of Duffy's flychasers were good "run-getters," the term applied to players who were able to generate runs through their batting and baserunning skills. A talented run-getter was given a level of respect by Deadball Era fans that later was reserved for an "RBI-man." The three Phillies outfielders averaged 105.7 runs scored per man. Roy Thomas had the second highest total in the league with 118. Sherry Magee tied for fifth with 100, and John Titus was seventh with 99.

Roy Thomas, the center fielder, was the team's only holdover from the Phillies teams of the 1890s, when they were an offensive juggernaut led by the great Ed Delahanty. Roy scored 137 runs in 1899, his rookie year. That relatively high total ranked only third in the league, reflecting the highscoring nature of the game during those years. We've already noted that Thomas's ability to foul off pitches was a factor in bringing about the foulstrike rule in 1901, charging a strike for the first two fouls, rather than having them basically count for nothing. The rule led to a significant decline in batting after it was effective but, ironically, didn't affect Roy much at all. He walked at a rate of one walk per 4.6 at-bats in 1900, the last year under the old rule, and at an average rate of one walk per 4.7 at-bats over the next three seasons. He led the National League in walks every year, except one, from 1900 to 1907—the exception being 1905, when he walked "only" 93 times, ranking third in the league.[54]

Although he hit for a good average every year through 1905, Thomas rarely punched out an extra base hit. He got lots of hits every year, but almost all of them were singles, and a significant portion of his singles were bunts. But since his specialty at bat was to lead off, that didn't matter much. His ability to draw walks put him on base frequently—his lifetime on-base percentage of .413 ranks 28th all-time—and his speed and savvy on the bases enabled him to rank in the top ten of the National League every year from 1899 through 1906 in runs scored. It is highly unlikely that the reader has heard Thomas mentioned as one of the great leadoff hitters of all time, but Bill James rated him as the twelfth best leadoff hitter ever, virtually on a par with Pete Rose, Don Buford and Rod Carew.[55]

In the field Thomas finished among the leaders in putouts among the outfielders nearly every year through 1906. He finished first in that category three years in a row, from 1903 to 1905. A description of a catch he made against the Pirates offers an insight as to why he did so: "The most sensational play of the game was Roy Thomas' catch of Phillippe's drive toward the flagpole in center in the third inning.... When the ball left the bat it looked like a sure enough two-bagger, Thomas made a lively sprint toward the flagpole and stretching his [ungloved] left hand down within a few inches of the ground gathered in the ball, though he took a headlong slide in the grass after making his desperate effort."[56]

Left fielder Sherry Magee was only 20 years old in 1905, which was his first full year in professional baseball. According to a *Baseball Magazine* article written a few years later, Duffy took young Magee under his wing and showed him how to generate more power with his swing. Thomas helped him with the fine points of playing the outfield, and Kid Gleason imparted tips on how to play scientific baseball. Combined with Magee's immense natural talent, the result was one of the top players in the league. In the spring of 1905 Philadelphia's *Sporting News* correspondent reported, "Magee is slugging the all in great shape down South, thus fulfilling the predictions made for this youngster last fall that he is cut out to develop into a second Delahanty as a slugger."[57] The youngster didn't quite develop into another Delahanty, but he certainly set a high standard as the first Magee. He finished in the top ten in the league in virtually every important batting category. He was second in triples (17), fourth in RBIs (98), and fifth in stolen bases (48) and runs scored (100). His slugging percentage (.420) was tenth-best in the league.

John Titus was one of those quiet players who tend to hang in the background while other players get the attention. Philadelphia sportswriters called him "Silent John." In his first couple of years with the Phillies he got almost as many comments about his blond locks, bushy mustache, and the ever-present toothpick he kept in his mouth as he did about his play on the diamond.[58] He was a fine defensive player with a great arm—he had over 20 assists every year from 1904 through 1909—and a good hitter with above average power. He had a good eye at the plate and was willing to get knicked by an inside pitch often enough to rank high in reaching base by that method. Grover Cleveland Alexander, a teammate late in Titus's career said of him, "Titus had one of the best batting eyes I ever saw. He would take his position

Sherry Magee contributed to the Phillies greatly improved record in 1905 with his outstanding work at the plate and in the outfield (Library of Congress).

at the plate with the easiest and most confident air in the world. If the ball was an inch outside of the plate, he would watch it go by and never bat an eyelash. If it was an inch inside he wouldn't move. He would just draw in his stomach and let the ball pass. But if you put the ball over the plate, he would whale the cover off."[59]

Second Only to the Babe: Cincinnati

Cincinnati (79–74)

Regular Lineup	AVG	OBP	SLG	R	RBI	SB
Miller Huggins, 2b	.273	.392	.326	117	38	27
Shad Barry, 1b*	.304	.352	.371	100	66	21
Joe Kelley, lf	.277	.346	.346	43	37	8
Cy Seymour, cf	.377	.429	.559	95	121	21
Tommy Corcoran, ss	.248	.277	.329	70	85	28
Fred Odwell, rf	.241	.293	.359	79	65	21
or Jimmy Sebring, rf	.286	.329	.406	31	28	11
Harry Steinfeldt, 3b	.271	.329	.367	49	39	15
or Al Bridwell, ut	.252	.309	.272	17	17	8
Admiral Schlei, c	.226	.285	.280	32	36	9
or Ed Phelps, c	.231	.306	.301	18	18	4

Leading Pitchers	W	L	Pct	IP	H	ERA
Orval Overall	18	23	.439	318	290	2.86
Bob Ewing	20	11	.645	311.7	284	2.51
Charlie Chech	14	14	.500	267.7	300	2.89
Jack Harper	9	13	.409	179.3	189	3.86
Tom Walker	9	7	.563	144.7	171	3.24
Noodles Hahn	5	3	.625	77	85	2.81

*Includes record with Chicago

During the first decade of the 20th century Cy Seymour was one of the better outfielders in the major leagues. For four years during the previous decade he had been one of the top pitchers in the National League. In 1905 Cy had a monster season at bat for Cincinnati. He hit .377 in a year the entire league batted only .255, leading the league in batting average, slugging percentage, doubles, triples, total bases, and runs batted in, while coming in second in home runs and on-base percentage. Seven years earlier, in 1898, he had enjoyed a season on the mound that, if not quite a monster season, was at least a very good one. Pitching for a mediocre seventh-place team (in a 12-team league), he went 25–19 and led the league in strikeouts, while compiling a good 3.18 earned run average. In a *Baseball Research*

Journal article, Dan Kirwin pointed out that only one man in baseball history—Babe Ruth—had more pitching victories and more hits than Seymour. In three full seasons and three partial seasons as a pitcher, Seymour compiled a 61–56 record; during his 16-year career he totaled 1,724 hits, retiring after the 1913 season with a lifetime batting average of .303.[60]

As a pitcher Seymour featured one of the best fastballs in the league and a crippling overhand drop curve. Ed Delahanty called Seymour's drop "the most dangerous curve that I ever saw."[61] In the three full seasons he pitched in the National League Seymour was always among the hardest pitchers to hit. He allowed the fewest hits per game in 1897 (8.1), finished sixth in 1898 (7.9) and fourth in 1899 (8.3). He led the league in strikeouts per game in all three of those seasons, and in total strikeouts two of the three seasons.

But if batters had trouble making contact with his pitches, Seymour had almost as much trouble making contact with the strike zone. He led the league in walks in each of his three complete seasons. In May of 1899 he lost to Cincinnati in the tenth inning when his 13th walk of the game brought in the winning run. Near the end of the season he again put 13 men on base—he hit two and walked 11—in only seven innings. The opposing team could manage only five hits off him, but won the game 6–4, thanks to Seymour's wildness.

Seymour suffered a sore arm in the spring of 1900. He struggled along for almost half a season, allowing about a hit and a walk for each inning pitched and almost seven runs a game. The Giants tried to farm him to two minor league teams, but he was so wild and ineffective that neither kept him around for very long. Seymour was able to salvage his baseball career because he was a good hitter and had been willing to play the outfield when the Giants were hit by injuries. In 1898 he had played 35 games there, batting .276 and fielding adequately. He had hit over .300 in his last two years with the Giants, although most of his games were as a pitcher. In 1901, when John McGraw was busy signing players for his new American League team, he agreed to give Seymour a chance to make the team as an outfielder.

With the Orioles, Seymour was a solid player, but not one of the league's stars. He batted .303 for the Orioles in 1901, but in the expansion American League that wasn't good enough to make the top 20 in the league. He stood out in only one category—stolen bases. Cy stole 38 bases, the highest total of his career, and third best in the league. In 1902 Seymour was batting .268 when McGraw broke up the team. In July Seymour was given his release by the Orioles and signed with Cincinnati, where he seemed to find a home. He hit .340 over the remainder of the 1902 season, and posted .342, and .313 marks in the next two seasons.

Throughout the 1904 season Seymour complained of severe headaches which gave him a feeling of dizziness. In March 1905 he had an operation. Incisions were made in the skull and in the jaw below the ear, and an abscess was drained. "Mr. Seymour passed through the ordeal wonderfully well," the doctor reported after the surgery. "He is a splendid athlete and in fine physical condition, which helped him to stand the pain and confinement well. The trouble was a serious one, and the fact that he stood it as long as he did, meanwhile keeping his playing up to the top notch, speaks well for his constitution." The writer who reported on the procedure remarked that as soon as Seymour regained his strength, he would "be in better shape physically than he has been for some time. This might be the best year the fast gardener has had for many seasons."[62] The writer's cheerful forecast, of course, turned out to be an understatement, since Cy put up numbers that were above any that would be posted for years. His .377 average was the best in the National league during the entire Deadball Era. His 121 RBIs would be topped only by Sherry Magee in 1910 and Gavvy Cravath in 1913. (Honus Wagner had driven in 126 in 1901.)

As a defensive outfielder Seymour was probably a little above average. He was a fast runner and, naturally enough for an ex-pitcher, had a good throwing arm. He ranked high in assists several times during his career, leading the league while with the Giants in 1908. While he was with the Orioles the Baltimore correspondent for *The Sporting News* said of him, "Seymour is a great fellow. While he is in a game he knows nothing else; he is intensely absorbed in winning. And I don't think I ever saw another man who was all the time putting forth his every energy to the utmost. I have sometimes wondered that 'Sy' [sic] has not burst a blood vessel trying to reach a fly ball, or to get to a base."[63]

Seymour's intensity may have worked against him with respect to playing scientific baseball. While aggressive baserunning and proactive defensive tactics were generally applauded, Cy tended to overdo both, with negative results. He was often thrown out trying to advance on the bases, and he had more than his share of throws that went to the wrong base or were inaccurate. After he was traded away from Cincinnati in 1906, Cincinnati sportswriter Jack Ryder remarked, " Though a great natural batter, Cy was never a good man for the Reds. Only a moderately good fielder and a wretched baserunner, he canceled much of his strong work at the bat by fumbling and wild throwing in the field and stupid work on the sacks."[64]

Although Seymour may have had his shortcomings, his performance was undoubtedly the highlight of the 1905 season for Cincinnati fans. The Reds spent most of the season lodged in fifth place, rarely moving more than a few games over the .500 mark. Cy's hitting added a great deal of

Jack Taylor II: St. Louis

On the mound Jack Taylor was a bulldog; off the field he was more like one of those nervous little house dogs who are always growling and snapping at visitors. Taylor was a great competitor, unfazed by bad innings or his teammates' errors, never willing to give in to the batter. He had the misfortune to spend almost all of his career with mediocre teams, but he usually had a pretty good earned run average and managed to win 20 games in a season four times in a ten-year career. Taylor tended to be a bit grumpy, ready to find fault and complain. Although they admired his pitching skills, baseball writers who covered his teams weren't particularly fond of Taylor personally.

St. Louis (58–96)

Regular Lineup	AVG	OBP	SLG	R	RBI	SB
Jack Dunleavy, rf	.241	.328	.303	52	25	15
or Josh Clarke, ut	.257	.361	.353	31	18	8
Spike Shannon, lf	.268	.327	.309	73	41	27
Homer Smoot, cf	.311	.359	.433	73	58	21
Jake Beckley, 1b	.286	.333	.370	48	57	12
Harry Arndt, 2b	.243	.290	.313	40	36	13
George McBride, ss*	.217	.267	.258	31	41	12
or Danny Shay, inf	.238	.331	.288	30	28	11
Jimmy Burke, 3b	.225	.275	.276	34	30	15
Mike Grady, c	.286	.360	.434	41	41	15
or John Warner, c	.255	.301	.321	9	12	2

Leading Pitchers	W	L	Pct	IP	H	ERA
Jack Taylor	15	21	.417	309	302	3.44
Chappie McFarland	8	18	.308	250.3	281	3.81
Jake Thielman	15	16	.484	242	265	3.50
Buster Brown	8	11	.421	178.7	172	2.97
Wish Egan	6	15	.286	171.3	189	3.57
Win Kellum	3	3	.500	74	70	2.92

*Includes record with Pittsburgh.

Maybe Taylor's mood when he was around the reporters was affected by the fact that, in the press, he never got to be just Jack Taylor from Lancaster, Ohio. When he reached the National League near the end of the

1898 season, the league already had a well-known Jack Taylor—Brewery Jack—a good pitcher and out-sized character who had been gathering headlines for several years with his pitching and off-field antics. Jack Taylor from Lancaster, Ohio almost immediately became known as Jack Taylor II. One small consolation for Number Two came in the two matchups between the Jack Taylors. Number Two beat Number One 5–4 in ten innings at the end of the 1898 season and repeated the feat in April of 1899, winning by an 8–4 score. Those were the only two matchups featuring the Jack Taylors. Brewery Jack became ill during the 1899 season and died the next February.

Connie Mack had discovered Jack Taylor II during a barnstorming trip after the 1896 season. Taylor had held Mack's team of major league players to three hits. Impressed by Taylor's performance, Mack offered him a contract to play with Milwaukee of the Western League. After a 9–6 record in 1897, his first professional season, Taylor became one of that league's top pitchers in 1898. He won 28 games, while losing only 13. Knowing he would lose Taylor in the major league draft following the season, Mack shopped Taylor around. He concluded a deal with Louisville, but later had that deal nullified and sent Taylor to Chicago instead. The next spring Taylor grumbled to reporters that Mack had reneged on an agreement to give him a $600 bonus if he pitched well. "I pitched 38 games, winning 25 [sic], but Connie Mack didn't give me one cent of that $600. Evidently I don't know what good ball playing is," Taylor complained. He was also unhappy about the amount Chicago had offered for the 1899 season, He had won all five games he started for the Orphans at the end of the 1898 season, and thought he was worth more than the $1,800 Chicago was offering. "Sooner than that I would go back to railroading, where I can make $95 to $110 a month the year around, besides pitching Sunday ball for semi-professional teams at $25 per. I would rather pitch in the Western League for $1,000 a season than in the National for $1,800," he concluded. "It's not as hard work, and a man's arm lasts longer."[65]

Taylor went to spring training with the Cubs. Just before opening day he asked his manager to buy him a train ticket back to Chicago. When the manager asked why, Taylor replied, "Hart has not come to my terms and I don't propose to start the race without a contract." Hart was surprised when Taylor walked into his office. He refused Taylor's salary demand, which was now up to $2,100. Taylor grabbed his coat and started out of the office. Hart shouted to Taylor, telling him to come back. "If I had one more pitcher," he said, "I would never yield. Here is your contract for $2,100. But I'll never forgive you for writing me mean letters and showing such obstinacy."[66] Taylor barely earned his money, based on the pay standards of the time. He went 18-21 for a team that finished two games over .500. His ERA was a few points below the league average. In 1900 his 2.55 ERA was the third-lowest in the National League, but he gave up over five runs a game, one of the highest totals in the league. He probably wasn't nearly as bad as his 10-17 record would indicate, and probably wasn't as good as his ERA would suggest.

While his won-lost record didn't seem like much to brag about, Taylor gradually won respect around the league for his talents. In July of 1900, after he shut out the hard-hitting Phillies, Chicago reporter Hugh Fullerton wrote, "The remarkable part of the performance was the pitching of Taylor." The Phillie batters seemed eager to swing at Taylor's pitches, Fullerton said, but couldn't hit them solidly. "The question which agitated the sluggers was this: 'What is he pitching?' He seemed to pitch nothing, but simply floated the sphere around the plate in a queer, twisting manner, and the harder the Quakers hit the ball the higher it went in the air." Three days later Taylor pitched another shutout, beating Boston 2-0. "Somehow Taylor is not a hero," Fullerton noted. "No matter what Taylor does the crowd does not become frenzied when he walks out to pitch nor cheer when he pitches well." Searching for an explanation, Fullerton wondered if it might be because of Taylor's lack of flair. "Perhaps because there is no style and no flourish to Taylor the crowd does not appreciate him. He pitches just as he used to twist a brake on a coal train down in Hocking Valley—as a matter of business and without passion."[67]

Taylor had another middling year in 1901, going 13-19 for a bad team. He had to put up with two different types of hardships that season. One was a team that regularly embarrassed itself in the field. The other was Rube Waddell. Rube's high-strung personality and flighty habits seemed to grate on Taylor. One hot, steamy day in St. Louis, Rube decided it was too hot to pitch. Taylor told him to quit loafing. That evening, after the two pitchers argued over the matter during the train ride back to Chicago, Taylor issued an ultimatum to his manager: he would pitch one more game for Chicago, then either he or Rube had to go. A few days later the two seemed to have made up. They were seen near the clubhouse playing catch and joking around with each other.[68]

That season Taylor began a streak that will probably never be broken. As Fullerton might have noted, the streak was not one that involved flashy performance. Rather it was one that might be associated with a brakeman on a coal train in Hocking Valley. Taylor just showed up for work regularly and did the job he was expected to do. After being knocked out of the box in his previous start, Taylor took the mound against Boston and pitched a complete game, losing to Vic Willis, 2-0. That was the first of 187 straight complete games. The next time Taylor failed to finish a game was in August of 1906, when he left a game against Brooklyn trailing 3–1 in the third inning.[69]

For Taylor the 1902 season was one in which everything went right. Probably the first thing that went right was the Cubs' hiring of Frank Selee to manage the team. Selee built his teams around pitching and defense. While the 1902 Cubs made almost as many errors as the 1901 team, they were a much snappier team on defense and held their own in the head games related to "scientific baseball." Since Taylor did not strike out many batters, he needed a team behind him that could handle the ball when it was put in play. When Taylor was on his game, as he was in almost every outing in 1902, his fielders had plenty of easy chances. A typical game for Taylor came on May 28, when he outpitched Bob Wicker of the Cardinals, beating him 5–1. Wicker fanned seven batters, while Taylor struck out only two. But the feature of the game, according to a St. Louis reporter, was Taylor's deceptive pitching. "While Wicker had him beaten in strikeouts, the Chicago pitcher was a harder proposition to hit safely," the reporter wrote. "This is shown by the fact that no less than seven of the St. Louis outs were made on pop foul flies, all but one of them going to the catcher or first baseman. Several of the other outs were easy pop flies to the infield."[70] Taylor allowed seven hits in that game, slightly less than his average of 7.5 per game for the season, the third best average in the league. He was also stingy with walks, and had the lowest on-base percentage in the league (.260). His 1.33 ERA led the league by almost a half-run per game. Although the Cubs were a weak-hitting team that finished a game under .500, Taylor won 23 games while losing only 11.[71]

Taylor had another good season in 1903, going 21–14, with the sixth-best ERA in the league (2.45). But after the season he became embroiled in a controversy that led to his being accused of throwing baseball games. The Cubs and White Sox had decided to take advantage of their intra-city rivalry by scheduling a few post-season games between the two cities. In keeping with the level of greed shown by club owners of this era, "a few" meant 15. In anticipation of possible post-season games, in 1903 players in both leagues had been signed to contracts that bound them to play for their teams through October 15, even though both leagues concluded their seasons just before the end of September.

Taylor pitched the first game for the Cubs, winning a blowout 11–0. He pitched three more times, losing each one. Two games were by lopsided scores (10–2 and 9–3) and, although the third was close (4–2), Taylor was hit hard in that one, too. The series ended with each team having won seven games. The Cubs' president, Jim Hart, and manager Selee refused to play a deciding 15th game, saying that transportation had already been arranged. That winter Taylor was traded to St. Louis.

When Taylor came to Chicago in May of 1904 for his first series against his old team he was greeted with catcalls from a group of Cub fans, who got onto him for losing to the White Sox in the intra-city series the preceding fall. Taylor yelled back to them that he had "got $100 from Hart for winning a game and $500 from Comiskey for losing it."[72] On July 30 of that season Taylor was unusually wild in a game against Pittsburgh. Although he gave up only seven hits in the game he walked five batters and hit one. He lost the game 5–2. When a Pittsburgh gambler won a lot of money on the game, rumors started swirling that the game had been fixed.

Near the end of the 1904 season, Comiskey suggested to Hart that the two Chicago teams schedule another post-season intra-city series. Hart refused to do so and hinted publicly that the 1903 series had not been on the up-and-up. Comiskey asked for proof. In response Hart issued a series of statements implying that Taylor had purposely lost to the White Sox in the 1903 series and suggesting that he had thrown the July 30 game in Pittsburgh. The case against Taylor was either very shaky or non-existent, depending upon a person's viewpoint. Regarding the intra-city series the evidence was Taylor's response to the razzing of the Chicago fans and the fact that he lost three games. To believe that Taylor threw the game, one also had to believe that Charlie Comiskey conspired to fix an exhibition game. As for the Pittsburgh game, the evidence was that he was wilder than usual and a Pittsburgh gambler won a lot of money on the game.

Taylor defended himself by denying the charges and attacking Hart who, Taylor said, had disliked him since 1899, when he demanded and got more money than Hart wanted to pay. The "Taylor case" came up as the 1904 season ended and supplied material for newspaper stories throughout the off-season. For his part Taylor talked freely—one reporter said he "babbled more like an old woman who wouldn't steal a biscuit from a parrot than like a hardened criminal who would throw games." Taylor admitted to getting drunk on several occasions and even said he had used loaded dice to cheat some ballplayers who had previously cheated him with marked cards.

With regard to the Chicago intra-city series, Taylor said he had tried his hardest to win but the White Sox just hit everything he threw. After the third loss, Hart called him into his office. Hart accused Taylor of "dissipation and gambling" and told the pitcher he thought he was crooked. Cincinnati player/manager Joe Kelley told a reporter that Taylor had told him about the meeting with Hart. Kelley related that Taylor had told him he had become angry at Hart's charges. According to Kelley, Taylor said that after hearing Hart's charges, on the impulse of the moment he had snapped back at Hart, saying yes, he had thrown the game, and, as Hart knew it, he was glad of it.

As for the Pittsburgh game, Taylor admitted that he and teammate Jake Beckley had spent the previous evening drinking and gambling. They did not get back to the hotel until noon on the day of the game. He said Manager Kid Nichols knew he was not in good shape but put him in to pitch anyway. Taylor attributed his wildness to his poor physical condition. A saloon keeper who thought he might have been the gambler whose big winnings prompted the rumors about the game told a Pittsburgh reporter that he had not talked to Taylor for about three years. He said he had gotten information that Taylor and Beckley had spent the night boozing and thought the odds of $100 to $65 on St. Louis offered a chance to win some good money. So he placed a sizeable bet on the Pirates.

Taylor and Hart sniped at each other all winter. While there was, of course, a wide of range of opinions expressed in the newspapers, the majority opinion was probably close to that of Sy Sanborn of the *Chicago Tribune*. Sanborn wrote, "There is no one who knows Taylor, Comiskey and all parties concerned in the scandal who does not believe the series was played and tied on the level. Not even Hart believes that Taylor was crooked, although he has allowed the opposite belief to grow here and has helped to increase it decidedly."

The National Commission heard evidence regarding the Pittsburgh game, issuing a curious decision. The Commission stated that there was a lot of testimony presented, but since a guilty verdict would cost a player his livelihood, after weighing the evidence carefully and giving Taylor the benefit of every possible doubt, they found him not guilty. But the Commission did find Taylor guilty of misconduct in Pittsburgh and fined him $300.[73]

Having weathered the storm of controversy over his behavior over the winter, Taylor was his usual imperturbable self on the mound, posting a workmanlike 15–21 record for a team that was severely challenged both at bat and in the field. Meanwhile the team was being battered by a tempest of management discordance and on-field uncertainty. In May player-manager Kid Nichols was informed that his services as a manager were no longer needed, but that he would be retained as a pitcher, even though Nichols was at the time sidelined with a sore arm. As part of the change in leadership shortstop Dave Brain was relieved of his duties as team captain. Third baseman Jimmy Burke was to assume both roles. Nichols and Brain were traded to Philadelphia and Pittsburgh, respectively, a couple months later. Burke remained in charge until early August, when he asked to be replaced as manager because he could no longer put up with micromanaging by owner Stanley Robison. Robison finished the season as the manager, retaining Burke as the captain. The changes made little difference in the Cardinals' performance. They settled into sixth place by the end of May and remained there for the rest of the season, struggling to win 40 percent of their games.[74]

True to his personality, after the season ended Taylor contributed his ten cents to the Cardinals' bickering. Told that Nichols had included him as one of several disturbing elements within the team, Taylor responded, "I am told that Burke, Shay, Grady and I were named by him as the disturbers. I am giving the Robisons a better tip than Nichols did. I deny that any of the four he mentioned is a disturber, but I frankly admit that the owners of the club would get better results if they put the Cardinals in the charge of a first-class manager and require him to maintain strict discipline. A manager of ability, fairness and firmness will have trouble with me just once unless he crawfishes when I make my bluff."[75]

Extreme Frugality: Boston

Boston (51–103)

Regular Lineup	AVG	OBP	SLG	R	RBI	SB
Ed Abbaticchio, ss	.279	.326	.374	70	41	30
Fred Tenney, 1b	.288	.368	.332	84	28	17
Cozy Dolan, rf*	.269	.319	.343	51	52	23
Jim Delahanty, lf	.258	.315	.349	50	55	12
Harry Wolverton, 3b	.225	.276	.300	38	55	10
Rip Cannell, cf	.247	.311	.286	52	36	17
Fred Raymer, 2b	.211	.232	.247	26	31	15
or Bill Lauterborn, inf	.185	.238	.200	11	9	1
Pat Moran, c	.240	.270	.341	22	22	3
or Tom Needham, c	.218	.293	.269	21	17	3
Leading Pitchers	W	L	Pct	IP	H	ERA
Irv Young	20	21	.488	378	337	2.90
Vic Willis	12	29	.293	342	340	3.21
Chick Fraser	14	21	.400	334.3	320	3.28
Kaiser Wilhelm	3	23	.115	242.3	287	4.53
Dick Harley	2	5	.286	65.7	72	4.66

*Includes record with Cincinnati.

Boston's owners, commonly referred to as the Triumvirs, had a well-deserved reputation for taking a frugal approach to running the team. Complaints about a poorly-maintained field were common, even in the years when the Beaneaters were dominating the National League and benefitting from a large attendance at their games. After the American League began pursuing the team's stars, the Triumvirs let most of them go to the new league, rather than paying them enough to retain them. One result, of course, was a the plunge down the standings. The few stars who remained with the team were good enough to help scratch out enough victories to avoid the cellar, but by 1905 last place seemed to be looming on the horizon. After the 1904 season Boston's manager, Al Buckenberger, was let go. The owners, who by then included only two of the Triumvirs, did not settle on a replacement until just before spring training. In February they asked Fred Tenney to handle the tasks of signing players for the upcoming season and making arrangements for preseason exhibition games.

Since he was handling the manager's duties, one day Tenney suggested he be signed to a manager's contract. "You've got your player's contract for $2,400," replied one of the owners. "Sign that and I'll see that you get what you deserve." Tenney accepted that somewhat vague offer. When he inquired about making some moves to strengthen the team, he was told, "We don't care where you finish, so long as you don't lose money with the team."[76]

Reportedly Tenney met his goal of avoiding red ink. One strategy for doing so was to cut down on the support staff by taking on extra duties himself. "Without doubt Fred Tenney is the busiest athlete who ever came down the pike," remarked a Philadelphia writer. "This is what the gifted Tenney does for Boston and does it without extra charge. Most teams on the road rate one or more business people to direct affairs; but Fred is the whole cheese. To begin with, he is second batter, field captain, resident and traveling team manager, financial and recording secretary, bookkeeper, business manager, treasurer, hotel bus and transportation agent, baggage hustler, pay master, kick adjuster, first baseman, war correspondent for three Boston papers, cartoonist and medical adviser.... The Triumvirs at home regard Fred as a good man and so he is–at least four of them rolled into one compact branch of brain and nerve and placed at the head of the Beaneaters."[77]

The biggest single item on a baseball team's expense account in the Deadball Era was the player payroll. Tenney saved a few bucks by carrying the minimum number he thought would be needed. In June, just as the team was about to leave on a western trip, catcher Pat Moran was spiked on a play and had to leave the game. Since the other Boston catcher was already out with an injury, Tenney brought outfielder Bud Sharpe in to catch. That left him one man short in the outfield, so he sent pitcher Kaiser

Wilhelm out to center field. The two substitutes finished that game without any problems, but in the second game of the doubleheader Wilhelm muffed a couple balls and Sharpe had big problems handling Vic Willis's overhand drop ball, contributing strongly to an 8–3 loss.

When the team headed out to Chicago, Tenney negotiated for a replacement catcher. He got one, but not from a minor league team. He got Cincinnati president Garry Herrmann to lend him catcher Gabby Street. Although he later became a fine catcher with Washington, Street had a miserable three games with Boston, committing four throwing errors in his first game, allowing six stolen bases in his second, and breaking a finger in his third, when the Cubs added seven more stolen bases to bring their total in the series up to 18. Street's misfortune caused Sharpe to go behind the plate one more game before the team's normal backup catcher, Tom Needham, recovered.

The desire to limit payroll costs probably contributed to a couple of negative records posted by the 1905 Beaneaters. With the small pitching staffs of the era, it wasn't all that unusual for a second-division team to have one or two 20-game losers. The Beaneaters had four. Even on poor teams of any era, there are usually a couple pitchers who manage to win more games than they lose. Not on the 1905 Beaneaters. Irv Young, widely considered the "find of the season" and a 20-game winner that season, managed to lose one more game than he won, going 20–21. Poor Kaiser Wilhelm had to suffer through a season in which he managed to win three games while coming out on the short end of the score 23 times. Wilhelm was never a great pitcher, but in 1908 he posted a 1.87 ERA with Brooklyn while going 16–22 with a team that was 53–101 for the season. In the spring of 1905 Wilhelm decided to add the spitball to his repertoire. The results were so ugly that by July Tenney told him to quit using the pitch. Tenney felt the experiment with the wet pitch had hindered Wilhelm's ability to throw his other pitches.[78] With almost any other team, Wilhelm would likely have been given time to work on the sidelines in an effort to regain his normal stuff, or would have been sent to the minors. But he was one of four pitchers Tenney kept on the Beaneaters' pitching staff for any extended period of time. Therefore he had to work out his problems while appearing regularly on the mound.

Tenney was one of several players of the early Deadball Era who refused to play on Sundays. The Beaneaters' captain on those days was Ed Abbaticchio, who had the distinction of being the first major league player of Italian descent. Interestingly, he also was the first Italian-American to play professional football. He had been a fullback and punter for the Latrobe Volunteer Fireman football team from 1895 to 1900. The Latrobe team is generally recognized as the first professional football team. Fielding Yost, a great coach for the University of Michigan, cited Abbaticchio as the first punter who was able to put a spiral on his punts, enabling the ball to travel farther.[79]

Boston acquired Abbaticchio from Nashville of the Southern Association near the end of the 1902 season. At that time his baseball skills were still a work in progress. In his first season with the Beaneaters he played second base, where his fielding was acceptable but not anything special. In 1904 and 1905 he was moved to shortstop. He led the National League in errors both seasons, booting 78

Ed Abbaticchio was the first major league baseball player of Italian descent (Library of Congress).

balls the first year and reducing that total to a mere 75 the second year. Part of the reason his error total was so high was that he went after everything hit his way, ranking second in both putouts and assists in 1904 and first and fifth, respectively, the next year. He seemed to be improving as he gained experience at the position. When Abbaticchio was first moved to shortstop late in the 1903 season, the *Boston Globe's* Tim Murnane remarked, "The new man has no idea of playing the position, continually holding back for the ground balls to come to him, and thereby losing his man at first. The man was never cut out for the position. He hits well and would fit in nicely at second base." By the middle of the 1905 campaign, Murnane was complimenting Abbaticchio's play, although not yet completely sold on his ability at shortstop. "There are days when Batty can play shortstop with the best of them," Murnane conceded. "Yesterday was one of those days."[80]

Abbaticchio refused to play with the Beaneaters in 1906, saying his hotel business in Latrobe required his full-time presence and that he could make more money in business than he was making in baseball. Reportedly he turned down a flattering offer from John McGraw to play for the Giants. In 1907 he signed with Pittsburgh. He was the regular second baseman for the Pirates for two years and remained in baseball through the 1910 season.[81]

This Recipe Ain't So Good: Brooklyn

There were no organized farm systems during the early Deadball Era. Farming was expressly prohibited in the regulations governing organized baseball. The major league clubs got around the anti-farming rule by releasing players to minor league teams with the understanding that they had the sole right to re-purchase the player, either at the end of the minor league season or after an agreed-upon date late in the season. Such arrangements would typically involve only a few players from any one major league source. A formal draft system was set up by which clubs could draft players from other teams at a lower level in organized baseball's hierarchy. The major league clubs usually tried to pre-empt the draft by arranging to purchase the best minor league prospects before the date set for the draft. The number of new players acquired each year might include at most about a half-dozen purchased players and a handful of draftees. At the end of each season the major league teams would submit a list of players reserved for the next season. When drafted and purchased players were added to the players already playing at the major league level, the total number of reserved players would be between 20 and 30 players.

Therefore, in September of 1904 when Brooklyn President Charles Ebbets announced that his club was reserving 57 players for 1905, he got everyone's attention. He also opened himself up to a lot of not-so-gentle kidding. The number of players he proposed to take to camp in 1905 happened to be the same as the varieties of different food products advertised by the Heinz food company. Baseball writers didn't see how the Superbas would be able to identify the best players with 57 guys milling around their training grounds in the spring. "Some people question our procedure in purchasing so many new players and are inclined to treat our efforts to secure a winning team as a joke," said Ebbets. "Now, if one were to start a racing stable he would go out and buy a couple of hundred yearlings with the object in view of getting four or five stake horses out of the lot. It is the same in baseball. A manager has to get a bunch of minor league players together with the object in view of getting half a dozen stars out of the lot.... We ought to get a good outfit out of 57 players."[82]

The man who was in charge of making a competitive team out of the mob of players hoping to wear Brooklyn uniforms in 1905 was, of course, Ned Hanlon, the Brooklyn manager. In the early 1900s, Hanlon was widely recognized as a superor manager because of his success in putting together the great Baltimore Orioles teams of the 90s and his two successive pennants with Brooklyn in 1899 and 1900.

The Orioles excelled at putting pressure on the opposition using the tactics of scientific baseball—the hit-and-run, bunting for hits rather than just sacrificing, stealing bases whenever the opportunity presented itself. With his championship teams Hanlon was among men who immersed themselves in the minutiae of their chosen profession. His morning practices featured conferences in which he would gather the players to discuss "baseball, as she was played." If a player suggested a new tactic or approach to teamwork, the suggestion would be critiqued pro and con, and might be tested to see how well it worked.[83]

Willie Keeler credited Hanlon with being the principal cause of the Orioles' success. "He used to lie awake nights thinking of new tricks to spring on the other fellows," Keeler said. "Hanlon, always on the lookout for the unexpected, would see us do a thing in practice, or in a game, and figure out whether it was worth trying. Then we would go to work and perfect ourselves in that particular play and spring it." Lave Cross, already a veteran when he came to the Superbas, confided to a fellow player that he thought he knew all about baseball until he had played a short time under Hanlon. He said he soon changed his mind, and added that he now believed that when he did finally know all about the game he would be too old to play.[84]

Brooklyn (48–104)

Regular Lineup	AVG	OBP	SLG	R	RBI	SB
John Dobbs, cf	.254	.304	.330	59	36	15
Jimmy Sheckard, lf	.292	.380	.398	58	41	23
or Bob Hall, ut*	.238	.280	.296	22	15	8
Harry Lumley, rf	.293	.340	.412	50	47	22
Emil Batch, 3b	.252	.285	.352	64	49	21
Doc Gessler, 1b	.290	.366	.369	44	46	26
Phil Lewis, ss	.254	.282	.305	32	33	16
or Charlie Babb, ut	.187	.303	.238	27	17	10
Charlie Malay, 2b	.252	.300	.292	33	31	13
Lew Ritter, c	.219	.255	.293	32	28	16
or Bill Bergen, c	.190	.213	.219	12	22	4
Leading Pitchers	W	L	Pct	IP	H	ERA
Harry McIntire	8	25	.242	308.7	340	3.70
Doc Scanlan	14	12	.538	249.7	220	2.92
Elmer Stricklett	9	18	.333	237.3	259	3.34
Mal Eason	5	21	.192	207	230	4.30
Oscar Jones	8	15	.348	174	197	4.66
Fred Mitchell	3	7	.300	96.3	107	4.76

*Includes record with New York.

The team Hanlon had to work with in 1905 was far different from his championship teams. His players were for the most part young and inexperienced. They lacked the skills necessary for the proper execution of scientific baseball tactics. Barely a month into the season Abe Yager of the *Brooklyn Eagle* noted: "Hanlon's young men are lamentably weak in bunting, not only on the ground of lack of execution, but also because they telegraph their intentions to the other fellows. It might be advisable for Manager Hanlon during the next week or so to permit his young men to play straight baseball instead of floundering through a lot of fancy tricks that appear to be sanscrit to them and an A.B.C. primer to their opponents."[85]

Instead of being able to gain an advantage through smart, aggressive play, the Superbas were much more likely to be the target of such tactics. The team's entire infield was new in 1905. First baseman Doc Gessler had played 78 games for two teams in 1904, all of them in the outfield. The two men who played the most games at second base were both rookies, as was shortstop Phil Lewis. Third baseman Emil Batch's league-high 52 errors and league-low .882 fielding percentage in 1905 demonstrated conclusively that he was placed in the wrong position.

In a game against New York, the *Eagle's* Yager commented on the Superbas' difficulty countering aggressive play, "Whenever a couple of Giants got on the bases the Brooklyns immediately lost their heads and forced the runners home by wild throwing," Yager wrote. "Donlin and Browne were the luckiest ones. In the third inning, Donlin was caught between second and third and was like a rat in a trap, but Batch made a wild throw that not only allowed Donlin to tally, but Browne came in from first base right on his heels. Again in the fourth these two were on bases when Gessler dropped two flies in succession, due to his anxiety to throw the ball somewhere. He got a chance later and fired the ball in the spot where it did the least good."[86]

As the losses mounted the Superbas' young players became demoralized. In mid-season Yager remarked, "If the Brooklyns were bad before they went away on their recent western trip, they are a joke now. Continuous disaster has made them calloused not only to defeat but to the sarcasm of the few remaining loyal fans and it would exhaust the prevailing supply of ginger to even face the treasurer on payday.... They are beaten these days before they even start a game of ball."[87]

Morale on the team dropped so low that three players decided to take their talents elsewhere. After two months of suffering with the Superbas, pitcher Doc Reisling jumped to the Coatesville team of the independent Tri-State League. Before another month had passed second baseman Reddy Owens and shortstop Phil Lewis joined other teams in that league. Lewis returned after a short hiatus with the Harrisburg Tri-State team, but later he left the team twice without giving prior notice.[88]

Yager explained the desertions by pointing to the low salaries being paid by the Superbas. In addition to paying the youngsters little more than they could get from minor league teams, Ebbets had cut the pay of several veteran players, who responded by holding out and then bringing sour attitudes with them when they finally agreed to report. Even Hanlon, who was a minority owner, had been forced to take a substantial cut, his $12,500 salary chopped down to $6,000.[89]

According to Yager, Hanlon was trying his best under very discouraging conditions. "No manager ever treated ballplayers better than Foxy Ned," Yager claimed. " He has pampered them and catered to them as a trainer would a turf star, looking after their every comfort and at times digging deep into his own bank roll in order to get out all the playing abilities they possess. When a man showed abilities above the average the old general treated him like a son and spent his time scheming to keep him at the top notch of his playing. Thus he wagered with Harry McIntire that the pitcher refrain from cigarette smoking in order that the twirler might develop into one of the season's stars, and he worked a similar scheme with Lewis, so that the shortstop would keep in the straight path. He went to headquarters on behalf of Elmer Stricklett when the little spitball merchant wanted to quit because he was underpaid and secured a substantial increase for him, because the little fellow showed indications of being a star."[90]

It was evident, however, that Hanlon found his situation very trying. As early as April he had begun discussions with Garry Herrmann about becoming the Cincinnati manager in 1906, but made no firm commitment. For the rest of the year, he vacillated between staying in Brooklyn to continue the struggle to build a winning team and moving to Cincinnati, where he would be given a free hand to do things his own way. Going into the winter meetings in December, Hanlon thought he had ironed out an agreement with the Superbas to remain with the team. But after Ebbets and majority owner Henry Medicus failed to show up for several scheduled meetings with him, he decided it was time to end his connection with Brooklyn. He signed a contract with Herrmann to manage the Reds in 1906.[91]

Four

1905, American League

Spitballs! Spitball Pitchers Everywhere!

Jack Chesbro's 41 wins in 1904 cast a giant shadow over major league mounds the next spring. Every team had at least one pitcher throwing the spitball when the 1905 season started. Every pitcher on the St. Louis Cardinal staff was throwing it and every Cleveland hurler except Addie Joss was using it. Three weeks into the season the editor of *The Sporting News* estimated that 75 percent of the pitchers were using it.[1]

Efforts to have the pitch declared illegal were stymied early in the season when the two league presidents, Ban Johnson and Harry Pulliam, each released statements saying there were no rules prohibiting its use. Pulliam said he thought the manner of its use was "not consistent with good taste." He instructed his umpires to see to it that pitchers did not moisten the ball in an ostentatious manner, such as holding the ball in one hand and deliberately wetting the fingers of the other hand like he might lick a postage stamp. In such a case, Pulliam said, a balk should be called.[2]

Some baseball people, including Pulliam, found the name "spitball" objectionable. Baseball writers, as well as the players themselves, were happy to offer alternatives—though most of those sound worse to the modern ear than the original. The pitch was at times called a "wet ball," mostly to avoid repetitious use of the same term for it. The term "slippery elm pitch" came into use fairly quickly, being based, naturally, on the substance used to generate saliva. At other times it was called a "vapor float," a "spray ball," and an "eel ball." It's not hard to guess which of these labels was applied in 1906 when Cleveland's rookie pitcher, Harry Eells, threw the pitch.[3]

It wasn't long before a spitball pitcher's game became a sort of "foreign substance" war. Cleveland had used mustard oil against Chesbro shortly after he started having great success with the pitch. In 1905 the countervailing substance of choice seemed to be licorice, which when combined with saliva would make the ball sticky and hard to control. Detroit manager

Bill Armour, one of the first to employ licorice, got Ban Johnson to state officially that if it was legal for a pitcher to apply saliva to the ball, then it was also legal to use other substances. Tabasco sauce also found its way onto the ball in some games. Another liquid, benzine, also came into use. It was used by spitballers and their teammates to remove the licorice. The umpires, who at first took a "hands off" approach to the situation, eventually started inspecting the doctored balls and throwing some of them out of the game.[4]

The spitball was the proverbial double-edged sword. Even a pitcher who had mastered the pitch could suddenly lose control of it for an inning or two. The weather could affect a pitcher's ability to throw the ball. Cold weather or a light rain could hinder its use. The pitch's sudden break was rough on the catcher. At times he had to jump around to contain the pitch, making it easier for baserunners to steal. The ball's movement also caused the backstop to incur injuries at a higher rate. Fielders at times found it difficult to get a good grip on the ball, causing their throws to go off the mark.[5]

Perhaps worst of all, the pitch seemed to cause some pitchers to come down with sore arms. The White Sox' Doc White, the Boston Americans' Norwood Gibson, and the Senators' Casey Patten were among the pitchers who quit using the pitch because it hurt their arms. A couple months into the 1905 season John McGraw instructed his pitchers to cease using the spitball because he was convinced it would cause injuries. In mid–1906 Tim Murnane of the *Boston Globe* observed, "Few pitchers are now using the spitball, as it was found to lame the arm and ruin the pitchers' ability to curve."[6]

Eventually, batters made adjustments that enabled them to deal with the pitch more effectively. In August 1907, a Washington reporter commented, "It is beginning to dawn on everyone that the use of the spitball no longer assures success. The spitter is just as hard to hit now as it was when it was first sprung on the unsuspecting batsmen, but the batters have learned to wait out a spitball pitcher and his lack of control loses him many a game."[7]

The spitball remained, however, a very effective pitch. A year after the above comment was made, the White Sox' Ed Walsh won 40 games with the spitter serving as his primary pitch.

1905 American League Standings

Team	W	L	Pct.	GB
Philadelphia	92	56	.622	—
Chicago	92	60	.605	2
Detroit	79	74	.516	15.5
Boston	78	74	.513	16
Cleveland	76	78	.494	19

Team	W	L	Pct.	GB
New York	71	78	.477	21.5
Washington	64	87	.424	29.5
St. Louis	54	99	.353	40.5

Aging Well—With an Injection of Youth: Philadelphia

The A's were growing old. Lave Cross was 39—ancient for a ballplayer in 1905—Monte Cross was 35, Socks Seybold was 34. Four other Athletics were in their early 30s. Good, solid players usually reached the end of their careers in their mid-30s in the days before weight training and an emphasis on eating properly. Even now, with better training regimens, a player in his 30s is seen as having lost some of his physical ability. Connie Mack knew he had to bring in some young blood. He added two new players who were about half of Cross's age and were coming to the A's without any previous professional experience. Outfielder Bris Lord was 21 in 1905, which means he had time to pick up some experience at the semi-professional level. Infielder Jack Knight was all of 19 years old, and had spent the previous season playing for a local high school.

Philadelphia (92–56)

Regular Lineup	AVG	OBP	SLG	R	RBI	SB
Topsy Hartsel, lf	.275	.409	.346	88	28	37
Danny Hoffman, cf	.261	.312	.333	66	35	46
or Bris Lord, of	.239	.285	.298	38	13	3
Harry Davis, 1b	.285	.334	.422	93	83	36
Lave Cross, 3b	.266	.299	.332	69	77	8
Socks Seybold, rf	.274	.341	.402	64	59	5
Danny Murphy, 2b	.277	.339	.389	71	71	23
John Knight, ss	.203	.227	.274	28	29	4
or Monte Cross, ss	.266	.332	.349	28	24	8
O. Schrecongost, c	.271	.278	.345	30	45	9
or Mike Powers, c*	.156	.182	.162	11	12	4

Leading Pitchers	W	L	Pct	IP	H	ERA
Eddie Plank	24	12	.667	346.7	287	2.26
Rube Waddell	27	10	.730	328.7	231	1.48
Andy Coakley	18	8	.692	255	227	1.84
Chief Bender	18	11	.621	229	193	2.83
Weldon Henley	4	11	.267	183.7	155	2.60

*Includes record with New York

Both youngsters were good defensive players. Mack undoubtedly intended for them to give the older players a rest now and then, counting on them to do the job in the field while furnishing whatever offense he could get out of them. Essentially that is how things worked out for Lord, who played all three outfield positions while posting a batting average that was comparatively low, but not embarrassing. For Knight, events brought a different role.

On opening day Monte Cross leaned into a curve from Cy Young and was hit on the wrist on a pitch the umpire ruled was a strike. Cross completed the at-bat, but had to leave the game the next inning with an injury later diagnosed as a cracked wrist. Knight replaced him at shortstop. To everybody's surprise Knight played a big part in the A's fast start—they won five of their first six games. Knight had a game-winning hit and a key home run in those games. Through the A's first eight games he hit .407, good enough to lead the league. After that Knight's average dropped steadily, reaching .230 in mid–June and staying just below that level for the next several weeks. That was not an average to brag about, but it was in the acceptable range for a Deadball Era shortstop. Mack seemed satisfied with Knight's work. When Monte Cross recovered from his injury, Mack continued to play the ex-schoolboy. It was not until the second week of August, after the Athletics had moved into first place, that Cross returned to the lineup on a regular basis. After the season ended Mack offered the opinion that young Knight's hitting in the early weeks of the season had played a big part in the team's ability to capture the flag.[8]

Another young player who contributed significantly to the pennant drive was Danny Hoffman, the swift outfielder Mack had foreseen as a potential star until he suffered a fractured cheek when hit by a pitched ball in 1904. Hoffman never quite recovered his eyesight after the beaning. A left-handed batter, he found it particularly difficult to follow pitches from a lefthanded pitcher. Therefore, Mack set up a platoon arrangement whereby Hoffman would play center field against righthanders and Bris Lord would face the lefties.

Hoffman was extremely fast. He teamed with Topsy Hartsel to give the A's speed at the top of the lineup. Hartsel was an excellent leadoff man. He hit .275, a decent batting average. His forte, however, was drawing bases on balls. He walked 121 times, as a result leading the league with a .409 on-base percentage and scoring 88 runs, the fourth-best total. Hoffman followed Topsy, giving the team two fast, aggressive men at the top of the order. Hoffman led the league in stolen bases with 46, Hartsel was fourth with 37. The number five man in the league, who trailed Topsy by one steal, batted third for the A's. That was Harry Davis, who wasn't a particularly fast runner, but was very savvy on the bases. Davis was not only one of the better baserunners in the league, he also led the league in most of the important power categories. He was number one in doubles (47), home runs (8), runs batted in (83), and runs scored (93). He had the most extra-base hits, but ranked fourth in slugging percentage because most of his extra-base hits were doubles.

The next three batters—Lave Cross, Socks Seybold and Danny Murphy—were all good at the hit-and-run game and had above-average power. Cross was the number two man in the league in runs batted in with 77, and Murphy ranked sixth with 71. Seybold and Murphy tied for fourth in the league in home runs with the modest total of six. Half of Socks' homers came when he hit for the circuit in three consecutive games against Cleveland in August.[9] Knight and Monte Cross batted seventh in the order, each contributing some clutch hits over the course of the season. The number eight batter was Ossee Schrecongost, who was Rube Waddell's friend, sometimes drinking buddy and fellow oddball. Schrecongost didn't have the kind of personality that would make him a patient hitter. He seemed to have very little desire to wait out the pitcher. In 1905 his batting average was .271. His on-base percentage was only .007 higher, a result of walking only three times in 424 plate appearances.

No Deadball Era team was going to win a pennant without a good pitching staff. Mack had three pitchers who would later be voted into the Hall of Fame—Eddie Plank, Rube Waddell, and Chief Bender. Due to injuries and illness in 1905 he had to be creative in using them. That season Plank was the anchor of the staff. He started 41 games—the most of any American League pitcher—and completed 35 of them. His 24 wins were second-highest in the league, trailing only his teammate, Waddell. Eddie stumbled a lit-

Danny Hoffman suffered permanent damage to his vision as a result of a beaning in 1904, but continued to play for the Philadelphia Athletics and New York Highlanders for several years after being injured (Library of Congress).

tle at the beginning of the season losing as often as he won, but beginning in June he put together an eight-game winning streak. He won won about as many as he lost from mid–July through August 23, then put on a finishing kick, winning nine of his last ten decisions.

Waddell came out of spring training with a sore arm. He was able to pitch when the season opened, but was used only in relief during the first three weeks, Mack evidently choosing to build up his arm strength slowly. During that time the Athletics had a three-man starting rotation—Plank, Chief Bender, and Andy Coakley. Waddell relieved in four of the team's first 12 games, finishing up three of Coakley's starts and one for Bender. Rube made his first start on May 4, pitching a two-hitter against Washington. After that he took his turn regularly.

At this point in his managerial career, Mack insisted he didn't use a rotation, that he chose the pitcher who could be most effective considering the opposition.[10] Still, his choices resembled a rotation, since the amount of rest a pitcher had since his last game was an important component of his ability to pitch well. After Waddell recovered his arm strength, Mack started his three Hall of Famers and worked in Coakley and Weldon Henley whenever he felt they were needed. Coakley forced his way into the group of regular starters again in June by running off a string of eight straight wins. He remained in the group throughout the rest of the season. Henley was unable to gain any consistency, his 4–11 record with a pennant-winning team paving the road for a trip back to the minor leagues.

Mack used Chief Bender as both a starter and as the go-to guy when a reliever was needed. The Chief started on opening day, beating Boston 3–2. He had picked up the spitball during the spring. It was at times a very effective pitch for him, but like other pitchers who used the "wet ball," he could lose control of it in mid-game. In late June, after Bender went through a rough stretch, Mack suggested he quit using the pitch.[11] Over the next couple of months, the Chief was used infrequently, partly because of physical problems. In September, however, he played a key role in nailing down the pennant, winning five games in the last three weeks of the season.

From May until Labor Day Waddell was the team's big winner. Rube picked up two victories while working in relief and won his first eight starts, beginning the season with a 10–0 record. Being Rube, his first loss couldn't come in an ordinary game. On June 9 he hooked up with Chicago's Doc White in a pitchers' duel that lasted 14 innings. The only runs scored by the White Sox in the first nine innings came when Rube fell down fielding a bunt, then made a bad throw into left field trying to get the baserunner at second. That runner scored as a result of Rube's error and the batter came around when Topsy Hartsel added another throwing error to the play. A bunt hit, infield out, and a double in the 14th gave Chicago the victory. Rube lost another tough game in his next outing, bowing to Detroit and Wild Bill Donovan, 1–0.[12]

On July fourth, Rube celebrated the nation's birthday by going up against Cy Young. The two great pitchers had several memorable matchups over the years, and this was one of the longest and best. Rube gave up two runs in the first inning, but held Boston scoreless for the next 19. Harry Davis hit a two-run home run in the sixth for the only runs off Young until the 20th inning. In that round the Americans fell apart, committing three errors that led to two runs, giving the A's and Rube a 4–2 victory.[13]

In August Rube notched a five-inning rain-shortened no-hitter against the Browns. He lost his next game, then threw three straight shutouts, adding in 7⅔ scoreless innings in two relief appearances. His streak came to an end on September 5, when he struck out 17 batters in a 13-inning game against Boston. In that game the Americans pushed across two runs in the ninth with the help of three fielding miscues by the A's infield. Those runs broke a streak of 44 consecutive scoreless innings pitched by the big lefthander. Boston won the game four innings later on a walk, sacrifice and Jimmy Collins' line drive to the fence.[14] Rube's next start came only two days later, and it went poorly. He lasted only two innings, giving up two runs on a home run.

That game closed out the series with Boston. After the game the A's boarded a train, heading for New York. The train stopped in Providence, where Andy Coakley was to join the team after enjoying a day off to visit with his family in that city. When he met the train Coakley was wearing his straw hat, evidently unaware of a custom dictating that straw hats be retired the day after Labor Day, the symbolic date for the end of summer. Among ballplayers the custom was enforced by grabbing and smashing hats worn after the holiday. Waddell noticed Coakley wearing the proscribed headgear, and immediately made a beeline for it. Coakley saw Rube coming at him and ran for the train door. Rube lunged for the hat. In the mixup that followed, Rube fell and hit his shoulder. Afterwards Rube took a seat next to a window, exposing his shoulder to the cool air. The next day he could barely raise his arm.

As newspaper reporters became aware of Rube's condition, rumors began to circulate that New York gamblers had gotten to the erratic lefty. Supposedly he was going to be paid for not facing the Giants in the World Series, which was still a month away. The rumors ignored the possibility that Waddell's absence could very well ruin the A's chances of even getting to the series. Neither Mack nor Rube's teammates believed the story, but that didn't stop it from being repeated and its authenticity thoroughly debated.[15]

The A's held a 4½-game lead over the White Sox the evening Waddell was injured. When the two teams opened a three-game series on September 28, they were in a virtual tie for the lead, the A's holding an advantage of .003 percentage points because Chicago had won two more games than Philadelphia and lost two more. Eddie Plank started the first game and won with the help of overwhelming stuff and Topsy Hartsel's glove. Plank struck out 12 Chicago batters, a very high total for him. As for Topsy's glove, it was dropped to the ground as the leftfielder came in from the field to start the bottom of the seventh inning with the score tied, 2–2. That was customary practice in the early Deadball Era and for many decades afterwards. Ossee Schrecongost started that inning with a double and went to third on Plank's sacrifice. Hartsel drew a walk. Bris Lord hit a bounder to third on which Schreck was cut down at the plate. The rally seemed to be about over. But Harry Davis rapped a liner into left field. The ball was hit hard enough that Hartsel should have been out trying to score. But Topsy's glove was lurking at the exact spot needed to assist its owner in his trip around the bases. The ball hit it, slowing down just enough so that despite a great throw to the plate, Hartsel was safe "by the narrow margin of a gnat's heel."[16]

The next day no furtive glove tricks were needed. The A's pounded Nick Altrock and Ed Walsh for 11 runs while Chief Bender held the Windy City team to a single run. Plank tried to come back on one day's rest in the final game of the series, but came up short, losing 4–3. Connie Mack's team entered the last week of the season with a one-game lead over the White Sox and both teams slated to end the season against St. Louis and Washington, the two tailend teams. Waddell was not available to play the hero's role for his team, so someone else had to play that part. Chief Bender, probably the quietest, most reserved Athletic stepped forward.

Andy Coakley whitewashed the Browns in the first game of the next series. Weldon Henley started out all right the next day, but began to wobble in the sixth inning, giving up a run and loading the bases before getting the third out while clinging to a 3–1 lead. After Henley opened the seventh by walking the leadoff man, Mack brought Bender into the game. The Chief hit the first batter he faced and gave up a run-scoring single to the second. A sacrifice put runners on second and third with only one out. Bender got out of the inning without further trouble by fanning the next two batters. He closed out the game by striking out four more batters over the next two innings. Plank won the next game, 4–1, giving up only five hits. Chicago had lost one game in its series with Washington, dropping two games off the pace. The A's traveled to the nation's capital hoping to hold on to that lead.

On October 5, Bender blanked the Senators 8–0 in the first game of a doubleheader, getting three hits as well as throwing a shutout. Coakley started the second game, but gave up three runs in the first two innings. The Chief was sent in to pinch-hit for Coakley in the third, and responded with a triple, driving home Monte Cross. He scored on Hartsel's single to pull within a run, 3–2. Then he went to the mound, where he showed signs of fatigue, since he had already pitched a complete game earlier in the day. At bat, though, he was still strong. He doubled in two runs in the fourth inning to give his team a 5–4 lead. The A's continued to pound the Senators' Casey Patten and Bender held on for a 9–7 victory. The White Sox were idle that day, but now trailed by three games.

Coakley started the third game of the Washington series. He was ineffective. After three innings, with the game tied 4–4, Mack decided to bring Waddell into the game to see how he could do. Rube was wild, walking five batters and throwing two wild pitches while giving up six runs in five innings of a 10–4 loss. Meanwhile the lowly Browns beat the White Sox 6–2 in St. Louis, enabling the A's to clinch the title.

The following day Mack took another look at Waddell. Rube started the first game of a doubleheader. He was lifted after one inning, after giving up two runs on two hits and showing that he was not up to pitching against top-level competition, and certainly not ready to face the Giants in the World Series.[17]

Hitless? Not Quite; Wonders? Almost: Chicago

In the spring of 1905 most baseball people had a negative attitude toward the spitball. White Sox owner Charlie Comiskey, however, had a different view. "Granting that this spitball will cut as big a hole into batting as everyone predicts, it will help my team more than it will hurt," Comiskey remarked. "We weren't the worst batting team in the league last year, and if the spitball cuts down the batting the other teams are going to hit less, too. There wasn't a team in the league which could beat us in fielding and baserunning last year, and if the other fellows can't hit this year, why, we ought to win the pennant on our fielding and speed on bases."[18]

Chicago (92–60)

Regular Lineup	AVG	OBP	SLG	R	RBI	SB
Fielder Jones, cf	.245	.335	.327	91	38	20
Frank Isbell, 2b-of	.296	.335	.440	55	45	15
or Ducky Holmes, lf	.201	.258	.259	42	22	11
George Davis, ss	.278	.353	.340	74	55	31

Regular Lineup	AVG	OBP	SLG	R	RBI	SB
Jimmy Callahan, lf	.272	.336	.368	50	43	26
or Danny Green, rf	.243	.345	.309	56	44	11
Jiggs Donahue, 1b	.287	.346	.349	71	76	32
Billy Sullivan, c	.201	.239	.269	25	26	14
or Ed McFarland, c	.280	.345	.364	24	31	5
Lee Tannehill, 3b	.200	.274	.244	38	39	8
or George Rohe, inf	.212	.310	.248	14	12	2
Gus Dundon, 2b	.192	.248	.228	30	22	14

Leading Pitchers	W	L	Pct	IP	H	ERA
Frank Owen	21	13	.618	334	276	2.10
Nick Altrock	23	12	.657	315.7	274	1.88
Frank Smith	19	13	.594	291.7	215	2.13
Doc White	17	13	.567	260.3	204	1.76
Ed Walsh	8	3	.727	136.7	121	2.17
Roy Patterson	4	6	.400	88.7	73	1.83

Comiskey's men didn't quite fulfill their boss's hope, but they came close. They spent most of the season in second place, within a week-long hot streak of the top spot. Cleveland led most of the summer, although they shared the lead with the White Sox about half of the time in July. Philadelphia surged past both Cleveland and Chicago the second week of August and held on to a very small lead the rest of the year. The White Sox came to within a half-game of catching the A's near the end of September but, as described above, lost a key series between the two teams.

Unlike some team leaders, Comiskey didn't object when his pitchers showed an inclination to experiment with the spitball. Three of his six pitchers used the pitch at some time during the season. Frank Smith made it a central part of his pitching arsenal. Doc White used it regularly at the start of the season, but after about a month said the pitch hurt his arm, and therefore he would use it only in emergencies. Ed Walsh, still a "project" who remained with the team because of his immense potential, worked on the pitch all season without bringing it entirely under control. A fourth member of the staff, Roy Patterson, also seemed to be working on it but probably didn't use it in live action yet. The team's two top winners, Frank Owen and Nick Altrock, stuck with their tried and true stuff.[19]

Comiskey was "country when country wasn't cool"—that is, he was among the first to use the bunt and aggressive baserunning as weapons when he managed the St. Louis Browns, winning the American Association pennant four years in a row from 1885 through 1888.[20] He wanted his teams to employ the same kind of offense. They led the American League in stolen bases each of the first four years the American League operated as a major league. Unlike managers like Ned Hanlon, John McGraw, and Connie Mack, who didn't particularly like the sacrifice bunt, Comiskey encouraged his managers to use it as a central element in their team's offense. One statistic about the 1905 White Sox that stands out is that the team's number three hitter, George Davis, had 40 sacrifices, the second-highest total in the league, trailing only Wee Willie Keeler. The White Sox had four players ranking among the top ten in sacrifices, all players who hit in the heart of the team's batting order. They led the league with a total of 241. (As a point of reference, in 2017 Colorado led the National League with 62 sacrifices, 42 of those by pitchers. Chicago led the American League with 35.)

George Davis was close to being the ideal man for the type of offense the White Sox employed. Davis had an unsavory side to his character. While playing with the New York Giants in the 1890s, he developed a reputation for using minor injuries as an excuse for skipping games. He used his position as the Giants' manager to borrow money which he then forgot to pay back. Off the field He seems to have had at least a couple of affairs with married women. Later in life he was committed to the Pennsylvania State Hospital suffering from a mental illness which evidently was a result of having contracted syphilis years earlier.[21] He was, however, an extremely talented baseball player. He hit for a good average and with good power for the Deadball Era. Every year he sprinkled a good number of walks among his hits, could work the hit-and-run when needed, and while not noted as an exceptionally fast runner, he stole a respectable number of bases each year. To top it all off, he had good hands as a shortstop and was adept at defending against the tactics of scientific baseball.

Davis's broad range of skills gave him the ability to boost his team's attack in a variety of ways. On April 28, he came up in the 13th inning with Ducky Holmes on first and one out. On a hit-and-run play he rapped a single to right, sending Holmes to third. He then drew a throw to second on a delayed steal. Davis slid into second safely while Holmes crossed the plate before the return toss reached the catcher.

On May 1, the White Sox held a 2–0 lead over Detroit in the third inning. Ducky Holmes was at third base and Danny Green at first. Davis laid down a squeeze bunt that scored Holmes. In his rush to make a play on Davis's deft bunt, the Detroit pitcher made a poor throw, putting Davis on second and Green on third. Both men scored on a single, turning a close game into a rout.

A month later, Davis figured in a "buntation" attack to begin a game against Cleveland. Fielder Jones led off with a bunt single. Holmes followed with another bunt, which he beat out. Davis chipped in with a third bunt, which went for a sacrifice. A single followed, giving the White Sox a two-run advantage to round out the first inning.

Davis contributed his share of extra-base hits, also. On June 9 he ended Rube Waddell's 10-game winning streak by cracking out a double in the 14th inning. A couple weeks later he contributed two doubles and a single to an 8–2 blow-out victory over Cleveland. His 29 doubles over the course of the season gave him the eighth highest total in the league.

Although Davis was certainly a better all-round player, the top White Sox hitter in 1905 was Frank Isbell, a development that would have been utterly unpredictable before that season. Isbell was a fixture with the White Sox, having been with the franchise in St. Paul before Comiskey moved it to Chicago. He had begun his career as a pitcher, but was moved to first base after failing in a brief stay with the Chicago Colts of the National League in 1898. "Izzy" helped the White Stockings win the first American League championship in 1901, leading the team in runs scored (93) and RBIs (70), and topping the league in stolen bases with 52 purloined sacks. And he did this while batting .257, which was 20 points below the league average. Izzy had a pretty good year at bat—for him—again in 1902, posting a .252 average. He stole 38 bases, ranking fourth in the league. After the American League adopted the foul strike rule in 1903, however, he struggled. His average dropped to .242 that season and plunged to .210 in 1904.

But hitting was not Isbell's forte. He was known as one of the best fielding first basemen in baseball. Tim Murnane, the noted baseball editor of the *Boston Globe*, described him as one of the finest first basemen ever seen in Boston. "With a long range, a sure catch, and a fast true throw," Murnane said, "this man need ask no odds from the best that ever toed the initial cushion." When the White Sox infield was thrown into disarray in 1903 because George Davis defected to the Giants (more specifically, to New York's race tracks), Isbell was credited with stabilizing Lee Tannehill's play at shortstop by flagging down most of Tannehill's erratic throws to first.[22]

Isbell's hitting woes eventually cost him his job at first base. After his mediocre 1903 season Izzy was a holdout through most of spring training the next year. When he returned to the team his job had been given to Jiggs Donahue, who was about as good a fielder as Izzy and was a far better hitter. Isbell became the team's all-purpose utility player, filling in at second base and in the outfield, as well as playing 57 games at first base while Donahue was injured.

While Isbell was bouncing around the field filling in for injured players and sitting on the bench waiting for a chance to play, he was experimenting with his batting style. He had been tinkering with it since at least mid-1902, when a writer noted that he had moved up to the front of the batter's box, trying to meet the ball before it broke. He had some success with the change, but the improvement was only temporary, as shown by his declining averages. In late August of 1904, a Chicago writer again noted that Isbell seemed to be hitting much better. He attributed the change to a long period of rest. Again Isbell hit well for a while and then went into a deep slump.[23] But in 1905 Izzy made an adjustment that worked just fine. He had been using a thick-handled bottle bat. Someone—possibly Charlie Comiskey—suggested that he switched to a bat with a big barrel but slimmer handle. He played sparingly in the first third of that season. When he finally got into the lineup he hit better than he had ever hit before. This time he was able to maintain the higher level of production throughout the rest of 1905 and into 1906, when he would make a large contribution to the success of one of baseball's most memorable teams.[24]

The Comedic Touch: Detroit

One of the new players joining the Tigers in spring training in 1905 was a stocky, energetic infielder named Herman Schaefer, who became better known by his nickname, "Germany." Schaefer was an experienced minor leaguer, having already played four seasons at the Class A level (then the highest minor league classification), as well as spending 1902 with the Chicago Cubs. Although he batted poorly for the Cubs, putting up a meek .196 batting average, he hit well with St. Paul and Milwaukee of the Western League during the next two years. One writer called him "the crack minor league hitter of 1904."[25]

Detroit (79–74)

Regular Lineup	AVG	OBP	SLG	R	RBI	SB
Duff Cooley, cf	.247	.297	.332	25	32	7
Chris Lindsay, 1b	.267	.315	.316	38	31	10
Matty McIntyre, lf	.263	.330	.325	59	30	9
or Ty Cobb, cf	.240	.288	.300	19	15	2
Sam Crawford, rf-1b	.297	.357	.430	73	75	22
Bill Coughlin, 3b	.252	.309	.317	48	44	16
or Bobby Lowe, ut	.193	.255	.254	17	9	3
Germany Schaefer, 2b	.244	.302	.318	64	47	19
Charley O'Leary, ss	.213	.259	.242	47	33	13
Lew Drill, c	.261	.366	.303	17	24	7
or John Warner, c	.202	.252	.269	12	7	2

Leading Pitchers	W	L	Pct	IP	H	ERA
George Mullin	21	21	.500	347.7	303	2.51
Ed Killian	23	14	.622	313.3	263	2.27
Bill Donovan	18	15	.545	280.7	236	2.60
Frank Kitson	12	14	.462	225.7	230	3.47

Schaefer fit in well with the Tigers. He and shortstop Charley O'Leary had lived near each other in Chicago's South side. They had played sandlot ball together and had long hoped to play alongside each other in the major leagues. Germany became a favorite subject for Detroit sportswriters before spring training was far along, relating his experiences at his various baseball stops. He and O'Leary became a smooth-working team on double plays, which led Schaefer to tell one of the writers that he would "have his name changed to Lajoie before the season is over." Of course, that was his way of saying he hoped to become good enough to be compared with the best second baseman in baseball. By coincidence, near the end of Detroit's first series with Cleveland, one of that city's writers remarked, "Schaefer's catch of Flick's high fly to short right was a spectacular piece of work. The German has rivaled Larry [Lajoie] throughout the series in the ease and grace with which he covers the keystone corner."[26]

Germany Schaefer liked to interact with fans. Here he has borrowed a camera from a professional photographer and is likely offering helpful hints to its owner (Library of Congress).

The experience Schaefer had accumulated in the high-level minor leagues showed up early in the season. One of the hallmarks of a good middle infielder in the Deadball Era was his ability to deal with the delayed steal. On one such play against Cleveland Germany got the ball at second too late to tag the runner coming down from first, but quickly fired it back to the catcher in time to cut down the runner trying to score from third on the throw. He was applauded for the great play. After he cut off two rallies by making running catches off potential Texas Leaguers, Joe Jackson of the *Detroit Free Press* commented, "Schaefer is certainly the best on those short outfield flies that has worn the Tigers' stripes for many years."[27]

Schaefer liked to interact with the fans and he became energized by their response. As one writer put it, "the German gathers ginger as he gathers hits." The active mind that created the continual repartee with fellow teammates, reporters, and fans also created some innovative plays on the diamond. In a game against Cleveland, Germany was on third base when the squeeze play was called. He started for home with the pitch. The batter, John Sullivan, tried to bunt but missed the ball. Schaefer kept coming and slid to the front side of the plate, avoiding the tag and scoring the run. On another squeeze play later in the year, against the Athletics, Schaefer was the batter, with Tom Doran on third and Duff Cooley on second. Both runners took off as the pitch was delivered. Germany bunted toward the right side, past the pitcher. First baseman Harry Davis fielded the ball. He saw he had no play at the plate, so he held the ball for an instant while second baseman Danny Murphy sprinted over to cover first. Schaefer was out at first. Meanwhile Cooley had continued to run and beat Murphy's throw to the plate. The *Philadelphia Inquirer* reporter called it "the swellest presentation of the squeeze play seen in these parts."[28]

In a game against Cleveland in July, Germany came out to the field at the start of the game wearing a green feather in his cap. The fans roared and his teammates laughed. But for the Detroit players the joke wore thin as he continued to wear it while the team absorbed a 14–3 shellacking. Schaefer defended himself by saying the feather helped him at bat, having collected three hits in the game. Although by season's end in 1905 he was already being identified as "the German comedian," the feather incident was the only stunt of note pulled off that season. More were to come.

In May of 1906, again with the Naps as the opponent, Germany came to bat in the first inning wearing a set of false long yellow whiskers. The umpire allowed him to finish the at-bat, in which he fouled out, but when Schaefer went to the coaches box the next inning wearing the whiskers he was ordered to take them off. Six weeks later, Germany was called upon to pinch-hit in the ninth inning against Chicago's Doc White. Two men were out, the Tigers trailed 2–1, and Schaefer's buddy, Charley O'Leary was on first base. Schaefer walked up to the plate, paused, and returned to the bench to get a new bat. He returned to the plate, stepped in the batter's box, and promptly smashed White's first pitch "a mile and a half over [left fielder] Hahn's head into the left field bleachers," winning the game. According to the reports in the *Detroit Free Press* and *Chicago Tribune*, Schaefer trotted "gloatingly" around the bases, wearing a big smile on his face. He had been trading barbs with the Chicago fans all day long while on the coaching lines, but after the home run he was given a hearty ovation.[29]

That was the story according to two newspapers covering the game. Davy Jones, Schaefer's teammate, added some colorful details six decades later when describing the event. (The reader should feel free to take them with a couple boulder-sized grains of salt.) According to Jones, when Schaefer paused on the way to the batter's box, he took off his cap, turned to the grandstand and announced, "Ladies and gentlemen, you are now looking at Herman the Great, acknowledged by one and all to be the greatest pinch hitter in the world. I am now going to hit the ball into the left field bleachers. Thank you."

After delivering on his promise, according to Jones, Germany raced to first base, slid headfirst into the bag, jumped up and yelled, "Schaefer leads at the quarter!" He got up and made the circuit of the bases, sliding into each and announcing his lead, as if in a horse race. After sliding into home plate, he arose and yelled, "Schaefer wins by a nose!" Jones went on to relate that the next day Schaefer struck out three times before coming to bat in the ninth. The *Detroit Free Press* account conforms with that of Jones, adding that Schaefer also fanned in the ninth for the fourth straight time.[30]

A week later the Tigers were playing Cleveland, which seemed to be Germany's favorite foil, when it began raining. Soon the grounds became very wet and slippery. The Tigers, who trailed by several runs, appealed to umpire Billy Evans to call the game. Evans refused. In the bottom of the sixth Schaefer trotted out to second base wearing a raincoat. Evans was not persuaded. When the half-inning ended Cleveland shortstop Terry Turner came up to Schaefer and borrowed the raincoat. At that point Evans called the game.[31]

In 1905 Schaefer's comedic nature added a much-needed light touch to a season that otherwise sputtered along, presenting as many losses as wins until September and as many bad moments as good ones. In April star outfielder Jimmy Barrett suffered a knee injury that turned out to be career-ending. In July a feud erupted between slugger Charlie Hickman and manager Bill Armour. The two men had clashed when both were with Cleveland in 1904. Their differences were resolved by Hickman being traded to the Tigers. Armour moved to Detroit over the winter. On July 1, Hickman left the team, saying he wanted to play elsewhere. Hickman complained that Armour criticized him continually in all aspects of his game. "He found fault with everything I did," he said. "I could not stand at the plate to suit him, or did not hold my hands right to get a ball. Everything I did was a fault-finder for him." Once again Armour solved his "Hickman problem" by moving him to a different team, this time selling him to Washington.[32]

The Tigers spent most of the season bobbing around the .500 mark. For the first three months that was enough to put them in fourth place, a few games above sixth and well ahead of Washington and St. Louis, who were battling each other to keep out of the cellar. In August the Tigers slumped, dropping to 51–60 on August 28. Something clicked for them after that. They finished the season by winning two-thirds of their remaining games, finishing in third place, albeit well out of pennant contention. The Detroit correspondent of *The Sporting News* spread the credit for the improvement widely, citing the addition of Chris Lindsay at first base and Jack Warner at catcher as stabilizing factors, general improvement by the team's pitchers, and the clutch hitting of Sam Crawford. Over the last six weeks of the season Wahoo Sam hit .333 and scored 22 runs in 42 games.[33]

From Champions to "Roly-Polys": Boston

Some of us have learned that age can catch up with a person quickly. For the 1905 Boston Americans it came like a boulder dropping off a cliff. In October of 1904 they were two-time champions of the American League and still the defending World Champions, since the Giants refused to play them in a series that fall. A few months later they were struggling to break even in spring training exhibition games, losing four times to minor league teams. When the games counted, they lurched into the new season by losing their first six games. They were in last place as late as May 27. The team rallied a bit after that, but it didn't reach .500 until August 4. In September a poor month dropped them back under the break even mark. After losing the opener of a doubleheader on September 30, they were in sixth place with a 70–74 mark. They salvaged a small bit of respect by winning their last eight games, moving into fourth place three days before the season ended.

Such a rapid fadeout naturally brought analyses from the press. They generally focused on the fact that Manager Jimmy Collins had stayed too long with the same men, age and an associated weight gain resulting in a team that was slow and out of touch with the changes in the way the game was played. "The champions are clearly not in shape to play fast and winning ball," one writer said. "Most of them are fat and slow. Stahl. Selbach, Parent, and Collins himself look altogether too heavy. These men are stocky built, and ordinarily look beefy, but their movements indicate that they are slower than ever before."[34] Another writer made the same point, but with a much sharper barb. "The adipose athletes of beanburg dug their way into the error tabulation four times," he wrote, "and their mistakes were the kind to make them puff and wheeze like the contestants in a fat man's sack race at a Fourth of July picnic." The next day he called Collins' team "the stout ones" and the "Roly-Polys."[35]

Boston (78–74)

Regular Lineup	AVG	OBP	SLG	R	RBI	SB
Kip Selbach, rf	.246	.355	.342	54	47	12
Freddy Parent, ss	.234	.296	.277	55	33	25
Jesse Burkett, lf	.257	.339	.344	78	47	13
Jimmy Collins, 3b	.276	.330	.370	66	65	18
or Bob Unglaub, inf	.223	.260	.281	18	11	2
Chick Stahl, cf	.258	.332	.308	61	47	18
Buck Freeman, 1b-rf	.240	.316	.338	59	49	8
or Moose Grimshaw, 1b	.239	.293	.323	39	35	4
Hobe Ferris, 2b	.220	.253	.361	51	59	11
Lou Criger, c	.198	.322	.272	33	36	5
or Charlie Armbruster, c	.198	.336	.242	13	6	3

Leading Pitchers	W	L	Pct	IP	H	ERA
Cy Young	18	19	.486	320.7	248	1.82
Jesse Tannehill	22	9	.710	271.7	238	2.48
George Winter	16	17	.485	264.3	249	2.96
Bill Dinneen	12	14	.462	243.7	235	3.73
Norwood Gibson	4	7	.364	134	118	3.69

Even when the Americans won their pennants they were criticized for not playing scientific baseball. Naturally, those criticisms intensified, and the team's failed efforts at those tactics only hurt them. By May they had messed up the squeeze play four times in a row. In September, Tim Murnane, of the *Boston Globe*, noted that Boston had usually failed to stop the squeeze play when it was tried against them. Murnane counted six times in seven attempts when their opponents succeeded in pulling off the play. An old criticism was again made—that Jimmy Collins was the only Boston player who was adept at the hit-and-run. The team's attempts at sacrificing also came in for criticism. "Open and shut sacrifice hitting is being overdone by the champions," Murnane wrote. "Bang the ball past the third baseman now and then just to keep him guessing. That's up-to-date baseball."[36]

While advancing age was clearly a problem for Boston, the "old man" of the team, Cy Young, escaped criticism. He received sympathy for the way his good pitching was poorly rewarded. Young turned 38 during spring training, but he still possessed overwhelming speed and great control. He lost seven of his first eight starts, but pitched only one bad game over that stretch. In six of the seven losses he gave up three or fewer runs. Evidence that his stuff was as good as ever is shown by his strikeout totals which included one 12-K game and another with 10. Over the course of the season he struck out more batters per nine innings than any other American League pitcher except Rube Waddell, and he tied Eddie Plank for second in total strikeouts, both trailing Rube in that category. He had the third lowest earned run average in the league (1.82). In the more modern statistic of WHIP (walks and hits per inning pitched), he led the league with 0.867. In late August Cy strained his arm throwing a shutout against the Browns. He pitched in only one game, a 5–3 loss to the A's over the next three weeks. When he returned to the rotation on a regular basis he threw two consecutive shutouts, relying chiefly on his fastball, but mixing in a few spitballs—which he had previously refused to use because he feared it would hurt his arm—when he felt the situation called for it.[37]

Although Young probably pitched better than any other member of the Boston staff, the team's most successful hurler in what counts most—winning games—was Jesse Tannehill. In a way, it figures that Tannehill would be less affected by his teammates' struggles than the other players. Jesse was very much a "loner." After the 1904 season a Boston reporter noted, "Jesse isn't a man to say much or to make many friends, but he is staunch to those he pledges his friendship and his motto seems to be few friends but good ones." Tannehill assumed a standoffish attitude toward the writers who covered his teams. One of them wrote that Jesse had a habit of "sneering at all reporters." He quoted Tannehill as saying, "They are like umpires—all bad," and the writer added the observation that "Jesse always acted as though he believed in the sentiment he was charged with uttering."[38] Although his overall personality was undoubtedly a major factor in Tannehill's attitude, it was likely at least partly also due to the treatment he received in his rookie season.

He was still a month short of his 20th birthday and playing for a local semi-pro team when the Cincinnati Reds signed him in the middle of the 1894 season. He did well in his first couple of appearances with the Reds. After winning his first major league game, Jesse went to the park the following day expecting to be congratulated for his achievement. Instead, he was frozen out. "Why, for a time I thought that the players of the Cincinnati team had forgotten me," Tannehill later recalled. "At first not a member of the team spoke to me. They passed by without so much as a nod of the head. Most of them turned their heads another way when they passed me. Those who did look at me did so with a stare that seemed to say, 'What are you doing here anyhow?'" Thinking back, Jesse explained, "I was only a green kid, and this kind of treatment broke my heart. I felt I couldn't do anything with the team."

Jesse pitched only five games with the Reds. The next two seasons he pitched for Richmond in the Virginia League. He was very successful there, going 22–10 in 1895 and 27–14 in 1896. He was drafted by Pittsburgh after the 1896 season. When he joined the Pirates in the spring of 1897, he got another cold reception from the veterans on the team. This time Tannehill reacted differently. "I was no longer the green kid I was when I joined the Reds," Jesse said later. "When they started to freeze me I just froze them back. I said to myself, 'I have come here to paddle my own canoe. I am going to do my part and let the others take care of themselves.' I gave back a stare for every one I received and made up my mind to hustle for dear life, and in a short time I was on an even plane with the best of them."[39]

After going 9–9 his first season in Pittsburgh, Jesse blossomed into one of the best pitchers in baseball. He went 25–13 in 1898, pitching 326 innings, and 24–14 in 1899, throwing 322 innings. Tannehill was not a big man. He stood five feet eight

Jesse Tannehill never quite got over the hazing he received as a rookie. He decided to "paddle his own canoe," becoming a loner with only a few friends among his teammates (Library of Congress).

inches tall and weighed about 150 pounds. The heavy workload took its toll on him. In September of 1899 he went out with a sore arm. He never again approached the number of innings he pitched in those two years with the Pirates, his high-water mark after that being the 281 frames he hurled for Boston in 1904. That would be considered a big workload for modern pitchers but in the Deadball Era it was only a moderate total.

Jesse's manager from 1900 through 1902 was Fred Clarke, who didn't use him as an innings-eating staff ace. Clarke had Deacon Phillippe and

Sam Leever for that role. He started Tannehill regularly, but also utilized his fielding and batting talents at times when a substitute was needed in the outfield. Jesse played 30 games in the outfield during the three years he pitched for Clarke. He hit .336, .244 and .291 in those years. In his prime job, left-handed starter, Jesse went 20–6, 18–10, and 20–6. He led the National League in 1901 with a 2.18 ERA, and had an even lower figure in 1902 (1.95). After he jumped to the New York Highlanders in 1903, Jesse compiled a relatively poor record for him, going 15–15. He and manager Clark Griffith happily parted ways after just one year, and Jesse returned to his winning ways with Boston.

Tannehill didn't have a great fastball. Instead, he relied upon changing speeds and fooling batters with a sharp-breaking curve ball. After Jesse beat Chicago 8–1 in a game, Chicago writer Hugh Fullerton commented, "Chicago had no chance to win because Tannehill was pitching a deceptive curve. Loftus's batters were always expecting Tannehill to pitch something, but he never pitched anything, thereby deceiving the sluggers and keeping them popping the ball in the air through all the game."[40]

In the same vein, after Jesse moved to the American League a reporter observed, "Mr. Tannehill is one of those pitchers about whom opposing batsmen are wont to say, as they prepare for the trip to the plate, 'ain't got a thing.' He doesn't burn the air with speed, and his catcher doesn't give imitations of the prize winner in an amateur night prize buck and wing competition while grabbing for the fag end of elusive curves. He just serves a dinky floater with a whole lot of crimp to it. It's easy to hit, but hard to hit safely." Tannehill had a smooth motion that made his delivery more deceptive. An opposing batter said, "It is this careless yet graceful delivery which helps Tannehill's effectiveness. He is apparently just tossing the ball to the catcher but there is much more speed on it than one would suppose from the stands."[41]

The characteristic that best defined Jesse's pitching was his winning percentage. With a decent team behind him, he was very hard to beat. He won over 70 percent of his decisions in three different seasons. His career record was 197–117, for a won-lost percentage of .627, the 59th highest percentage in baseball history for pitchers with at least 100 decisions.[42] Jesse had only nine seasons in which he started more than 20 games. He notched at least 20 victories in six of those nine seasons.

The Answer Is Elmer Flick, .306 in 1905: Cleveland

The Naps once again followed the path ordained for them during this period–start out the season appearing to have a great chance to win the flag, then drop out of contention as injuries decimate the team. If anything, their 1905 season was marked by exaggerated hopes and a sharper fall. They led the league until August 1, despite the onset of the injury plague a month earlier. When their slide began, a few days before slipping out of the lead, they had posted a 53–31 record. Over the remainder of the season they were 23–47.

All but a couple of the Naps missed significant time because of injuries. But the most damaging incident occurred on July 1, when Charley O'Leary accidentally spiked Nap Lajoie in the foot while sliding into second base. The wound soon developed blood poisoning. At one point it was feared that the leg would have to be amputated. With his team struggling badly, in late August Lajoie tried to return to the field at first base. But he lasted only a few games before fouling a pitch off his foot. He collapsed in pain, his season over, after having appeared in only 65 games.[43]

Cleveland (76–78)

Regular Lineup	AVG	OBP	SLG	R	RBI	SB
Jim Jackson, lf	.256	.317	.317	60	31	15
Harry Bay, cf	.301	.349	.370	90	22	36
Elmer Flick, rf	.308	.383	.462	72	64	35
Nap Lajoie, 2b	.329	.377	.418	29	41	11
Bill Bradley, 3b	.268	.321	.354	63	51	22
Terry Turner, ss	.265	.289	.360	49	72	17
Charlie Carr, 1b	.235	.266	.310	29	31	12
or George Stovall, 1b-2b	.272	.295	.357	41	47	13
or Nick Kahl, inf	.215	.248	.259	16	21	1
or Otto Hess, of-p	.254	.291	.347	15	13	2
Fritz Buelow, c	.172	.198	.209	11	18	7
orHarry Bemis, c	.292	.344	.376	27	28	3
or Nig Clarke, c*	.208	.275	.292	12	10	0

Leading Pitchers	W	L	Pct	IP	H	ERA
Addie Joss	20	12	.625	286	246	2.01
Earl Moore	15	15	.500	269	232	2.64
Bob Rhoads	16	9	.640	235	219	2.83
Otto Hess	10	15	.400	213.7	179	3.16
Bill Bernhard	7	13	.350	174.3	185	3.36
Red Donahue	6	12	.333	137.7	132	3.40

*Includes record with Detroit

The frustration the Cleveland players must have felt is shown by a comment made by interim player-manager Bill Bradley in mid–August, when Lajoie had recovered enough to resume managing the team. "If I had that team a week longer," Bradley said, "there would not be a player able to put on a uniform. As it is, I have succeeded in killing off five."[44]

While it was a season the Naps wanted to forget, for one Cleveland player it became a season that would become a part of his baseball identity.

For over six decades Elmer Flick was the answer to a trivia question: Which major league batting champion had the lowest batting average? Flick held that distinction from 1905 through 1967. His .306 batting average in 1905 was the league's highest, and one of only three that exceeded .300. In 1968 Carl Yastrzemski replaced Elmer as the owner of that dubious honor when he was the American League's only .300 hitter, winning the championship with a .301 average.

Years later, when a reporter asked him about his 1905 batting average Flick responded, "A lot of people remember me for that puny .306 average because it was in the record book. But I hit .378 in 1900 with the Phillies and didn't win the championship." Flick possessed a momento of the 1900 season which, he claimed, showed his leadership in another batting category that season. He showed off a silver pitcher with the engraving: "Elmer Flick, champion home-run hitter, 1900." The cup had been presented to Flick during the last game of the 1900 season. "I had 14 or 15 [home runs] that year and was awarded this cup," Flick said. "But you know how records were kept in those days—not very good. A couple of years later Herman long, who had 11 homers in 1900, was given credit for being champ. They said he had 12. I was given 11 and he's in the books now as the fellow who led the league. Well, he got the honor and I've got the cup."[45]

Flick was drafted by the Philadelphia Phillies in 1897, after batting .386 for Dayton of the Interstate League. When he reported to spring training in 1898, the Phillies thought they would use him as a backup to Sam Thompson, one of the great hitters of the 19th century. Thompson had missed most of the preceding season with back problems, but the Phillies were hoping he had fully recovered. Elmer was the sensation of the Phillies' training camp, batting .526. In his first eight spring training games he had nine extra-base hits, including four home runs. When he reported to the Phillies, Elmer had trouble playing the sun field—a big problem if he needed to replace Thompson. Fortunately for Elmer, Thompson was not one of those veterans who resented younger players. Thompson volunteered to help him learn how to deal with the sun's glare. "Sam took me in hand," Flick said, "and, first equipping me with sun glasses, showed me every wrinkle of the game. I do not remember ever losing a ball in the sun and I used to get lots of sun balls on the old Philadelphia grounds."[46] Elmer started the season on the bench, as planned, but Thompson's back started acting up after only a few games. He retired before the season was very old, and Elmer became the regular right fielder.

It didn't take long for Flick to establish himself as one of the game's better players. In June he attracted attention by slamming three triples and a single in one game. In July a reporter claimed, "Thompson is no longer missed in right, as Flick is his equal, if not his superior in fielding, batting and running. Flick has been doing fielding of the Fogarty-Curt Welch order lately." (Jim Fogarty and Curt Welch were often cited as two of the best fielding outfielders of the 19th century.) In September Elmer stole three bases in one game, inspiring a comparison with Billy Hamilton, the top base thief of the 90s.[47]

Flick hit .302 in his rookie year and raised his average to .342 the next year. By the beginning of 1900, his third year in the National League, he had gained recognition as one of the best

For six decades Elmer Flick owned the lowest league-leading batting average. His .306 average in 1905 (since adjusted to .308) was superseded by Carl Yastrzemski's .301 in 1968 (Library of Congress).

players in the league. In May of that year Cincinnati reporter J. Ed Grillo, after describing two outstanding catches made by Flick despite the glaring sun of Cincinnati's notorious right field, remarked, "Flick is regarded as the greatest sun fielder in the league. He seems to be able to play a sun field just as well as he does an ordinary field. The fact of the matter is that Flick is a great ballplayer."[48]

Flick had one of the better throwing arms in the game. While he was with the Phillies he learned to play a shallow right field in the Baker Bowl, which had a short right field fence. He picked up a few extra assists by fielding sharply hit balls and throwing out the batter at first base. After he moved to Cleveland his strong arm figured in a quite different type of play, one a writer called "either the cleverest thing of the season or else the sheerest accident and bit of bullhead fortune." The White Sox had men on first and third when a batter hit a fly to Flick. The ball did not go quite far enough to enable the runner to score from third. But Flick fired toward the plate anyway. As the throw came to the plate the catcher, Nig Clarke, "stood like a statue, never touched the ball, and let it go to the stand." Seeing the overthrow, the runner on third quite naturally broke for the plate. While fans and players alike were following the path of the ball, the pitcher, Red Donahue, had quietly sprinted past Clarke all the way to the backstop. Flick's throw came straight to Donahue, who caught it, and fired the ball back to Clarke in time to tag out the surprised runner. "What made the play seem intentional," said the Chicago writer, "was the fact that Clarke did not rush madly back after the ball when it passed him, as the catcher always does when a wild throw happens, but made no move to get it, and then, stepping to the plate, stood ready for the return."[49]

Flick played four years with the Phillies. He jumped across town to the Athletics in 1902 but, because of the injunction levied as part of the Lajoie decision, ended up in Cleveland by the beginning of May. He remained with the Naps through the 1910 season, but played only the equivalent of about a half-season over his last three years. After the 1907 season he came down with a severe stomach ailment that doctors eventually diagnosed as "acute gastritis." He played in only nine games in 1908. The next season his condition stabilized long enough to enable him to appear in 66 games, but he had lost much of his speed and was able to hit only .255. In 1910, after Elmer hit .265 in 24 games, he was released by the Naps. Elmer played in the minor leagues for two more years before retiring.

As time passed Flick became pretty much a forgotten part of baseball's past. In the Hall of Fame voting he got one vote, in 1938. Then, when Ty Cobb died in 1961, articles about the Georgia Peach mentioned that he was almost traded even up for Flick just before the 1907 season. That longforgotten non-event brought renewed attention to Flick's career. When the Hall of Fame Veterans Committee voted in 1963 they announced the selection of four old-timers. One of them was Flick. Elmer's selection surprised just about everyone, including Elmer, who by that time had already celebrated his 87th birthday. When he received the telephone call informing him of his selection, Elmer's response was, "You're kidding. I don't believe it." Later that afternoon, talking to a reporter in his living room, Elmer said, "I just hope it's true. Me in the Hall of Fame? It's hard to believe. I wonder if it's really a joke."[50]

The Veterans Committee's selections—Sam Rice, Eppa Rixey, John Clarkson, and Flick—were not universally applauded. *The Sporting News* printed an editorial stating that, while the four had good credentials, others had done better. The paper called for a limit on the number of players admitted to the Hall.[51] Since then Flick's selection has at times been cited as a mistake.

On the surface it's relatively easy to question Flick's qualifications for the Hall of Fame. Although he played 13 seasons in the majors, he was mostly inactive in three of those seasons, leaving him with barely more playing time than the minimum requirement of ten years. And while Flick's .313 career batting average ranks relatively high in the all-time ranks, he did not consistently stand out in any of the major batting categories. He won one batting crown, led the league in runs scored once, and in stolen bases twice. Although he led the league in triples three times, since the end of Deadball Era that category has become viewed as sort of a quirky stat that is more a mark of speed afoot than long-ball hitting ability.

To truly appreciate Flick's talent, it is necessary to do a little digging. Flick's ability was somewhat hidden in a couple of ways. First, although Elmer was one of the better hitters in baseball for ten years, he was never the best hitter on his own team. With the Phillies both Ed Delahanty and Nap Lajoie were justly recognized as better hitters; with Cleveland Lajoie was better. Elmer was often among the top hitters in his league, but the only time he won the batting championship was when he hit "that puny .306" in 1905. And while Elmer twice led the league in stolen bases, the speed merchant on the Cleveland team was Harry Bay. As a result, Elmer received significantly less attention from the baseball press than he might have received on other teams. Secondly, Elmer was a versatile hitter who helped his team in a number of ways that weren't apparent in the statistics available to most fans until recent decades. Elmer's batting averages earned him a reputation as a good hitter, and the writers of his day noted his speed, his patience at bat and his extra-base hit totals. But there were no statistics at the time that adequately reflected the totality of his offensive talents.

If he were still alive, Elmer might be surprised at the summary of his batting record currently listed in baseball reference sources. Most of his batting averages are different than those listed while he was playing—varying by a few percentage points up or down—and his extra-base hit and stolen base totals have changed slightly. Flick's trivia-question 1905 average is now listed at .308, rather than .306, and his 1900 average was revised downward, from the .378 he recalled to .367. More importantly, new categories have been added that capture much better than the statistics of his day just how good a player Flick was. When he batted in the middle of the batting order, rather than at the top, he excelled at driving in runs, a statistic not compiled in his day. Modern statistics, such as on-base percentage, slugging percentage, OPS (On-Base-Plus-Slugging-Percentage), as well as runs batted in, show clearly that he was one of the best hitters in baseball from 1898 through 1907.

Take, for example, Flick's 1898 rookie season. Elmer hit .302 that year, a solid average but only the fourth-best on his own team. But with Flick, the closer you examine his record the better it looks. While his batting average wasn't among the top 20 in the league, Elmer walked 86 times and was hit by a pitch 15 times. He had the fourth-best on-base percentage in the league (.430). Elmer also rapped out 13 triples and eight home runs, to rank seventh and sixth in the league in those categories. He had the sixth-best slugging percentage in the league (.448). His OPS, a good short-hand indicator of overall batting effectiveness, was the third-best in the league, trailing only Hamilton and Delahanty.

It was like that for Elmer throughout the ten healthy years of his career. He combined a top-notch batting average with enough patience to draw a good number of walks and enough power to rank high in total bases. He seldom led the league in any category, but his name is sprinkled throughout the list of leaders every year. The following are the number of times he finished among the league's top hitters in major offensive categories during his ten healthy years:

Category	*Top Ten*	*Top Five*
Batting Average	seven times	four times
On-Base Percentage	eight times	six times
Slugging Percentage	seven times	six times
OPS	seven times	six times
Total Bases	seven times	six times
Doubles	five times	three times
Triples	nine times	six times
Home Runs	six times	three times
Runs Scored	six times	twice
Runs Batted In	five times	once
Stolen Bases	six times	three times

In his book *The New Bill James Historical Baseball Abstract*, Bill James rated players by "win shares," based on a statistical system he devised. James created a list of the top 100 players at each position based on his system, reserving some wiggle room for subjective evaluation. His list includes career win share totals for each player and win share totals for each player's top three and top five seasons, as well as a career win share projection for a 162-game season. James ranks Flick number 23 among the game's right fielders. Just ahead of him at numbers 21 and 22 are Tony Oliva and Dwight Evans; just behind him at numbers 24 and 25 are Rusty Staub and Pedro Guerrero.

When the focus is narrowed, however, Flick moves up in the rankings. (The following comments are the author's and are based solely on the number of win shares—James does not rank or comment further than Flick's number 23 ranking). Flick's win-share total for his top five years puts him number ten among right fielders. Only two of the players with higher totals than Elmer's are not in the Hall of Fame. One is Pete Rose, who certainly had a Hall-of-Fame career. The other is Ken Singleton, who almost certainly did not. If the focus is narrowed further, to win shares per 162 games, only one player rates ahead of Flick. That player is Babe Ruth. There are two matters that should be noted about this last ranking. First, Barry Bonds was not included in the rankings. Second, while James' system yielded this result, it is clearly a statistical aberration that overstates Flick's performance.[52]

The point is that Flick was a top-flight player during his ten healthy years. He had a short career by Hall of Fame standards. His place in the Hall of Fame can legitimately be questioned based on the length of his career. It is much harder to question it based solely on his performance during the years he played.

Flick was 87 years old in 1963, when he was selected for the Hall of Fame. Despite his advanced age he was able to travel to Cooperstown for the induction ceremony. Commissioner Ford Frick introduced him as an "eternally young 87 year old." Elmer hadn't planned on making a speech, but as he accepted his plaque he became aware that he was expected to say a few words. He thanked the Commissioner, saying, "I was introduced as being young, but I don't think I look it the way I walk with a cane. This is a bigger day than any I have ever had before. I'm not going to try to find words to explain what the Hall of Fame means to everyone in baseball." He concluded his short speech by saying, "This is America. I did my best, and results came along." Later, after the ceremony ended and he had a chance to look over his Hall of Fame plaque, which listed some of his accomplishments, Elmer smiled. "I guess I was a pretty fair player at that," he said.[53]

Oh, What a Relief: New York

Clark Griffith was not afraid to "think outside the box." In 1905 he is credited with two innovations that impacted the way baseball was played in the Deadball Era and beyond. One we have already mentioned. He decided in spring training to make the squeeze play a part of his team's routine strategy. "Clark Griffith has taught his band of Highlanders a play that has won a couple of practice games for them," a reporter noted. "Griffith claims it's a great thing with one run needed to tie or win, and the team hitting lightly. He calls it 'the squeeze' because it should be tried only when in a tight place." The *Boston Globe's* Tim Murnane later explained that the play was old, "but certainly has been perfected by the Highlanders." It did not take long before most of the major league teams had incorporated it into their tactics, but baseball reporters continued to identify the play with Griffith and his team, one referring to it as "Griffith's famed play."[54]

New York (71-78)

Regular Lineup	AVG	OBP	SLG	R	RBI	SB
Patsy Dougherty, lf	.263	.319	.335	56	29	17
or Ed Hahn, of	.319	.426	.350	32	11	1
Willie Keeler, rf	.302	.357	.363	81	38	19
Kid Elberfeld, ss	.262	.329	.318	48	53	18
Jimmy Williams, 2b	.228	.306	.343	54	62	14
Hal Chase, 1b	.249	.277	.329	60	49	22
Joe Yeager, 3b	.267	.330	.342	54	42	8
or Wid Conroy, inf-lf	.273	.329	.395	55	25	25
Dave Fultz, cf	.232	.308	.277	49	42	44
Red Kleinow, c	.221	.284	.281	23	24	7
or Deacon McGuire, c	.219	.291	.268	9	33	3

Leading Pitchers	W	L	Pct	IP	H	ERA
Al Orth	18	16	.529	305.3	273	2.86
Jack Chesbro	19	15	.559	303.3	262	2.20
Bill Hogg	9	13	.409	205	178	3.20
Jack Powell*	10	14	.417	231	236	3.27
Clark Griffith	9	6	.600	101.7	82	1.68
Ambrose Puttmann	2	7	.222	86.3	79	4.27

*Includes record with St. Louis

The other innovation was not planned, but more or less forced on Griffith by the brittleness of his 1905 pitching staff. The previous year Jack Chesbro and Jack Powell had shouldered very heavy workloads, the two combining for 845 innings out of 1381 pitched by the entire Highlander staff. Both men struggled to even pitch at the outset of the 1905 season. Chesbro started the opening game against Washington. He seemed ready to have another fine season, as he held Washington to five hits and struck out seven batters in a 4–2 victory. His next outing did not go all that well. He gave up seven runs and 14 hits in a 7–6 loss to Philadelphia. The weather was quite unpleasant, a strong, cold wind sweeping over the field as "Happy Jack" and Eddie Plank both struggled against the elements. Two days later he was sent back to the mound to face Washington, again in nasty weather.

This time the game was played despite a steady rain, and with a brisk wind blowing. Soon pools of water formed on the field. In the top of the fourth Chesbro stopped the game momentarily so he could exchange his soggy glove for a dry one. Washington scored three runs in that inning, after which the game was called.[55]

Chesbro evidently injured his arm in this game. Later in the season, responding to critics who blamed the spitball for his sore arm, Jack insisted that report was erroneous, that he hurt his arm pitching in the rain. Five days after the rained-out game, Chesbro took the mound again even though, a reporter noted, his arm "has not been in the best of shape recently." He blanked the A's for seven innings, but lost his effectiveness in the eighth, giving up a walk and two singles before being relieved by Powell. The next day his arm was so sore from the shoulder to the elbow that he "couldn't stand the pain of usual massage and the electric treatment was decided on."[56]

This being the Deadball Era, when pitchers were not supposed to let a little pain get in the way of taking their normal turn, Happy Jack didn't remain on the sidelines very long. A week later he pitched against Boston, allowing only two runs in seven innings before giving way to a reliever. That outing was so successful that Griffith started him again on just two days' rest. Not surprisingly, the sore-armed twirler's "soup bone" gave out after three innings.[57] At that point both the intrepid pitcher and his manager seemed to realize that some time off was needed. Chesbro rested for about four weeks before returning. For about a month after that he required some careful handling, being relieved in several starts because he didn't seem to have his normal stuff. In July the summer heat, which in the Deadball Era was considered a panacea for healing veteran pitching arms, did its magic. Chesbro pitched well in most of his outings through the remainder of the year.

On the surface Chesbro's year doesn't look too bad. He tied for ninth highest number of wins in the league (19), had the tenth best ERA (2.20), and ranked ninth in strikeouts per nine innings (4.6). But whereas previously he had finished almost every game he started each season, in 1905 he completed only 24 of 38 starts. And several of his appearances were ugly affairs in which he was hit pretty hard.

Powell's case was slightly different than Chesbro's. His complaint was that he had a "kink" in his arm – that is, that he was unable to get loose and use his natural, easy delivery. He blamed the chilly Northeastern weather. "I have had no trouble with my arm," he told a reporter in late May. "And as soon as the weather warms up I'll get to going.... Our park is on the Hudson River and the spring breezes are cutting and chilly. I did not have a sweat until I came to St. Louis and no pitcher can do himself justice until he perspires freely while in action." Griffith used Powell primarily as a reliever the first month of the season. Jack lost his only two starts over that period, giving up eight runs on 14 hits to the A's in one of them and losing 4–2 to Boston in the other game, in which a reporter said he "did not have enough speed to break a pane of glass."[58]

In mid–May Griffith seemed ready to use Powell as a starter on a regular basis, but Jack didn't pitch well enough to continue very long in that role. From then until mid–September he was used in relief along with Griffith and the Highlanders' younger pitchers, and plugged in for starts seemingly at the manager's whim. On September 11, the unhappy Powell was sold to the St. Louis Browns, his former team. That winter Jack complained about the way he was used in New York. "Griffith certainly adopted wrong tactics with me," he said. "As soon as I would give a base on balls or two or a couple of hits was made off me in an inning, I would be benched. Why, I have always begged to be kept on the firing line when the score was against me. All the managers I worked for except Griffith gave me my way, and many a game have I saved that seemed hopelessly lost." Powell predicted he would do much better with the Browns, which he did in terms of pitching effectively, if not so much in wins.[59]

Powell's complaint went to the crux of Griffith's innovative approach to using his staff. Other managers of the era, faced with the loss of a couple reliable starters, would have simply substituted other men in their places and let them pitch their games. Griffith didn't do that. If he didn't think his pitcher had good stuff, he would take him out and send in another man to try his luck. Similarly, if the Highlanders trailed by a run or two and the pitcher was due to bat in the middle of a rally, Griff might decide to send up a pinch-hitter, necessitating the use of a reliever. This is what managers have done for a century now, but that wasn't the way pitchers were handled before 1905. Then the starting pitcher was given the ball and the game was in his hands, period. About 85 to 90 percent of starts resulted in complete games. In 1905 Highlanders pitchers completed what they began only 58 percent of the time.

Griffith used almost all of his staff in relief roles. The two exceptions were Chesbro and Al Orth, who each relieved in only three games. Everybody else had about the same number of relief appearances as starts, except for Griff himself. The Old Fox relieved in 18 of the 25 games he pitched. The wide distribution of relief appearances played a part in another unusual feature of the Highlanders' pitching in 1905. The staff really had no rotation to speak of. Orth and Chesbro—once he recovered (more or less) from his sore arm—started regularly. Powell and rookie Bill Hogg slipped in and out of the rotation during the course of the season, Powell starting 23 games and Hogg 22. Ambrose Puttmann started nine times and Griffith seven. Puttmann also served as a left-handed relief man, appearing in eight games in that role. Doc Newton, who was recalled from the minor leagues in August, filled a role similar to Puttmann's over the final two months of the season.

Another unusual feature of Griffith's use of relievers was the high number of innings pitched by the relievers when they were called into action. Of 64 games in which Griff took out the starting pitcher, relief pitchers (usually one) pitched five innings or more in 24 games. In 20 other games relievers pitched either three or four innings. Relief duties were so widespread among members of the Highlanders' pitching staff that it is difficult to discern a pattern to Griff's strategy. The only guiding principal that emerges is that if the Old Fox thought his starter didn't have good stuff he was going to get a relatively quick hook.

The 88 complete games the Highlander staff pitched in 1905 was 25 fewer than any other major league team. (Pittsburgh's staff completed 113 for Fred Clarke; John McGraw and Connie Mack each let their starters finish 117.) Griffith's strategy of fully employing his pitching staff through frequent use of relief pitchers was not duplicated by other managers right away. His strategy did not spark a revolution in the use of pitchers. But it apparently was the beginning of an evolutionary change. The number of complete games started to decline slowly each year after 1905. By 1911 a staff total of 88 complete games would become about the median for a major league pitching staff.

Mission Accomplished! Washington

Washington (64–87)

Regular Lineup	AVG	OBP	SLG	R	RBI	SB
Charlie Jones, cf	.208	.254	.267	68	41	24
Hunter Hill, 3b	.209	.278	.254	37	24	10
or Rabbitt Nill, 3b-2b	.182	.269	.251	46	31	12
Charlie Hickman, 2b*	.277	.311	.405	69	66	6
or Jim Mullin, 2b	.190	.214	.307	18	13	5
John Anderson, rf**	.279	.323	.361	62	52	31
Frank Huelsman, lf	.271	.333	.397	48	62	11
or Punch Knoll, of	.213	.247	.295	24	29	3
Jake Stahl, 1b	.250	.311	.371	66	66	41
Joe Cassidy, ss	.215	.250	.262	67	43	23
Mike Heydon, c	.192	.261	.265	20	26	5
or Malachi Kittridge, c	.164	.213	.197	16	14	1

Leading Pitchers	W	L	Pct	IP	H	ERA
Casey Patten	14	21	.400	309.7	300	3.14
Tom Hughes	17	20	.459	291.3	239	2.35
Jack Townsend	7	16	.304	263	247	2.63
Barney Wolfe	9	14	.391	182	162	2.57
Beany Jacobson	7	8	.467	144.3	139	3.30
Cy Falkenberg	7	2	.778	75.3	71	3.82

*Includes record with Detroit
**Includes record with New York

Desperate times call for desperate measures.

Given the team's terrible record in 1904, it was obvious some changes were in order for the Washington franchise. After 18 months spent under the stewardship of Ban Johnson and the American League, the team was turned over to a group of local owners. That was a start, but since the businessmen involved in the deal were too old and not talented enough to score many victories on the ball field, more had to be done. The next step was to follow the time-honored tradition of bringing in a new manager. So Patsy Donovan was out; Jake Stahl, a bright 26-year-old college graduate with less than two years of major league experience, was in. After that it was time to get serious. The team nickname, the Senators, had too long been associated with losing. It had to go. Fans were invited to help choose a new one. They voted for "Nationals," a name used in the good old days of the 1870s and 1880s, when Washington teams bearing that moniker had actually been winners.

And just to ensure that the players would try hard to win—as if they hadn't been doing that—the new owners promised a $1,000 bonus to be divided by the players if the team rose as high as seventh place in the standings. An additional $50 was to be tacked on for each additional rung the team climbed up.[60]

Although it might appear that these measures would fall short of bringing about a marked increase in performance, the first month of the 1905 season seemed to show they had wildly exceeded anyone's expectations. After losing their first three games the Senators—oops, make that the Nationals—won ten of the next 13 to move into first place. They remained at the head of the American League procession until May 11. Manager Jake Stahl was being hailed as a "born leader," and when the team returned from a brief road trip their fans filled the park. Upon receiving praise for the club's great start, Stahl modestly attributed the teams' success to his pitchers. "All of them have been doing good work. Then they have been receiving some elegant support, for the team is batting in timely form, just when runs are needed, and we have wasted few hits this season. Besides, our fielding is of the best. We are playing good ball." The reporter who interviewed

Stahl noted that Stahl's players considered him one of the top managers, and added, "the youngest manager in major league baseball has one proud distinction, viz., he has shown a few of the veterans how the game can be played and with success."[61]

The Nationals' success was well received all around the circuit. "No young player in either league gives more promise of soon becoming one of the stars of the baseball world than youthful Joe Cassidy," said a Boston writer. "Cassidy has been a sensation since he made his debut with Washington last year.... He is a slightly built chap, but covers an immense lot of ground and hits the ball hard." In Philadelphia three of the other young Nationals drew praise. "Hill, Nill, and Knoll, besides keeping the letter L reasonably busy, fretted our southpaw much," wrote Charley Dryden. "Mr. Hill, who hails from the knolls of Texas, was there with two singles, and Mr. Knolls, from the hills of Tennessee, whacked off a pair of bruising doubles. Mr. Nill grasped a couple of our timely misplays and scored twice." Casey Patten, Beany Jacobson, and Jack Townsend, all employing the nefarious spitball, were giving the batters fits. Townsend, nicknamed the "Delaware Peach" by baseball writers, had a pet name for his spitter. "He calls it the Delaware peach seed," said a Washington reporter. "One peculiarity of the peach seed delivery is the way it has of shrinking as the fooler nears the plate. It grows invisible, and being moist at the same time, the slaughter is fearful."[62]

It wasn't long, however, before reality began setting in. The Nationals weren't hitting very well even while they were marching into first place. The team was getting by on good pitching, great defense, and more than their share of luck. Their young infield, which performed brilliantly in the early going, started making more of the mental and physical errors expected from inexperienced players. The spitball began playing havoc with Patten's arm and Townsend's control. Jacobson came down with appendicitis. The Nationals started drifting down the standings, bumping into the cellar in June.

In mid-summer Washington's new ownership decided something needed to be done to get some hitters into the team's lineup. At the end of May, John Anderson was purchased from New York. A month later Charlie Hickman came from Detroit. Both men could hit, though they had deficiencies in other parts of their game. Together with Jake Stahl and outfielder Frank Huelsman, they gave the Nationals four big guys who could sting the ball. Noting the size of these four men, a Detroit reporter quipped that it looked like Stahl was configuring the Nationals along the lines of a football team.[63] Later Stahl added another big player, pitcher Cy Falkenberg, who could have been a basketball player since he stood 6'5" tall.

The highlight of the year may have been Tom Hughes' pitching against the Cleveland Naps. Long Tom started ten games against "Larry's Larrupers." His record was a creditable 6-4 in those games. Of his six wins five were shutouts. In August he pitched back-to-back two-hit shutouts against the Naps, three days apart, fanning ten men in one of those games and six in the other. Hughes pitched one other shutout, against Detroit, giving him a total of six for the season, the third highest total in the league.

After the Nationals dropped into last place in June they stayed there only for a couple of days before edging into seventh, ahead of the St. Louis Browns. Those two teams traded places a few times over the next six weeks. On July 25, the Nationals began a streak in which they won 11 of 13 games, moving five games ahead of the Browns. That lead held up to the end of the season (though, of course, the Nationals did not move any higher in the standings than seventh.)

True to their word, after the season ended the Nationals' ownership group handed out a bonus of $1,000 to the Washington players. The team had accomplished the goal laid out for them at the beginning of the season—escaping last place.[64]

The Man for the Job: St. Louis

Harry Howell brimmed with confidence. When Jack Chesbro became the wonder of the baseball world because of the spitball, it was inevitable that Harry would give the pitch a try. And likely he would master it.

St. Louis (54–99)

Regular Lineup	AVG	OBP	SLG	R	RBI	SB
George Stone, lf	.296	.347	.410	76	52	26
Ike Rockenfield, 2b	.217	.340	.255	40	16	11
or Charlie Starr, 2b	.206	.260	.206	9	6	0
Emil Frisk, rf	.261	.342	.336	58	36	7
or Ike Van Zandt, of	.233	.252	.295	31	20	7
Bobby Wallace, ss	.271	.324	.349	67	59	13
Tom Jones, 1b	.242	.290	.282	44	48	19
Harry Gleason, 3b	.217	.269	.262	45	57	23
Ben Koehler, cf	.237	.285	.297	55	47	22
or Tubby Spencer, c	.235	.285	.278	6	11	2
or Frank Roth, c	.234	.274	.262	9	7	1

Leading Pitchers	W	L	Pct	IP	H	ERA
Harry Howell	15	22	.405	323	252	1.98
Fred Glade	6	25	.194	275	257	2.81
Barney Pelty	14	14	.500	258.7	222	2.75

Leading Pitchers	W	L	Pct	IP	H	ERA
Willie Sudhoff	10	20	.333	244	222	2.99
Jim Buchanan	5	9	.357	141	149	3.50
Cy Morgan	2	5	.286	77.3	82	3.61

Harry literally grew up with a baseball in his hands. His father had played with the Eckford's, one of the top teams in baseball's early years. Harry started learning the game as soon as he was old enough to hold a bat and ball. In 1898 he obtained his first job in professional baseball from Jack Chapman, who owned the Meriden team in the Connecticut League. "I had to give him a great game of talk before I could persuade him to take me along," Howell later said. "I told him I could stand in the pitcher's box and put a ball through a six inch ring suspended above the plate five times out of six. Chapman told me I was either a liar or a phenom, and after trying me he took me to Meriden with him."[65]

Howell turned out to be somewhat of a phenom, going 18–13 with Meriden. It earned him a shot with a major league team. He was sold to the Brooklyn-Baltimore franchise of the National League, which assigned him to their Baltimore side. Harry immediately took the opportunity to send a letter to Baltimore manager John McGraw, who shared it with Baltimore reporter Frank Patterson. "Howell writes that that he not only expects to be among the league's greatest pitchers, but also among the leading batters, and feels that he will find it easy to hit above .300," Patterson wrote. "How is that for a youngster? He says he will be with Brooklyn next year as Hanlon will be glad enough to get him, after the record he expects to make this season. Here's hoping that Mr. Howell may be all and more than he expects to be. If he is, we will pitch him every other game and win the pennant sure."[66]

Once again, Harry delivered on his promise—more or less. As late as August he had the best won-lost record in the National League, winning nine of his first ten decisions. But it appears he benefited from a generous portion of good luck. In that tabulation of his record, he was awarded victories in two games in which he was taken out of the box while trailing. Also a few of his wins were more a result of good Baltimore hitting rather than his pitching.[67] Harry finished the season with a record shown in modern listings as 13–8, which probably excludes any games in which he was taken out while trailing the opposition. Nevertheless, his performance was good enough for Ned Hanlon to keep him with the Brooklyn Superbas when the National League reduced to eight teams in 1900, eliminating the Baltimore team, along with three others.

After being used essentially as an extra pitcher by Hanlon in 1900, starting ten games and relieving in 11 while going 6–5, Harry jumped to

Baltimore in 1901, reuniting with his previous manager, McGraw, who started him regularly and also used him in a utility role. Howell went 14–21 as a pitcher and played 18 games at other positions. When McGraw abandoned the Orioles midway through the next season, many of his top players followed him to the National League, jumping either to New York or Cincinnati. Their absence enabled Howell to demonstrate his versatility. He volunteered to play wherever his new manager, Wilbert Robinson, needed him. Robby needed players everywhere, so Harry played everywhere, catcher excepted. In addition to pitching 26 games, in which he posted a 9–15 record—not that bad considering the makeshift character of the post–July Orioles—he played 45 games in the field and put up a .268 batting average.

The Orioles franchise moved to New York in 1903. Harry, of course, went with it. American League president Ban Johnson stocked the Highlanders with as many good players as he could acquire, so Howell was again relegated to a secondary role on the pitching staff. He pitched fairly well, going 9–6, but started only 15 games, while relieving in ten. His time in New York, however, proved to be valuable for Harry's career. It was there that he observed Chesbro trying to master the spitball. Harry tried the pitch himself, but did not learn to control it until the last few weeks of the 1904 season, by which time he was in St. Louis.[68]

Harry went to St. Louis as part of a deal for Jack Powell. Newspaper descriptions of the transaction wouldn't have done much to boost Howell's ego. "Secretary Hedges has sold Powell to the New York club for $6,000 and to give the transaction the semblance of a deal Howell comes to the St. Louis club," reported *The Sporting News*. After describing why St. Louis had to make the trade, the publication concluded, "Howell has the best wishes of St. Louisans who trust that Powell will be the Highlanders' premier pitcher, but Harry is far from the first flight of twirlers."[69] By the end of May, however, Harry had won over many of his critics. After he shut out the Athletics 2–0, besting Rube Waddell in a pitcher's duel, Charley Dryden of the *Philadelphia North American* remarked, "Howell simply put the Athletics in a can and pasted an appropriate label on the outside. Harry wants to live down the rumor that he figured as 80 cents in the deal for Powell. He is much stronger than that. When a man buys a suit of clothes the merchant sometimes throws in a pair of suspenders. This is more like it, for Howell has done a lot to brace the Browns."

Then Dryden analyzed Harry's methods. "How does Howell do it? Easiest thing in the world. The next time he's on the slab just study his method. He does it all with his trousers. Before the delivery he stands hitching at the bloomers, after the manner of the stage sailor. Then when Harry stops hitching to pitch, the batsman is absorbed in the trousers, waiting for them to fall off, and forgets to swing fairly at the ball. The batsman hits it where somebody is instead of ain't."[70] Near the end of the season, of course, Harry came up with a more efficient way of putting away batters, having, of course, mastered the spitball.

Harry quickly became one of the most heralded "purveyors of the vapor float." In his first outing in 1905 he shut out Chicago for ten innings before losing in the 11th on a walk, sacrifice, and throwing error following a short passed ball. Harry followed up with another 11-inning game, this time shutting out Cleveland's hard-hitting Naps, 1–0. The White Sox manager, Fielder Jones, claimed Harry had "the most complete control of the spitball of any pitcher in the country, not excepting Jack Chesbro."[71] But Howell encountered the same issues with the pitch as other spitballers. After completely dominating the Naps the first time he faced them, in their second confrontation Howell lasted only five innings, allowing six runs on eight hits. The Naps had applied licorice to the ball, making it so sticky that Harry could not throw the spitball. A couple starts later Detroit tried the same tactic, but in that game the umpire threw out the licorice-coated ball. Harry won the game 9–4.[72]

There were other games in which Howell lost control of his spitter even though the opposition did not resort to substances such as licorice or mustard oil. That happened to all spitball pitchers. Harry also suffered from poor throws by the fielders behind him because they could not control the slippery ball. Harry may have had more incidents of that sort because of the amount of saliva he applied to the ball. He chewed slippery elm to produce a steady supply of saliva. Eddie Collins remarked that "Howell used so much slippery elm we could see the foam on his lips and on hot days some of the boys thought he was about to go mad."[73] Like all spitball pitchers, Harry induced many ground balls. In one of his games the Browns had 20 assists.[74] While, in general, that was a good thing, for a Browns pitcher it was a mixed blessing. The infield supporting them had "the King of Shortstops" in Bobby Wallace and two of the worst-fielding players in the league at second and third bases. They booted a lot of plays, and even Wallace had a comparatively large number of errors, many coming on plays where he would have normally yielded to one of the other infielders. As a result, Harry's excellent earned run average (1.98) told only part of the story of his pitching in 1905. The other part was 38 unearned runs scored off his pitching, giving him an average of 3.04 runs scored each nine innings. That part of the story goes a long way toward explaining his 15–22 record in 1905.

Harry continued to be one of the league's top pitchers through the 1908 season, posting earned run averages below 2.00 in two of the next three seasons. In 1909 he injured his shoulder taking infield practice at third base, bringing his pitching career to an end. After trying to rehabilitate the injury for a year, he had surgery in 1910, but the operation failed to restore his arm sufficiently to resume pitching. Ever resourceful, Harry extended his career one more season by playing the infield for Louisville and St. Paul of the American Association in 1911.[75]

"The Matty Show": 1905 World Series

After New York refused to play an American League team in a post-season series following the 1904 season, the presidents of the National and American leagues, got together with Garry Herrmann of the National Commission to establish rules for an annual post-season meeting between the champions of the two leagues. This time John T. Brush went along with the idea, undoubtedly swayed by the prospect of pocketing a huge wad of dollar bills from the series.[76] Baseball fans expected to see another set of hard-fought games between the two league champions, the New York Giants and the Philadelphia Athletics. What they got was a very convincing demonstration that Christy Mathewson was not just a great pitcher—he was a GREAT pitcher.

The opening game was played in Philadelphia before a sell-out crowd of 17,955 fans, who overflowed into the outfield bringing into play ground rules allowing only two bases on fly balls hit into the crowd. Such conditions at times led to high-scoring games, but neither Mathewson nor Eddie Plank was bothered too much by them. Matty allowed only four hits, walked none and struck out five A's. Three of the A's hits were doubles, two of them leading off innings. Matty wasn't fazed, however. In the sixth inning, after Ossee Schrecongost led off with a double and was sacrificed to third, he struck out Danny Murphy and got Monte Cross on a grounder to third. In the eighth Murphy started the inning by lining a double into the crowd. Mathewson responded by fanning Cross, retiring Schreck on a fly to right field, and whiffing Plank to end the inning. The A's third double was by Harry Davis, with two men out in the bottom of the ninth. Matty induced Lave Cross to bounce a grounder to shortstop and the game was over.

The Giants gave Mathewson a lead by scoring two runs in the fifth. Matty led off with a single over second base. He was forced by Roger Bresnahan, who promptly stole second. After George Browne popped to Monte Cross for the second out, Mike Donlin drove in Bresnahan with a double into left field. Dan McGann drew a walk. Sam Mertes scored Donlin with a double into the crowd in center field. New York scored an insurance run in the ninth. Billy Gilbert singled past Monte Cross and was sacrificed to second by Mathewson. Bresnahan, who was to be exceeded only by Matty as the star of the series, dribbled a single through the middle, bringing Gilbert home.[77]

Game two, played in New York, attracted another sell-out crowd. Attendance was announced as over 30,000 by the Giants' management, but the official count was revealed to be 24,187 when it came to paying the players their share of the proceeds. This game also resulted in a four-hit shutout, and a 3–0 score, but the winning twirler was the A's Chief Bender, who fanned nine Giants, while walking three. Bris Lord did some clutch hitting for the Athletics, driving in two of their three runs.

It was back to Philadelphia for game three. Mathewson, pitching on two days' rest, threw another four-hit shutout, this time in a lop-sided 9–0 win. He struck out eight batters, walked one and hit one. Danny Murphy had a rough game, making three costly errors, two of them in the five-run fifth inning.

Joe McGinnity, who had lost game two to Chief Bender, continued the shutout streak in game four, stopping the A's on five hits, 1–0. Eddie Plank allowed the Giants only four hits. Once again faulty fielding hurt the A's. The Giants' only run

Christy Mathewson demonstrated his great ability by throwing three shutouts against the Philadelphia Athletics in the 1905 World Series (Library of Congress).

scored in the fourth, when Monte Cross bobbled Mertes' grounder. After Dahlen flied out, Art Devlin advanced Mertes to second on a probable hit-and-run play, knocking a grounder that Plank fielded but only after it was too late to get a force play on Mertes. Gilbert, normally the Giants' weakest hitter, came through with a bad-hop single past Monte Cross, scoring Mertes with the game's only run.

With a 3–1 lead in the series, McGraw sent Mathewson to the mound in game five to finish off the A's. Pitching his third game in six days and on only one day's rest, Matty didn't quite do as well as in the first two games– he gave up five hits, rather than four, while pitching his third shutout of the series, beating Chief Bender 2–0. Once again weak-hitting Billy Gilbert got a key hit. In the fifth inning Bender walked Mertes and Dahlen to open the inning. Devlin sacrificed. Gilbert drove a fly ball deep enough to left field to score Mertes for the lead run. New York's second run came in the eighth. With one out Matty walked. Bresnahan drove the ball deep to left field for a ground-rule double. Browne followed with a hard grounder that Bender tried to field with his bare hand. He succeeded only in deflecting the ball to second baseman Murphy, whose only play was to first base as Matty scored the second run.[78]

Mathewson's performance was, of course, the sensation of the series. In 27 innings he allowed no runs and only 13 hits. Not one Athletic baserunner got past second base. In a year dominated by pitching nobody pitched better than Matty during the regular season, and he added an exclamation mark to the season with his World Series performance.

Five

1906, National League

An Historic Season—116–36! Chicago

In an interview before he left to return to his home in California after the 1905 season, Frank Chance said, "We need more good hitters. Of course our club at present is in great condition, and we haven't got a single kick, but we want none but the best stick handlers." Chance thought he might find the men he wanted among the Pacific Coast League players.[1] He found them, but not out west.

1906 National League Standings

Team	W	L	Pct.	GB
Chicago	116	36	.763	—
New York	96	56	.632	20
Pittsburgh	93	60	.608	23.5
Philadelphia	71	82	.464	45.5
Brooklyn	66	86	.434	50
Cincinnati	64	87	.424	51.5
St. Louis	52	98	.347	63
Boston	49	102	.325	66.5

He had already picked up a pretty good player in a deal arranged near the end of the season. The Cubs traded Jake Weimer, their top winner over the previous two seasons, to Cincinnati for third baseman Harry Steinfeldt and outfielder Jimmy Sebring. On paper the deal seemed to favor the Reds. Steinfeldt had fallen off in his batting the previous two years and missed many games because of sickness and injuries. Sebring was potentially a good hitter and a skilled outfielder, but he had jumped the Reds to play with his hometown Williamsport team in the outlaw Tri-State League.

At the winter meetings in December, Cubs owner Charles Murphy told reporters that when he had discussed prospective deals with Chance, the manager had told him, "I want just two men." Those two were Jimmy Sheckard of the Brooklyn Superbas and Pat Moran of the Boston Beaneaters. The Cubs swung deals for both men, though they paid a steep price for each of them. They sent four players to Brooklyn to get Sheckard. Gone were third baseman Doc Casey and right fielder Billy Maloney—both starters at their positions—Jack McCarthy, the team's substitute outfielder, and Buttons Briggs, who had started 20 games for the Cubs in 1905. For Moran, they sent Big Jeff Pfeffer, an outstanding pitching prospect who had gone 4-4 for the Cubs in 1905, and veteran catcher Jack O'Neill.[2]

Although the players the Cubs got in the deals were all good players, none seemed at the time to be the key to catching the Giants. Moran was a fine catcher, but he wasn't going to beat out Johnny Kling for the starting job in Chicago. Sheckard had enjoyed a good season in 1905, but had played inconsistently for the preceding three years. Sebring was an unknown quantity—it wasn't certain that he would even report to the Cubs, which he, in fact, refused to do. Steinfeldt, like Sheckard, had enjoyed a couple good seasons, but had not played consistently good ball over the course of his career, and had missed many games in 1904 and 1905 due to sickness and injuries.

As it turned out, Chance's judgment was right on the mark. The three veteran players obtained in the trades all contributed greatly to the team's historic success in 1906. And Sebring's failure to report had little impact. The man he might have replaced, Frank Schulte, had an excellent season in 1906 and went on to play 15 years in the major leagues.

The new acquisition who had the greatest impact in 1906 was Harry Steinfeldt. Coming into that season, if you were to ask a baseball man about Steiny, it is likely the first thing mentioned would be his throwing arm. He could zip the ball across the diamond faster than any other infielder. "That snap throw with which Steinfeldt hurls the ball from third to first, is in my humble opinion, the greatest I have ever seen," said veteran infielder Tom Daly. "If you will notice there is hardly any motion to Steinfeldt's arm when he delivers the ball, yet it shoots across the diamond at terrific speed. There are no players whom I have seen that are to be compared with Steinfeldt when it comes to throwing." Cincinnati baseball writer Charley Zuber made a similar comment. "I have been on the field on several occasions when Steinfeldt has made throws past where I was standing," Zuber wrote. "The ball fairly whistles through the air and goes almost on a straight line from his hand to the man to whom he is throwing."[3]

Chicago (116–36)

Name	AVG	OBP	SLG	R	RBI	SB
Jimmy Slagle, cf	.239	.324	.279	71	33	25
or Solly Hofman, ut	.256	.326	.328	30	20	13
Jimmy Sheckard, lf	.262	.349	.353	90	45	30
Wildfire Schulte, rf	.281	.324	.396	77	60	25
or Doc Gessler, of*	.250	.346	.319	11	14	7
Frank Chance, 1b	.319	.419	.430	103	71	57
Harry Steinfeldt, 3b	.327	.395	.430	81	83	29
Joe Tinker, ss	.233	.293	.289	75	64	30
Johnny Evers, 2b	.255	.305	.315	65	51	49
Johnny Kling, c	.312	.357	.420	45	46	14
or Pat Moran, c	.252	.281	.319	22	35	6

Leading Pitchers	W	L	Pct	IP	H	ERA
Mordecai Brown	26	6	.813	277.3	198	1.04
Jack Pfiester	20	8	.714	250.7	173	1.51
Ed Reulbach	19	4	.826	218	129	1.65
Carl Lundgren	17	6	.739	207.7	160	2.21
Jack Taylor**	20	12	.625	302.3	249	1.99
Orval Overall***	16	8	.667	226.3	193	2.74

*Includes record with Brooklyn
**Includes record with St. Louis
***Includes record with Cincinnati

Steinfeldt made his major league debut in 1898 at the age of 20. Cincinnati sports writers were intrigued by the gifted young player, confidently predicting a great future for him, but his role on the Reds in 1898 was only that of a utility player. Cincinnati had future Hall-of-Famer Bid McPhee at second base, fielding whiz Tom Corcoran at shortstop, and a solid veteran in Charlie Irwin at third base. The Reds were expected to contend for the National League pennant, and manager Buck Ewing did not intend to turn a key infield position over to a rookie. Steiny filled in at every infield position, including first base, and played 29 games in the outfield. He hit .295, which was only a decent average in 1898. Still, Cincinnati writers trumpeted him as the best utility player in baseball, and held high expectations for Steinfeldt's future.

Unfortunately, the next few years were disappointing ones for Steinfeldt. In 1899 he missed two months with malaria. His batting average dropped into the .240s and stayed there for two more years. McPhee retired after the 1899 season, Corcoran missed most of the 1901 season because of illness, and Irwin slumped and was traded to Brooklyn the same season. Yet Steinfeldt continued as a utility player, splitting his time between second and third. The high expectations for Steiny turned into disappointment. "This man Steinfeldt is a puzzle as a hitter," a writer noted. "He will bat like a Lajoie for a few weeks, and then fall to nothing. He stands up to the plate well, has a good swing and picks out good balls, yet he has never batted as he should."[4]

Steiny seems to have had a tendency to overswing. When he was hitting well, someone would point out that he had a nice short, snappy swing. Then he would slump again, only to rediscover the need to shorten his swing. After his rookie year Frank Selee said Steinfeldt was already a good hitter and would surely improve in the future. "He just snaps at the ball and does not make a long swing," Selee said. "He is a great youngster, and another year will make him a corker." But another year brought Steinfeldt a .246 average. A couple years later, Steinfeldt got into a hot streak with the bat. Cincinnati reporter J. Ed Grillo pointed out that Steiny had benefited from advice given to him by John McGraw, who had told him to lean back more and snap at the ball. But the hot streak ended and once again Steinfeldt's batting dropped off. In 1902 Steinfeldt was put on third base and allowed to stay there for the entire season. His hitting picked up somewhat. He raised his average to .278, but there still seemed to be room for improvement.

After watching Steinfeldt closely for the last couple months of the 1902 season, manager Joe Kelley told him the bat he was using was too heavy. During spring training of 1903 Kelley got Steiny to change bats and worked

Harry Steinfeldt was noted for his great throwing arm, a baseball reporter commenting that "the ball fairly whistles through the air" (Library of Congress).

with him on his swing. As before, the objective was to get him to cut down on his swing and use a shorter, snappier motion. Steinfeldt responded with the best season of his career up to that point, batting .312 and leading the league in doubles with 32.[5] As before, though, success at bat was a passing phenomenon for Steiny. His average dropped to .244 in 1904. That was the year in which he narrowly escaped disaster because of a natural gas leak in his hotel room furnace and then later suffered leg and arm injuries. Steiny played in only 99 games that season and in 114 the following season, when he raised his average to .271, but again suffered from injuries.

The trade sending Steinfeldt to Chicago was arranged before the 1905 season ended, although it didn't become official until late October. When a Cincinnati sportswriter asked about the deal during the Cubs' last swing through the Ohio city, Chance replied that he had been anxious to get Steinfeldt for some time and was very happy about having secured him. "We need a few men who can hit long flies at critical times," Chance told the reporter.[6] Steiny more than fulfilled his manager's expectations. He hit plenty of long flies, and a lot of them fell in for base hits.

The 1906 season was by far the best of Steinfeldt's career. His batting average was among the top five in the league during the entire season, and he led the league for most of August, before falling behind Honus Wagner. He finished with the second-highest batting average, as well as the fourth-best slugging percentage and sixth-highest on-base percentage. Steiny shared the league lead in RBIs with Joe Nealon, and was fifth in runs scored. He trailed only Wagner in total bases. He even led the league in the painful category of being hit by pitches.

Steinfeldt batted fifth in the Cubs batting order. His role was to drive in runners who were in scoring position and to contribute to rallies started by the men ahead of him. Jimmy Sheckard, Chance's other prize acquisition, had a completely different role, one suited to a man who fit the description related by former Cub executive Jim Hart. "In Sheckard," Hart said, the Cubs "now have the greatest living outfielder who has the Hanlon style of play down pat." The "Hanlon style of play" was basically a reference to scientific baseball as practiced in 1906. Sheckard was inserted in the all-important number two spot in the Cubs' batting order. His job was to move Jimmy Slagle down to second base, if Slagle was on first, as he often was, or to ignite a rally by getting on base himself.

Sheckard was much more at home doing that than he was being the man charged with making the key hit. As we mentioned above, when he inherited a leadership role with the Superbas in 1904, he responded with the worst season of his career. Hanlon helped Jimmy's individual performance by appointing him captain in 1905. Jimmy rebounded at bat and in the field, but became unpopular with his teammates. According to one of his ex-teammates, he became impatient with his fellow players, telling them they should not be looking for him to make the big plays, but should be making those plays themselves. Both Sheckard and many of his teammates welcomed his trade to Chicago.[7]

The addition of two accomplished batters, Schulte's emergence as a top hitter in the number three spot in the batting order, and Chance's continued excellence at bat and on the bases, gave the Cubs an offense unequaled by any other team in baseball. In May, the *Chicago Tribune* summarized a 5–1 victory over Pittsburgh by remarking, "The Murphys [Cubs]were smoking hot. Their brilliant, dashing, slashing style of play swept the Pirates off their feet at the first break." The "dashing" and "slashing" in that game referred to the relentless attack that became a hallmark of the Cubs' 1906 offense. In the fourth inning the Cubs got a run on back-to-back line drive doubles by Sheckard and Schulte, followed by a short fly to an open spot in left by Chance, which sent Schulte to third. Then Chance distracted the Pittsburgh pitcher by racing to second, facilitating a wild pitch that scored Schulte. Two innings later Slagle started by beating out a bunt. Sheckard sacrificed. Slagle scored on a single by Schulte to center, with Schulte moving up to second base on the throw home. Schulte then scored on Chance's ground ball single through the box.[8]

A week later the Cubs rolled over the Superbas, beating them 10–1. They trailed 1–0 in the second when Chance led off with a walk. He stole second. Steinfeldt waited out another base on balls and Joe Tinker sacrificed. Johnny Evers drove home the two baserunners with a double, and went to third on a short single by Johnny Kling. The Cubs' catcher then took off for second base on a double steal, arriving safely as Evers beat the return throw to the plate for another run. In the fifth Sheckard walked and stole both second and third bases. He scored when Chance placed the ball into short left, legging out the hit for a double. The boss Cub scored on a single by Steinfeldt, who stole second and scored on Evers' single. In total, the Cubs netted eight stolen bases in the game, taking advantage of the Brooklyn pitcher's inability to stop them from gaining long leads off first.[9]

The Cubs' attack featured aggressive play. They stole lots of bases, moved runners along with sacrifices and the hit-and-run, and tried to take advantage of any opening that presented itself. Sometimes the aggressive tactics backfired, but a few outs did not lessen the team's commitment to pushing the envelope. The day after their "dashing" and "slashing" play downed Pittsburgh, 5–1, the Cubs had two men cut down trying to take extra bases. Trailing 1–0 in the fourth, Steinfeldt singled. Tinker lined out a double, but Steiny was thrown out trying to score. Two innings later,

Schulte lined a hit to the outfield, but ran the hit into an out trying to stretch it into a double. Chance then smashed a long drive to center. He made three bases easily, but wasn't satisfied with a triple. Wagner's relay of Tommy Leach's throw seemed to be in time to get the Cub manager at home plate, but struck the umpire. The ruling on the play put Chance back on third base. He scored on a single by Steinfeldt. A wild pitch gave Steiny second base, but he wasn't content with that, continuing on to third base on the play, beating the startled catcher's throw. Tinker brought him home with a long fly to center field. After that display of relentless baserunning, the Cubs won the game in the next inning on a single, sacrifice, another wild pitch and a single—textbook baseball.[10]

Against the Giants, in a show-down series early in August, the Cubs went into the ninth inning tied 1–1. Sheckard led off the inning with a base on balls. After Schulte went out, Chance drew another walk. Both runners took off on a pitch to Steinfeldt, who tapped the ball slowly toward Giants pitcher Dummy Taylor, who threw to Dan McGann at first. By the time McGann got the ball, Sheckard was already half-way home. Jimmy easily beat the throw home, while Chance went from first to third on the play. After the game the Cubs players and their home town writers joked about whether they should call the play a "two-base hit squeeze" or a "quadruple steal."[11]

A few days later Chance's men introduced a new variation on an old tactic. Three times while bunting in obvious sacrifice situations, they tried to tap the ball past the men who were rushing in to field the ball. Tinker picked up two base hits that way and Chance got one. The play was used several times over the next couple of weeks, usually with good results, once leading to a double play.[12]

In addition to spicing up the Cubs' offense, the new men strengthened an already formidable defense. Steinfeldt led the National League third basemen in fielding percentage. Many baseball experts considered him the top fielding third baseman in the National League. Sheckard was a fine fielder and possessed an excellent arm. Perhaps best of all, he had no trouble playing in the sun field. One day Cincinnati manager Joe Kelley complained about the difficulty of playing left field in Chicago. "I wouldn't play the sun regularly for any money," said Kelley. "It hurts your eyes and makes you fall off in your hitting. Sheckard plays this field without glasses, but he hardly knows himself how he does it." Young Schulte was about as good in the field as Sheckard and also had a great arm. In a game against Philadelphia on July 31, the Phillies twice chose to hold a runner at third base, rather than challenging first Sheckard's arm and then Schulte's. The next day they threw caution to the wind and had two runners thrown out at the plate, one each by the two strong-armed outfielders.[13]

As good as the Cubs were on offense—they scored 79 more runs than any other National League team—and on defense, where they had a top-notch defender at every position (two at catcher) and led the league in fielding average by five percentage points, the most impressive part of the team may have been the pitching staff. Cubs pitchers combined for a team earned run average of 1.75—almost a run below the league average of 2.62, and the third-best in modern baseball history. (The lowest ERA was posted by the Cubs staff in 1907 [1.73] and the second-lowest [1.74] by the 1909 Cubs pitchers.) There were six hurlers who threw over 144 innings for the Cubs. Only one of them had an ERA over 2.00. And that was Carl Lundgren, who limped along with a won-lost record of 17–6, prevailing in only 73.9 percent of his decisions.

This was the season that Mordecai "Three-Finger" Brown established himself as the leading rival to Christy Mathewson for recognition as the National League's top pitcher. For this one season the honor was not up for debate. Brown won 26 games and lost only 6. Joe McGinnity won one more game than Mordecai, but lost twice as many. Teammate Ed Reulbach edged Brown out for the top won-lost percentage, going 19–4 (.826) to Mordecai's .813 figure. But Brown had the lowest ERA in the league (1.04). Only one other pitcher since 1893 has had a lower ERA, Dutch Leonard allowing only 0.96 runs per nine innings for the Boston Red Sox in 1914. Brown also led the league with nine shutouts. He threw two one-hitters, a two-hitter, and five three-hitters, thus allowing three or fewer hits in one-fourth of his starts. Mordecai's "WHIP" (walks and hits per inning pitched) was accordingly the lowest in the league at 0.934. Sy Sanborn of the *Chicago Tribune* called Brown a "pitching marvel," and compared his 1906 record favorably to that put up by Mathewson in 1905.[14]

Enjoying a great year in 1906, Mordecai "Three-Finger" Brown became the leading rival to Christy Mathewson for recognition as the National League's top pitcher (Library of Congress).

Brown was only one of six

pitchers who had outstanding records for the Cubs. It's a toss-up as to whether Jack Pfiester or Ed Reulbach was the next best Cub hurler. Pfiester posted a 1.51 ERA to Reulbach's 1.65, and won one more game, but Reulbach's 19–4 won-lost record was superior to Pfiester's 20–8. Pfiester's 0.941 WHIP was second only to Brown's, but Reulbach gave up only 5.3 hits per game to Pfiester's 6.2. Pfiester showed his overwhelming stuff on May 30, when he struck out 17 Cardinals in a 15-inning game, fanning 13 batters in the first nine innings.

Of course, this is just quibbling over details, tantamount to debating which flavor of ice cream is the yummiest. With the exception of Bob Wicker, who had a 3–5 record and 2.99 ERA when he was traded to Cincinnati, every pitcher on the staff pitched excellent ball. Jack Taylor and Orval Overall, whose records listed above include their totals with the Cardinals and Reds, respectively, both were 12–3 with the Cubs. Taylor's ERA for the Cubs was 1.83, Overall's was 1.88. Fred Beebe, who was sent to St. Louis in exchange for Taylor, had a 6–1 record when traded.

Given all the superlatives associated with their season, including the fact that they finished 20 games ahead of the second-place Giants, it's somewhat surprising to note that the Cubs did not pull away from the rest of the league until August. They broke even in their first 12 games, before launching a ten-game winning streak, which opened up only a short-lived, half-game lead over New York. The Cubs and Giants battled on pretty even terms through the month of May, with neither team being able to open up much of a lead over the other and with Pittsburgh and Philadelphia both needing only a hot streak to catch up. The Cubs edged into the lead on May 25, when Steinfeldt's triple brought a 2–1 win over Boston, while the Giants were losing to the weak Cardinals. They were clinging to a one-game lead when they arrived at the Polo Grounds on June 5 to open a four-game series with the Giants. Three-Finger Brown started the showdown with a convincing three-hit shutout, beating McGinnity 6–0. The next day Frank Schulte went five-for-six as the Cubs hammered Dummy Taylor, 11–3.

The third game loomed up as a pitchers' duel between Christy Mathewson and Pfiester. It didn't quite turn out that way. Matty, who was still feeling the effects of a serious illness contracted over the winter, failed to get a batter out. He walked Slagle to start the game. Sheckard and Schulte followed with singles and Chance reached first when Devlin's throw for a forceout on his grounder was too late to get Schulte at second. Steinfeldt came through with a single and Tinker with a double. Four runs were home, two men on base and still no outs. To stop the bleeding, McGraw rushed in his other star pitcher, the man he long had turned to in big games, Joe McGinnity. The Iron Man got Evers to hit a grounder to Bill Dahlen at shortstop. Dahlen threw to the plate to get Steinfeldt, but Steiny retreated, forcing a rundown on which he scored after third baseman Art Devlin's throw hit him in the back. Pat Moran followed with a double, scoring two more. More hits followed. The Cubs batted around against the two New York aces, and then two-thirds of the way through the order a second time. When the Giants came to bat in the bottom of the first, they trailed 11–0.

The next day the *New York Sun* noted, "The sixth inning of yesterday's ball game at the Polo Grounds was momentous. It was momentous, not because of what was done, but for what was not done. The Cubs did not score in that inning. It was the first inning of the game in which they did not score, and there were appreciative yells, possibly slightly tinged with derision." At that point the Cubs led by 18 runs. They added another tally two innings later. When the carnage ended, the Cubs had annihilated the Giants, 19–0.[15]

It was only one game, and New York came back to win the next game, but the thrashing of the Giants when both of their aces were on the mound changed the complexion of the pennant race. After the game, the *Tribune's* Sanborn remarked, "So great has become the worship of the Giants' prowess that it was thought nothing ever could beat them even without the great Mathewson in condition. This was the opinion in New York and outside, too, in some cases. But Chance and his men have shattered the Gotham idols, and it will be a long day before New Yorkers get over the humiliation of their pets in three out of the four games of their last series."

Sanborn concluded his verbal victory lap with a cautionary note. "Local fans already have consigned New York to the scrap heap and are watching the Pittsburgh scores more closely than those of McGraw's men. The Giants never have been under stiff pressure before, and what they will do is an unknown quantity, consequently it will be wise to suspend judgment until after another trip."[16] Caution was indeed the word of the day, for both the Giants and the Pirates shadowed the Cubs' pace through the rest of the summer.

The Cubs held only a 2½-game lead when they opened a six-game matchup against the Pirates with a July 4 doubleheader. In the first game Brown and Lefty Leifield both pitched one-hitters, the Cubs winning, 1–0, on their only hit–a single by Slagle–followed by a sacrifice and two infield grounders. They took the afternoon contest by the same score, Lundgren throwing a five-hitter and the only run coming in the same fashion as in the first game. Sheckard singled, went to second on a sacrifice, and scored when Chance's grounder bounced off the second baseman's glove. The Pirates hung on to split the four remaining games, but their best chance of overtaking the Cubs had passed them by.[17]

Chicago was 5½ games ahead when they visited the Polo Grounds for a four-game series in August. Time was running out on the Giants, and they responded by winning the first game 7–4, behind Mathewson. The Cubs bounced back, however, with a 3–1 victory. This was the game in which Sheckard scored from second base and Chance went from first to third on the "two-base hit squeeze/quadruple steal." McGraw was not on the field to witness the play, having been thrown out of the game earlier for arguing a call at home plate. The next day he refused to let the offending umpire enter the Polo Grounds, thus giving his rivals another win, this time by forfeit.[18] These two victories began a streak in which the Cubs won 37 of their next 39 games. When the streak ended, on September 18, they had built their lead up to 16 games over the Giants and 20½ over the Pirates and the only question was how far they would go in setting a new record for games won in a season.

The answer was, of course, that the Cubs would exceed the Giants' 1905 win total by ten games. Their 1906 won-lost record is still the best in modern baseball history. The Seattle Mariners matched their 116 wins in 2001, but needed 162 games to do it. Seattle's won-lost percentage of .716 pales in comparison to Chicago's .763, as does that posted by any other modern major league team. The next best percentage was posted by Pittsburgh in 1909 (110–42, .724). The 1954 Cleveland Indians own the best record in the American League (111–43, .721).

Bad Breaks: New York

Somehow it seems incongruous to describe a 96-win season as a disappointment. But that was undoubtedly how New York fans felt. Their team won ten games fewer in 1906 than they had the previous year, and they finished 20 games out of first place. The Giants' season started unraveling— again, if that term can be applied to a team that won so many games—before spring training began.

New York (96–56)

Name	AVG	OBP	SLG	R	RBI	SB
Roger Bresnahan, c-cf	.281	.419	.356	69	43	25
or Spike Shannon, lf	.254	.342	.279	42	25	18
George Browne, rf	.264	.304	.302	61	38	32
Dan McGann, 1b	.237	.344	.304	62	37	30
Sam Mertes, lf*	.241	.315	.329	57	52	31
or Mike Donlin, cf	.314	.371	.397	15	14	9

Name	AVG	OBP	SLG	R	RBI	SB
Bill Dahlen, ss	.240	.357	.297	63	49	16
Art Devlin, 3b	.299	.396	.390	76	65	54
Billy Gilbert, 2b	.231	.341	.257	44	27	22
or Sammy Strang, ut	.319	.423	.435	50	49	21
Frank Bowerman, c	.228	.274	.284	23	42	5
or Aleck Smith, c	.179	.207	.179	0	2	1

Leading Pitchers	W	L	Pct	IP	H	ERA
Joe McGinnity	27	12	.692	339.7	316	2.25
Christy Mathewson	22	12	.647	266.7	262	2.97
Hooks Wiltse	16	11	.593	249.3	227	2.27
Luther Taylor	17	9	.654	213	186	2.20
Red Ames	12	10	.545	203.3	166	2.66
Cecil Ferguson	2	0	1.000	52.3	43	2.58

*Includes record with St. Louis

Mike Donlin had been comparatively well-behaved throughout the 1905 season. One year of good conduct was about his limit. After the 1905 World Series a group of Giants went on a barnstorming trip in New Jersey. While they were in Trenton a group of businessmen held a banquet for the players. Afterwards Donlin had some drinks, becoming intoxicated. He got into an argument with a waiter and punched him in the jaw. Friends tried to intervene and they also became targets for his wild swings.[19] Later that fall Donlin joined teammate Billy Gilbert in running a saloon in Harlem. Mike wasn't the kind of guy who could stare temptation in the face every day without giving in to it—every day, more or less. He started drinking regularly. In February he became involved in a drunken incident on a train, in which he threatened a porter with a gun. He spent that night in jail, and had to pay a fine, but escaped further punishment.

Donlin's drinking continued in spring training, when McGraw was compelled to suspend him for several days. After the season started, however, Mike got his drinking under control well enough to play at his usual all-star level. He was batting .339 on May 15 when he got his leg twisted while sliding on a steal attempt. He broke his ankle and had to be carried off the field. By the time he returned to action in mid–September the Cubs had already locked up the pennant.[20]

A second, and possibly even more damaging, loss occurred during spring training. Christy Mathewson came down with an ailment that he at first thought was a cold, but which turned out to be nasal diphtheria. He was confined to his brother-in-law's home in New Jersey, and didn't join the Giants until the second week of the season. He made his debut on the mound on May 5, against the league's doormat, the Boston Beaneaters, allowing three runs in seven innings. He had some speed, but clearly lacked his normal strength. He pitched again nine days later, as McGraw began to use him regularly. But he was not the old Matty. A Pittsburgh writer remarked, "The famous twirler does not look like his old self. He is thin and wan and the flush of perfect health, which always adorned his cheeks, has given way before a sallowness that is not pleasant to see."[21]

Matty slowly recovered his strength as the season progressed, but as late as July 14 he was still getting batters out with his knowledge of their weaknesses and his skill in locating the ball. On that day he held the Cardinals to five hits while shutting them out 4–0. "It may be that the former champion of the pitchers has returned to his form. If so he just did arrive on Saturday [the day of the game]," remarked a St. Louis reporter. "There was nothing about his speed or curves that savored of former greatness. He had little of the one and much less of the other."[22] By early September, however, Matty's stuff seemed to improve, if strikeouts are evidence of that. In a 6–2 victory on September 6, he whiffed 14 Superbas. He fanned nine batters in his next start, against the Beaneaters, and eight Superbas in his following game. In his last five outings he returned to his more normal 1906 level of four Ks or less.

Forced to cope with Donlin's absence, McGraw made two deals to bring in new outfielders. On July 12, he shipped $12,000 to Cincinnati to obtain Cy Seymour, the 1905 batting champion. Seymour's batting average had dropped precipitately in 1906, but the real problem in Cincinnati was that Ned Hanlon wanted to school the Reds in his scientific baseball tactics, and Seymour wasn't that type of player. McGraw, on the other hand, was quite willing to accept Cy's periodic baserunning gaffes in exchange for his drives into the outfield gaps. Seymour hit .320 in 71 games for the Giants, after putting up only a .257 average while trying to adapt to Hanlon's style. The other outfielder brought to the Polo Grounds was Mike Shannon, who came from the Cardinals in exchange for Sam Mertes and utiltyman Doc Marshall. McGraw was trying to inject more speed into the Giant lineup and Shannon's game was built around speed. Mertes, on the other hand, had started to show his age (34). His batting average had dropped over 40 points, to .237, and McGraw undoubtedly wanted to unload him while he could still command a decent player in exchange.[23]

The Christy Mathewson who took the mound for the Giants in 1906 turned in a solid performance that would have made him the ace of most pitching staffs. But that was still a step or two below the first-tier Hall-of-Famer of former (and future) years. Joe McGinnity made up for part of the difference by returning to the form he had shown before 1905. Already 35 years old in 1906, the Iron Man pitched the second-highest number of innings in the National League and led the league in victories with 27. His ERA (2.25) was not outstanding in a season when six pitchers posted numbers under 2.00, but it was still very good considering the number of innings he pitched.

McGraw once again used one of his young pitchers as a designated reliever, again with the emphasis being to relieve the strain on other hurlers' arms rather than saving games. His 1905 designated "reliever," Claude Elliott, had been returned to the minor leagues. The new man given this role was Cecil Ferguson. McGraw used Ferguson in relief 21 times. The young pitcher finished 19 Giants games and is listed in modern statistical sources as the National League leader in saves with seven. But the reader should react to that stat with a slight chuckle. Fourteen of Ferguson's 21 relief appearances came while the Giants were trailing, usually by large scores. In six of the seven games in which he came in to "save" the game for the Giants, he was called on to preserve a lead of at least six runs. In one game he pitched the ninth inning of a 5–4 Giants victory–a legitimate save.

During the 1906 season the Giants followed their usual tactic of trying to browbeat favorable decisions from the umpires. In April, Brooklyn writer Abe Yager remarked, "Bresnahan kicked on the first ball pitched and kept it up with lots of assistance right through the game. They evidently propose to fight every inch of the way, those Giants." A few weeks later, after McGraw and two players were suspended for three days for vociferously arguing a call, another writer said, "The fact is, [National League] President Pulliam has been quite lenient. No other manager or players in the league would dare to go to the extremes that McGraw and his men have gone since the season opened, for the reason that they would have been pounced upon long ago. Complaints have been heard from every city in which the Giants have played thus far and the worst have come from their own grounds in Manhattan, where they have run roughshod over the umpires."

In mid–July Roger Bresnahan became upset with a fan who had been heckling him throughout a game in Chicago. Bresnahan ran over to the stands and punched the fan, who it turned out was a New Yorker. Ten days later, Joe McGinnity gave up four runs to the Pirates in as many innings. As he was leaving the field at the end of the fourth, he and Heinie Peitz, who was coaching at third base for the Pirates, began exchanging barbs. Then the Iron Man slugged Peitz in the face. Peitz responded in kind. The umpire had to call in the police to end the scrap, and McGinnity was arrested and taken to a police station, where he was charged with disorderly conduct. The league's punishment was a ten-day suspension and $100 fine. National League President Harry Pulliam must have believed Peitz was only half as much to blame as McGinnity. The Pirate was suspended for five days and fined $50.²⁴

No Giants season could be considered complete without at least one act by John McGraw that offended the sensibilities of upstanding baseball fans. McGraw's 1906 outburst occurred on August 7, a day after Muggsy was thrown out by umpire Jim Johnstone for arguing the call on a play at home plate. When Johnstone and fellow umpire Bob Emslie arrived at the Polo Grounds, they were told that Johnstone would not be allowed to enter the park. Upon learning that Johnstone was barred from umpiring that day's game, Emslie also refused to enter the park. McGraw then appointed Sammy Strang as the umpire. He asked the opposing manager, Frank Chance, to name one of his men as the second umpire. Chance refused. Strang, acting as the duly appointed umpire, ordered the game to start. When Chicago refused to go along with the charade, he then declared the game forfeited to New York. Johnstone, acting for the National League, also declared the contest forfeited, but to Chicago rather than the Giants. McGraw was already under suspension for his conduct of the previous day. As further punishment for barring Johnstone, Pulliam kept him under an indefinite suspension for 20 days before allowing him to return to the field.²⁵

Competing While Rebuilding: Pittsburgh

The Pirates continued their slow-motion rebuilding job in 1906. The team was changing a bit at a time while continuing to contend for the pennant. By opening day of that season four of the regular starters from 1903 had been displaced. First baseman Kitty Bransfield, right fielder Jimmy Sebring, and catcher Ed Phelps had been traded to other teams. Tommy Leach was still with the Pirates—and still playing most games when healthy—but he was now splitting time between third base, which he could no longer play well because of difficulty making the throw to first, and the outfield, where he was still in a learning mode. Only two pitchers remained from the 1903 champions—Sam Leever and Deacon Phillippe. Both were still effective pitchers, but they were now in their mid-30s and could not shoulder the heavy workload associated with staff leaders in the Deadball Era.

Bransfield's replacement at first base in 1906 was Joe Nealon, a highly-regarded prospect from the Pacific Coast League. Standing 6'2" tall, Nealon was a big man for the era. He was agile and was able to haul in wide throws with his long reach. He seemed to do well in his rookie year, leading the league in RBIs with 83 and scoring 82 runs, the league's fourth-highest total, but his .255 batting average didn't stand out, and Pittsburgh fans weren't convinced he was up to Bransfield's standard.²⁶ Bob Ganley was another rookie starter, winning the right field spot when Otis Clymer broke his ankle early in the season. Ganley was a Willie Keeler wannabe. He was an expert bunter and had great speed. He fit in well with Fred Clarke's aggressive game on the bases, but didn't hit enough balls out of the infield to be very valuable at bat. Tommy Sheehan took over at third base when Leach was injured or in the outfield. He was an excellent fielder, but like Ganley, did not hit very well.²⁷ The catching job was split between young George Gibson and old Heinie Peitz. They both followed the theme of good defense, not much hitting.

Pittsburgh (93–60)

Name	AVG	OBP	SLG	R	RBI	SB
Ginger Beaumont, cf	.265	.311	.332	48	32	1
or Dutch Meier, of	.256	.298	.326	32	16	4
Bob Ganley, rf	.258	.316	.295	63	31	19
Fred Clarke, lf	.309	.371	.412	69	39	18
Honus Wagner, ss	.339	.416	.459	103	71	53
Joe Nealon, 1b	.255	.327	.353	82	83	15
Tommy Leach, 3b-of	.286	.333	.342	66	39	21
or Tommy Sheehan, 3b	.241	.284	.289	28	34	13
Claude Ritchey, 2b	.269	.369	.339	46	62	6
George Gibson, c	.178	.225	.208	8	20	1
Or Heinie Peitz, c	.240	.321	.304	13	20	1
or Ed Phelps, c*	.247	.308	.323	12	17	3
Leading Pitchers	W	L	Pct	IP	H	ERA
Vic Willis	23	13	.639	322	295	1.73
Sam Leever	22	7	.759	260.3	232	2.32
Lefty Leifield	18	13	.581	255.7	214	1.87
Deacon Phillippe	15	10	.600	218.7	216	2.47
Mike Lynch	6	5	.545	119	101	2.42
Homer Hillebrand	3	2	.600	53	42	2.21

*Includes record with Cincinnati

Clarke managed to put together a strong pitching staff in 1906. During the winter he traded two players to get a pitcher who had just completed successive seasons in which he lost 25 and 29 games, respectively. Ordinarily that would not seem to be a good move for a team with pennant-winning aspirations. But in this case the pitcher had long been one of the top pitchers in the National League. Vic Willis had gone 25–13 as a rookie with Boston in 1898, when the Beaneaters won the pennant for the fifth time in the 90s. In his sophomore season he was 27–8, with a league leading ERA of 2.50.

In 1900 Vic tried to pitch through shoulder and back pain, his record suffering from the effort, as he put up a 10–17 record. He came back to win 20 games in 1901, and in 1902 appeared in 51 of the Beaneaters' 140 games. He started 46 games that season and completed all but one of them. His 45 complete games has only been exceeded once since 1900, by Jack Chesbro in 1904. He hurled 410 innings, the fifth-highest total since 1900.

Willis's marathon effort in 1902 brought a return of his back pains and another sub-par season in 1903. Although he led the National League in losses in 1904 and 1905, with records of 18–25 and 12–29, the defeats were more because of the miserable support he received from the Beaneaters than from poor pitching. Still, the burden of pitching for a chronic loser had started to affect Willis's attitude. In an interview with a Pittsburgh writer at the start of spring training Willis said he never quit giving his best while pitching for Boston but, nevertheless, pitching for a losing team was mighty discouraging. "Many a time," Vic said, "I have worked my head off to win a game, and just when I thought I had things sewed up, someone would commit some error, for which there was no excuse seemingly, and things would go up in the air." It would be different with Pittsburgh, he said. "With a team like the Pirates behind me, I believe that I will win the big percentage of my games. At least, I will do my best."[28]

His best turned out to be pretty good. His 23–13 record gave him the third-most wins in the league and his 1.73 ERA was bettered only by three Chicago pitchers.

Another addition to the Pirate pitching staff was Lefty Leifield, who had made his major league debut in September of 1905. Leifield emerged as the best of several young pitchers Clarke looked at early in the season. In fact, although he had a couple rough outings early in the year, Lefty proved to be one of the best pitchers in the National League. He threw eight shutouts, a number exceeded only by Three-Finger Brown in 1906 and by only five left-handed pitchers in modern baseball history. His 1.87 ERA was the fifth-lowest in the league. On September 26, he held the Phillies hitless in a game that was limited to six innings by a previous agreement between the two teams. Earlier he had pitched a one-hitter against the Cubs, a game he lost 1–0 as Three-Finger Brown also threw a one-hitter.[29]

Throughout the early Deadball Era the Pirates entered every season with a marked advantage over all the other National League teams. That advantage was named Honus Wagner. It wasn't just that Wagner was the best hitter in the league—in terms of both average and power—and one of the top baserunners. It was that he combined league-leading talent at bat and on the bases with top-flight defense at a position where glovework was considered much more important than the ability to hit. The difference between Wagner's batting marks and those of other shortstops was enormous. In 1906 Honus's batting average of .339 made him the league leader in that category. He finished fourth in on-base percentage (.416), and second in slugging percentage (.459). No other National League shortstop came anywhere close to those marks.

The best shorthand summary of batting is a player's on-base-plus-slugging percentage. Wagner posted an .875 mark—the best in the league. The Giants' Bill Dahlen was second to Honus among shortstops with a mark of .654, mostly because he walked 76 times, The third-best shortstop, Brooklyn's Phil Lewis, posted a measly .588, almost 300 points below Honus's figure. On the bases, Wagner racked up 53 steals. The Cubs' Joe Tinker stole 30 bases. No other shortstop got more than 16.

It was like that every season for the rest of the decade. In 1907 Honus was at .921, Lewis was second with .675. In 1908 Wagner bested Al Bridwell, by then a Giant, .957 to .683. In 1909 the difference was .909 to 724, again with Bridwell coming in second among shortstops.

In their book *The Diamond Appraised*, Craig Wright and Tom House argue that Wagner was the most valuable player in baseball history—including Babe Ruth—when all aspects of the game are considered.[30] Dissenting cases can be made for a handful of players—Ruth, Barry Bonds, Willie Mays, and Ty Cobb, for example—but it is obvious that Wagner's skill set was of enormous value to the Pirates. When a team can put in a man who is always among the leaders in batting and baserunning, while the opposition is fielding players

Combining top-level hitting with the ability to play great defense at the game's most demanding fielding position, Honus Wagner gave the Pirates a marked advantage over their opponents going into every season (Library of Congress).

whose offensive abilities range from mediocre to terrible, that team has a lead of more than a few games before the first ball is pitched on opening day.

Don't Mess with the "Kid": Philadelphia

> The Kid settled in at the bar. He needed a cold one. The day had been rough. The guys on the other team had been all over the team's young pitcher. They even threatened to punch him in the jaw. The Kid had covered the youngster's back, at one point inviting the hecklers to try him first. When they refused his invitation, the Kid went after them. Now he needed to relax. He was standing with his back to the barroom door, facing the big mirror behind the bartender.
>
> The kid heard a noise behind him. He looked up into the mirror. Three of the opposing players had burst through the door and were heading towards him. On the bar in front of him stood a glass of beer. Lifting this as though to drink it, the Kid suddenly threw it over his shoulder into the face of the nearest of his opponents. Then wheeling, he knocked all three down before they had recovered from their surprise. As fast as they started to get up he knocked them down, until they stayed on the floor. Then the Kid calmly walked out and told the corner cop to go in and clean up the remains.[31]

"The Kid" in this account was Kid Gleason, the Phillies' veteran second baseman. The story is almost certainly apocryphal. It was written a few days after his death in 1933, and was intended to capture one of the foremost elements of Gleason's character. He was a "fighter" who didn't take guff from anyone. But the tale was not made up from whole cloth. The author found at least two accounts of Gleason engaging in fights. In one of them a teammate recalled an encounter he witnessed. "I saw him [Gleason] in a fight with a six-foot tough in St. Louis one night, and he punched the big fellow groggy in a half-dozen blows."[32]

Gleason dealt with issues in a straightforward manner. He could be loyal to those he felt had treated him well, but was quick to protest and defend himself when he thought he had been wronged. When his baseball career appeared threatened, he recreated it in a new position. He worked hard at his game, played with energy and intelligence, and carved out a long career despite relatively ordinary physical skills.

Philadelphia (71–82)

Name	AVG	OBP	SLG	R	RBI	SB
Roy Thomas, cf	.254	.393	.302	81	16	22
Kid Gleason, 2b	.227	.281	.269	47	34	17
or Joe Ward, inf	.295	.321	.450	12	11	2
Kitty Bransfield, 1b	.275	.300	.353	47	60	12

Name	AVG	OBP	SLG	R	RBI	SB
John Titus, rf	.267	.378	.339	67	57	12
or Johnny Lush, p-of	.264	.310	.307	28	15	6
Sherry Magee, lf	.282	.348	.407	77	67	55
Mickey Doolin, ss	.230	.270	.297	41	55	16
Ernie Courtney, 3b	.236	.315	.276	53	42	6
or Paul Sentell, inf	.229	.292	.281	19	14	15
Red Dooin, c	.245	.274	.305	25	32	15
or Jerry Donovan, c	.199	.236	.223	11	15	2

Leading Pitchers	W	L	Pct	IP	H	ERA
Tully Sparks	19	16	.543	316.7	244	2.16
Johnny Lush	18	15	.545	281	254	2.37
Bill Duggleby	13	19	.406	280.3	241	2.25
Lew Richie	9	11	.450	205.7	170	2.41
Togie Pittinger	8	10	.444	129.7	128	3.40

Gleason began playing professional ball in 1886, pitching and filling in as a utility player for Williamsport in the Pennsylvania State League. After two minor league seasons he attracted the attention of Harry Wright, the Philadelphia Phillies' manager. Wright gave him a tryout and signed him for the 1888 season. Gleason was a back-of-the-rotation starter for the next two years, posting a losing record both years. When the Players' Revolt came in 1890, Gleason was asked to jump to the Players League. He refused, saying, "Harry Wright gave me my chance two years ago when I was just a fresh kid playing coal towns, and I'm not running out on him now." In 1890 Gleason broke through, posting a 38–17 record, undoubtedly benefiting from the relative weakness of the National League in a season when many of the league's better players had defected to the new league. Gleason remained the Phillies' top starter in 1891, when defecting players returned from the Players League, going 24–20. He was traded to the St. Louis Browns in 1892. There he pitched well for a team mired in the second division.[33]

While playing for the Browns, Gleason quickly learned that in baseball loyalty is pretty much a one-way street leading to the owners' coffers. In the fall of 1892 he was released by the Browns as part of a league-wide effort to bring down player salaries. All the National League teams had agreed not to sign players released by other teams, so the released players had no recourse other than to sign new contracts at lower salaries. In addition, St. Louis owner Chris Van der Ahe began fining his players for minor or even imaginary offenses as a way of saving money. When Gleason was traded to Baltimore early in the 1894 season, he announced that he would report only if he got $500 from the sale price as reimbursement for unjust fines withheld from his salary by Van der Ahe. Gleason, of course, meant what he said.

After he held out for a month, he received the $500 and reported to Baltimore.[34]

Gleason's holdout might have been a good thing for him and for the Orioles. He had been suffering from pain in his pitching arm since midway through the 1892 season. He dealt with the pain by undergoing "galvanic battery treatment" and rubbing in various types of liniments, some of which left his arm raw. After going 2–6 with the Browns before the holdout, Gleason was 15–6 with Baltimore, contributing greatly to the team's first pennant.

When the 1895 season began, the Kid's arm was again giving him trouble. After the Orioles' second baseman, Heinie Reitz, broke his ankle, manager Ned Hanlon used Gleason as a replacement. Gleason played so well he remained at the position for the rest of his career.[35]

That winter, with Reitz returning for the 1895 season, Hanlon did Gleason a favor by trading him to New York, where he was needed at second base. The Kid, pugnacious as ever, again proclaimed that he was in charge of his own destiny. Asked about the trade, he responded, "Next summer is a long ways off, and I may never play in New York. I am getting to be an old man now [he had just turned 29], and I want the magnates to understand they cannot move the 'Kid' around wherever they want him." Gleason said Arthur Irwin, the New York manager, had asked him to come to New York for a meeting. "Did I do so?" the Kid asked himself

Kid Gleason, shown here as a coach with the White Sox in 1912, was a "fighter" who worked hard at his game and played with energy and intelligence (Library of Congress).

rhetorically. "Not on your life! If he wants to see me, he has to come after me, and if he does find me and talks about signing a contract, I will just say, 'I am not ready to sign just yet, so you had better go on about your business.' They can't monkey with me, I tell you. If I don't want to play in New York, I won't play there—that's all there is about it." Two months later Gleason signed a New York contract, playing there for the next five years.[36]

Gleason was a popular player for New York, well-liked by both his teammates and the fans. His disputatious personality might have made him less than popular, however, with team officials. One spring day in 1897 when team president Andrew Freedman decided to join the players in a game of catch, he made the mistake of firing the ball at Gleason at close range. Gleason responded by repeatedly burning the ball back at Freedman at top speed. Freedman continued the exchange for several minutes before excusing himself. The President's hand remained swollen for a couple days afterward. A couple years later a reporter stated that the Giants' president considered Gleason to be a "disorganizer."[37]

During the 1900 season Gleason was named as one of a half-dozen Giants players who refused to take orders from manager Buck Ewing. The players, all veterans, disagreed with Ewing's tactics and often ignored his instructions. Gleason and team captain George Davis took the disagreement to president Freedman, ultimately resulting in Ewing's firing. Reportedly Gleason then quarreled with Davis, who was Ewing's successor. After the season, Davis announced that he would make no effort to re-sign three veteran Giants, one of them being Gleason.[38]

As he gained experience at the position, Gleason developed into one of the best defensive second basemen in the game. He was noted for his range and for his quick hands in turning a double play. He was a very active player—backing up plays, positioning himself for relays, helping out wherever he could. As a batter he usually finished in the middle of the pack among second basemen. He was considered a good "scientific" player, adept at sacrificing and working the hit-and-run play.[39]

With Detroit in 1901 he teamed with shortstop Norman "Kid" Elberfeld to give Detroit outstanding defense in the middle of the infield. The Tigers led the American League in double plays that season by a wide margin. The two pugnacious "Kids" were a major pain to American League umpires, protesting virtually any call going against the Tigers and just generally making a nuisance of themselves. Chicago owner Charlie Comiskey praised the two for their fiery play, while conceding that their desire to win "drew them to the edge of rowdy ball."[40]

Gleason stayed with the Tigers two years. After the 1902 season he was traded to the New York Giants. But the Kid decided he didn't want to play in New York. He refused to report, instead remaining at his home in Camden, New Jersey, just outside Philadelphia, until a deal was arranged between the Giants and Phillies. Shortly after the 1903 season began a Philadelphia writer remarked, "The Gleasonized Quakers—Gleasonized is the newest synonym for the infusion of dash and ginger, again played fine ball."[41] The Kid, who was already 36 years old when he returned to Philadelphia, had two of his best years at bat with the Phillies, batting .284 in 1903 and .274 in 1904. In 1905 his average fell to .247, but he contributed by sacrificing 43 times. His last season as a regular player, 1906, his average dropped to .227 and his advanced age of 39 cut down on his range and baserunning ability.

During spring training of 1907 Gleason suffered a groin injury. His replacement, Otto Knabe, played very well while the Kid was recuperating. Billy Murray, the Phillies manager, came to the conclusion that Knabe should become the regular second baseman. He called Gleason aside one day and said, "Kid, I'm thinking that young Knabe looks pretty good there, and..." Gleason interrupted his manager, saying, "Bill, the boy is better than me and deserves the job. I was going to mention that to you the other day, but I thought you might think I was trying to run things for you."[42]

After Gleason was consigned to the bench, a writer familiar with the Phillies suggested the Kid could help in another way when the team faced the Cubs. "If some person of influence would induce Bill Gleason to bite a piece out of Mr. Chance's left ankle the old town might fall back into her stride."[43]

Gleason served as a coach and manager for many years after retiring as a player. He is probably best remembered as the manager of Chicago "Black Sox," who conspired to throw the World Series in 1919.

The Early Deadball Era's Dave Kingman: Brooklyn

Brooklyn (66–86)

Name	AVG	OBP	SLG	R	RBI	SB
Doc Casey, 3b	.233	.306	.291	71	34	22
Billy Maloney, cf	.221	.286	.272	71	32	38
Harry Lumley, rf	.324	.386	.477	72	61	35
Tim Jordan, 1b	.262	.352	.422	67	78	16
Jack McCarthy, lf	.304	.347	.351	23	35	9
or Emil Batch, lf	.256	.311	.350	23	11	3
Phil Lewis, ss	.243	.309	.279	40	37	14
Whitey Alperman, 2b	.252	.284	.338	38	46	13
or John Hummel, ut	.199	.289	.259	20	21	10
Bill Bergen, c	.159	.175	.184	9	19	2
or Lew Ritter, c	.208	.263	.239	22	15	6

Leading Pitchers	W	L	Pct	IP	H	ERA
Elmer Stricklett	14	18	.438	291.7	273	2.72
Doc Scanlan	18	13	.581	288	230	3.19
Harry McIntire	13	21	.382	276	254	2.97
Mal Eason	10	17	.370	227	212	3.25
Jim Pastorius	10	14	.417	211.7	225	3.61

Dave Kingman was known as an "all-or-nothing" hitter. He either hit a home run or he struck out. (In fairness to Kingman, it should be noted that his style of hitting has become widely accepted. While his strikeout totals were quite high for his playing days, currently they would likely attract very little, if any, comment.) In his day Kingman was a controversial hitter. While he frequently walked back to the bench having accomplished nothing other than striking out, when he managed to hit the ball he racked up some pretty good numbers in the two most important hitting categories—runs scored and runs batted in. Lots of people thought that made him a good hitter. Others thought he wasted too many at-bats without getting on base or moving up a runner.[44]

In the early Deadball Era nobody hit many home runs. Power hitters were batters who legged out doubles and triples, with a few home runs added in for good measure. Fans liked to see extra-base hits, and so did managers. But the trait most sought-after in baseball players was speed. As we have mentioned above, fast running was a central element in the tactics of the day.

For most players, speed on the basepaths and in the field was just one element in their set of baseball assets. For at least one player, however, speed was basically his game. That player was Billy Maloney. In a way he was the Deadball Era equivalent of Dave Kingman. He gave his team a much-sought-after talent, but little beyond that. His talent was such a big part of the way the game was played, however, that for a while he was able to make a valuable contribution to his team.

Given that he was one of the fastest men in baseball, it is surprising to discover that Maloney began his career as a catcher. He was signed by the Milwaukee Brewers in 1901, the American League's inaugural season as a major league. Billy had been a catcher and outfielder for Georgetown College, which at the time fielded one of the best college baseball teams in the country. He had also been a sprinter for the Georgetown track team.[45]

When the 1901 season opened Maloney was used as a utility player. His role was to back up the team's two more experienced catchers and be ready to go into the outfield when needed. He didn't start catching with any regularity until mid–June. Within a month, though, he was getting rave reviews from the Milwaukee press, which generally didn't have a lot of kind words for their hapless team. Looking for a silver lining after a typically messy Brewer loss in late July, a Milwaukee writer noted: "Maloney is throwing to bases with wonderful accuracy and speed, and the baserunners are making little headway against him." By September, the same writer said, "Maloney's throwing to the bases is becoming one of the most interesting features of local games. Yesterday he again managed to catch a man off base." Near the end of the season, when Clark Griffith and Connie Mack raised the issue of an American League all-star team, Maloney's name was mentioned as a good candidate to be the mythical team's catcher.[46]

When the Milwaukee franchise moved to St. Louis in 1902, Maloney went with them, spurning a lucrative offer to jump to the New York Giants. In St. Louis he found himself playing for a new manager, Jimmy McAleer, who preferred to use veteran Joe Sugden as his primary catcher. Sugden was a good defensive catcher who had caught for the champion Chicago White Stockings in 1901. Early in the season Maloney played sparingly for the Browns, appearing mostly as an outfield substitute. In one of the few games he caught, the Cleveland Blues stole four bases off his throws. On June 18, his hand was injured by a foul tip. He had not yet recovered a month later when the Browns released him.

Maloney was quickly signed by the Cincinnati Reds. But again his work as a catcher was mediocre at best. The Reds put him behind the plate for a few games, then decided he might be more successful in the outfield. There he played poorly, losing a couple games by his errors. Offensively, Maloney showed little, batting only .247 with the Reds after having struggled to a .205 average with the Browns. When the 1902 season ended, with the

Billy Maloney used his one great talent, terrific speed, to make some spectacular plays (Library of Congress).

baseball war still raging, the Reds hurried to sign all their players. Except one, that is. They made no effort to sign Maloney. Neither did anyone else. In one short season Maloney had gone from being a great young player to being a failure undesired by any major league team.[47]

Even as he was playing poorly, however, Maloney had made a deep impression with his great speed. His hometown writers did not fail to praise his running ability, even while criticizing other aspects of his game. In his short stay at Cincinnati, he showed a glimpse of the daring baserunning style that was to later become his hallmark. He stole eight bases in only 27 games. In one game, after reaching first base, he took off for second on a pitch and scored all the way from first base on a single to center field.[48]

After being released by the Reds, Maloney caught on with Kansas City of the American Association. Playing 66 games for the Cowboys in 1903, he stole 24 bases and scored 57 runs. He was traded to Minneapolis in mid-season. With the Millers he scored 21 runs in 25 games, although batting only .234. In 1904 Billy raised his average to .317 and scored 103 runs for the Millers. In August of that year a Cleveland reporter noted, "Under the teaching of Watkins at Minneapoliis, he [Maloney] has developed into a star."[49] The Chicago Cubs selected Billy in the draft that fall.

Maloney's timing in joining the Cubs was pretty good. This was the Cubs team that Ira Sanborn called "the Zephyrs." Frank Chance was the team's leader for most of that season, and Chance believed in trying to exploit every baserunning opening that presented itself—which was exactly Maloney's approach. An example is shown in the summary of a game against Cincinnati in June. "The Cubs ran bases like deer.... The prettiest work on the bags was done by Slagle and Maloney. They were on second and first respectively in the eighth inning, and made a clever double steal, Slagle sliding into third by the back door and eluding the eager Bridwell. He scored a moment later on a wild pitch, and Maloney, the wing-footed, followed him over like an antelope, coming all the way from second on a ball that Phelps partially stopped so that it just rolled to the stand. Maloney also scored from second on the scratchiest kind of a hit to Huggins in the sixth inning."

Perhaps Maloney's most striking play came against the Giants in August. With men on first and second and no outs, Billy was given the signal to sacrifice. He did, but beat out the bunt to load the bases. Chance followed with a fly ball that right fielder Sammy Strang almost caught. Bob Wicker and Jimmy Slagle, the Cubs on third and second, respectively, held their bases in case the ball was caught. Maloney, however, ran almost to second base while the ball was in the air. When the fly eluded Strang's grasp, Wicker scored easily and Slagle raced from second base also trying to score on the play. Maloney followed him only a step or two behind. Strang chased down the ball and fired to catcher Roger Bresnahan, who made the putout on Slagle. But an instant after Bresnahan tagged Slagle, Maloney came sliding over home plate just under Slagle's body. Maloney's caper stunned both Bresnahan and the umpire, who called Slagle out and Maloney safe.[50]

The 1905 season would be the highlight of Maloney's career. Billy hit .260, a solid average for that year, and led the league with 59 steals. That winter he was part of a four-player package sent to Brooklyn for Jimmy Sheckard. With Brooklyn, Maloney displayed the same aggressive style of baserunning he had performed for Chicago, as well as the ability to make sensational plays in the outfield. In one game in late September his play evoked a semi-poetic outburst from normally staid Brooklyn reporter Abe Yager: "Out of the smoke of defeat there flashed one burning ember that blazed effulgently throughout the gloomy afternoon. This was Billy Maloney. There may be those who railed at Brooklyn's center fielder because of his inability to line 'em out, but when it comes to fielding his position or breezing around the bases, Maloney is in a class by himself. He covered acres of territory yesterday. Not only did he haul down sizzling liners and Texas Leaguers with rare brilliancy in his own bailiwick, but he frequently scampered into right and left fields and performed similar feats of electrical display. Seven times he hauled down drives that appeared to be sure hits, robbing the Red batters right and left without fear or favor."[51]

A couple weeks into the 1907 season, however, Yager's analytical side offered a different and more sobering description of Maloney's abilities. "The first principle of an outfielder's usefulness to a team is his ability to hit," Yager asserted. "The fielding is secondary. Maloney is the fastest center fielder in the National League—very few will dispute that. But there his usefulness, thus far at least, has ended.He is the fastest baserunner, too, but he gets on first so infrequently that he doesn't get much chance to show his speed."[52]

The Brooklyn reporter thus placed his finger—so to speak—on the Achilles tendon in Maloney's game. With the Cubs Billy had hit well enough to allow his team to benefit from his daring baserunning. With the Superbas, his average dipped to .221 in 1906 and .229 in 1907. His stolen base totals dropped to 38 and 25. He managed to score 71 runs for the Superbas in 1906, a dropoff of only seven from his Chicago total, but in 1907 he scored only 51 times. His strikeout number, on the other hand, rose from 84 in 1905, to 116 in 1906, to 97 in 1907—all three league-leading totals. While that many whiffs would not be remarkable the way baseball is now played, in the Deadball Era they were truly "Kingmanesque."

In 1908 Billy's batting slipped to a level that no team could accept from an outfielder, regardless of his baserunning abilities. He hit only .195 and fanned 71 times in 402 plate appearances. After that season he slipped back into the minor leagues, where he remained until calling it quits after the 1914 season.

Ned Hanlon's "Weeding Out"; Frank Chance's Revenge: Cincinnati

Worn down by years of trying to shape a winning team out of a group of players lacking talent and/or experience, and frustrated by a budget too slim to go after players who might bring a brighter future, Ned Hanlon quit as manager of the Brooklyn Superbas, signing with Cincinnati within hours of informing his fellow Brooklyn owners of his decision. (Yes, he still owned stock in the Superbas while managing the Reds.) Hanlon explained his decision by saying he had been assured by Cincinnati owner Garry Herrmann that he would have a free hand to do whatever he thought was necessary to build a winning team.

Cincinnati (64–87)

Name	AVG	OBP	SLG	R	RBI	SB
Miller Huggins, 2b	.292	.376	.338	81	26	41
Joe Kelley, lf	.228	.300	.323	43	53	9
or Fred Odwell, rf	.223	.286	.287	20	21	11
Frank Jude, rf	.208	.261	.263	31	31	7
or Shad Barry, 1b-of*	.269	.329	.335	64	45	17
Cy Seymour, cf**	.286	.339	.378	70	80	29
Jim Delahanty, 3b	.280	.371	.364	63	39	21
or Hans Lobert, 3b-ss	.310	.366	.366	39	19	20
or Paddy Livingston, c	.158	.259	.223	8	8	0
Tommy Corcoran, ss	.207	.242	.249	29	33	8
Snake Deal, 1b	.208	.228	.251	13	21	15

Leading Pitchers	W	L	Pct	IP	H	ERA
Jake Weimer	20	14	.588	304.7	263	2.22
Bob Ewing	13	14	.481	287.7	248	2.38
Chick Fraser	10	20	.333	236	221	2.67
Bob Wicker***	9	16	.360	222.3	220	2.79
Charley Hall	4	8	.333	95	86	3.32
Jack Harper***	1	4	.200	37.7	38	4.06

*Includes record with St. Louis
**Includes record with New York
***Includes record with Chicago

Cincinnati fans were elated to see their team under the direction of a man who was considered by many to be the foremost baseball leader in the country. "With Hanlon at the helm the local fans are counting heavily upon the team's success," wrote Cincinnati's *Sporting News* correspondent. "They are not claiming a pennant.... But one thing is certain, Ned Hanlon has shown repeatedly that he is capable of getting their best out of a bunch of ball players and if the championship timber is in the men Hanlon will produce it."[53]

However, the mood of optimism that pervaded the team through the spring dissipated quickly. After splitting their first eight games, the Reds lost eight of their next nine. By the end of April it was becoming clear that the team, as it was composed, did not have the makings of a winning ball club. It was reported that after a long discussion Hanlon and Herrmann had agreed that a "weeding out of players" was needed, and that at least six Reds players would be sent elsewhere before long. A week later a note to a game summary stated, "Manager Hanlon is thoroughly downcast over the continued poor work of some of the men on the team, and expects to have a couple of changes completed early next week."[54]

The first move was fairly innocuous. Prospect Carl Druhot, a small man with a big fastball, was sold to the Cardinals. Druhot pitched well for a while in St. Louis before injuring a tendon in his arm. Next, Gus Dorner was traded to the Beaneaters for veteran Chick Fraser. Dorner was a borderline major leaguer. He pitched very well with Class A teams (the highest minor league classification in the early 1900s), but was mediocre at the major league level. Dorner lost his only decision with the Reds and then lost 25 games with the Beaneaters, posting a combined 8–26 record in 1906. Fraser was a good pitcher, but he had rebelled against the miserly ways of the Boston owners, choosing to play in the outlaw Tri-State League rather than accepting the lowball salary offered by the Beaneaters.

The churning of ballplayers continued for the rest of the season. Few places in the lineup were spared. Catcher Ed Phelps, first baseman Charlie Carr, right fielder Fred Odwell, center fielder Cy Seymour, left fielder Bill Hinchman, utilityman/first baseman Jack Barry, reserve outfielder Johnny Siegle, and pitchers Jack Harper, Orval Overall, and Charlie Chech were all told to catch trains to various destinations. Former Detroit star outfielder Jimmy Barrett joined the team in May and left 11 days later after demonstrating that he had not yet recovered from a knee injury. Third baseman Jim Delahanty was moved to the outfield in August to make way for rookie Mike Mowrey, and then was traded to the St. Louis Browns in December. Tom Corcoran, the team's shortstop since 1897, made it through the season before going to the Giants at the winter league meetings. Joe Kelley, Hanlon's predecessor as manager and captain of the 1906 Reds, was given his release at the same time, going to Toronto as player-manager.

As the season neared its end, *Cincinnati Enquirer* reporter Jack Ryder reviewed the season. He explained that Hanlon had hoped to finish as high as fourth place with the team he inherited. "Manager Hanlon was as much disappointed as anyone in his failure to develop a system that would land the team higher in the race," Ryder said. "He attributed this largely to the number of veterans in the club who were set in their ways and could not be taught a dashing style of play such as distinguished the old Baltimore champions. Hence the weeding out." Ryder pointed out that only a few veterans would be left when the team opened its 1907 season. "All the rest will be young players, some like Lobert, Mowrey and Jude, with a season's experience in fast company, others still green as grass. Here will come the test of managerial ability."[55]

Of all the deals Hanlon made, only two created much controversy; one at the time it was completed, the other much later. Fans and sportswriters alike were surprised that Cy Seymour was allowed to leave the team without getting a solid player in return. Seymour had led the National League in batting in 1905 with an outstanding .377 average–the highest posted in the National League between the 1900 and 1921 seasons. He was batting only .257 for the Reds in July, when Hanlon sold him to the Giants for $12,000, but everyone knew he was a better hitter than that. "Cincinnati is 'strengthening' for the remainder of the present campaign in a manner never before heard of," remarked a Pittsburgh reporter. "Will the fans of Cincinnati stand for the sale of Seymour? Wonder if the Pittsburg fans would stand for the sale of Wagner to the Chicago club?" he asked rhetorically. The reporter answered his own question by pointing out that John McGraw "was not in the habit of picking up baseball corpses," and predicting that Seymour would hit well for the Giants, which proved true, as Seymour hit .320 for McGraw over the remainder of the season.

Hanlon's thinking may have been mirrored by Jack Ryder of the *Cincinnati Enquirer*. "Though a great natural batter, Cy was never a good man for the Reds. Only a moderately good fielder and a wretched baserunner, he canceled much of his strong work at the bat by fumbling and wild throwing in the field and stupid work on the sacks," Ryder said. "Cy was never a timely hitter. Of an extremely nervous and high-strung disposition, the fact that there were men on bases and two out found him at his worst."[56]

When Jack Harper was sent to Chicago in May, few people thought Hanlon had made a mistake. In fact, the deal didn't really become controversial until a decade later. In 1915 Hugh Fullerton wrote a short article for *Sporting Life* supporting the Federal League's suit against the National

League. "The case of Jack Harper is one the Feds will tell," Fullerton wrote. "In one game he hit Frank Chance three times with pitched balls, the last one rendering Chance unconscious. Chance accused Harper of hitting him purposely and informed the pitcher of his intention of 'putting him out of the business.' That winter President Murphy made a trade with Cincinnati. Chance insisted upon having Harper in the trade." According to Fullerton, the Cubs cut Harper's pay from the $4,500 he had been making with the Reds to $1,500. When Harper objected, Fullerton wrote, Chance told Harper, "he had him, he could either sign that contract or quit. Harper appealed to the [National] Commission, which declined to hear his case and he was out of baseball, and never has been back."[57]

The story of Harper's mistreatment by Chance has been told in several more recent works, almost always as an illustration of Chance's tough, competitive nature.[58] But intentionally ending a man's career is pretty extreme. Did Chance really do that? Also, what was Harper's story—what did he do before Chance allegedly squashed his baseball career?

Harper seemed to become embroiled in unusual situations with some regularity. Take the 1899 season for example. Jack didn't seem to be pitching all that well in the minors that year. He went 12–29 with the Grand Rapids Furniture Makers/Springfield Wanderers/Columbus Senators of the Interstate League. (That was one team; it meandered through three cities in search of fans.) Yet in September Patsy Tebeau signed Jack to pitch for the St. Louis-Cleveland syndicate. Tebeau assigned him to the Cleveland side of the organization. He probably thought Jack's experience with the wandering Grand Rapids team would help him fit in with the Cleveland team—which earned the nicknamed Misfits in 1899. The Misfits were so bad they were forced to play 112 of their 154 games on the road. After joining the Misfits in September, Jack went 1–4, his .200 won-lost percentage far surpassing the team won-lost percentage of .130 (on a 20–134 record). His lone win broke a 24-game losing streak for the Misfits.[59]

When the National League contracted in 1900, Tebeau couldn't find room on his team for a pitcher with a combined record of 13–33 the preceding season. He farmed Harper to Ft. Wayne in the same League where Jack had performed so well in 1899. Jack went 20–15 for Ft. Wayne, ending the season with an iron-man feat of pitching and winning three games in the last two days of the season to clinch the Interstate League pennant for his team.[60]

St. Louis gave Jack another chance in 1901. He was an immediate success, leading the team in victories with a 23–13 record. He was the team's top pitcher, but with an asterisk. In a day when pitchers finished what they started, Jack was taken out of nine of his 37 starts. By later standards his

28 complete games and 308 innings pitched would be taken as a sign of great durability. But In 1901 the nine incomplete games were seen as evidence that his record was not quite legitimate. After Harper jumped to the American League in 1902 a reporter commented, "Jack Harper has no Donovan with him this year. Patsy padded his record last year by yanking him out of games as soon as the opposing teams began to do any batting."[61]

Jack was still in St. Louis in 1902, but with the Browns rather than the Cardinals. He received a handsome salary—reportedly $5,000, but probably less—for moving across town. For that much money his new Manager, Jimmy McAleer, expected a workhorse, someone who could pick up the slack when other pitchers faltered. Instead, Jack was one of the guys who struggled once the Browns managed to get in the middle of the pennant race. He had streaks of wildness that led McAleer to pull him from a few games in the early and middle innings, and he didn't respond well when McAleer started trotting him out to the mound every three days. By August he was suffering from a sore arm. Near the end of that month a reporter wrote, "Harper's miserable showing after the amount of money paid him to jump and expended in litigation to hold him has been a keen disappointment to both the management and the patrons of the game. It is variously attributed to illness and an aggravated case of sulks." Jack's "miserable showing" wasn't really all that bad. His record was 15–11 on August 30, when McAleer shut him down for the rest of the season.[62]

By early September reports were circulating that Harper had agreed to play with Cincinnati in 1903. St. Louis owner Robert Hedges was asked about those reports while he was accompanying the team on a road trip. He replied, "I know nothing except that before we left St. Louis Harper told us of Cincinnati's offer and asked me what I would give him. I told him, and it was not what Jack thought he was worth. Then I told him to go where he could get the most money."[63] Harper signed with Cincinnati for $3,000, probably a reduction in pay from 1902.

During spring training in 1903 Cincinnati Manager Joe Kelley expressed confidence in Harper. Kelley thought Jack had been less effective in the American League because it had not yet adopted the new foul-strike rule the National League began using in 1901. Harper tended to be somewhat wild. He benefited from the foul-strike rule because he threw a good fastball high in the strike zone. Those pitches tended to be fouled off more often than low pitches, Kelley said. They would be strikes in the National League but weren't in the American League in 1902. Kelley might have been right about the foul-strike rule, but he overlooked another rule change. In 1903 both leagues enforced a rule prohibiting a pitcher from taking a step back of the rubber while delivering the ball. Jack had trouble adjusting to the rule. Lacking control, he would get behind in the count, take something off his fastball to get it over the plate, and then give up lots of hits. Late in the season, he began overhauling his pitching motion. He eliminated the full swing he had been using, and began pitching with an abbreviated motion. But by then the 1903 season was almost over. Jack's record in 1903 was a mediocre 8–9, with a poor 4.33 earned run average.

Just before he left Cincinnati to go home for the winter, Jack admitted there had also been another problem in 1903. He had carried too much weight. "I worked hard all the time, but it seemed impossible for me to get down to weight without greatly weakening myself," he said. Jack vowed that 1904 would be different. "I am going to start hard training at home about the first of the year, and when I report here next spring I will be lighter than I was at any time this season."[64]

Harper lived up to his pledge. In 1904 he was in top condition when he reported to spring training. He regained the outstanding fastball he had possessed in 1901. He opened the season by winning his first eight decisions. He and Joe McGinnity were both undefeated on June 4, when he battled the Giants ace to a 2–2 tie in 11 innings. In late August his record was 18–4. He slumped somewhat after that, but finished the season at 23–9, with a 2.30 ERA. It looked like Jack's career was back on track.[65]

It is here that we come back to Fullerton's account of Frank Chance's revenge. It is true that on May 30, 1904, Harper hit Chance three times in the first game of a doubleheader. Chance was unconscious for several minutes after being hit the first time. After he regained consciousness, he remained in the game and was hit two more times. In the second game of the doubleheader Cincinnati pitcher Win Kellum hit him again, making a total of four times Chance was plunked in one day. (Chance was hit by a pitch 16 times in 1904, 137 times in his career.) But that winter there was no trade involving Harper. Indeed, Chance was not yet in a position to arrange a trade. He was not yet Chicago's manager—that came in the summer of 1905. Instead, Harper signed with the Reds, anticipating another season along the lines of 1904.[66]

That was not to be the case. He had a bad season in 1905, going 9–13. Once again his season ended early. His last start came on August 11. He had battled a sore arm all season long. After resting the second half of August he encountered a malicious insect that bit him on the lip and hand. A Cincinnati reporter said it was a "kissing bug"; a club official thought it was a tarantula.[67] Regardless, Jack ended a painful season in more pain than ever. His problems continued in 1906. He started five games for the Reds, losing four of them. In May the Reds traded him to Chicago. With the Cubs Jack got into one game, against the Giants on June 6. He lasted one inning before a line drive injured his pitching hand. The injury was serious enough that Jack was given permission to go to his home in Oil City, Pennsylvania, to recover. While he was gone the Cubs ran away from the rest of the league, ending the season with a record 116 wins against only 36 losses. Jack spent most of that record-setting season in Oil City, before notifying the team he had recovered and would join his teammates in Boston on September 19, about two weeks before the end of the season. Chicago management told him not to bother.[68]

That winter a Chicago reporter wrote that Chance was looking forward to Harper's return to full capacity in 1907. But as spring training drew to a close Chance told reporters, "No team can have too many pitchers, if they are good ones. The slightest injury throws a pitcher off his form and there is no telling when half of a twirling corps may be out of condition. We closed the season last year with seven pitchers—Brown, Reulbach, Pfiester, Lundgren, Overall, Taylor and Harper. Harper couldn't get into shape to pitch and will not be with us this year." In mid-April the Cubs sold Jack's contract to Columbus of the American Association. At first Jack refused to report to Columbus, objecting to the salary offered. But he finally gave in and began working out with his new team. After a couple weeks of training, he got into one game with Columbus, losing it 3-0. He pitched seven innings, giving up seven hits and six bases on balls, while striking out two batters. A week later Columbus returned his contract to the Cubs. The sale had been contingent upon Harper's ability to pitch. Columbus claimed Jack had not been able to get into pitching condition, even though he had been given a month to do so. The Cubs had no room on their team for Harper, so he returned to Oil City, his baseball career ended.[69]

Once again we return to the tale of "Frank Chance's Revenge." It doesn't seem to hold water. In his short biography of Harper, completed for the Society for American Baseball Research's Biography Project, Phil Williams calls the story "a memorable myth that has wound its way through a century of baseball history." Harper may well have signed for $1,500 in 1907, but that would have been with Columbus. And after Columbus returned Harper to Chicago there was a report that St. Paul, another American Association team, had purchased Harper's contract, though Harper doesn't seem to have pitched for St. Paul.[70] If Chance was intent upon gaining revenge against Harper, he seems to have become distracted, possibly by the 1907 pennant race.

And what did Harper have to say about the ending of his baseball career? In a *Sporting News* story printed after his death, he was quoted as saying he quit after he came down with arm trouble. "Guess they'd call it a chipped bone in the elbow," he explained.[71]

Like Fine Wine: St. Louis

St. Louis (52–98)

Name	AVG	OBP	SLG	R	RBI	SB
Al Burch, cf-rf	.266	.339	.287	40	11	15
Pug Bennett, 2b	.262	.334	.318	66	34	20
Spike Shannon, lf*	.256	.339	.275	78	50	33
Homer Smoot, cf**	.252	.300	.327	52	48	3
or Jack Himes, cf	.271	.307	.329	10	14	4
or Red Murray, of	.257	.305	.438	18	16	5
Jake Beckley, 1b	.247	.283	.334	29	44	3
Harry Arndt, 3b	.270	.320	.391	30	26	5
or Art Hoelskoetter, ut	.224	.238	.262	21	14	2
George McBride, ss	.169	.215	.208	24	13	5
or Forrest Crawford, ss	.207	.248	.241	8	11	1
Mike Grady, c-1b	.250	.369	.332	33	27	5
or Pete Noonan, c***	.172	.237	.250	8	9	1
or Doc Marshall, c*	.227	.278	.284	14	17	8

Leading Pitchers	W	L	Pct	IP	H	ERA
Buster Brown	8	16	.333	238.3	208	2.64
Ed Karger	5	16	.238	191.7	193	2.72
Fred Beebe***	15	10	.600	230.7	171	2.93
Carl Druhot**	8	9	.471	155.3	144	2.90
Gus Thompson	2	11	.154	103	111	4.28
Wish Egan	2	9	.182	86.3	97	4.59

*Includes record with New York
**Includes record with Cincinnati
***Includes record with Chicago

As a blue-collar kind of guy, he probably didn't drink very much of it, but Jake Beckley was a little like fine wine—he got better with age. He was attentive to the changes that were occurring in baseball as he matured, and he modified his skills to remain competitive to an advanced baseball age.

The 1906 season was Beckley's 19th year in the major leagues. He had first played in the National League in 1888 with the Pittsburgh Alleghenys. Jake was an unabashed slugger in those early days. He didn't quite have the power of Dan Brouthers, Roger Connor, or Sam Thompson—the top sluggers of the time—but he got lots of extra-base hits. In the Deadball Era a batter's home run total was highly dependent upon a combination of having a short fence in the home ballpark and just plain luck. Long-ball hitters didn't necessarily have high home run totals, but they did have lots of doubles and triples, as well as a few home runs. The total number of extra-base hits and the total bases made on those hits were the measure of a slugger.

Jake did well in both. In 1890 he led the Players' League in extra base hits with 69, ten more than the runner-up. In other years through 1895 he ranked in the top ten in the National League.

In 1892 Jake said he was pleased with his batting, but felt he should be able to sacrifice better. "I believe in sacrifice hitting," Jake said, "but I hit the ball too hard and can't run fast enough to first base." By the end of the year, a Pittsburgh reporter noted that Beckley had learned to sacrifice. In 1894, the first year official sacrifice records were kept, Jake had 22 sacrifice hits, the third highest total in the league.[72]

Beckley had a poor season in Pittsburgh in 1896. He was batting only .253 midway through the season when the Pirates decided to trade him. They sent him to New York. Although he hit fairly well with the Giants the rest of 1896, he got off to a slow start again in 1897. After only 17 games the Giants released him. He caught on with Cincinnati, and began to work on refining his bunting touch, this time trying to place the ball where he had a chance to beat it out. His manager, Buck Ewing, later recalled that Beckley was very awkward at bunting when he came to the Reds, but became a good bunter after about a month's practice. Beckley had an unusual bunting style. As the ball approached, he would flip the bat around and bunt the ball off the handle, using the smaller end to deaden the ball.[73]

About this time Jake also gradually changed his entire approach at the plate. In 1900 John McGraw noted that Jake had become a different type of hitter. "It is only a few years ago when Beckley was a pronounced right-field hitter," McGraw said. "He would never get a ball nearer to left field than right center." Jake asked McGraw, a left-handed batter like Beckley, how he was able to shove the ball over to left field so often. McGraw replied that he had learned to do it through lots of practice. Jake decided to give it a try, and began pushing the ball towards left field in morning practices. "In every game that I played against him I could see him improving," McGraw said, "and now I suppose that he has it down as well as any man in the business."[74]

The adjustments Beckley made through the years sacrificed some power, but helped him to maintain a good batting average. In fact, in comparison with the rest of the league, Jake's batting averages in his 30s were better than those he put up in his 20s. He finished in the top ten in the National League in batting average five times during his career; in 1892, and then again every year from 1900 through 1904, except for 1901, when he hit .307, still a good average. From 1902 through 1904 he hit .330, .327, and .325. In those years the league as a whole hit .259, .269, and .249.

Jake usually batted in the middle of his team's batting order. He finished in the top ten in RBIs 12 times in his career, including every year from 1899 through 1904.

The Cardinals acquired Beckley after the 1903 season. Although he was already 36 years old when the sale was completed, Jake was still a productive hitter then and one of the league's better fielding first basemen. Essentially, the deal was made because Cincinnati player-manager Joe Kelley wanted to move from the outfield to first base. At the time, Beckley was criticized as not being a "scientific" player. "Jake is one of the old school of players," a Cincinnati writer asserted. "He plays the game as it was 20 years ago, and, of course, that sort of ball is not going to win any pennants these days."[75]

Jake's "old-fashioned" game worked out pretty well in his first year with the Cardinals. He had the third-highest batting average in the league (.325), ranked eighth in on-base percentage (.375), and tenth in slugging percentage (.403). That season marked the 13th time Jake posted a batting average over .300. The next year his batting average dropped to .286, which was still 31 points above the league average. Jake's fielding was always considered one of his strong points. In June of 1905, after he made several good plays, a St. Louis writer remarked, "If Jake Beckley has any peers at the initial station, they have not shown here this year. The Mayor of Hannibal has years to spend before the mast if his capers yesterday is a line on his form." Another writer praised him for his work around the bag a year later. "Beckley did great work on wide and hurried throws from Arndt and McBride and, in the first inning, made a grand return of Arndt's throw to third, getting Mertes, who tried to make the sack from second while Arndt was throwing Dahlen out at first."[76]

The latter comment was a rare instance of Beckley being complimented for a throw. Jake was notorious for having a poor throwing arm. In Cincinnati one of the writers at times mentioned that Jake had made one of his "famous rainbow throws," usually describing an error or a play in which a runner reached base safely when he should have been out. One time Jake complained about having a sore arm. He was worried, he told some teammates, that if he went into the game, he would not be able to do any throwing. "The other players assured him," a reporter said, "that this would be a blessing, rather than a calamity."[77]

Although Beckley played the entire 1906 season with the Cardinals, it was becoming obvious as the season progressed that he was reaching the end of the road. "Men may come and men may go, but Tennyson's brook and Byron's ocean alone go on forever. Hence it is the time has come almost to the passing of Jake Beckley," a writer began an article about Beckley. "Old Jake has been a good man for St. Louis, too. Never a clever ballplayer, he has always been full of life, energy and spirit. A good mark to throw at and a good man to hit—that is until this year—he has always been a favorite with the people. His 'Work hard. Hustle all the time. Come on. Come on.' may not play much ball, but it makes a hit with the spectators. There is not a more popular man on the Cardinal club than old Jake." But, the writer concluded, "this year he has not hit. Experts say that his eye is not as bright as it once was nor his stride to first as springy. Be that as it may. It seems that the days of this great and honorable player are about numbered."[78]

Jake made it through the 1906 season with the Cardinals, although he played only 87 games and posted a .247 batting average. After he could manage only a .209 average in 32 games the next spring, he was given his release. Jake left behind a career average of .308, having accumulated a total of 2,938 hits, only 62 short of the magic 3,000 hit number.

In 1971 Beckley was one of seven players selected by the Veterans Committee for induction into the Baseball Hall of Fame. Few people knew much about him, and some questioned his qualifications. David Fleitz summarized Jake's accomplishments in his book *Ghosts in the Gallery at Cooperstown*: "The Veterans Committee examined his statistics and found a 20-year veteran with nearly 3,000 hits a batting average over .300, and the career leader in games played at his position. There are many position players in the Hall who cannot claim any of those distinctions, and Jake's stats added up to a powerful argument in favor of his induction."[79]

Bright Spots in a Dreary Season: Boston

For a while it looked like the Beaneaters might have a decent season. They won their first four games, beating up on Brooklyn, one of their rivals for sixth place—the highest position they could realistically aspire to. As late as April 28, their record was 7–7—not great, but hey, that's .500 ball. They were 12–16 on May 16, when they beat Cincinnati, 6–5. Catcher Tim Needham won the game with a long smash into center field, the ball bouncing into the bleachers for a home run. The winning pitcher was Gus Dorner, who didn't get his next victory until June 9. That was also the Beaneaters' next win, following 19 losses in a row. The long losing streak dropped the team into last place, where they remained for the rest of the season, even though they followed Dorner's streak-breaking win by winning five of their next seven games. The Beaneaters' brief rally lasted until June 23, when they were 21–39. After that, it was a steady drip, drip, drip of losses, with a few wins interspersed among the shower of defeats.

Boston (49–102)

Name	AVG	OBP	SLG	R	RBI	SB
Al Bridwell, ss	.227	.297	.251	41	22	6
Fred Tenney, 1b	.283	.357	.340	61	28	17
Dave Brain, 3b	.250	.293	.333	43	45	11
Johnny Bates, cf	.252	.315	.349	52	54	9
Del Howard, lf-2b	.261	.306	.330	46	54	17
Cozy Dolan, rf	.248	.318	.299	54	39	17
or Gene Good, of	.151	.246	.151	4	0	2
Tom Needham, c	.189	.230	.242	11	12	3
or Sam Brown, c	.208	.262	.242	12	20	4
or Jack O'Neill, c	.180	.243	.222	14	4	0
Allie Strobel, 2b	.202	.273	.262	28	24	2

Leading Pitchers	W	L	Pct	IP	H	ERA
Irv Young	16	25	.390	358.3	349	2.91
Vive Lindaman	12	23	.343	307.3	303	2.43
Big Jeff Pfeffer	13	22	.371	302.3	270	2.95
Gus Dorner*	8	26	.235	288.3	280	3.53

*Includes record with Cincinnati

One of the few rays of hope for the Beaneaters in this dreary season came from their left-handed ace, Irv Young. It was almost inevitable that a Boston pitcher name Young would end up with the nickname of Cy—since the Americans' ace had long been one of baseball's elite hurlers. In his rookie year (1905) Irv Young immediately became "Cy Young the second," "young Cy Young," and even "Cy Young, Jr.," although he was no relation to the venerable Denton T. Young. Cy the second was a very different pitcher from the original Cy. The most basic difference, of course, was his throwing arm—the left one rather than the right one. His style was also different. He really wasn't a "Cy"—which denoted a pitcher with an exceptional fastball. Irv had a good fastball, but he was successful because he had good control on his sidearm delivery and his fastball had natural movement, like many lefties.[80]

Young Cy had enjoyed a very successful rookie season. He had gone 20–21 with a team that won only 51 games. He pitched seven shutouts, second only to Christy Mathewson. He was so good that manager Fred Tenney used him like a proven veteran, rather than a first-year man. He started 42 games and completed all but one. Those 41 complete games still stand as a record for a rookie pitcher, as does his total of 378 innings pitched.

At first it appeared Young would be even better in 1906 than he was in 1905. He opened the season by pitching a one-hit shutout against Brooklyn. He won his first five games, the fifth being another one-hit shutout of the Superbas. At that point he owned all but two of Boston's wins, the Beaneaters being 7–7 and Young Cy 5–0. His record was 6–3 when the Beaneaters went into their 19-game freefall. He lost six games during that streak, three of his losses being blowouts, two of the other three by 2–1 scores. Young Cy held his own against the rest of the league until mid-August, when his record stood at 14–16. He won only two of his last 11 decisions, one of the wins being his third one-hit shutout of the season.

The late season slump Young Cy encountered in 1906 foreshadowed the difficult season he endured in 1907, when his ERA jumped up by a run and he turned in a dismal 10–23 record. He was traded to Pittsburgh in 1908 and dropped back to Class A ball in 1909. He was acquired by the White Sox in 1910, finishing his career with them as a part-time starter that year and the next.

Another player who gave Beaneaters fans something to smile about was rookie Johnny Bates. The young center fielder didn't wait long to get started. In his first time at bat in the majors he drove one of Harry McIntire's pitches over the right field fence. His home run turned out to be the game winning hit, the only run in Young Cy Young's opening day 1–0 victory over Brooklyn. Game-winning home runs were not a common occurrence in the Deadball Era, a condition that flowed down from the fact that home runs of any kind were uncommon. That said, Bates won three more games with home runs in 1906.

On June 18 Johnny had a walk-off home run in the bottom of the ninth to defeat Ed Reulbach and the Cubs 2–1. A couple weeks later He repeated the feat, leading off the bot-

Irv Young, known as "Cy Young the second" and "Young Cy Young," was a bright spot in a couple of dreary seasons for the Boston Beaneaters (Library of Congress).

tom of the ninth with a drive over Boston's left field fence for the only run in a 1–0 victory over the Phillies. It took another month for him to bop another game-winning four-bagger. This one came in the sixth inning against the Reds' Bob Wicker. With a man on first Bates hit a high fly that just managed to clear the fence as right fielder Frank Jude looked up at it. The two runs gave Boston a 2–1 victory. Bates had two other home runs in 1906, giving him a total of six on the year, tying him with Sherry Magee for fifth place in the league.[81]

Bates played in the major leagues for nine years. He never hit more than six home runs in a season, duplicating his 1906 number in 1913, when that total was only enough to rank 15th in the league. By that time Johnny had been traded twice, first to the Phillies in 1909 and then to Cincinnati after the 1910 season. Over the course of his career Bates proved to be a slightly above average hitter with pretty good power, which in the Deadball Era usually translated itself into doubles and triples rather than home runs.

Six

1906, American League

Hitless Wonders: Chicago

1906 American League Standings

Team	W	L	Pct.	GB
Chicago	93	58	.616	—
New York	90	61	.596	3
Cleveland	89	64	.582	5
Philadelphia	78	67	.538	12
St. Louis	76	73	.510	16
Detroit	71	78	.477	21
Washington	55	95	.367	37.5
Boston	49	105	.318	45.5

For over two months it looked like the 1906 season would be very forgettable for the White Sox. It appeared to be a transition year, one in which the team tried to find two adequate outfielders and figure out how to get more hitting from the infield. Ducky Holmes and Jimmy Callahan, who had split the left field job in 1905, were gone—Holmes becoming a player-manager at Lincoln in the Western League, Callahan preferring to own and play for a semi-professional team in the Chicago City League. Danny Green, the team's regular right fielder since 1902, had declined as a hitter and could no longer make the long outfield throws. Green was loaned to Milwaukee of the American Association. When it was later suggested that he be brought back to the White Sox, a writer remarked, "that would necessitate keeping a player in short right to throw the balls back for Dan."[1]

Manager Fielder Jones made Frank Isbell his regular at second base, replacing light-hitting Gus Dundon. He eventually decided to stick with Lee Tannehill at third base, feeling that Tannehill's outstanding glove work outweighed his poor hitting. Because of an injury and time spent substituting at shortstop, Tannehill played only 99 games at third, but he still led the American League in assists.

The men initially projected to replace Holmes and Callahan in the outfield didn't pan out. Rube Vinson fielded a sparkling .600 in left field, fumbling four of his ten chances before being benched. Frank Hemphill fielded well enough, but didn't hit. Bill O'Neill, the youngster who failed as a replacement for Patsy Dougherty for the Boston Americans in 1904, became the regular in right field. The White Sox loved his speed, which was tremendous, but didn't think too much of his hitting, which was relatively light. In May Charlie Comiskey purchased Ed Hahn from the New York Highlanders. Like many of his new teammates, Hahn didn't post a high batting average, but he drew lots of walks and ran the bases well. In July, Patsy Dougherty was added to the team. Dougherty had jumped to the Tri-State League from the Highlanders. Comiskey talked him into coming to Chicago, and purchased his contract from New York.[2]

The team's pitching staff also suffered at the beginning of the season. Doc White, who had posted the lowest ERA on the staff in each of the two preceding years, had received permission to coach the Georgetown University baseball team and did not make his first start until May 21. Frank Smith, a 19-game winner in 1905, struggled with control of his spitball through most of the season, seemingly having mastered it at times, only to lose it again a short time later. Nick Altrock injured his ankle in April, but continued to pitch despite the injury.

These pitchers' difficulties created an opportunity for Ed Walsh, who had been working on his breaking pitches, and especially his spitball, while serving as an extra pitcher for two years. Walsh didn't exactly seize the opportunity in the spring, but he offered a glimpse of the good things that could result in the future if he gained control of a breaking pitch. In his first start he lost a close game to Detroit, 3–2. Then he relieved Frank Owen in the eighth inning of a 4–2 loss to the Tigers and let in an insurance run on a wild pitch. In his next appearance he allowed six runs in seven innings against Cleveland. After losing to Detroit again, 2–1 in 10 innings, Big Ed shut out Cleveland, allowing only one hit, but relying almost entirely on his fastball, abandoning the spitter after the first inning because he couldn't control it. The next turn in his roller coaster season was a steep drop. He gave up eight runs in three innings as the Sox took a 15–1 pounding from the Naps. He injured his side in that game, putting him on the sidelines for two weeks. He didn't make another start for three weeks, then lost his next two games. On June 3 his record stood at 1–5.[3]

While the White Sox treated the .500 mark like an impenetrable ceiling until deep into June, they remained part of a six-team group that harbored pennant aspirations. Only the hapless Senators and the nearly helpless Boston Americans were considered out of contention. On June 12 Chicago was 20–24, but trailed first-place New York by only 8½ games. Ten games later they had spurted to 29–25, moving up to fourth place, 4½ games behind Cleveland, which had taken over first place.

Chicago (93–58)

Name	AVG	OBP	SLG	R	RBI	SB
Ed Hahn, lf-rf*	.221	.331	.257	82	28	23
Fielder Jones, cf	.230	.346	.302	77	34	26
Frank Isbell, 2b	.279	.324	.352	71	57	37
George Davis, ss	.277	.338	.355	63	80	27
Jiggs Donahue, 1b	.257	.320	.318	70	57	36
Patsy Dougherty, lf*	.226	.278	.298	33	31	11
or Bill O'Neill, rf	.248	.301	.276	37	21	19
Billy Sullivan, c	.214	.262	.297	37	33	10
Lee Tannehill, 3b	.183	.254	.220	26	33	7
or George Rohe, 3b	.258	.316	.289	14	25	8
or Gus Dundon, 2b	.135	.224	.146	7	4	4

Leading Pitchers	W	L	Pct	IP	H	ERA
Frank Owen	22	13	.629	293	289	2.33
Nick Altrock	20	13	.606	287.7	269	2.06
Ed Walsh	17	13	.567	278.3	215	1.88
Doc White	18	6	.750	219.3	160	1.52
Roy Patterson	10	7	.588	142	119	2.09
Frank Smith	5	5	.500	122	124	3.39

*Includes record with New York

Despite their struggles, these were still the White Sox—a gritty team that fought until the last man was out. In April, after Chicago topped St. Louis by beating out three bunts in a row, and then scoring the tying and winning runs on a single, a *Post-Dispatch* writer remarked, "The White Sox will again bear watching. They are as tenacious in sticking to a game as a burr to a mule's tail."[4] By mid–June, the team began attracting an unusual amount of attention for their ability to win games in which they did little hitting. In a 1-0 victory over New York, Owen topped Al Orth, allowing eight hits. Orth, on the other hand, allowed only one hit, and that came in an inning in which the White Sox did not score. The lone run came on a hit batter, an error on an infield grounder, a fielder's choice, and another error, this time on a hot ground ball off the first baseman's glove. A few days later, after taking two games from Washington in which they managed three hits in each game, a Washington writer commented, "It is growing more and more apparent as the joyous summer days simmer past, that the Sox do not require hits to win the games they bag.... At the end of the sixth they had a run and nary a hit. They got a run by the aid of three safeties in the seventh, but it was superfluous. They would have won anyway."[5]

At about this time, the term "hitless wonders" began to be applied to the White Sox. They had been able to stay within reach of the top teams despite having the worst batting average in the league—on June 20, the Chicago team batting average was .220, the next worst mark was Boston's .239. In a somewhat envious tone, a Cleveland writer remarked, "Had Cleveland the ability, luck or whatever it is that the White Sox have to score runs on a few hits, the Naps would be so far ahead of the other seven teams in the American League that nothing short of a cyclone could stop them. Just think of a team than can field and bat like the Naps that also had the scoring knack that Fielder Jones and his teammates possess. Here they are about the weakest hitting team in the league, but season after season, they finish in the first division, even giving the pennant winners a battle. Game after game they win when they are outbatted anywhere from two to eight to one." At a time when Chicago had a total of 33 wins, the writer counted 12 games the White Sox won while being outhit by their opponents. "Primarily, the ability to pull off the right play at the right moment is the secret of the White Sox' success but at the same time there is more or less luck to many of their victories. They call them the 'hitless wonders' because they have been known to win many a game in which none of their runs were scored by aid of base hits. Many a run is scored by Chicago on a base on balls, a stolen base, a sacrifice and a fly to the outfield. If an opposing player makes an error, it is sure to happen when Chicago has men on bases. Oftimes, it is a wild throw that lets Chicago score two or three runs."[6]

At that point in the season the White Sox had been able to stay in contention without doing much hitting, but they remained near the end of a tightly packed group of six teams still having a good shot at winning the flag. On July 4, after winning five of their last seven games, they were in fourth place with a 37–31 record, five games behind the first-place Cleveland Naps. Nearly a month later, on August 1, they were still in fourth place, their 50–43 record putting them 7½ games behind the new leaders, the Philadelphia Athletics, but only three games ahead of the sixth-place St. Louis Browns. The next day the White Sox started a notable streak, Doc White shutting out Boston 3–0, as Frank Isbell drove in two of the Sox runs and scored the other. On August 3, Ed Walsh whitewashed the Americans, 4–0, not allowing a hit until one man was out in the ninth inning. Patsy Dougherty knocked in the winning run with a double and scored two of Chicago's four runs. The following day Roy Patterson notched the third straight shutout for the Chicago pitching staff, and Dougherty drove in the game's only run with a ninth-inning single.

Next came the league-leading Athletics. The White Sox swept them in a five-game series, in which Walsh and Patterson each threw shutouts for the second game in a row. Walsh allowed only three hits in his game. The sweep moved the White Sox to within 2½ games of the A's, but New York was also ahead of them, only a half-game out of first. That was no problem, they were headed for New York. Walsh topped Jack Chesbro, 2–1, in the opening game of the series, holding the Highlanders to five hits, while giving up his first run in three games. Patsy Dougherty, who had played a key role in the five-game sweep of the A's, tripled and scored the first run. Walsh scored the winning run himself. Owen won the second game of the series, 8–1, as the "Hitless Wonders" battered three New York pitchers. On August 12, Walsh came back on one day's rest to pitch another shutout, defeating Al Orth 3–0. The win was the tenth straight for the White Sox and moved them past the Highlanders and A's into first place. The next day Doc White and Chesbro fought to a scoreless tie in a game called after nine innings.

After a day off spent traveling to Boston, the White Sox resumed their winning ways. Walsh, pitching his third game in six days, threw another shutout, beating the Americans, 6–0. After adding two more victories over the Americans, the Sox moved on to New York for another big confrontation with the Highlanders. Walsh again opened a series with a whitewashing job, a 10–0 blowout with Chesbro on the losing end. White outpitched Orth 4–1 in the second game. With the help of a Sunday off-day and rain on Tuesday, Big Ed came back on three days' rest to beat Chesbro again, 6–1, in the first game of a doubleheader. Owen won the second game, 11–6.

Now for Washington. Patterson extended the winning streak to 19 in a row with a 4–1 victory in the opener, giving the team a 5½-game lead over the A's. However, all good things must come to an end sometime. Rain and a Sunday day off gave the Senators time to regroup. On Monday, August 25, Frank Smith, pitching for the first time in several weeks, took a 3–0 lead into the sixth. With two down and a man at first, he gave up four straight singles, plating two runs before getting the third out. That was the cue to turn once again to Big Ed Walsh, who breezed through the seventh and eighth without being touched. Meanwhile Chicago added another run to go into the bottom of the ninth leading 4–2. Big Ed entered the ninth having won nine games in a row and having allowed only two runs in his last 63 innings. John Anderson led off with an infield hit that George Davis just missed. After taking two strikes, Charlie Hickman doubled, sending Anderson to third. Two singles followed, tying the score and putting Jake Stahl on third. Pitcher Charlie Smith ended the suspense by smashing another single, bringing in Stahl with the run that ended the White Sox's 19-game winning streak. The Senators added insult to injury by also winning the second game of the doubleheader, knocking Roy Patterson out of the box in the first inning and saddling Doc White with the loss by a 4–3 margin.[7]

Chicago held a four-game lead after their streak ended. But they staggered a bit entering September. They split a two-game series in Philadelphia, then lost three out of five games against Cleveland. Meanwhile New York was in a stretch in which they won 15 straight games and 19 out of 20. By September 8, when the Highlanders reached the end of that 20-game set, they led the White Sox by 1½ games. To make matters worse, while they were dropping behind New York, the White Sox lost the services of two key players. Catcher Billy Sullivan had the thumb of his throwing hand smashed by a foul tip and third baseman Lee Tannehill dislocated his knee. When asked if, in the face of these developments he was worried about the Highlanders, Fielder Jones replied that he wasn't concerned. "They've got to play us. We beat them in Chicago and we beat them in New York. We will dispose of their chances in our own series, regardless of what happens elsewhere."[8]

That series began on September 21. By then, the White Sox had put together a seven-game winning streak and held a one-game lead over New York when the two teams clashed. The matchup didn't quite go the way Jones had envisioned. In a series-opening double header, Walsh and Owen went down to defeat. With the score tied, a man on first, and two men out in the ninth inning of the first game, two errors, a hit-batter and a single brought in three New York runs for a 6–3 win over Walsh. New York's 4–1 win in the second game came with some help by Frank Roth, who had taken Sullivan's place behind the plate. Doc White came off the injured list to win the next game of the series, but when Walsh lost a pitchers' duel, 1–0, in the final game, the series ended with the Highlanders in first place by a game.

At this juncture of the season a casual fan might believe the White Sox were ready to fade away, having fallen short after a spirited run at the pennant. A more knowledgeable fan might think back to the St. Louis writer's comment about the Sox "sticking to a game as a burr to a mule's tail." This team was filled with scrappy players. Having just blown the big series with New York, they responded by winning seven of their next eight games. The Highlanders, meanwhile, lost seven out of ten. The White Sox clinched the pennant on October 3, watching rain fall outside their hotel rooms in St. Louis while New York split a doubleheader with Philadelphia.

The White Sox had won the pennant despite posting a .230 team batting average—seven points below the next worst team, the Boston Americans, who managed only 49 wins and finished 45½ games behind the Sox. The rarity of that achievement has made the "Hitless Wonders" one of the most memorable teams in baseball history.

Not Again! New York

It would be hard to judge which group of rival fans were most disappointed by the last week comeback by the "Hitless Wonders." New York, Cleveland, and Philadelphia all seemed to have taken charge at some point in the race. Perhaps, since their team saw its lead disappear at the last moment for the second time in three years, Highlanders fans might have suffered the most.

The Highlanders, who were also at times already called the "Yankees," had three hot spells that carried them into the lead. The first, which can be characterized as an explosion of offense appropriate for the emerging nickname, began on May 15, when they won the last game of a three-game series with Cleveland, 5–4. They then swept four games from St. Louis, winning the last two games by scores of 14–4 and 8–3. Chicago interrupted the incipient winning streak by pounding Jack Chesbro and reliever Clark Griffith, 7–6. The Highlanders bounced back the next day with an 8–2 victory. Ten more wins followed, including games in which the Highlanders scored 15, ten, ten, and 14 runs. When the 17-game streak began they were in sixth place, with a 9–12 record, trailing first place Philadelphia by 5½ games. After the loss that ended it, they were in first place a half-game ahead of the A's. For the 17 games played during that time they averaged 8.1 runs per game, a terrific performance for the early Deadball Era.

New York (90–61)

Name	AVG	OBP	SLG	R	RBI	SB
Willie Keeler, rf	.304	.353	.338	96	33	23
Kid Elberfeld, ss	.306	.378	.384	59	31	19
or Joe Yeager, inf	.301	.407	.366	20	12	3
Hal Chase, 1b	.323	.341	.395	84	76	28
Frank LaPorte, 3b	.264	.300	.368	60	54	10
or George Moriarty, 3b	.234	.298	.340	22	23	8
Jimmy Williams, 2b	.277	.342	.373	61	77	8
Frank Delahanty, lf	.238	.282	.345	37	41	11
or Wid Conroy, ss-of	.245	.303	.332	67	54	32
Danny Hoffman, cf*	.254	.318	.319	38	23	33
Red Kleinow, c	.220	.287	.276	30	31	8
or Deacon McGuire, c	.299	.365	.333	11	14	3
or Ira Thomas, c	.200	.258	.243	12	15	2

Leading Pitchers	W	L	Pct	IP	H	ERA
Al Orth	27	17	.614	338.7	317	2.34
Jack Chesbro	23	17	.575	325	314	2.96
Bill Hogg	14	13	.519	206	171	2.93

Leading Pitchers	W	L	Pct	IP	H	ERA
Walter Clarkson	9	4	.692	151	135	2.32
Doc Newton	7	5	.583	125	118	3.17
Clark Griffith	2	2	.500	59.7	58	3.02

*Includes record with Philadelphia

The offensive outburst was obviously a team affair. But Kid Elberfeld was given special kudos for the club's success. He led the team in hitting and trailed only the Browns' George Stone in the American League at that time, with a 374 batting average. But many baseball people felt Elberfeld's contribution went far beyond his own individual performance. "Elberfeld is a cross-grained little fellow with a hot temper, who says and does things at times which make him look bad, but he's never played greater baseball in his life than at present. He is game and a fighter. His hitting is simply great, and he stands near the top of the American League batsmen," wrote Joe Vila, the Highlanders' correspondent to *The Sporting News*. "Elberfeld is a natural leader, and as Griff's righthand man he wants to win all the time. He has put a lot of ginger into the Yankees."[9]

Over the next three weeks New York's bats cooled down and the team dropped into third place, three games behind Cleveland. Then another hot streak began, this one lasting for a couple weeks in which they won ten of 12 games and moved past Cleveland and Philadelphia into first place, albeit by only a half-game. This time Hal Chase, the team's young first baseman, was singled out for praise. "Chase has flashed upon the Eastern baseball horizon as no other young player ever did and has instantly won the favor of the public as well as the press," wrote a New York journalist. "He can cover more ground than any other 'initial sacker' that I ever remember seeing, unless perhaps, Charlie Comiskey." The writer described three plays Chase made in a recent game. On one play, with men on first and second, Chase assumed his regular position off the bag, and then dashed to first to take a pickoff throw and tag out the runner. He followed that play with a diving grab on a grounder to his right, and ended the inning with a jumping catch of a line drive far over his head. "Anyone watching those three plays could not help thinking he (Chase) was a past master in the 'Lodge of First Basemen.' As far as I can see he is in a class all by 'him's lonesome.'"

Chase was in his second season with New York, and widely viewed as the best first baseman in the game. A Cleveland writer was one of several who echoed the New Yorker's praise for Chase's defensive skills. "It seems to be the opinion of about all the Cleveland fans who saw the New York games that, in Hal Chase, Clark Griffith has the best first baseman who ever pulled in bad throws. He is certainly a marvel about that sack and the way he covers bunts could not be improved upon. In fact, his every move is a picture, and many a fan did not take his eyes off the California boy while he was fielding."[10]

At the end of this hot streak Chase was batting .345, fourth-highest in the league. He finished the season with the third-highest average (.323), ranked fifth in RBIs, and stole 28 bases. Griffith seems to have had great confidence in Chase's ability to make contact. The New York manager employed the squeeze play more often than any other manager, and Chase was frequently called upon to lay down the squeeze bunt. Griffith called for the squeeze play at least 24 times, including one game in which he tried it four times (and failed on all but one attempt). "Prince Hal" was on the bunting end of the play at least 13 times.

The Highlanders third hot streak came as the pennant race was reaching its climax. It was the one in which they won 19 out of 20 games and edged past Chicago into first place. As related above, they slipped back into second place going into a series with the White Sox, but took over first again by taking three out of four games. Their one-game lead evaporated quickly, however, in Detroit. The team's most dependable starters, Jack Chesbro and Al Orth, each blew late inning leads to lose the first two games. They were shut out in the third game by John Eubank, who accomplished little else during a season in which he posted a 4–10 record. The Highlanders stumbled through the remainder of their schedule, losing four out of seven decisions before being mathematically eliminated from the race.

The fact that New York almost won the pennant was somewhat surprising given the state of their pitching staff. Griffith had not yet reconstructed his pitching staff. He again went to the bullpen much more often than managers had previously done. He allowed his pitchers to complete 99 of their 156 games, but when he pulled the starter he used an average of over two relief pitchers in the game. He relied very heavily on two pitchers—Chesbro and Orth. Although Chesbro started the most games in the league, Griffith didn't seem to have complete confidence in his former ace. The spitball artist completed only 24 of his 42 starts, a ratio more appropriate for a fringe starter than a staff's mainstay. Although Chesbro won 23 games in 1906, he had a tendency to lose effectiveness suddenly after five or six innings. Griff seemed to be on the lookout for signs that Happy Jack was losing his stuff, and was ready with a quick hook, causing a reporter to comment, "All season long Griff has been carrying a portable derrick for use on days when Chesbro pitches."[11]

The Highlanders' top pitcher in 1906 was Al Orth, who had been around so long he had already gone through two well-recognized nicknames. Early in his major league career, which began in 1895, he gained the nickname "The Curveless Wonder." From the stands it appeared as if he should be easy to hit. He had neither overpowering speed nor impressive breaking pitches. But when a writer decided to get into a position where he could judge Orth's pitches for himself, he found that Orth had a variety of breaking pitches. "They took just enough bend to completely fool the batsman," he said. "These short curves, together with his change of pace and his knowledge of the batsman, have made Orth a valuable pitcher."[12]

As the 90s came to an end, Orth picked up a second nickname. He became "Smiling Al," probably because he had a big, toothy grin that reminded people of Theodore Roosevelt, then of Rough Rider fame. "Orth gives his own signals to the catcher," explained a *Chicago Tribune* reporter. "He has a smile which is sometimes as narrow as W. J. Bryan's, and at others as all-pervading as Teddy Roosevelt's. When he intends to pitch a fast straight ball he smiles in such a manner that his mouth is just a line reaching from ear to ear. When he wants to pitch a curve he smiles a 26-tooth smile, and [catcher Ed] McFarland understands."[13]

Orth pitched for mediocre teams most of his career, spending seven seasons with the Phillies and two and a half with the Senators. He was considered an above-average pitcher, but not a top-notcher. His best two years prior to 1906 came while he was in Philadelphia. In 1899 he went 14–3 and in 1901 he posted a 20–12 record. He came to New York in 1904, in time to contribute an 11–6 record to the Highlanders' pennant drive. He began using the spitball during the 1905 season, when he threw six shutouts, three of which came in consecutive outings. Early in the 1906 season, after Christy Mathewson's splendid World Series performance had made the "fadeaway" the new fad in baseball pitches, a Boston writer claimed Orth had invented a new pitch–the "spit fall away."[14]

Smiling Al led the American League in victories in 1906, his 27 wins being four more than the second-best total, which belonged to his teammate, Jack Chesbro. He also led in complete games and innings pitched (338⅔). His earned run average (2.34) was good, but did not rank among the league leaders. Orth's best season turned out to be his last good season. In 1907, a poor season for the Highlanders, he could only manage a 14–21 record, and he followed that with a disastrous 2–13 mark in 1908. He was released in August of that year. The next year he served as player-manager for Lynchburg in the Virginia League until mid-year when the Highlanders' new manager, George Stallings, offered him a chance to return to his old team. Throughout his career Orth had been a good hitter, appearing at times as a pinch-hitter and occasionally playing in the outfield. Stallings used him in that role. Smiling Al appeared on the mound in one game that season, giving up four runs in three innings.[15]

A "Classic" Team: Cleveland

It is easy to imagine Cleveland sports writers busily rummaging through their files in late August trying to locate copies of articles they had written at that time of the year each of the previous two or three summers. Once again it was time to list the injuries and illnesses that had caused the Naps to fall back in the pennant chase. If anything, the 1906 version of the Naps' collapse was more dramatic than ever before. On paper, the Cleveland team statistics demonstrated that it was the best team in the league. The Naps led in hitting with a .279 batting average, 30 points above the league as a whole. Four of the top eight batting averages belonged to Naps players. They led in pitching with a 2.09 earned run average. Three of the top six in that category wore Cleveland uniforms and all three had ERAs below 2.00. They had the highest fielding average. Their keystone combination, second baseman Nap Lajoie and shortstop Terry Turner each led the league in assists, double plays and fielding average. The 1906 Naps looked so good on paper that a century later they were the subject of an article in the *Baseball Research Journal* that called them a "classic underachieving team."

Cleveland (89–64)

Name	AVG	OBP	SLG	R	RBI	SB
Elmer Flick, cf-rf	.311	.372	.441	98	62	39
or Harry Bay, cf	.275	.337	.325	47	14	17
Jim Jackson, lf	.214	.290	.259	44	38	25
or George Stovall, inf	.273	.288	.339	54	37	15
Terry Turner, ss	.291	.338	.372	85	62	27
Nap Lajoie, 2b	.355	.392	.465	88	91	20
Claude Rossman, 1b	.308	.338	.359	49	53	11
Bunk Congalton, rf	.320	.361	.396	51	50	12
Bill Bradley, 3b	.275	.324	.361	32	25	13
or Jap Barbeau, 3b	.194	.257	.279	8	12	5
Harry Bemis, c	.276	.311	.374	28	30	8
or Nig Clarke, c	.358	.404	.486	22	21	3

Leading Pitchers	W	L	Pct	IP	H	ERA
Otto Hess	20	17	.541	333.7	274	1.83
Bob Rhoads	22	10	.688	315	259	1.80
Addie Joss	21	9	.700	282	220	1.72
Bill Bernhard	16	15	.516	255.3	235	2.54
Jack Townsend	3	7	.300	92.7	92	2.91
Harry Eells	4	5	.444	86.3	77	2.61

In that article the authors—Rod Caborn and Dave Larson—mention nine factors that contributed to Cleveland's underachievement. These included a relatively poor record against left-handed pitchers, inability to break even in one-run games and extra-innings games, and a losing record against Chicago and New York. They concluded, however, that injuries to key players hurt the team most.

The first of these injuries involved Harry Bay. The fleet center fielder missed two weeks with a split finger suffered on June 13. The injury hindered his performance over the next three weeks after he returned. On July 19, Bay wrenched his knee trying to avoid a collision with shortstop Terry Turner on a short pop fly to the outfield, and was out for the remainder of the season. That same day, third basemen Bill Bradley was hit by a pitch, fracturing his arm just above the wrist. He was also gone for the rest of the year. Bay's absence meant that Elmer Flick moved from right field to center. Flick was a very good outfielder, so there wasn't much of a drop-off defensively. The other two outfield spots were manned by, Jim Jackson, Bunk Congalton, and Ben Caffyn. Jackson was a pretty good fielder, but not much of a hitter. Congalton hit .320, the fourth-highest batting average in the league, but he was a poor fielder and a slow baserunner. Caffyn had his problems both at bat and in the field. The result was a big decline from Bay's level of play, both on offense and defense. Bradley's main replacement was Jap Barbeau, who hit .194 and fielded .830. Barbeau only lasted a little over a month at third base, but then the position became a revolving door, as manager Nap Lajoie searched for an adequate replacement. He played 15 games there himself, which weakened two positions. He finally settled on George Stovall, a smooth-fielding first baseman who had become a utility player because he could not hit as well as Claude Rossman. Stovall was mediocre at third base. He played 30 games there for the Naps in 1906, but returned to the position in only three games over the remaining nine years of his career.

Another damaging injury was the sore arm suffered by Addie Joss in July. Reportedly, he "caught cold" in his arm pitching against Boston on July 24. A "cold" in the arm was a generic term used at the time when a pitcher experienced discomfort. Two days later Joss filled in as a substitute in center field in a game at Washington. When the team returned to Cleveland, he was given permission to rest at his home in Toledo for a week. He came back on August 6, shutting out Boston, 4–0, even though he "did not appear to have much outside of control and the proverbial prayer." Addie rested eight days and tried again, but lasted only three innings against Washington, giving up six runs in a game the Naps pulled out, 9–8. Three more weeks of rest followed that outing, and seemed to solve the problem.

In his next appearance Joss threw a six-hit shutout against St. Louis. He pitched at his normal level during the last month of the season. While Addie was struggling with his arm problems the Naps went 17–17, while both the White Sox and Highlanders were putting together winning streaks.[16]

One of the Naps' young players whose individual excellence helped to make the Naps' season a "classic underachievement," rather than just a plain ol' third-place finish, was Terry Turner. In his third season with the Naps, Turner hit more like an outfielder than a banjo-hitting Deadball Era shortstop. He ranked fifth in the league in doubles, ninth in total bases, eighth in runs scored and tenth in RBIs. In addition, he was one of the team's better baserunners, taking extra bases when given a chance, and stealing 27 bases. And that was the part of his game that seldom drew a comment, because his sparkling defensive play attracted so much attention.

He seemed to respond especially well to the crowds in New York. Each visit to that city seemed to bring plaudits for his fielding stunts. "Turner gave as finished an exhibition of shortstopping as has been seen here this or any other season," said one reporter after a game in the Big Apple. "His stops and throws were clean-cut and the danger of an error when he went after a batted ball never lurked in the minds of the spectators. Inning after inning he fairly hurled his lithe body at the flying sphere and by a long reach or a fast sprint he got his hands on the ball and retired the runner at Rossman's station by snappy and accurate flings. His nimbleness and faultless play earned merited applause for him on half a dozen occasions."

Fans in Boston were also impressed. "The honors of the game fairly belonged to shortstop Turner, for the superb game he played at short by all odds was the finest game seen in Boston this season," a reporter wrote. "The amount of ground that the little chap covered was phenomenal and he earned the bursts of applause that greeted

Terry Turner played outstanding defense at shortstop for the Cleveland Naps for several years before illness and injuries limited his playing time (Library of Congress).

his plays and the splendid reception he got when he stepped to the bat in the ninth."

Even an umpire felt compelled to praise the youngster. "Terry Turner is the sensation of the circuit," said Tom Connolly. "They go simply crazy over him at Boston, New York, and Chicago, and think that no other shortstop is in a class with 'Cotton.' For myself, I know I have never seen his work surpassed."[17]

Turner's batting average slipped down to .242 in 1907. The next season he was seriously injured when he was hit in the head by a pitch. He missed a significant number of games almost every season after that due to illness or injury. After 1910 his primary position became third base, although he also played second base and shortstop on occasion. He usually batted around .250, although in 1912 he hit .308. He was considered accomplished as a "scientific hitter," once leading the league with 38 sacrifices even though he played in only 121 games that season. He became one of Cleveland's most popular players, remaining with the Naps/Indians until 1918. Connie Mack brought him to Philadelphia in 1919, but Terry appeared in only 38 games for the A's.[18] In 1913 an article appeared in *Baseball Magazine* celebrating Turner's defensive skill at every infield position except first base, his small stature preventing him from being stationed at that position. Terry "has won his greatest laurels by his all but impossible fielding skill," the author noted. "No more easy, graceful and spectacular fielder ever lived with the exception possibly of his teammate Lajoie."[19]

Lave's Absence and Rube's Thumb: Philadelphia

Lave Cross was unhappy with his situation in Philadelphia. He was the A's captain, but Connie Mack relied on Harry Davis for advice about the team. In mid-season of 1905 Cross went to his manager and told him he would like a change of scenery, and wanted to play in Washington if a deal could be worked out. After trying in vain to get Lave to change his mind, Mack gave the veteran permission to talk to Washington manager Jake Stahl. An agreement was worked out in which Cross was to finish the season in Philadelphia, but would then be transferred to Washington in exchange for cash. "There was no other reason than that I liked Washington and thought a change would do me good that the change was made," Lave explained. "I always liked Philadelphia, however, and was fairly treated there. No ballplayer ever received better treatment anywhere than I got in Philadelphia and for that reason I feel rather sorry to make a change. There has never been the least friction between Connie Mack and me."[20]

Philadelphia (78–67)

Name	AVG	OBP	SLG	R	RBI	SB
Topsy Hartsel, lf	.255	.363	.334	96	30	31
Bris Lord, cf	.233	.281	.302	50	44	12
or Harry Armbruster, of	.238	.353	.306	40	24	13
Harry Davis, 1b	.292	.355	.459	94	96	23
Socks Seybold, rf	.316	.367	.418	41	59	9
Danny Murphy, 2b	.301	.341	.404	48	60	17
O. Schrecongost, c	.284	.305	.358	29	41	5
or Mike Powers, c	.157	.170	.162	5	7	2
Monte Cross, ss	.200	.291	.272	32	40	22
John Knight, 3b	.194	.250	.273	29	20	6
or Rube Oldring	.241	.263	.310	15	19	7
or Art Brouthers	.208	.240	.257	18	14	4

Leading Pitchers	W	L	Pct	IP	H	ERA
Rube Waddell	15	17	.469	272.7	221	2.21
Chief Bender	15	10	.600	238.3	208	2.53
Jimmy Dygert	11	13	.458	213.7	175	2.70
Eddie Plank	19	6	.760	211.7	173	2.25
Jack Coombs	10	10	.500	173	144	2.50
Andy Coakley	7	8	.467	149	144	3.14

Cross was 40 years old in 1906. Although the veteran had played well enough the preceding year, Mack had planned on trying out a couple younger players at third base that season. He would either move Jack Knight to third or try out a minor league recruit, Rube Oldring. When the season started, another new recruit, Art Brouthers, was at third. Brouthers was supposed to be a good fielder, but he made a rash of errors early in the season. The fans started getting on him about his fielding, which only made matters worse. After about a month Connie went to plan B, which was moving Knight to third. Jack responded by trying to top Brouthers in the error department, making three in his first appearance at third. "Manager Mack made a change in his team yesterday, sending Knight in to play third in place of Brouthers," a Philadelphia writer noted. "It is a toss-up which is the poorer player of the two and third base is at present a spot which is causing Mack some worry."

Mack wasn't going to undermine Knight's confidence by pulling him after one bad game. He kept the youngster at third for about two months. Knight, however, didn't produce. He fielded poorly and was batting about .170 in the first week of August when Connie went to Plan C. That was Eddie Lennox, who was signed away from Lancaster in the outlaw Tri-State League. Lennox lasted about a week, making one hit in 17 times at bat and fielding .909. On to plan D. Rube Oldring finished the season as the regular third baseman, but made errors galore—his fielding average was .897—and batted a mediocre .241.

Third base was not the only area of instability that became a concern in 1906. Another one was Rube Waddell's mind. During the off-season Rube's wife had sued for a divorce, which seemed to make Rube even more restless than usual. His season included a very busy nightlife. In spring training, while investigating the delights of the local bar scene, he wandered onto a side street. Afterwards, Rube couldn't say for sure what happened, but he had a six-inch gash on his head and was $40 poorer than before.[21]

His misadventures continued into the season, which included some periods of brilliant pitching and others of frustrating developments. Waddell and the A's started the season playing well. Rube's first two appearances were in relief. He pitched eight innings in relief of Jimmy Dygert in the second game of the season, holding Washington to three hits and striking out eight. A few days later he came into a game in the sixth, after Eddie Plank and Jimmy Dygert had been pounded for ten runs, and held the Senators scoreless for four innings before giving up the losing run of a 11–10 slugfest in the tenth inning. Rube then pitched shutouts in three of his next four starts. In the last of those shutouts, Ty Cobb led off a game with a bunt single. Rube held the Tigers hitless through the remainder of the game.

When Waddell next took the mound, on May 21, the A's had won 11 games in a row and were in first place, leading his opponent, the Cleveland Naps by 3½ games. Rube held the Naps to one run and struck out 13 batters in nine innings before being lifted for a pinch-hitter in the bottom of the ninth. Chief Bender, who relieved in the ninth, allowed only one hit, a home run in the 13th, losing 2–1. The next day Rube decided to relax by going for a ride in a horse-drawn carriage. As he was crossing an intersection, a delivery truck cut in front of him. Seeing that a collision was inevitable, Rube jumped out of the carriage, catching his left thumb in the whip socket, injuring it seriously. X-rays seemed to indicate that the injury was only a sprain, which meant the big hurler might be out for a week or two.[22]

It proved to be a couple weeks before Rube felt up to pitching. Meanwhile, the A's stumbled a bit, losing eight of their next 13 games. They were in second place, a game and a half behind New York, when Rube decided he was ready to pitch again. He lasted only three innings against Chicago, giving up five runs on seven walks and three hits. Disappointed, Rube drowned his sorrows at several pubs in Chicago and St. Louis. In one of them he decided to challenge a professional wrestler to an impromptu match. The encounter ended with Rube being body-slammed, hurting his back. Two weeks passed before Waddell's battered body was up to another attempt to pitch.[23]

This time Rube seemed to have recovered. He shut out Cleveland, allowing the hard-hitting Naps seven hits in a 2-0 victory over Addie Joss. The win put the A's back into first place by a half-game. Rube began pitching regularly, winning five of his next six starts, including two games in which he struck out 11 batters. During practice before his next game, Rube injured his tender thumb while hitting fungos. Although the thumb was swollen, he wanted to test it in the game. He lasted three innings, giving up four runs before leaving. Over the next three weeks—from July 14 to August 6—Waddell went to the mound twice, but could manage only one inning in each contest before requiring relief. During the last week of July he had the thumb lanced. The doctor discovered the bone had been split.[24]

Rube was ready to go again on August 7. At that time the A's were still hanging onto first place, but serious trouble was just over the horizon. They had lost the first two of a five-game series to Chicago. Rube held the "Hitless Wonders" without a hit for four innings before giving up two runs in each of the next two innings. He lost to Ed Walsh, 4-0. The A's, mired in a hitting slump, lost the next two games to the White Sox and three more to St. Louis, making eight losses in a row. Rube was scheduled to pitch the first game of a doubleheader on August 13. He won easily, shutting out the Browns, 8-0. He felt "fit as a fiddle," so he insisted upon pitching the second game also. Mack agreed to let him do it, but after Rube gave up four runs in the second inning, he sent in rookie Jack Coombs to finish the game.[25]

Waddell's recovery might have given the A's the boost they needed to win the pennant had it not been for other misfortunes. Eddie Plank, who was enjoying a fine season, came down with a sore shoulder. He pitched only one game after August 8, a five-inning outing against Boston in mid–September. Although he missed almost two months because of the injury, Plank was the A's top winner, with a 19-6 record. The team's other star pitcher, Chief Bender, who had been suffering from digestive problems since at least mid–July, also injured his arm. He pitched one game after August 21, mixing slow curves with slower change-ups in a 10-3 win over Washington.[26]

Over the last six weeks of the season the A's starting rotation was Waddell—who didn't pitch up to his normal standard—and rookies Jimmy Dygert and Jack Coombs. Mack gave a start to a minor league hopeful every week or so. As a result the A's dropped back into fourth place, not figuring as a contender for the pennant after mid–September. Waddell, whose record was 12-6 when he returned to action on August 7, won only three games while losing 11 over the last two months of the season.

He Don't Look Like a Hitter: St. Louis

St. Louis (76–73)

Name	AVG	OBP	SLG	R	RBI	SB
Harry Niles, rf	.229	.297	.281	71	31	30
or Ben Koehler, cf-rf	.220	.322	.237	27	15	9
Tom Jones, 1b	.252	.290	.315	51	30	27
George Stone, lf	.358	.417	.501	91	71	35
Charlie Hemphill, cf	.289	.338	.383	90	62	33
Bobby Wallace, ss	.258	.344	.345	64	67	24
Pete O'Brien, 2b	.233	.293	.277	44	57	25
Roy Hartzell, 3b	.213	.266	.230	43	24	21
Branch Rickey, c	.284	.345	.393	22	24	4
or Tubby Spencer, c	.176	.205	.218	15	17	4
or Jack O'Connor, c	.190	.199	.190	8	11	4

Leading Pitchers	W	L	Pct	IP	H	ERA
Harry Howell	15	14	.517	276.7	233	2.11
Fred Glade	15	14	.517	266.7	215	2.36
Barney Pelty	16	11	.593	260.7	189	1.59
Jack Powell	13	14	.481	244	196	1.77
Beany Jacobson	9	9	.500	155	146	2.50
Ed Smith	8	11	.421	154.7	153	3.72

George Stone had an odd batting stance. Almost every other batter in the major leagues stood straight up with feet spread wide enough to provide a firm balance. There were a few batters who took somewhat longer, hard swings at the pitch, but most players favored a short, choppy swing. Not Stone. He had a pronounced crouch, with his legs spread far apart. He moved his arms and hips some as the pitch approached, and took a hard, but quick and relatively short swing. A St. Louis reporter described his approach as follows: "This Stone is the funniest hitter I ever saw. Half the time the pitcher fools him, yet he hits successfully. He will guess it a slow and then start to hit it that way. The ball will come fast and he will stumble, fall down, swing, re-swing, cover up, feint a few times and hit safe. Same way if he guesses a fast one and it is a slow. He will duck his nose in the ground, change his feet, give his hips a twist and hit like Hades.... I never saw such a queer hitter. The old boys were wont to guess it right and hit. Stone guesses it wrong and still hits."[27]

Stone told reporters the crouch gave him the advantage of putting his eyes "in a better position to follow the ball, as they are almost on a direct line with any delivery that comes over the plate." One observer attributed his success to his strong arms and wrists, which gave him the ability to use a heavy bat and still hit the ball very hard with a short swing. Stone also had very good speed, allowing him to beat out bunts and infield hits.[28]

Although he had posted some outstanding batting marks in the minor leagues, Stone's style was so unusual that many knowledgeable baseball people doubted he could succeed in the major leagues. After he hit .346 in the Class A Western League in 1902, the Boston Americans purchased his contract. Boston Manager Jimmy Collins wasn't impressed by the new recruit's stance. After George struck out in two pinch-hitting appearances in April he was sent to Milwaukee, where he hit .298 in 1903. The next year Stone led the American Association with a .406 average, the highest average in the league's history. When St. Louis approached Boston about a deal for Stone, Collins agreed to trade the top minor league hitter for Jesse Burkett, who had been a great hitter, but was obviously nearing the end of the line. In the spring of 1905, after St. Louis manager Jimmy McAleer saw his new acquisition take his position at the plate, he began to worry that Collins had put one over on him. Once the season began, however, Stone's performance allowed his manager to relax. In a May series against the Highlanders George reached base 14 times in 18 plate appearances. His batting average ranked among the league leaders and he showed good power. In June he hit two home runs in a series against Detroit. A month later, a St. Louis reporter commented, "Stone's opportune hitting is little short of sensational. In two days he has tied up the score by a double which scored two runners.... He is rapidly developing into the most remarkable hitter in the American League."[29] George's final batting average in 1905 was .296, the sixth-highest in the league, and only 12 points behind Elmer Flick's league-leading average. He led the league in hits and total bases.

In 1906 Stone was outstanding. He was batting over .400 as late as mid–May. In June he encountered a slump that dropped his average to about .350, which provoked a St. Louis writer to blurt out: "The mighty Stone seems done. Truth to tell, the writer never could see how Stone got them. All spring he was making base hits when the pitchers were deceiving him grossly. He would swing at what he thought was a fast one, find it a slow, stop his slap, take another pass and paste it. He was swinging at balls an hour too soon yet getting base hits with one hand. When pitchers keep on out-guessing a man how can he hit?"[30]

Aided by his speed and bunting ability, Stone soon ended the slump. On June 23, he beat out three bunts against Cleveland. He also got bunt hits in several other games and began driving the ball once again. Soon his average was up around .370. And he continued to get his hits in an unorthodox manner. "Stone hit that prodigious pelt to left center with one hand," said one game summary. "He took a full swing, was too quick, but by letting go with his left followed through, on the scoffled [sic] golf basis, caught it fair and hit it one mile. It was a huge boost, but was hit so hard and traveled so fast that [Chick] Stahl could not get under it. Truly a beautiful bash."[31]

It would be hard to argue that Stone wasn't the top hitter in the American League in 1906, even if he wasn't very stylish in doing so. He was number one in batting average (.358), on-base percentage (.417), and slugging percentage (.501). He finished in the top ten in 14 different offensive categories, including stolen bases and hit-by-pitches. One man can only do so much to help a team win, but he played a big part in the Browns jumping to fifth place with a 76–73 record in 1906 after finishing last in 1905 with 99 losses and only 54 wins.

Another player who contributed to the Browns' improvement was a young catcher named Branch Rickey. Like Stone, Rickey was unorthodox, but in a different way. Stone was a committed ballplayer who had a different approach to the game. At this stage of his career, Rickey was a somewhat confused young man who thought maybe he would play baseball a year or two before moving on to another career, such as law. Rickey had signed with the Reds in 1903, but had only sat on the bench for them for a few days before he announced that he didn't believe in playing baseball on the Lord's day. His manager, Joe Kelley, responded that he didn't believe he needed Rickey on the team. The Reds sold Branch's contract to Dallas in the Texas League. The young catcher played part of the 1904 season with Dallas, and coached football and baseball teams for Allegheny College during the remainder of the year.

Meanwhile Rickey's contract had been obtained by the Chicago White Sox, who traded him to the Browns in 1905. Branch informed the Browns he would be available only between June 15 and September 15, due to his

Although he had an unusual batting stance, George Stone enjoyed several fine seasons with the St. Louis Browns. He was the American League's top hitter in 1906 (Library of Congress).

college commitments, and that he did not play ball on Sundays. Despite those demands, the Browns signed him. He appeared in one game before an emergency arose taking him away again. His parents had become ill, and he was needed at home to care for them. While he was looking after his parents, the Browns farmed him back to Dallas. When his parents recovered, late in the summer, Branch caught for the Texas League team, batting .295 in 37 games.[32]

The Browns needed a catcher, so they invited their reluctant young backstop to spring training in 1906. This time Rickey made it through most of the season with St. Louis. He played in a little less than half of the Browns' games over the first third of the season. Although he hit only .224 through those games, he made a good impression around the league. A Detroit writer, ignoring a poor throw that contributed to a 2–1 Tiger victory, remarked, "This Rickey looks like a good man with the stick. His drive in the sixth, on a line to Crawford, was as well-hit as either of his two safeties." In Boston, the *Globe's* Tim Murnane said Rickey had caught a clever game and "went after fouls like a terrier after a rat." Washington sports fans were informed that Branch had been "a revelation to St. Louis fans," and had forged ahead of the other three Browns catchers. A *St. Louis Post-Dispatch* writer noted that Boston fans were "in love" with Rickey. "His praises are in the mouth of every man who sees the games. Hitting like a fiend, fast as an outfielder, throwing like poor Martin Bergen, noisy as old Tom Tucker behind the bat and a fellow who is always fit and in condition to catch, he has made the hit of years in Boston. His work in this series has been grand. That a young fellow from a fifth-class league should jump into the breach when the old catchers, O'Connor and Spencer, were unfit for play, catch game after game against the best teams in America and teams he never saw before is regarded as one of the wonders of baseball."[33]

But the St. Louis writer also mentioned another fact about Rickey. "Certainly for peculiarity Branch Rickey, the backstop, is in a class by himself. While the Ravens were in Cleveland Rickey, who has absolutely no respect for the letter 'R,' filled up on oysters. Then symptoms of ptomaine poisoning showed themselves. Mr. McAleer excused Rickey and the latter went to his home in Portsmouth, Ohio. Yesterday the news was flashed across the wire that Mr. Rickey had taken unto himself a wife."[34]

The Browns' young catcher could be an innovative and subtle thinker, but when it came to batting he kept things simple. He grabbed a long bat just above the handle and swung hard. And, in 1906 at least, it worked. He hit .284, with a .393 slugging percentage—both pretty good for any batter in 1906 and outstanding for a Deadball Era catcher. Among catchers with at least 200 at-bats, Rickey tied Osee Schrecongost for the top batting average and slugged .053 higher than any other backstop. (Nig Clarke batted .358 and slugged .486 for Cleveland, but had only 179 at-bats.)

As good as his hitting was, Rickey had a gigantic hole in his game. "This young catcher has an arm of steel and shoots the ball at the mark with accuracy and speed, but he has the fault of most young catchers, he does not get the ball away from him quickly," said a reporter. "Rickey, when he poises for a throw, is very picturesque, almost a model. He draws his arm very far back, throws out his chest, puts his left foot in proper position and then lets go at the mark. When Rickey completes these preliminary passes the runner generally has a start which is an advantage." The White Sox took advantage of that weakness to steal five bases in two innings in a September game. That event and similar ones brought a less analytical but more direct comment: "Rickey's throwing was immense in practice, but pusillanimous in action. He could pick a fly off second in exhibition, but could not hit a barn in actual endeavor."[35]

Rickey parted ways with the Browns the next spring when he was traded to the New York Highlanders. During the winter he injured his throwing arm while working out in a gym. As a result, his mediocre throwing deteriorated into a record-breaking low level. On June 28 the Washington Senators decided they would test his arm. He responded by giving up 13 stolen bases, a single-game record that still stands. Branch got into 52 games with the Highlanders, only 11 as a catcher. He was able to compile a batting average of .182 in the last full year of his playing career. (He put himself into two games as a pinch-hitter while managing the Browns in 1914.)

Rickey gave up baseball for a while after that season. He studied law and coached baseball at the University of Michigan. He became a special assistant to Browns owner Robert Hedges in 1913 and, near the end of the season, became the team's manager. In 1917 he moved to St. Louis's National League team as the Cardinals' president. He became noted for developing the first modern farm system with the Cardinals, transforming that franchise from a yearly second-division finisher to an annual contender. Later, of course, he became the general manager who brought Jackie Robinson into organized baseball with the Brooklyn Dodgers.[36]

A Fighting Team: Detroit

The trouble began in spring training. Ty Cobb, although only 19 years old, seemed about ready for a job as one of the team's regular outfielders. He had put on about 25 pounds over the winter and still had his outstanding speed. Cobb had joined the Tigers at the end of August in 1905. He got into

41 games. Although he had batted only .240, he had shown great promise. In his first spring training with the Tigers, Cobb became convinced that a clique of veteran players, led by outfielder Matty McIntyre and Ed Killian, were trying to drive him off the team. According to Cobb, they made him the butt of petty jokes, played cruel tricks on him, and showed a general attitude of animosity towards him. Ty reacted by separating himself from other members of the team, becoming a loner who avoided places where he might encounter his teammates.[37]

While Cobb placed the blame solely upon the "clique" that he thought was out to get him, others saw the matter differently. "We weren't cannibals or heathens," said Sam Crawford decades later. "Every rookie gets a little hazing, but most of them just take it and laugh. Cobb took it the wrong way. he came up with an antagonistic attitude, which in his mind turned any little razzing into a life-or-death struggle. He always figured everybody was ganging up against him."

"Ty didn't have a sense of humor," said Davy Jones. "Especially, he could never laugh at himself. Consequently, he took a lot of things the wrong way. What would usually be an innocent-enough wisecrack would become cause for a fist fight if Ty was involved."[38]

Detroit (71–78)

Name	AVG	OBP	SLG	R	RBI	SB
Davy Jones, cf	.260	.347	.310	41	23	21
Germany Schaefer, 2b	.238	.290	.296	48	43	31
Sam Crawford, rf-1b	.295	.341	.407	65	66	24
Matty McIntyre, lf	.260	.338	.343	63	39	29
or Ty Cobb, of	.316	.355	.394	45	41	23
Bill Coughlin, 3b	.235	.293	.297	54	60	31
Chris Lindsay, 1b	.224	.293	.265	59	36	18
Charley O'Leary, ss	.219	.253	.271	34	41	8
or Bobby Lowe, ut	.207	.233	.248	11	13	3
Fred Payne, c	.270	.316	.338	24	22	4
or Boss Schmidt, c	.218	.242	.264	13	10	1
or John Warner, c*	.227	.288	.293	20	18	7

Leading Pitchers	W	L	Pct	IP	H	ERA
George Mullin	21	18	.538	330	315	2.78
Red Donahue	13	14	.481	241	260	2.73
Ed Siever	14	11	.560	222.7	240	2.71
Wild Bill Donovan	9	15	.375	211.7	221	3.15
Ed Killian	10	6	.625	149.7	165	3.43
John Eubank	4	10	.286	135	147	3.53

*Includes record with Washington

Six. 1906, American League   255

The feud between Cobb and his teammates lasted throughout the season. It formed the backdrop to several incidents and undoubtedly undermined the team's overall performance. The first public demonstration of the turmoil roiling the team came on May 5. The Tigers and Browns were playing in Detroit, but had a game against each other scheduled the next day, a Sunday, in St. Louis. Manager Bill Armour agreed to call the game at 5:00 so the two teams could catch a train. Two hours was normally enough time to complete a game, but this one turned out to be a high-scoring affair. With the score tied 7–7 in the last of the ninth, the Tigers had a man on second and no outs when the game was called. Detroit officials were so upset about the outcome of the game that Secretary Navin publicly criticized Armour for entering into the agreement. Armour responded by wiring his resignation from St. Louis. After discussing the matter further with Navin, the manager soon changed his mind, and the club announced that he would continue in the position with absolute authority over the team. It later became known that Armour was to finish the current season with the Tigers and then be replaced.[39]

While it was not mentioned as part of Armour's discontent, the bickering among his players had to play a role. On June 24 Armour announced that he had suspended McIntyre indefinitely because of his indifferent work. Matty batted behind Cobb in the Tigers' batting order. All too often, with Cobb on base, McIntyre seemed to be making little effort to advance him. A catcher on an opposing team told a reporter that Matty had once told him, "You don't suppose I going to help that ... to the plate, do you?" He then struck out, seemingly on purpose. Armour had spoken to McIntyre several times about his lack of effort. Matty retorted that he hated Cobb and did not care to play on the same team with him. After a week McIntyre became sufficiently contrite to gain reinstatement.[40]

Ed Killian, mentioned by Cobb as a co-leader of the clique opposing him, had a run-in with the young outfielder after Ty made a bad throw to third, leading to a run. After the inning ended, Killian had words with Cobb on the bench. He punctuated his remarks by throwing a punch, and the two had to be separated by other players.[41]

On August 9, after being absent from the team for two or three days, Killian entered the clubhouse, evidently very drunk, and smashed the furniture. Security guards restrained him from going out on the field. After being suspended indefinitely, Killian went to Chicago and began pitching for a team in the city semi-pro league at $100 a game.[42]

When they announced Killian's suspension, the Tigers also said they had sold catcher Jack Warner to Washington. Warner was released, the club said, to restore harmonious conditions. The veteran catcher had been telling McIntyre he was being treated unjustly and had been a bad influence on the team's younger players. One writer commented that Warner had a reputation for getting involved with cliques wherever he played, and as a result he had been traded a half dozen times.[43]

Dissension among the Detroit players continued until the end of the season. The team's last game was a meaningless encounter with St. Louis. In the seventh inning, with a man on first base, George Stone lined a drive into left-center, between McIntyre and Cobb. Neither man made an effort to get the ball, which rolled to the fence while Stone and the baserunner circled the bases. Detroit's pitcher, Ed Siever, blamed Cobb. He confronted Ty at the hotel that evening. The two exchanged angry words and then punches. Cobb proved to be much the better street fighter of the two, giving Siever a black eye and kicking him in the face when Siever went to the floor.[44]

Despite all the turmoil swirling around him—maybe invigorated by it—Cobb showed superior baseball skills. Still a teenager, he had the sixth-highest batting average in the league (.316) and the ninth-best on-base percentage (.355). He impressed baseball men with his speed, being timed at 3.2 seconds going to first base. A Detroit writer remarked that Sam Crawford would be leading the league in hitting if he had Cobb's speed. "The Georgian's speed helps him and makes base hits of a lot of balls that would be outs for many batsmen," he added.[45]

But He Can Hit the Ball a Long Way: Washington

Wherever he played, the fans loved Charlie Hickman. During the Deadball Era there was much talk about the wonders of scientific baseball, but deep-down the fans loved to watch batters who could hit the long ball. And when he caught one solidly, Hickman could knock the living bejabbers out of the ball. Scarcely a season passed without Charlie being credited with "the longest hit of the year" in at least one park, and in his good years he would earn that distinction at two or three locations. Late in the 1902 season Jimmy McAleer, whose career dated back to the late 1880s, described Hickman's game-winning home run in a recent game in Cleveland as the longest drive he had ever seen. "Hickman met the ball half way, wrapped his club around it and pushed. The ball went over the fence, over a house and a bunch of trees, and the last I saw of it I thought it would surely land in Youngstown," said McAleer. The next season Charlie hit another one about that far. Facing Al Orth, the "Curveless Wonder," in another game in Cleveland, he smashed a ball reported as "the longest ever made at League Park since Cleveland has been in the American League, clearing the left field fence by at least ten feet and dropping a hundred feet outside the park."[46]

Charlie was among the leaders in the slugging categories each year from 1900 through 1906, with the exception of 1901, a year in which he was kept busy trying to learn the fundamentals of playing virtually every position on the field except catcher. During those years he was always among the top six in his league in slugging percentage, except for 1901. He was among the top five in home runs five times, finishing second three times and fourth twice. Charlie enjoyed a great year in 1902, when he hit .361, finishing behind only Nap Lajoie and Ed Delahanty. That year he led the league in hits and total bases and was second in home runs and RBIs.

Washington (55–95)

Name	AVG	OBP	SLG	R	RBI	SB
Rabbitt Nill, inf	.235	.340	.273	37	15	16
Charlie Jones, cf	.241	.283	.326	56	42	34
or Harry Schlafly, 2b	.246	.345	.329	60	30	29
Dave Altizer, ss	.256	.324	.307	56	27	37
Lave Cross, 3b	.263	.303	.322	55	46	19
John Anderson, lf	.271	.296	.343	62	70	39
Charlie Hickman, rf	.284	.311	.421	53	57	9
or Joe Stanley, rf	.163	.236	.199	18	9	6
Jake Stahl, 1b	.222	.266	.274	38	51	30
Howard Wakefield, c	.280	.303	.355	17	21	6
or Mike Heydon, c	.159	.238	.221	14	10	2
Leading Pitchers	W	L	Pct	IP	H	ERA
Cy Falkenberg	14	20	.412	298.7	277	2.86
Casey Patten	19	16	.543	282.7	253	2.17
Charlie Smith	9	16	.360	235.3	250	2.91
Long Tom Hughes	7	17	.292	204	230	3.62
Frank Kitson	6	14	.300	197	196	3.65

Had Hickman been even average on the basepaths and in the field, his powerful bat probably would have kept him in one city and he would be remembered as a player who was the darling of the fans in that city for a decade or so. Instead he became a baseball nomad. After brief trials with the Boston Beaneaters as a pitcher in 1898 and 1899, he caught on with the New York Giants in 1900. Charlie jumped to the Boston Americans in 1902, but was sold to Cleveland after a couple of months. After about two years in the Forest City, he was shipped across Lake Erie to Detroit. There he was reunited with manager Bill Armour, who had been critical of Charlie's weak fielding in Cleveland. When the criticism was renewed, Hickman became angry and left the team, bringing about his sale to Washington in July of 1905.[47]

Charlie's build wasn't conducive to great speed and no amount of work during practice time could make him a good fielder. After complaining that Charlie had "pounded out many a three-bagger that with a fast runner would have been a homer," a reporter explained to his readers that "Hickman's underpinning is a little weighty for speed around the bags." Charlie's short, thick "underpinnings" led writers to tag him with the nickname "Piano Legs."[48]

Hickman was with the Senators for a little over two years, so their fans were able to experience the full range of his abilities. On the day of his arrival a writer told them what to expect: "Washington will not find in Hickman a sure fielder or a clever baserunner. He is prone to fall over himself in turning the bases and scrambling after fielding chances. His forte is hitting the ball on the nose, and therein he is a valuable man for the Nationals and worth the big price paid for him."[49]

Although he had played primarily at first base and in the outfield while with Cleveland and Detroit, the Senators decided to put Charlie at second base, a position he had tried with moderate success while with Cleveland. Shortly after his debut with the Senators, Charlie gave an example of what he could do as a second baseman. In the fourth inning, with his team leading 1–0, he made a fine play to cut off an incipient White Sox rally. Ducky Holmes was on first with one man out when George Davis hit a sizzling grounder near second base. The *Tribune* game summary described Charlie's reaction: "Hickman transformed himself into a long distance telescope and, by shooting out his full length, just managed to scoop the ball up and toss it to Cassidy, forcing Holmes out, then fell flat and slid twice his length in the dust back of second base." Later in the game, though, Charlie fumbled two grounders, one of which started the rally that won the game for the White Sox.[50]

Later, against his former Cleveland teammates, Hickman made some great plays. "The game was featured by Charlie Hickman, who gave a wonderful exhibition of playing second base with one hand," remarked a reporter. "Once he made a one-handed catch of a fly ball away back of second. Again he grabbed a line drive by Flick with one wing, and he ended up by making a regular Lajoie one-handed pickup of a grounder hit by Bradley." Charlie's play in that game drew some favorable comments by Cleveland writers, who were still kindly disposed towards him. A St. Louis reporter, however, was not so kind after an 11–6 victory by the Browns: "'Cheerful Charlie' Hickman played like a lobster at second. At times he could hardly get out of his own way. He slipped, stumbled, fumbled and tripped. Out of nine fielding chances he fell down on five." Charlie played 85 games at second base for the Senators in 1905, fielding .922—about 20 points below an acceptable average for the position. Over the next season and a half, he played there in only four more games.[51]

Six. 1906, American League 259

While Charlie's fielding at second base was a mixed bag, his hitting for the Senators was great. His batting average with the Senators was .311, which was three points higher than Elmer Flick's league-leading average. His slugging percentage of .447 while in a Washington uniform trailed Flick's .462, but was better than anyone else's. This comparison, however, ignores Hickman's numbers with Detroit. He batted only .221 for the Tigers. Nonetheless, Charlie hit well enough with the Senators to bring his overall numbers up among the leaders. His season-long batting average was .277, which ranked 11th in the league. His slugging percentage (.405) ranked sixth. He ranked third in number of extra base hits (53).

In 1906 Washington manager Jake Stahl decided Charlie's best—or, maybe, least-worst—position was right field. A snippet from the game summary of a 6–3 loss to the A's demonstrated the perils of that decision: "In the seventh Hickman received a skyscraper from Monte Cross, or rather he didn't receive it. So far no university has conferred the degree of E. F. (eminent fielder) upon C. Hickman, and it is not believed that any will this year. That ball from Cross stayed up in the air like a tariff reform committee. It seemed glued to the azure. Finally it came straight down toward the expectant but erratic C. Hickman. By a wonderful contortion he so twisted his neck and arms that the sphere passed right between his nose and hands and fell to the ground without being touched. It was a magnificent exhibition of how not to play right field."[52]

A couple throws to the wrong base and some difficulty dealing with the sun contributed to a stretch in which Washington lost 12 of 14 games. Among a reporter's suggestions for avoiding streaks of that sort in the future was removing Charlie from his station in right field. "Charlie Hickman has yet to give a reason why he should be retained in the field. Hick is one of the sweetest dispositioned players in harness. In Cleveland he numbers his friends by the thousands. A perfect gentleman and a dandy fellow, but Charley should not be kept in right field. Personal feelings and friendship are severed in baseball. There is no sentiment. Hick was late coming around last season, and until the sun gets lower in right field the fat boy should be allowed to rest up."[53]

Of course, Charlie wasn't standing out there in right field because of his fielding ability. He was out there waiting for a chance to bat. And he did his part in that phase of the game. A few days before the non-catch described above, Charlie hit one of his "longest hits ever" drives, "a four-bagger that went over the 'man-in-the-moon' sign, three feet from the top of the fence. It was the longest drive seen on these grounds in many years." About a month later he hit another one, with Lave Cross on second base: "The last time Lave saw the pill it looked like a speck off on the horizon.

Then came a dull thud and the horsehide danced off the boards and rolled toward the score sign. It was one of those 'longest hits seen on the local grounds this season,' but it sent over two runs and gave the District gang a lead of three runs." On a trip to Cleveland in June, Charlie hit the first ball to clear the left field fence in 1906. The next day he hit the second. In July he lined one off the center field fence in Washington. That drive didn't qualify as a "longest hit ever," but a Washington writer thought it was "a peach." In late September Hickman drilled another one, this time in St. Louis. "The wallop was about the longest seen here since Jake Stahl drove his famous clout over the bleachers and into the street."[54]

In 1907 Charlie injured his knee in spring training. The injury evidently reduced his power somewhat and undoubtedly affected his play in the field. On August 1, he was sold to the Chicago White Sox, who planned on using him primarily as a pinch-hitter. Hickman's major league career was nearing its end on December 21, 1907, when the White Sox sold him to Cleveland. A Cleveland reporter greeted the news by saying, "As a Christmas present to the Cleveland fans, the local club announced this evening that the release of Charlie Hickman, one of the most popular men that ever wore a Cleveland uniform, had been purchased from Chicago." The reporter explained that Hickman would be used as a utility fielder and pinch-hitter. "When he was traded for Charlie Carr, a few years ago, a great howl went up from the local public, although the fans admitted that Charlie had lost many a game in consequence of his errors." Cleveland fans had remained fond of Charlie, the reporter noted. "Ever since then he has been applauded every time he went to bat in Cleveland as a member of the Detroit, Washington and Chicago clubs, and it is a sure thing that the Cleveland club's action in securing him will be commended."[55]

Hickman hit .234 for Cleveland in 1908, his last season in the majors. He was sold to Toledo in mid-season. There he hit .409 in 47 games. He played for Toledo and Milwaukee through the 1911 season, hitting for a good average and knocking out plenty of extra-base hits.

Thud! Boston

Boston (49–105)

Name	AVG	OBP	SLG	R	RBI	SB
Jack Hayden, rf	.248	.292	.301	22	14	6
Freddy Parent, ss	.235	.277	.297	67	49	16
Chick Stahl, cf	.286	.346	.366	63	51	13
Hobe Ferris, 2b	.244	.262	.360	47	44	8

Name	AVG	OBP	SLG	R	RBI	SB
or Jimmy Collins, 3b	.275	.295	.408	17	16	1
Jack Hoey, lf	.244	.274	.288	27	24	10
or Kip Selbach, lf	.211	.277	.268	15	23	7
Moose Grimshaw, 1b	.290	.332	.383	46	48	5
or Buck Freeman, rf-1b	.250	.302	.349	42	30	5
Red Morgan, 3b	.215	.270	.264	20	21	7
or John Godwin, inf	.187	.215	.207	11	15	6
Charlie Armbruster, c	.144	.242	.184	9	6	2
or Bob Peterson, c	.203	.277	.254	10	9	1
or Bill Carrigan, c	.211	.252	.211	5	10	3

Leading Pitchers	W	L	Pct	IP	H	ERA
Cy Young	13	21	.382	287.7	288	3.19
Joe Harris	2	21	.087	235	211	3.52
Bill Dinneen	8	19	.296	218.7	209	2.92
George Winter	6	18	.250	207.7	215	4.12
Jesse Tannehill	13	11	.542	196.3	207	3.16
Ralph Glaze	4	6	.400	123	110	3.59

The Boston Americans' fall from first to fourth in 1905 was certainly painful to their players and fans alike. But that season was pleasant compared to what transpired the next year. The Americans finished eight games out of seventh place. The team's collapse was so thorough as to be almost unbelievable, reaching to every aspect of their game and involving all but a few players on the team.

The bad news started over the winter when catcher Lou Criger began suffering severe pain emanating from his spinal cord. "There were two choices—to cut or burn," a reporter explained. "To have cut the fiber would have paralyzed his right side and this would have meant death to a man of Criger's activity. He chose the other alternative and was seared with hot irons along the full length of the spine from top to base." Criger was assured that the operation was a success, and that he would be able to play before long. But the pain returned. He was unable to join the team until mid-August, and then he promptly injured a finger. He played a total of seven games in 1906.[56]

Boston had no adequate replacement for Criger, who was widely recognized as one of the top defensive catchers in baseball. All season long, opposing teams took liberties on the bases, succeeding in stealing plenty of bases and drawing wild throws that eventually led to runs. Boston catchers led the league in errors and passed balls. Poor catching was probably the worst of the team's many weaknesses—*Boston Globe* writer Tim Murnane estimated it cost the team 20 games before August 1.[57] Four players, excluding Criger, were tried and none of them did the job, although one—Bill Carrigan—would later develop into a very good catcher.

Catching was probably the most important defensive position in the early Deadball Era. Close behind it was third base. There the Americans played most of the season with men who couldn't find the range to first base. Jimmy Collins opened the season at third, but hurt his knee early in the season. He tried to play through the injury, but couldn't get to balls hit to either side and had trouble stabilizing himself for the throw to first base. He played only 32 games at the position over the entire season.[58] One of his replacements, Red Morgan, led the league's third basemen with 41 errors, even though he played only 88 games at the position. Morgan's fielding average was a dismal .866. His play caused a Detroit reporter to assert, "Anything that looked like a bunt caused chills on Boston's infield. This fact being discovered by Detroit, ample opportunity was furnished Messrs. Morgan and Young to handle taps. They did their best, but the result was something weird. By mixing bunts and bingles, the victory was secured."[59]

In the outfield, left fielder Kip Selbach played well enough defensively during the time he was with the team, although he had put on weight and lost speed, but he hit only .211. He was released at the end of June. His successor, Jack Hoey, who came straight from college ball, had a very rough time in the field. Like third baseman Morgan, he led the league in errors despite playing only a few games more than half a season. Comments in game summaries included complaints that Hoey had trouble judging balls chopped to left field by left-handed batters, had trouble dealing with glare from the sun, misplayed ground balls, and was slow in getting rid of the ball on throws.[60] Other than that he seemed to play just fine.

When a team has a very weak fielder in a position, it puts pressure on the men around him and usually leads to a decline in their effectiveness. That almost certainly happened with Boston, especially since they were very weak in three positions—four when Buck Freeman was playing, since Buck was a poor fielder in both the outfield and first base. Boston made 45 errors more than any other American League club, their .949 fielding average being .005 worse than any other team's.

At bat, the Americans managed to outhit one team—Chicago's pennant-winning "Hitless Wonders." Boston's batters collectively averaged .237, while the White Sox could manage only .230. But the pale hose didn't just swing away at the ball. They coaxed 87 more bases on balls than any other team. They moved runners along with sacrifices and stolen bases. Jimmy Collins' team didn't do that stuff. They were dead last in walks, sacrifices, and stolen bases. They stole only 99 bases, while the seventh place team in that category, the A's, stole 166. As a result they scored 55 fewer runs than any other team; 104 fewer than the White Sox, who finished third in runs scored despite their low team batting average. In August, after the Americans were shut out for the fourth consecutive game, a writer called them "the Runless Wonders."[61]

Given the weaknesses in other aspects of the team's performance, it is hard to judge how far Boston's pitching slipped in 1906. They had the worst team earned run average in the league, naturally. But individually, the pitchers got some pretty good performance evaluations over the course of the season. Cy Young, who was 39 years old when the season began, had the worst won-lost record of his career and posted his highest earned run average since 1897, when teams scored at a much higher level than in the Deadball Era. He was hit pretty hard in at least a half-dozen games. But he had several games in which game summaries described him as possessing as much speed as ever. Of his 21 losses, nine came in games in which he gave up three runs or less. In late June Tim Murnane commented that Young and Bill Dinneen "were pitching fine ball" and would have had winning records if the Americans were able to generate runs.[62]

The only Boston pitcher who posted a winning record was Jesse Tannehill, who once again "paddled his own canoe." Jesse went 13-11, but he got pounded in a few games, just like Old Cy did. The biggest difference between the two was that the Americans averaged about 1.5 more runs scored per game behind Jesse. Tannehill suffered a couple of injuries during the season that limited him to only 26 starts and one relief appearance.

For the team's veteran pitchers, the season was mostly a blot on otherwise successful careers. For rookie Joe Harris, however, it was career-defining. He had joined the Americans late in 1905. While he lost two of his three decisions, he seemed to have a bright future. After he lost his debut with the Americans, a 2-1 loss to St. Louis in which he gave up only six hits, manager Jimmy Collins proclaimed him the "pitching find of the season." He lost his next game, but then beat Detroit 4-1, holding the Tigers to three hits in a seven-inning contest in which he struck out eight Tigers.

Harris began the 1906 season in a relief role, pitching well his first couple of outings. He didn't make his first start until May 10, when he lost to Philadelphia 5-1. He was somewhat wild, and was handicapped by Bob Peterson's poor catching. The A's stole three bases off Peterson and moved runners into scoring position on a passed ball and an errant pickoff throw. Joe started—and lost—about one game a week in May. Then injuries to other pitchers led to a regular spot in the rotation. Harris pitched well enough—even though he continued his losing ways–but had a tendency to lose his stuff in the late innings. He also showed a damaging lack of ability to field bunts. On July 30, he held St. Louis to one hit over the first five innings. He had a 4-0 lead when he opened the sixth by throwing 12 straight balls, to fill the bases. Cy Young was rushed into the game without having sufficient time to warm up. He allowed three runs to score in the sixth, but blanked the Browns in the final three innings, preserving Harris's first win of the season after 14 straight losses. Joe lost his next start, 4-0 to Chicago, but on August 9 blanked Cleveland 1-0, for his second—and last—win of the season.

On September 1, Joe hooked up with Philadelphia rookie Jack Coombs in a pitchers' duel. In the third inning, Harris fell down fielding a bouncer off Coombs' bat. Boston's catcher once again undermined Joe's pitching, Bill Carrigan making a bad throw to second on Coombs' steal attempt. The opposing pitcher than went to third on a grounder back to Harris. He scored when Harris was late covering first base on a grounder. That was the only run Joe gave up until the 24th inning, when in the gathering darkness the A's pushed home three runs to win 4-1. Harris sprained his ankle in practice the next day and pitched only two more times in 1906, losing both games, of course. He finished the season with a 2-21 record. That was a pretty bad won-lost record but, somewhat surprisingly, others have done worse. In 1916, the year after Connie Mack broke up his championship team in response to sharp increases in player salaries due to competition from the Federal League, the A's suffered through the worst season in modern baseball, going 36-117. Jack Nabors posted a 1-20 record. Teammate Tom Sheehan was 1-16. Harris's .087 won-lost percentage positively shines in comparison to their .048 and .059 records. Joe came back in 1907 to add seven more losses, without a win, giving him a career mark of 3-30, the fourth worst among modern pitchers.[63]

For manager Jimmy Collins, the Americans' humiliating losing season was too much to bear. The team went 6-7 to open the season, then began a losing streak that went on for almost a month, and lasted 20 games. The response from Boston fans was exactly what could be expected—they blamed the manager. And they were probably right to a great extent. Collins had preferred veteran players to younger ones. He traded away two young guys—George Stone and Jake Stahl—who who played well for their new teams. He had not been much interested in taking time out to scout the minor leagues. The team had little depth to draw upon when age and misfortune struck. The team had won two pennants because of their excellent pitching and good power hitting. When the hits came less frequently the players were unable to resort to the "scientific baseball" tactics that would have enabled them to score more runs.[64]

Weighed down by disappointment over his inability to perform at his normal level because of his injured knee and battered by the constant losing coupled with withering criticism from fans and reporters, Collins began staying away from the ball park. Club officials covered for him at first, giving him permission to rest his knee for a couple of weeks. But when he remained absent long after he was expected back he was suspended. Before August ended he was relieved from his duties as manager.[65]

The "Slugging Wonders": 1906 World Series

Like the comic book character who shed his Clark Kent disguise to emerge as Superman, in the World Series the White Sox shed their weak-hitting exterior to reveal the power within. You could say that for the final two games of the series they became the "Slugging Wonders."

During the first four games the Sox played their brand of ball. The "dope" on the Cubs was that they had trouble hitting left-handers and spitball pitchers. So White Sox manager Fielder Jones selected Nick Altrock and Doc White, his two lefties, along with spitballer Ed Walsh, as his starters in all six games. Altrock outpitched Mordecai "Three Finger" Brown in the first game, a 2–1 nail-biter. Reserve third baseman George Rohe and Frank Isbell were the batting stars of the game. Rohe was playing because the regular third baseman, Lee Tannehill was filling in at shortstop for George Davis, who was suffering from a recurrence of his back pains. In the fifth inning he hit a ground-rule triple into the crowd in left field. He scored when Patsy Dougherty topped a ball down the third baseline, being called safe as Johnny Kling dropped Brown's throw on a close play. In the sixth, Altrock walked and went to second on Eddie Hahn's sacrifice. Jones hit a low fly into short center for a single. Altrock tried to score, but was thrown out by Solly Hofman, who substituted for injured Jimmy Slagle in center field throughout the series. Jones took second on the throw and went to third on a passed ball. He scored the winning run when Isbell singled along the left field foul line.[66]

Doc White started the second game for the White Sox, but the Cubs showed that they weren't easy marks at bat just because a twirler threw the ball with his left hand. They pounced on White in the second inning. After Chance had struck out, Steinfeldt rapped a single. Tinker surprised the White Sox with a bunt, making first without a throw being made. Evers hit a sharp grounder that Isbell fielded, but threw poorly on an attempted back-hand throw to second. Steinfeldt scored on the play, Tinker went to third, and Evers to second. After Kling was given an intentional walk, Reulbach squeezed Tinker home with a hard bunt that Isbell fielded and was just able to get Reulbach at first. Hofman drove in Evers with the third run of the inning on a ball that Tannehill just got to. Hofman beat the throw to first, but Kling was out trying to score from second on the play.

Frank Owen replaced White after the third. The Cubs got to him for four more runs, using the aggressive baserunning and scientific batting tactics that had enabled them to win 116 games. They stole five bases in the game, which they won 7–1, and forced Billy Sullivan, the top defensive catcher in the American League, into making two bad throws.[67]

Still performing in their characteristic "Hitless Wonders" style, the White Sox regained the lead in the series by taking game three, 3–0. Ed Walsh baffled the Cubs with his "vapor float," holding them down to two hits, both coming in the first inning, and fanning a dozen Cubs. George Rohe was again the batting star for the Sox. In the sixth inning Tannehill led off with a sharp single past Steinfeldt. Jack Pfiester, expecting a sacrifice attempt from Walsh, tried to tempt him into going after a bad pitch, but ended up walking his rival pitcher. Hahn, failing to judge an inside pitch correctly, was hit in the nose with the ball. He was forced to leave the game, Bill O'Neil running for him. Pfiester almost pitched his way out of the jam, getting Jones on a foul and striking out Isbell. But Rohe duplicated his ground-rule triple of the first game, clearing the bases.[68]

Game four went to the Cubs, 1–0. Three-Finger Brown showed the form that made him the premier pitcher of 1906, shutting out the White Sox on two hits. Johnny Evers sparkled on defense, making a great play to cut off a possible run-scoring hit, and a number of other fine stops. "From second base to short right field behind Chance, Evers tore up the turf back and forth, and always was found where most needed," commented a Chicago reporter. Evers also drove in the game's only run. Chance led off the seventh with a single. He went to third on successive sacrifices by Steinfeldt and Tinker. Evers brought him home with a line single to left.[69]

Although the fifth game of the series was played on the Cubs' home field, Chance's men came out wearing their road uniforms. They had decided to wear gray, rather than the prescribed white, because they had won both games played on the South Side. After the Cubs scored six runs on just six hits a reporter remarked, "Chance's sluggers took up the roles laid down by the Sox and became 'Hitless Wonders' themselves." The White Sox seemed to have also changed their persona. They became sluggers, driving out 12 hits, eight of them for extra bases, and scoring eight runs. Both teams began putting runs on the scorecard as soon as they could. The Sox scored a run in the top of the first, but the Cubs answered with three in the bottom of that inning. The pale hose tied the score in the third and then pulled ahead by four an inning later. Chance's pseudo "Hitless Wonders" pecked away at the lead, but couldn't quite catch up.

The White Sox were led by Frank Isbell, who knocked out four successive doubles. In the first inning he smashed one to right field, knocking in Hahn with the game's first run. In the third he led off with a double and scored on Davis's double. Later in the inning Davis and Pat Dougherty pulled off a double steal that scored the veteran shortstop. In the fourth, Isbell drove out his third double with men on first and second. Davis followed with his second double, giving the American Leaguers a four-run lead.

Isbell's fourth double came in the sixth, with one out. He went to third on a ground out and scored the Sox' last run on Rohe's single. Ed Walsh was the beneficiary of all this slugging. He gave up six runs and had allowed a leadoff double in the seventh inning when Doc White came to his relief. White shut down the Cubs over the last three innings, preserving the 8–6 victory.[70]

Chance turned to Three-Finger Brown in an effort to even the series in game six. This time Brown didn't seem to have much on the ball. He was buried under an avalanche of hits, allowing seven hits and seven runs in an inning and two-thirds. Doc White held the Cubs to single runs in the fifth, eighth and ninth innings, as the White Sox won the game, 8–3, and became the champions of Chicago and the baseball world.[71]

Seven

1907, National League

Depth: Chicago

"No team can have too many pitchers, if they are good ones," remarked Frank Chance during spring training. "The slightest injury throws a pitcher off his form and there is no telling when half of a twirling corps may be out of condition."[1] By then Chance had already ensured that his team would have a deep and effective pitching staff. At that time most teams were using a four-man starting rotation–a recent development–and had one or two extra pitchers available to fill in when an injury sidelined one of the starters. Chance opened the 1906 season with seven reliable, experienced starters. He kept them all busy, all of them appearing often as starters and helping out in relief at times.

1907 National League Standings

Team	W	L	Pct.	GB
Chicago	107	45	.704	—
Pittsburgh	91	63	.591	17
Philadelphia	83	64	.565	21.5
New York	82	71	.536	25.5
Brooklyn	65	83	.439	40
Cincinnati	66	87	.431	41.5
Boston	58	90	.392	47
St. Louis	52	101	.340	55.5

Chance was also careful to ensure that he had an adequate bench in case of injury to his regular players. But in that case he didn't necessarily rely on having a dugout full of substitutes. His secret weapon in that respect was utility player Art "Solly" Hofman, who was virtually a one-man bench.

After having a cup of coffee with Pittsburgh in 1903, Hofman was picked up by the Cubs near the end of the 1904 season. He played mostly in the outfield in his brief trial that September, but, according to a *Tribune* reporter, the next spring he remained with the team because of his ability to play the infield. The reporter suggested that Hofman might replace Joe Tinker as the regular shortstop.[2] Instead, he got most of his playing time at second base because of an injury to Johnny Evers. Foreshadowing his role over the next several years, however, over the course of the season Hofman played at least one game at every position except pitcher and catcher.

In August of that year Hofman was playing second base. The Beaneaters had runners on first and second and one out when the batter

Arthur "Solly" Hofman was virtually a one-man bench for the Cubs in 1907. That season he was at times cited as the team's most valuable player. Behind Hofman is pitcher Jack Pfiester (Library of Congress).

rapped a short fly just over the keystone bag. "There wasn't any chance for any ordinary mortal to get anywhere near it, so the runners put on a full head of steam," said a *Tribune* writer. But Hofman "ran back, jumped a couple or three yards in the air, and stretched his six feet three stature out to twice that length. This enabled him to just reach the ball with his bare hand. He squeezed it in the air, and before touching earth again performed some sort of a contortion feat which enabled him to throw the ball to Tinker at second while at least half of his anatomy was facing the clubhouse. Cannell was at the plate before he knew that he had been doubled at second." The writer exclaimed that the play would cause Hofman "to be known forevermore by the pseudonym Circus Solly." The nickname became commonly used by Chicago fans.[3]

Hofman quickly gained recognition for his versatility. "The club is amply protected against the ordinary, casual accident, because it has in Hofman one of the greatest all round utility men in the game," remarked a reporter early in 1906. "He can play any position on the infield with speed and accuracy, and is even better in the outfield. With any one of the regulars laid off, the team will not be seriously crippled, although the team work will be deranged a bit." When Jimmy Slagle was injured late in September, Hofman took his place in center field. He played there every game of the World Series, doing so well that some baseball men were suggesting he might supplant Slagle as the regular. "The real feature of the series was the discovery of young Hofman's real worth," said a correspondent to *The Sporting News*. "He subbed for Slagle in center and Slagle probably will sub for Hofman next spring. In this lad Chance has one of the most promising outfielders in the game. His fielding suggests that of Barrett, when Jimmie was at his best. Like Barrett, he is away with the crack of the bat, and times a ball perfectly. He has a fine arm, is fast, and can throw."[4]

Chicago (107–45)

Name	AVG	OBP	SLG	R	RBI	SB
Jimmy Slagle, cf	.258	.359	.294	71	32	28
or Solly Hofman, ut	.268	.328	.311	67	36	29
Jimmy Sheckard, lf	.267	.373	.324	76	36	31
Wildfire Schulte, rf	.287	.339	.386	44	32	7
Frank Chance, 1b	.293	.395	.361	58	49	35
Harry Steinfeldt, 3b	.266	.323	.336	52	70	19
Joe Tinker, ss	.221	.269	.271	36	36	20
Johnny Evers, 2b	.250	.309	.313	66	51	46
Johnny Kling, c	.284	.342	.386	44	43	9
or Pat Moran, c	.227	.271	.278	8	19	5

Leading Pitchers	W	L	Pct	IP	H	ERA
Orval Overall	23	7	.767	268.3	201	1.68
Mordecai Brown	20	6	.769	233	180	1.39
Carl Lundgren	18	7	.720	207	130	1.17
Jack Pfiester	14	9	.609	195	143	1.15
Ed Reulbach	17	4	.810	192	147	1.69
Chick Fraser	8	5	.615	138.3	112	2.28
Jack Taylor	7	5	.583	123	127	3.29

Hofman was at times cited as the Cubs' most valuable player in 1907. The team suffered a number of serious injuries and illnesses. Hofman filled in effectively at several positions. He was the shortstop on opening day because Joe Tinker was still recovering from an appendicitis operation. When Tinker came back, in mid-May, Hofman was switched to right field. That became his position for about three weeks, although he also filled in at first base, third base, left field, and center field for a game or two during that time. Although he was considered a substitute player, Hofman played in every game through June 30, when he had to sit out because of his own injury. By the end of the season, Solly had been in 134 games, the fifth-highest total of any Cub, playing 42 games at shortstop, 69 in the three outfield positions, 18 at first base, and a handful at the other two infield positions.[5]

By the last day of June, when Hofman sat out his first game of the season, Chicago was well on the way to their second straight pennant. The season had followed the pattern of recent National League seasons: New York and either Chicago or Pittsburgh exploding out of the gate and pulling well ahead of the pack, with the winner of that opening two-month sprint holding on to take the pennant, while everyone else dropped well off the pace. At first it appeared the Giants would be the team that would leave everyone else in their tracks. They put together a 17-game winning streak that gave them the lead on May 18 with a 24–3 record. The Cubs, however, were only a game back of them at 23–4. The two teams sparred on pretty even terms until the beginning of June, when Chicago started pulling ahead. They were eight games ahead of the Giants when Hofman took his first rest and slowly increased their lead after that. By August the contest that most enthralled Cubs fans was between the 1907 team and their 1906 predecessors—could they match or beat the record they had just established. Of course, they fell short by nine games in that matchup.[6]

A quick glance at the team statistics listed above would seem to indicate that none of the Cubs had a particularly fine season, especially when it is noted that the three top hitters didn't have very high runs scored and RBI totals. That was because two of the three—Frank Chance and Frank

Schulte—missed large chunks of the season because of injuries and the other—Johnny Kling—was given time off to recover from the rigors of catching. On the other hand, a broader view would show that Joe Tinker was the only regular whose batting average was below the league-wide mark—a weak .243. Nobody was doing much hitting, which meant the Cubs secondary offensive talents, such as sacrificing and stealing bases aggressively, had a larger payoff than ever. In each of those categories the Bruins had three men ranking among the top ten.

Johnny Evers provided an example of how the team's aggressive baserunning paid dividends. Although he batted a modest .250, Evers stole 46 bases, tying the Phillies' Sherry Magee for second in the league. Most notable, however, was that Evers stole home six times in 1907. Four of them were part of delayed steals, in which a man on first tries to steal second, drawing a throw from the catcher, and the man on third (in these cases, Evers) takes off for the plate as soon as the catcher starts his throw to second. Two of the steals were "clean" steals of the plate, in which Evers timed the pitcher's motion and beat the pitch to the plate. Evers also scored from second base on an infield out and scored on a play in which he went from first to third on a single by Tinker. On that play, he beat the outfielder's thrown to third on the hit. Tinker moved up to second on the outfielder's throw, and when the third baseman tried to head him off at that bag, Evers raced home, beating the second baseman's ensuing throw to the plate.[7]

In the low-scoring environment prevailing in 1907, team defense and pitching played a big part in any team's success or failure. Each of the Chicago regulars was noted for his defensive skills, as were backup catcher Pat Moran and backup-everywhere Solly Hofman. And the deep pitching staff that Chance put together paid off handsomely. In discussing the 1906 Cubs, we noted that Chicago's 1907 pitching staff had the lowest ERA in modern baseball. Five of the six lowest ERA's in the National League were posted by Chicago pitchers. Jack Pfiester led the league with a 1.15 ERA; Carl Lundgren was second with 1.17, and Three-Finger Brown followed with 1.39. Pittsburgh's Sam Leever poked his way in at number four with a 1.66 figure, then came Orval Overall at 1.68 and Ed Reulbach at 1.69.

The competitive spirit that drove the team was commented upon by veteran pitcher Jack Taylor after the season ended. Taylor was released in September. True to form, he complained that the team had shorted him one day's pay in his severance check. He continued to grumble to reporters deep into the off-season. "I was tickled to get away from the Champion Cubs as it's no cinch to pitch ball for a bunch of pennant winners," Taylor said. "I was never so unhappy in my life as during the time I was with the Cubs on this last probation. I was sick and tired of being crabbed at by

Johnny Evers and Tinker and one or two others when I was in the box. They'd roast me, kick at me, and advise me until I felt like throwing the ball over the fence and quitting the job. You've got to go too strong to suit me in order to please everybody concerned. I'd much rather be with a second-division club, where you don't have a lot of crabs jumping all over you all the time and where you don't have to wait two or three weeks before you hear the last of some game you lost."[8]

The hyper-competitive atmosphere probably caused strains in personal relations between other players, too—the most famous instance being long-standing animosity between Evers and Tinker. But, on the field, it worked for the Cubs. They won their third straight pennant in 1908, beating the Giants by one game in the year of "Merkle's Boner," finished second in 1909, and won their fourth pennant in five years in 1910, finishing 13 games ahead of the second-place Giants.

Improved Baserunning: Pittsburgh

At the beginning of spring training, Barney Dreyfuss was assessing his team. "Some of the fans are inclined to blame our downfall last season on the slab artists, but I cannot see it that way at all." He cited the number of shutouts as proof that the pitching staff did just fine. (Pittsburgh pitchers threw 27 shutouts, only the Cubs' staff exceeding that total, with 30.) And he mentioned that the Pirates had finished with the second-best batting and fielding averages. "It was in baserunning that we fell down," Dryfuss asserted. "In the past we had had a good baserunning team, but last season the boys fell down in that department and it resulted in our finishing where we did."[9]

Pittsburgh (91–63)

Name	AVG	OBP	SLG	R	RBI	SB
Goat Anderson, rf	.206	.343	.225	73	12	27
Tommy Leach, cf-3b	.303	.352	.404	102	43	43
or Bill Hallman, of	.222	.305	.255	39	15	21
Fred Clarke, lf	.289	.383	.389	97	59	37
Honus Wagner, ss	.350	.408	.513	98	82	61
Ed Abbaticchio, 2b	.262	.357	.331	63	82	35
Joe Nealon, 1b	.257	.301	.325	29	47	11
or Harry Swacina, 1b	.200	.240	.232	9	10	1
Alan Storke, 3b	.258	.295	.317	24	39	6
or Tommy Sheehan, 3b	.274	.341	.310	23	25	10
George Gibson, c	.220	.261	.301	28	35	2
or Ed Phelps, c	.212	.282	.221	11	12	1

Leading Pitchers	W	L	Pct	IP	H	ERA
Vic Willis	21	11	.656	292.7	234	2.34
Lefty Leifield	20	16	.556	286	270	2.33
Sam Leever	14	9	.609	216.7	182	1.66
Deacon Phillippe	14	11	.560	214	214	2.61
Howie Camnitz	13	8	.619	180	135	2.15
Nick Maddox	5	1	.833	54	32	0.83

Dreyfuss' analysis partially explained why his team parted ways with two of the core players from the championship teams of 1901–03 during the winter. Claude Ritchey and Ginger Beaumont were sent to Boston, along with pitcher Patsy Flaherty, for Ed Abbaticchio, who was slated to play second base for the Pirates. Ritchey was generally considered one of the top fielders at that position, but he had slumped a bit in his hitting and was not a fast baserunner. Abby, on the other hand, hit with some power and was fast and aggressive on the bases. Beaumont was included in the trade because back problems had taken away much of his speed in 1906, and both he and the team feared the condition might prevent him from taking the field in 1907.[10]

Even though the Pirates' stolen base totals had declined in relation to the rest of the league after 1902, when they led the league in steals, they had remained aggressive in going after extra bases when opportunities were presented. In 1907 they continued those tactics, but also stole 102 more bases than they had the preceding year, 29 more than any other team. They became the top scoring team in the National League, scoring 63 more runs than the second-best Cubs.

It didn't take long for the Pirates to give notice to the rest of the league that they were going all-out on the bases. On April 21, they trailed St. Louis 4–1 going into the seventh inning. With one out, Honus Wagner and Tommy Sheehan pulled off a double steal of second and third. Tommy Leach beat out an infield roller to second, scoring Wagner. Ed Phelps singled, scoring Sheehan and sending Leach to third. Wee Tommy scored on a delayed steal, Phelps drawing the catcher's throw and making second when the second baseman bobbled the throw. Three batters and two runs later, the Pirates tried their third double steal of the inning, but the Cardinals managed to nip the lead runner at third. Three weeks later they scored five runs in the first inning against the Beaneaters, the feature of the inning being a triple steal—Fred Clarke stealing home and two other runners moving up on the same play. By June 21, they had stolen 100 bases. That day they added five more to that total. A week later, they scored twice on double steals with men on first and third in the first inning against the Cubs.[11]

The emphasis on the running game helps to explain how Goat Anderson managed to get into 127 games with the Pirates in 1907. "Anderson is a player of the Willie Keeler style. Like Keeler he is not of the slugging kind, but on the order in which the New York player has made a name for himself, that of being able to beat out bunts," commented a reporter in April. He was right in stating that Anderson was not a slugger, but unlike Keeler the Pirate outfielder didn't do much else with his bat than beat out bunts, as indicated by his .206 batting average and his total of five extra base hits for the season. He was not as helpless at the plate, however, as those numbers would suggest. He walked 80 times and had an on-base percentage of .343, which put him among the top 25 in the league. His 73 runs scored ranked eighth. Unfortunately for "the Goat," his talents were too one-sided for Dreyfuss and Clarke. After the season ended he was sent to Rochester of the Class A Eastern League. Although he was never able to hit above .249, even in the minors, he remained in professional baseball until 1913.

With the trade of Ritchey and Beaumont, the Pirates had only three regular position players remaining from the 1903 world champions. (A fourth player, Ed Phelps, had been the primary catcher in 1903. Since then he had been traded to Cincinnati, re-acquired in 1906, and was a backup catcher in 1907.) The three regulars were Honus Wagner, Tommy Leach, and player-manager Fred Clarke. All three contributed heavily towards the Pirates' success in 1907.

Wee Tommy Leach, who was five feet, six inches tall and weighed all of 150 pounds, was one of the leading "sluggers" of the early Deadball Era. Tommy got his extra-base hits not so much because he hit the ball a long way, but because his speed enabled him to maximize the effect of hits that went between the outfielders. He finished among the top ten in triples six times during his career, and the same number of times in home runs. He enjoyed one of his better years in 1907, finishing fourth in batting average (.303) and sixth in slugging percentage (.404), triples (12), and home runs (4). He was second in runs scored (102) and fourth in stolen bases (43).

Like several of the Pirates, Leach was willing to take long chances on the basepaths. In June he led off an inning against the Beaneaters with a single. After the next two batters went out, he stole second. A walk followed. Then Goat Anderson laid down a bunt and beat it out. Tommy sprinted around third on the bunt and headed for home on the throw to first. He just managed to beat the throw to the plate with a headfirst dive. In a later game against Boston, he was on second base and Anderson was on third when Fred Clarke tried the squeeze play. Anderson scored easily on Clarke's bunt. Tommy also tried for the plate on the play, but this time he was tagged out. On at least a couple occasions he went from first to third on sacrifice bunts, and in one game against the Superbas he twice tried to get two bases on infield outs, making it one time and being put out the other.[12]

Clarke also finished in the top ten in batting average (.289), on-base percentage (.383), and slugging percentage (.389). Four of the top ten base stealers were Pirates. Wagner led the league with 61, Leach was fourth, Clarke sixth (37), and Abbaticchio (35) tied for seventh.

Wagner was his usual self—the best player in the league by far. He won his fifth batting title with a .350 average—.107 above the league average—and began a string of three consecutive seasons in which he would finish with the National League's highest batting average, on-base percentage, and slugging percentage. As a demonstration of his all-round ability, he also led in stolen bases in both 1907 and 1908, the latter season the fifth time he did so.

The two pitching holdovers from 1903, Deacon Phillippe and Sam Leever, were both 35 in 1907. They continued to pitch well, especially Leever who posted the fourth-lowest ERA in the league, but they were no longer asked to shoulder the heavy workloads of previous years. Vic Willis and Lefty Leifield were now the staff leaders.

Two pitchers who were to have big years in the future made their marks in 1907. Howie Camnitz had pitched briefly for the Pirates in 1904. He went 1–4, possibly because he overused his curve ball, not varying his pitches enough to keep batters off balance. After winning 22 games with Toledo of the American Association in 1906, he rejoined the Pirates near the end of the season, winning his only decision. He didn't make his first appearance with Pittsburgh in 1907 until June 11, when he saved a game for Sam Leever, pitching the last four innings of a 7–4 win over Brooklyn. He alternated relief appearances and starts for the next couple of months. Although he was somewhat inconsistent, he had some impressive outings. On

Although a small man, Tommy Leach was one of National League's top "sluggers," depending upon his speed to pick up extra bases on hits to the outfield (Library of Congress).

July 9 he gave up only one hit in six innings of relief against Philadelphia. Three weeks later he threw a two-hit shutout against the Phillies. On August 23, pitching the second game of a doubleheader, he held the Giants hitless in a game shortened to five innings because of travel arrangements. Over the next two weeks Howie pitched a four hitter, a five-hitter and a one-hit shutout, while also appearing twice in relief. In 1908 Camnitz went 16-9. The next season he led the Pirates to the pennant with a 25-6 record.

Nick Maddox made his major league debut on September 13 by fanning 11 batters and allowing only five hits while shutting out the Cardinals 4-0. He beat St. Louis again three days later, then threw a no-hitter against the Superbas. In three weeks with the Pirates, Maddox started and completed six games, finishing with a 5-1 record and an ERA of 0.83. In 1908 Maddox led the Pirates while posting a 23-8 record. Due to arm problems, he dropped to 13-8 in the pennant-winning season of 1909 and finished his big league career in 1910 by going 2-3.

Working at Their Craft: Philadelphia

Philadelphia (83-64)

Name	AVG	OBP	SLG	R	RBI	SB
Roy Thomas, cf	.243	.374	.301	70	23	11
or Fred Osborn, of	.276	.298	.325	22	9	4
Otto Knabe, 2b	.255	.339	.338	67	34	18
or Kid Gleason, 2b	.143	.200	.167	11	6	3
John Titus, rf	.275	.345	.382	72	63	9
Sherry Magee, lf	.328	.396	.455	75	85	46
Kitty Bransfield, 1b	.233	.262	.287	25	38	8
Ernie Courtney, 3b-1b	.243	.335	.314	42	43	6
or Eddie Grant, 3b	.243	.272	.280	26	19	10
Mickey Doolin, ss	.204	.243	.275	33	47	18
Red Dooin, c	.211	.252	.262	18	14	10
or Fred Jacklitsch, c-1b	.213	.312	.248	19	17	7

Leading Pitchers	W	L	Pct	IP	H	ERA
Frank Corridon	18	14	.563	274	228	2.46
Tully Sparks	22	8	.733	265	221	2.00
Lew Moren	11	18	.379	255	202	2.54
Buster Brown*	10	12	.455	193.7	175	2.74
Lew Richie	6	6	.500	117	88	1.77
Togie Pittinger	9	5	.643	102	101	3.00
George McQuillan	4	0	1.000	41	21	0.66

*Includes record with St. Louis

Frank Corridon, the Phillies' busiest pitcher in 1907, was often cited as the originator of the spitball. The editor of *The Sporting News*, in response to a question from a reader about the history of the pitch, explained that Elmer Stricklett had seen Corridon throw the pitch on the sidelines when both were in the Eastern League. Stricklett had practiced the pitch until he could control it enough to use it in a game. Jack Chesbro had picked up the pitch from Stricklett and popularized its use through his success with it in 1904. "Hence," the editor summarized, "credit for the spitball's discovery belongs to Corridon; for its development to Stricklett, and for its perfection to Chesbro."[13]

While Corridon seems to have been the man who first "discovered" the pitch, and deserves credit for doing so, mastering it was a different proposition. In 1902, he was experimenting with it on the sidelines when he drew Stricklett's attention. His other stuff, a decent fastball and good curve, were good enough to stymie Eastern League batters. He went 28–15 that year, and was drafted by the Chicago Cubs at the close of the season. Near the end of spring training in 1903 Frank came down with a case of flu that deteriorated into pneumonia. He missed the entire season because of the illness.[14]

In 1904 Frank was a back-of-the-rotation starter for the Cubs until July 20, when he was traded to the Phillies for Shad Barry. There is no indication that he used the spitball, but in a game he pitched against Boston, Sy Sanborn of the *Chicago Tribune* remarked, "Corridon used his peculiar and choice assortment of curves to good advantage for six rounds, shutting the Beaneaters out with three singles in that time."[15] With the Phillies, Frank pitched well enough to contribute to the turn-around that changed the Phillies from a doormat to a formidable opponent, going 6–5 with a 2.19 ERA.

In 1905, with the baseball world focused on the spitball, Corridon seems to have tried to incorporate it into his repertoire, evidently without much success. After he got off to a rocky start, a club official blamed his poor pitching on his inability to control the wet pitch.[16] He never quite regained the level of effectiveness he had shown the previous season, compiling a 10–12 record and having a relatively poor 3.48 ERA. During the off-season the Phillies sold his contract to Toledo of the American Association. Frank refused to go to Toledo, signing instead with Williamsport of the outlaw Tri-State League. His explanation to Toledo ownership was that "he was not treated right by [Philadelphia manager] Hugh Duffy, inasmuch as he was sold to Toledo without being consulted."[17] Corridon pitched well with Williamsport, posting a 22–12 record. The Phillies regained control of his contract in 1907, when the Tri-State League became a part of organized baseball.

Frank enjoyed the best season of his major league career that year. He opened the season for his new/old team by throwing a one-hit shutout against the Giants. A month later he improved on that performance by one inning, beating Boston 3–1 in ten innings, again allowing only one hit, the Beaneaters' lone run scoring on two errors and a sacrifice fly. After beating the Cubs on June 11, he had won nine games and lost only two. A few weeks later his friend and battery mate, Red Dooin, explained why Frank was pitching well: "Corridon needed just one addition to his pitching repertoire to make him a star. He has found it in the spitball, and there is today no pitcher in the business who is working better than he."[18]

It is likely the spitball was an important part of Corridon's pitching tool box in 1907, and not just an extra pitch. Because the "vapor float" broke sharply downward, batters tended to beat it into the ground, creating lots of ground balls when spitballers were on the mound. On April 30, in a 3–2 victory over Brooklyn, Corridon had nine assists and first baseman Kitty Bransfield had 15 of the 23 putouts that were not strikeouts. For the season, Frank led National League pitchers in assists with 99. Hot weather seemed to agree with Corridon. During the month of August he threw two four-hitters, two five-hitters, and a six-hitter, although his record in those five games was only 3–2.

Frank had two more good seasons with the Phillies, going 14–10 with them in 1908 and 11–7 in 1909. He was traded to Cincinnati and then to St. Louis during the winter of 1909–10. He was ineffective with the Cardinals in 1910, going 6–14 in his last major league season.[19]

The Phillies' top winner in 1907 was another pitcher who spent years developing his pitches before becoming successful. Frank "Tully" Sparks had first appeared in the major leagues in 1897, when he had a brief one-game trial with the Phillies. He pitched with Richmond of the Atlantic League in 1898, throwing a no-hitter and pairing with Jack Chesbro as the team's leading pitchers.[20] He and Chesbro were both purchased by Pittsburgh after the season. Tully spent the 1899 season with the Pirates, posting an 8–6 record with a 3.86 ERA—making him about equal to the average National League pitcher that year. When the National League reduced from 12 to eight teams in 1900, Tully was unable to find a place on a Pirate staff that included Deacon Phillippe, Sam Leever, Rube Waddell, Jesse Tannehill, and Chesbro. He signed with Milwaukee of the American League, which was in its last year as a minor league. He remained there in 1901, becoming a major leaguer when Ban Johnson declared that his league was now on a par with the National. Milwaukee didn't fare well in its only season in the American League for almost seven decades, and Tully suffered along with the rest of his teammates. The Brewers finished last with a 48–89 record,

Sparks went 7–17, winning an even lower percentage of games than his team managed to win. At this point in his career Tully did not have good control over his pitches. He walked significantly more men than he struck out in both of his first two major league seasons.

Sparks signed with the New York Giants in 1902, but was released after John McGraw took over the team in July. He quickly caught on with the Boston Americans. His record was mediocre with both teams. He went 4–10 with the last-place Giants, and was only 7–9 with the Americans, who finished in third place that season. When Tully appeared against Brooklyn in April, Abe Yager of the *Brooklyn Daily Eagle* commented, "A young pitcher named Sparks, who has been buffeted around the National League and the minor leagues for several years past, only to be dropped into New York, on the ebb tide caused by the American League raids, was turned loose on the Brooklyns yesterday. Mr. Sparks, in all his peregrinations, never gained a reputation for speed. He did get credit for being a heady twirler, which, in base ball parlance, means a pitcher who casts speed to the winds and mixes up what stock in trade he possesses so as to mystify the opposing batters."[21]

The "buffeting" continued in 1903, when Sparks signed with the Phillies, his sixth major league team. The Phillies were a poor seventh-place team that season, but Tully pitched well for them. He went 11–15, with a 2.72 ERA—by far the best on the staff. In 1904 he was one of the Phillies pitchers who rarely won a game before the August 21 "miraculous" change in the team's fortunes. He was pounded in four of his first five starts, all of which were losses. The last of those games was on May 21. He didn't appear in another game until June 29, when he relieved in the third inning of a game already lost. He joined the rotation shortly after that, adding four more losses before he managed to win a game. At the time of the team's turnaround Tully's record was 3–13. With the team playing better ball, he improved to 7–16 by the end of the season. His earned run average was pretty good (2.65), but it came nowhere near reflecting the amount of runs he allowed per game. He allowed only 59 earned runs in the 200⅔ innings he pitched, but he allowed 50 unearned runs, giving him a total of 4.89 runs allowed per nine innings. The latter number comes a lot closer to explaining his won-lost record than his official ERA.

It is likely that Sparks' relatively poor performance in 1904 was more a result of his teammates' inability to offer decent fielding support than a lack of ability on his part. As Abe Yager pointed out, Tully was a "heady" pitcher. Rather than trying to overpower the batter, he tried to elicit "soft contact" that his fielders could handle for putouts. In 1903, when he lost four more games than he won, the Phillies' team fielding average was .947.

In his disappointing 1904 season, the team fielding average dropped ten points to .937, by far the worst in the league. In 1905 that average jumped by 20 points, to .957. It stayed at that level or higher for the rest of Tully's time with the Phillies. From 1905 through 1907, backed by a much more solid defense, Tully's earned run averages were 2.18, 2.06, and 2.00, all in the top ten in the National League. His won-lost records for those seasons were 14–11, 19–16, and 22–8.

Over much of his career, Sparks' winning percentages did not seem to match the quality of his pitching. In 1906, after Tully got off to a good start, manager Hugh Duffy insisted that the wins were the result of a change in luck. "For a number of years Sparks was about as unfortunate as any pitcher that ever tossed a ball," Duffy said. "He usually pitched very fair ball, but nearly every time he was called upon to work, the team behind him would go to pieces, and no matter how well he performed he could not win. If the team was doing well, Frank would be sure to have an off day himself, and be hammered all over the lot." Duffy praised Sparks' pitching ability. "Sparks is the possessor of one of the best curved ball deliveries of any man in the business, and when right, no batsman dare take any liberties with him."[22]

That "curved ball delivery" attracted comments from around the league. "Sparks has a very wide outcurve which he has tamed carefully and trained to do his bidding," wrote a Cincinnati reporter. "When he starts this obedient beast toward the backbone of a right handed batter and it squirms around to starboard and floats modestly over the inside corner of the plate it looks mighty easy. But the effect produced is either a haughty stare on the part of the slugger at the bat and a called strike by his noble 'umps,' or a weak conflation between the ball and the handle of the bat with a popup as its result. With a left-hand batter the scheme is similar, only he hits the rolling sphere on the extreme tip of his stick more often than on the handle."[23]

Tully also had a good "slow ball," as the changeup was called at that time. In *Touching Second*, which as written by the Cubs' Johnny Evers in collaboration with sportswriter Hugh Fullerton, the authors described a technique of delivering the pitch with the ball held deep in the palm. Many pitchers had worked on the pitch, they said, "until its perfection was reached in the hands of [Three-Finger] Brown, Frank Sparks of the Phillies, and Doc White of the Chicago Americans."[24]

Sparks continued to pitch for the Phillies into the 1910 season. He had arm problems during the 1909 season, when he posted a poor 6–11 record. He appeared in only three games in his last year with the Phillies, failing to win a game while losing two.

Gee, That Sprint Took a Lot Out of Me: New York

New York (82–71)

Name	AVG	OBP	SLG	R	RBI	SB
Spike Shannon, lf	.265	.363	.308	104	33	33
George Browne, rf	.260	.308	.360	54	37	15
or Sammy Strang, ut	.252	.388	.382	56	30	21
Art Devlin, 3b	.277	.376	.324	61	54	38
Cy Seymour, cf	.294	.350	.400	46	75	21
Roger Bresnahan, c	.253	.380	.360	57	38	15
Dan McGann, 1b	.298	.383	.363	29	36	9
or Jack Hannifin, ut	.228	.303	.336	16	15	6
Bill Dahlen, ss	.207	.291	.254	40	34	11
Larry Doyle, 2b	.260	.320	.273	16	16	3
or Tommy Corcoran, 2b	.265	.288	.323	21	24	9
or Frank Bowerman, c	.260	.309	.299	31	32	11

Leading Pitchers	W	L	Pct	IP	H	ERA
Christy Mathewson	24	12	.667	315	250	2.00
Joe McGinnity	18	18	.500	310.3	320	3.16
Red Ames	10	12	.455	233.3	184	2.16
Hooks Wiltse	13	12	.520	190.3	171	2.18
Dummy Taylor	11	7	.611	171	145	2.42
Mike Lynch*	5	8	.385	108	105	3.00
Cecil Ferguson	3	2	.600	64	63	2.11

*Includes record with Pittsburgh

Older athletes can sometimes generate superior bursts of speed, but they usually find it difficult to sustain them over longer periods of time. If the 1907 Giants are an apt example, then it can be that way for teams too. McGraw's team was growing old. In the infield, third baseman Art Devlin was a hearty 27, but the three infielders to his left averaged 37 years old. Backup catcher Frank Bowerman was 38. Center fielder Cy Seymour was 34 and right fielder George Browne 31. On the mound, workhorse Joe McGinnity had been growing more mature for 36 years and Dummy Taylor for 32.

The Giants began the season as if they were going to lock up the pennant early, as they did in the two years before the Cubs pulled off that feat in 1906. They won seven of their first ten games and then ran up 17 wins in a row. Their record after beating St. Louis on May 18 stood at 24-3. But like an older man after finishing a long sprint, they seemed to be exhausted by the effort. They lost 11 of their next 14 games and were ten games under .500 for the part of the season that followed their great start.

Instead of being a memorable season resulting in either a championship or participation in a hot pennant race, the 1907 season turned out to be a transition year for the Giants. Half of the non-pitchers who took the field on opening day were gone by the beginning of the next season. Tommy Corcoran, who had been acquired from Cincinnati to replace Billy Gilbert at second base, was released in mid-season. Shortstop Bill Dahlen, first baseman Dan McGann, and right fielder George Browne were sent to Boston in December. The opening day pitcher—Joe McGinnity—had the most ineffective year of his major league career, followed by a reduced workload in 1908, his final year in the big leagues.

Two notable players were added to the team. After Tommy Corcoran was released in mid-July, McGraw reached deep into John T. Brush's moneybags to outbid two other teams for Larry Doyle, "the Three-I League phenom." Doyle spent the rest of the season adjusting to major league ball, batting a little above the league average and fielding below the standard for his position. But he became one of the game's top second basemen, playing until 1920 and posting a lifetime .290 batting average. In September, the Giants added first baseman Fred Merkle, of "Merkle's Boner" fame. While he is best known for the baserunning blunder that arguably cost the Giants the 1908 pennant, Merkle was an above-average player over a career that, like Doyle's, lasted until 1920.

Perhaps the most noteworthy accomplishment of the season by a Giants player occurred on opening day, when Roger Bresnahan walked onto the field wearing shin guards. Bresnahan was not the first catcher to wear protection for his legs, but the pair he wore were much sturdier than earlier versions, and were worn on the outside of his stockings, rather than under them. The new piece of equipment attracted considerable attention, with most but not all commentators suggesting they were a good idea. One man who didn't like them was Pittsburgh's Fred Clarke. In an early May game against the Giants, the Pirates' manager had tried to score on a squeeze play in which the batter failed to connect with the ball on a bunt. He slid into the plate and was out on a close play because Bresnahan had blocked him off, using his shin guards as a shield. Clarke protested to National League President Harry Pulliam, saying Bresnahan's innovation was illegal. Pulliam ruled in favor of the Giants catcher and his new equipment.[25]

Although shin guards became standard equipment for catchers before long, there wasn't the stampede to adopt them that one would expect. Pittsburgh's George Gibson was one of the catchers who was skeptical about them. Clarke had purchased shin guards for each of his catchers after Pulliam gave the go-ahead for their use. Gibson strapped them on, but didn't like them. He said he felt as if his legs were encased in plaster of Paris. "If

Roger Bresnahan attracted considerable attention for his use of shin guards in 1906. Here he is shown in a game against Pittsburgh a couple years later (Library of Congress).

I can't catch without these things," he said, "I guess I'll go back to Ontario [his home] and quit the game for good. I want to feel free to move about when I am behind the bat, and do not want to be handicapped by shin guards."[26]

Chicago's catchers had a different view. "As soon as I can muster up nerve enough, I intend to wear those shin guards," said Johnny Kling. "I believe they are a good thing and eventually every catcher in the country will use them just as they use the mask and chest protector. The roasting the rooters gave Bresnahan during the New York series here has taken away my nerve and I cannot muster up courage enough to wear them at home. I guess I will try them away from home first and then it won't be so bad." "It isn't often a catcher gets hit on the shins nowadays, but when he does it hurts," added Mike Kahoe. "I also believe there are more low fouls hit nowadays than there were two or three years ago, and one's shins are likely to get it any minute. Also they are a good protection when a man is sliding into the plate, although I have never been injured, to speak of, in this manner."[27]

In mid–June Bresnahan misjudged a pitch and was hit in the head. One of Andy Coakley's better pitches was a high fast ball that broke slightly inwards to a right-handed batter. Bresnahan's style was to crowd the plate and step into a pitch. On this occasion Roger didn't recognize the pitch and stepped right into it. The ball struck him behind the left ear, knocking him unconscious. He was taken to a Cincinnati hospital and was sidelined for almost a month. While he was recovering he conceived the idea of wearing protective headgear. He ordered a "Reach Pneumatic Head Gear" or football helmet, which he cut in half. Apparently, he never actually wore the contraption in a game, but in September Freddy Parent of the Boston Americans wore one after being hit in the head twice in 1907. Unlike the shin guards, the batting helmet didn't become widely used for half a century after Bresnahan introduced the concept.[28]

The Giants' great start was largely attributable to their pitching. None of their regulars hit over .300 during that period. Of their 24 wins, six came on shutouts and eight in games in which the opposition was limited to one run. As usual the staff leaders during the streak were the two aces, Christy Mathewson and Joe McGinnity, who both went 6–1. Mathewson continued to pitch well over the remainder of the season, despite a couple of minor injuries. He led the National League in victories (24), shutouts (8) and strikeouts (178). He had the second best WHIP (walks and hits per inning) at 0.962, trailing only Three Finger Brown. At the end of August, Matty's won-lost record was 20–7. He won only four of his last nine decisions, although he was hit hard in only one of them.

McGinnity continued to pitch well until about mid-June. He was still McGraw's "go-to guy," leading the team and the league in games finished (12) and in saves (4), as well as starting 34 times. But the appearances when the opposition pounded his offerings came much more frequently than in previous seasons. At the end of May the Iron Man's record was 8–1. By the end of August he had lost as many as he won and he finished the season at the .500 mark (18–18).

Comments appearing in game summaries suggest a widespread observation that batters were finding McGinnity's stuff far easier to hit than in preceding years. When he beat Brooklyn 4–1 in his second start of the season, holding the Superbas to six hits, a *New York Times* reporter remarked, "McGinnity's effective pitching discredits the carping critics, who have declared the Iron Man's arm is giving out." The string of victories over the next six weeks brought only positive comments, but by June a *Sporting News* editor was warning, "Mathewson and McGinnity are McGraw's only mainstays in the slab and neither seems to be able to stand the strain of working out of turn." In mid-July, as McGinnity was nearing the end of a period when he lost eight of nine starts, a reporter commented, "Old Joe was no mystery. He found himself up against a band of [Cincinnati] hitters who were determined to retrieve their lost reputations and he had to suffer for it." While Matty seemed to recover quickly from a couple of bad outings, McGinnity didn't seem to be the "Iron Man" he used to be.[29]

When it became apparent that the Giants were no longer championship material, McGraw seemed to lose interest in their games. New York writers reported that he was focusing more on the local horse races than on the National League pennant race. When the Cubs came to the Polo Grounds for a series in mid–August, one report stated, "Matty was in the box for the Giants and Muggsy McGraw, having seen two races run at the Empire City track, reached the Polo Grounds just in time to get into a uniform and assume control. Muggsy's head was filled with hoof beats all afternoon, but he didn't let on to the mob what he was thinking about." Later it was reported that McGraw missed all four games of a series against Brooklyn because he chose to remain at the track until the last race was run.[30]

Dan's Magical Elixir: Brooklyn

It wasn't as far-reaching or long-lasting as the wondrous transformation of the 1904 Phillies, but it was surely worth noting. We have testimony from reliable witnesses stating that the marked improvement in the Superbas' play in mid-season was a direct result of trainer Dan Comerford's homemade liniment. Harry McIntire swore that the ointment healed his sore arm, thus bringing him out of "the slough of despond" in which he considered quitting the game. After receiving several applications, Harry was able to throw successive shutouts against St. Louis and Cincinnati.

Elmer Stricklett had a similar experience. He was the first to try Dan's liniment. Afterwards he shut out the league's top three teams—New York, Chicago and Pittsburgh—in succession. Before his first treatment Elmer's record was 1-9. Then he racked up five straight wins before bowing 1-0 in a ten-inning nail-biter. Seeing the elixir's effects, all of the other Superba pitchers began using it and experiencing the hoped-for success. The only holdout was George Bell who, coincidentally, failed to emulate the others' improved performances.

Other Superbas added their praises. Infielder Whitey Alperman pointed out that his batting and fielding averages soared immediately after taking his first dose. Tim Jordan, who was mired in a season-long slump, began to hit after two applications. Harry Lumley said it cured his rheumatism.

Always helpful, Comerford volunteered to bring along a half dozen bottles to increase the attendance on the Superbas' next road trip.[31]

Brooklyn (65–83)

Name	AVG	OBP	SLG	R	RBI	SB
Whitey Alperman, 2b	.233	.266	.342	44	39	5
or John Hummel, ut	.234	.294	.313	41	31	8
Doc Casey, 3b	.231	.282	.279	55	19	16
Harry Lumley, rf	.267	.316	.425	47	66	18
Emil Batch, lf	.247	.291	.289	38	31	7
Tim Jordan, 1b	.274	.371	.363	43	53	10
Billy Maloney, cf	.229	.287	.283	51	32	25
Phil Lewis, ss	.248	.286	.276	52	30	16
Lew Ritter, c	.203	.255	.232	15	17	5
or Bill Bergen, c	.159	.165	.181	2	14	1

Leading Pitchers	W	L	Pct	IP	H	ERA
Nap Rucker	15	13	.536	275.3	242	2.06
George Bell	8	16	.333	263.7	222	2.25
Elmer Stricklett	12	14	.462	229.7	211	2.27
Jim Pastorius	16	12	.571	222	218	2.35
Harry McIntire	7	15	.318	199.7	178	2.39
Doc Scanlan	6	8	.429	107	90	3.20

The Superbas had an unusually streaky season, even for an era when long winning and losing streaks seemed to pop up nearly every season. They opened the season by losing 16 of their first 17 games. After 20 games they were 2–18. They had been shut out in seven of their 20 games and had scored a grand total of 23 runs. They closed the season by winning only three of their last 15 decisions. They were playing so poorly at the end that owner Charley Ebbets found a way to avoid playing a makeup doubleheader against Boston because he feared the team would lose them both and drop behind Ned Hanlon's Cincinnati Reds.[32] Between these two bookends to their season, however, the Superbas won seven more games than they lost.

It may have been just coincidental, but all but two of the season-ending losses came after the team's top slugger, Harry Lumley, injured his ankle sliding into the "hoodoo base" in Pittsburgh. Harry suffered a dislocation. About a dozen other players had succumbed to the curse that hovered over the bag, four of them fracturing their ankles.[33] Lumley's loss took away the team's top long-ball threat and leading clutch hitter. Lumley was completing his fourth major league season in 1907. He had ranked among the top three in the National League in home runs in each of those seasons, and had been among the leaders in slugging percentage in three of the four.

Harry didn't have a classic athletic body. He was slightly above average in height, but had a stocky build. One of the Brooklyn writers nicknamed him "Roly Poly." In his rookie year with the Superbas, manager Ned Hanlon promised to buy him a new suit of clothes if he would get his weight down to 180, which would have meant losing about ten pounds. The weight didn't seem to slow him down. One writer compared him to Billy Hamilton, saying he resembled the premier base stealer of the 1890s, both in build and speed. Lumley wasn't in Hamilton's class as a base thief, but he did steal over 30 bags in two of his first four seasons.[34]

From a personal perspective Harry's power had a side benefit. It kept his family well supplied with shoes. One of the Brooklyn merchants offered a pair of shoes for each home run hit by a Superba. Harry collected nine pairs in his rookie season, seven in 1905, and ten the following season. He was officially credited with only nine dingers in 1906, but one of them was a game winning hit in which a baserunner on first base scored the winning run, giving him only a triple in the box score. Perhaps that hit qualified for a homer under the merchant's reckoning. He probably picked up another nine pairs of shoes in 1907, although Brooklyn writer Abe Yager, who usually reported such matters, didn't seem to record it that fall.[35]

Lumley's ankle injury may have indirectly led to a rapid decline in his production. The injury still bothered him in the spring of 1908, keeping him from getting into proper condition. Later he suffered a charley horse in his other leg. He hit only .216 that season, with little power. In 1909 he became the Superbas' manager, playing in only 55 games and gathering only 11 extra base hits. He was replaced as manager in 1910 and drew his release in June after playing in only eight games.[36]

End of an Illustrious Career: Cincinnati

Cincinnati (66–87)

Name	AVG	OBP	SLG	R	RBI	SB
Miller Huggins, 2b	.248	.346	.289	64	31	28
Hans Lobert, ss	.246	.299	.313	61	41	30
Mike Mitchell, rf	.292	.339	.382	64	47	17
John Ganzel, 1b	.254	.297	.363	61	64	9
Art Kruger, cf	.233	.285	.322	25	28	10
or Lefty Davis, cf	.229	.293	.297	28	25	9
or John Kane, lf-3b	.248	.325	.347	40	19	20
Larry McLean, c	.289	.313	.361	35	54	4
or Admiral Schlei, c	.272	.347	.301	28	27	5
Fred Odwell, lf	.270	.336	.339	24	24	10

Leading Pitchers	W	L	Pct	IP	H	ERA
Bob Ewing	17	19	.472	332.7	279	1.73
Andy Coakley	17	16	.515	265.3	269	2.34
Jake Weimer	11	14	.440	209	165	2.41
Roy Hitt	6	10	.375	153.3	143	3.40
Del Mason	5	12	.294	146	144	3.14
Fred Smith	2	7	.222	85.3	90	2.85
Charley Hall	4	2	.667	68	51	2.51

Come springtime it was quite common for Cincinnati baseball writers to produce wildly optimistic accounts of the Reds' chances in the upcoming pennant race. In 1907 the team was so young and inexperienced that their predictions had to be leavened with a healthy dose of reality. "The local team is purely an experiment. There is entirely too much untried talent to venture a prediction. The team may finish at the bottom and then, again, if these youngsters come up to expectations, it may be a first-division aggregation," said the Cincinnati correspondent to *The Sporting News*. "One thing is certain, [Ned] Hanlon will get the chance he has been looking for ever since the old Orioles were disbanded. He had a bunch of the stars of the minor leagues. He has superintended the selecting of the bunch and it is now up to him to make a baseball team out of it."[37]

In a way the Reds' performance in 1907 was seen as a test of Hanlon's true ability as a manager. The decline of the Brooklyn team under his leadership had led many to question whether Hanlon really deserved credit for the success of his Baltimore teams. In 1905, after John McGraw won his second straight pennant in New York and Jack Dunn, who played for Hanlon in Brooklyn, topped the Eastern League as Baltimore's manager, New York writer Will Rankin remarked, "One local afternoon paper is giving Hanlon the credit for the brilliant work accomplished by McGraw and Dunn. Had Hanlon developed anything but a tailender during the past four years there might be a grain of fact upon which to make their claim, but as results have been it is not easy to see where Hanlon comes in. If one will look back a few years and review things it can be seen what McGraw did with a mixed-pickle team, that which Hanlon had failed to do at any time in the past few years." Rankin then stated an opinion shared by most of "Foxy Ned's" critics. "It looks to me as if Hanlon made his reputation off McGraw, Jennings, etc., or probably they robbed Ned of all his ability and that accounts for his failure since they left him." When Hanlon took charge in Cincinnati, one sportswriter commented, "Ned Hanlon won his spurs years ago and is known as the foxiest and best manager in the league, but it almost may be said he has to win them over again, after the disastrous spell he has been under in Brooklyn of late years."[38]

Hanlon's first year in Cincinnati didn't silence the doubters. Many questioned the wisdom of unloading several veteran players, most especially former batting champion Cy Seymour. One critic remarked, "Everybody wonders what Ned Hanlon is thinking about in making such a sweeping change in the Cincinnati team. Many hereabouts think this astute director-general is preparing to duplicate his Baltimore-Brooklyn feats in 1907—but I am inclined to the belief that they are doomed to disappointment. Looks as if the game had got past Hanlon."[39]

Foxy Ned saw the challenge somewhat differently than most outsiders. "I will be content to fail, if I have to, with any team made up of the right sort of men, ambitious and conscientious, because I will know that they are doing their best at all times," he said. He thought his team was promising, even if he had to concede that it might be somewhat weak on the mound. "We have a young and inexperienced team, but one that promises to be strong at the bat and on the bases," he concluded.[40]

The Reds' performance on the field was a mixed bag—it seemed to fulfill both the optimistic and the negative aspects of Hanlon's evaluation. The team settled into sixth place early in the season and remained there with little movement either up or down. The team's youth and lack of experience played a big part in the outcome of their games. They were very inconsistent. "It is getting so that it is a toss-up now as to whether the fans will get to see almost as good a game of ball as can be played or one that is as rotten as they get to be," said a Cincinnati reporter. "One thing that the fans like is that they are interesting. Either there are enough runs made by the opposing side to win easily and keep the Reds always fighting, or else the Reds put up a quality of ball that would do credit to any three-time winners. The peculiar part of it is that they cannot keep up their gait for two successive days."[41]

The Reds' young players were

Ned Hanlon gained fame as the innovative manager of the great Baltimore Orioles teams of the 1890s. He wound up his career in 1907, retiring after several disappointing seasons with Brooklyn and Cincinnati (Library of Congress).

not yet skillful in the tactics of "scientific baseball," which had long been the way Hanlon managed a game. After the Reds were shut out in a game despite smashing out 11 hits, coaxing a base on balls, and reaching on two errors, a reporter growled, "Ten Reds were abandoned on the sacks. The team is getting to be notorious for its numerous strikeouts and many failures to play inside ball effectively." Fans began to wish Hanlon would just forget the sophisticated tactics and let the kids swing away at the ball. After the team was swept by the Cubs in a four-game series to start July, and then lost seven of their next eight games, they began seeing Foxy Ned as part of the team's problems, rather than the solution. "The straight defeats of the Reds at Chicago was a heart-breaker," explained a reporter. The fans expected to break even, he wrote, because the team had done so before against the Cubs. "But Chicago came, and then Boston, and finally New York, and it was the same old story until the boys hereabouts simply said that something must be done, and their advice to Hanlon is to keep his hands off for just a little while and see what will be doing."[42]

The downward plunge seemed to bother Hanlon about as much as it did the fans. On July 21, he announced that he would no longer be the Reds manager after the 1907 season ended. A common assessment of his time as Cincinnati's leader was that he had been a dismal failure. The editor of *The Sporting News* noted that Hanlon's former team, the Superbas, had fared better under the management of Patsy Donovan than the Reds had under Foxy Ned, and asserted that "the highest salaried director of a team will close his major league career utterly discredited." Hanlon responded to criticism of his handling of the team by stating that he was willing to take the blame for the team's poor showing, but that he believed he had put together the nucleus of a good team. Jack Ryder of the *Cincinnati Enquirer* was among those who agreed with Hanlon's assessment. He praised Hanlon for imparting to his young players the tactics of scientific baseball. "Hanlon is a master of the finer elements of baseball play, and his teachings here have been all along the right line, and the only winning line," he wrote. "His successor, when he takes hold of the team, will find the Reds thoroughly grounded in the principles of successful play and must, to be successful himself, carry out Hanlon's policy along the same lines."[43]

A glance at the Reds' roster would seem to support Hanlon's claim that he had gathered the nucleus of a good team. He inherited second baseman Miller Huggins, one of the league's top second basemen, and Admiral Schlei, a good catcher. He added Hans Lobert and Mike Mowrey, both of whom became above average infielders. Unfortunately, both excelled at the same position—third base. Mike Mitchell and Dode Paskert, who was acquired near the end of 1907, were solid in the outfield. Mitchell twice led the league in triples. Larry McLean was a good catcher for several years. On the mound, Hanlon had three effective pitchers in 1907—Bob Ewing, Andy Coakley, and Jake Weimer. For the Reds to be successful, these three had to continue pitching well and one or two hurlers of equal caliber added to the staff. Instead, Coakley and Weimer each lasted only one more year. In 1908 Coakley combined a fine 1.87 ERA with an ugly 8–18 won-lost record before being traded to Chicago, where he was 2–0. Weimer appeared in only 15 games in 1908, going 8–7.

Hanlon had hoped that the corps of players he had collected would benefit from "judicious trades and purchases" over the next couple of seasons, thus providing Cincinnati fans with a first-division team. That didn't happen. The next time the Reds finished in the top half of the league standings was 1915.

As for Hanlon's reputation, which *The Sporting News* saw as being "utterly discredited," that fared far better than the team he left behind in Cincinnati. The disappointing seasons he encountered in his last three years in Brooklyn and with Cincinnati became overshadowed by the brilliant success he enjoyed with Baltimore and in his first four years with the Superbas. He was saluted for the five pennants he won over a seven year period and for fostering the development of a school of future managers, including John McGraw, Hughie Jennings, Wilbert Robinson, Joe Kelley, and Kid Gleason. Together his pupils won 18 pennants. When Hanlon passed away in 1937, *The Sporting News* declared that he was "the game's greatest strategist." "Hanlon's fame rests on three pedestals," the publication proclaimed, "his introduction and perfection of 'inside ball,' his development of players and managers who afterward became illustrious, and his winning of three pennants with the Baltimore Orioles and two with Brooklyn." Foxy Ned was credited with having "uncanny ability to judge players, a faculty of imparting to them his remarkable store of knowledge, a genius for inspiring his men to rise to the heights and a personality that enabled him to gain and hold the confidence of all with whom he came into contact."[44]

A Landing Zone for Ex-Pirates: Boston

About the time the 1906 season was coming to a blessful end, the Triumvirs sold their holdings in the Beaneaters to an ownership group headed by George and John Dovey. In response to the change, a new nickname was bestowed upon the club, which became the "Doves" for the next four years.

During the December winter meetings a trade was arranged with Pittsburgh that brought second baseman Claude Ritchey and pitcher Patsy Flaherty to Boston in exchange for Ed Abbaticchio, who had chosen to personally manage his hotel in Latrobe, Pennsylvania, rather than play for the Beaneaters in 1906. Later Ginger Beaumont was added to the deal. It was the second year in a row in which the two teams had engaged in a trade that sent Boston three players in exchange for one. When the 1907 season opened the Doves had ex–Pirates serving as half of their regular starters, and as two of their four starting pitchers. On opening day Ritchey was at second base, Dave Brain was at third base, Beaumont in center field, and Del Howard in left field. Patsy Flaherty and Vive Lindaman started the third and fourth games, respectively. The infusion of Pirates blood didn't make the team a contender—or even a first-division club—but it may well have avoided saddling the franchise with a losing season of epic proportions.

Boston (59–90)

Name	AVG	OBP	SLG	R	RBI	SB
Al Bridwell, ss	.218	.309	.242	49	26	17
Fred Tenney, 1b	.273	.371	.334	83	26	15
Dave Brain, 3b	.279	.324	.420	60	56	10
or Bill Sweeney, ut*	.254	.309	.264	25	19	9
Ginger Beaumont, cf	.322	.366	.424	67	62	25
Johnny Bates, rf	.260	.329	.367	52	49	11
Newt Randall, lf*	.211	.284	.271	22	19	6
or Del Howard, lf*	.254	.304	.304	30	26	14
or Frank Burke, lf	.178	.243	.194	6	8	3
Claude Ritchey, 2b	.255	.329	.317	45	51	8
Tom Needham, c	.196	.264	.246	19	19	4
or Sam Brown, c	.192	.250	.221	17	14	0
Leading Pitchers	W	L	Pct	IP	H	ERA
Gus Dorner	12	16	.429	271.3	253	3.12
Vive Lindaman	11	15	.423	260	252	3.63
Irv Young	10	23	.303	245.3	287	3.96
Patsy Flaherty	12	15	.444	217	197	2.70
Big Jeff Pfeffer	6	8	.429	144	129	3.00
Jake Boultes	5	9	.357	139.7	140	2.71

*Includes record with Chicago

The team's top performer was Ginger Beaumont, who was probably sent to Boston largely because in March both he and the Pirates had grave doubts as to whether he would recover sufficiently from a knee injury to be able to take the field in 1907. When Boston's *Sporting News* correspondent heard that Beaumont was to become a Dove, his reaction was one of skepticism. "I doubt if Beaumont will be much good to Boston," he wrote. "I can't imagine Beaumont being let go by Fred Clarke and Dreyfuss unless both were convinced that his days of usefulness as a ball player were over. When a star like Beaumont is let go by a club the very first question which suggests itself is 'What's the matter with him?'"[45]

That the ailment involved the knee was especially important for Beaumont. His game was built around his running ability. Ginger didn't look like a speedster. He was built more along the lines of a catcher. He was 5'8" tall, but weighed 190 pounds. Often he even moved around like a tired-out catcher. When he saw no need to run, Ginger walked at a very slow pace. When it was his turn to bat, he dragged his bat behind him as he almost crawled toward the plate. But when it was time to run, Beaumont sprinted as fast as any National Leaguer. He rarely put his full 190 pounds behind a swing. A left-handed batter, he took a short, quick cut at the ball. Boston writer Tim Murnane listed Beaumont among a group of scientific batters, "batsmen of the progressive order, who try to place the ball and hit at the ball in different ways, thereby keeping the pitchers and fielders on the guess."[46]

Pittsburgh writers at times referred to Beaumont's "specialty of beating out a bunt." Ginger showed that ability in a big way in his first full season. On July 22, 1899, he picked up six hits in six times at bat. Five of the hits came on bunts, three of which were so well placed the infielder didn't even bother to throw after picking up the ball. None of his hits left the infield, the sixth hit coming on an infield bounder. Three weeks later, Ginger showed that outfielders couldn't count on stopping his slap hits by playing close to the infield. He smashed out five hits against the Phillies, including three triples and a double. The hits were sprayed into each of the three outfield spots.[47]

Beaumont was one of the key contributors to the Pirates' three pennants of 1901–03. He led the National League in batting in 1902 and was among the top ten every year from 1901 through 1905. His knee injury hindered his running ability in 1906, and his batting average dropped to .265 as a result.

With the Doves Ginger surprisingly reverted to his form of the Pirates' championship years. In May a Pittsburgh writer remarked, "Beaumont has been hitting like a house afire all season. He is away above the .300 mark in slugging and is likely to remain up there all season, for there is no disputing that he is a great natural hitter. Beaumont has been getting two or three hits in almost every game, and, what is more significant of his return to form, he is stealing bases and contributing sacrifice hits with fine regularity." In a Pittsburgh series in September, Ginger and Honus Wagner engaged in a personal duel to see which one could outhit the other, since they were in a competition of sorts for the league batting championship. In one game each got three hits. After Wagner's third hit, he gave Ginger a big smile and received a tip of the cap in response. At season's end Beaumont ranked third, trailing both Wagner and the Phillies' Sherry Magee.[48]

Ritchey also played at about the same level as he did for the Pirates, which translated into a solid, workmanlike performance, rather than any flashy achievements. He combined with Fred Tenney at first base and Al Bridwell at shortstop to give the Doves top-notch defense in three of the four infield positions. In June, one writer remarked, "Ritchey has wonderfully braced up the infield, and he and Bridwell are playing together as if they had been lifelong pals." Ritchey's .255 batting average didn't seem all that great, but only one second baseman in the league surpassed it, and that was by only seven points.

After Beaumont, the Doves' top hitter was another ex-Pirate. Dave Brain was in his second year in Boston, having been part of a trade for Beaneater ace Vic Willis after the 1905 season. He had bounced around the majors by 1907, having played briefly for the Chicago White Stockings in 1901, the Cardinals from 1903 to mid-season of 1905, Pittsburgh for the rest of that season, and for Boston in 1906 and 1907. He had shown good power throughout his career, but had not hit for much of an average. He had played at both shortstop and third base, being somewhat error-prone in both positions. In 1905 he made a place for himself in the baseball record books that still stands. Twice that season he rapped out three triples in a game. Other players have hit three triples in a game, but only Brain did it twice in a season. Brain had his best season in 1907, leading the league with ten home runs, while batting .279—the 14th highest in the league.[49]

Patsy Flaherty led the Doves pitchers with a 2.71 earned run average. That was somewhat above the league average of 2.46, but Boston pitchers had the worst staff ERA by far, giving up 0.63 earned runs more per game than any other team. Flaherty had an unusual record. He could be pretty good one year and terrible the next—or vice-versa. In 1903, his first full major league season, Patsy went 11–25 for the Chicago White Sox. The next year he went 1–2 for the Sox before being sold to the Pirates, with whom he posted a 19–9 record, becoming a 20-game winner the season after losing 25. The following season his ERA increased by almost a run and a half per game, as his record dropped to 10–10. The Pirates sent him to Class A Columbus, where he stayed throughout the 1906 campaign. Patsy posted a 23–9 record that year and was rewarded by being recalled to Pittsburgh at the end of the season and traded to Boston.

Flaherty didn't have a world of stuff. He relied upon a decent fastball and his wits. He was noted for fooling batters with a quick pitch—that is, firing a pitch at the plate immediately after receiving the catcher's return. He was good at holding runners on base, and he was a good hitter for a pitcher, which of course is not quite the same as being a good hitter. On May 24 he hit a grand slam home run to beat the Giants 7–5. Since he was playing for a Fred Tenney team—which seemed to become shorthanded at some point every season—he was given the opportunity to play the outfield. He played eight games, receiving a compliment from a reporter for his play in at least one game. In August Patsy had a distinction he undoubtedly would have gladly foregone. He won the last game before the Doves went into their annual extended losing streak on August 2. Seventeen days later he won the game that ended the losing streak at 16 in a row.[50]

Although Vive Lindaman came to Boston in the Vic Willis trade, he had never pitched for the Pirates. He threw a spitball, and like many who used the wet ball, he tended to lose control of it at times. He walked 108 batters in 1907, third most in the league, and in the three complete seasons he pitched for the Doves he ranked among the top ten in wild pitches each year.

Del Howard, the sixth ex-Pirate to play for the Doves in 1907, was having a pretty good season when he was traded to the Cubs in July. Howard played 50 games for Boston, batting .273 and stealing 11 bases, a rate which would have given him about 33 steals over a full season. One of the players the Doves received for Howard, Bill Sweeney, remained with the team through 1913. Sweeney was then traded back to the Cubs for Johnny Evers, who became a key player on the 1914 Miracle Braves, a team that made a fabulous comeback to win the pennant after being in last place in mid-July.

A Potentially Great Player: St. Louis

St. Louis (52-101)

Name	AVG	OBP	SLG	R	RBI	SB
Bobby Byrne, 3b	.256	.307	.293	55	29	21
Shad Barry, rf	.248	.320	.279	30	19	4
or Tom O'Hara, of	.237	.286	.260	11	5	1
or John Kelly, of	.188	.245	.213	12	6	7
Ed Konetchy, 1b	.251	.317	.356	34	30	13
or Jake Beckley, 1b	.209	.222	.235	6	7	0
Jack Barnett, cf	.238	.296	.316	18	12	5
or Al Burch, cf*	.255	.325	.296	30	17	12
Ed Holly, ss	.229	.283	.279	55	40	16
Red Murray, lf	.262	.301	.367	46	46	23
Pug Bennett, 2b	.222	.272	.259	20	21	7
or A. Hoelskoetter, 2b	.247	.298	.292	21	28	5
Doc Marshall, c	.201	.246	.269	19	18	2
or Pete Noonan, c	.224	.252	.291	19	16	3

Leading Pitchers	W	L	Pct	IP	H	ERA
Stoney McGlynn	14	25	.359	352.3	329	2.91
Ed Karger	15	19	.441	314	257	2.04
Fred Beebe	7	19	.269	238.3	192	2.72
Art Fromme	5	13	.278	145.7	138	2.90
Johnny Lush**	10	15	.400	201.3	180	2.64
Bugs Raymond	2	4	.333	64.7	56	1.67

*Includes record with Brooklyn
*Includes record with Philadelphia

St. Louis was in a deep rebuilding mode. Like Ned Hanlon in Cincinnati, John McCloskey of the Cardinals had decided in 1906 that the group of players he inherited could never become a winning team. He got rid of most of them. As a result, the 1907 team was a collection of young players who were still trying to figure out how to compete at the major league level. One writer rather unkindly said of the team, "McCloskey's aggregation does not look much like a major league team. It is safe to say that there are men on the Cardinal team who would have the hardest kind of a time holding their own in the Eastern League or the American Association."[51] Therefore in June Cardinals fans were likely happy to learn that the team had obtained Johnny Lush, a player with seemingly unlimited potential.

Lush made his debut with the Phillies in 1904 at the tender age of 18. His baseball talents were multi-dimensional—he appeared to have the makings of an outstanding pitcher and a fine batter. The 1904 Phillies were a team looking for players at nearly every position, so they gave him every opportunity to show that he belonged in the National League. First they tried him on the mound. At first blush it would seem that Johnny didn't do so well—by the end of May his record was 0–6. But those were the Phillies who made errors by the bushel basketful. Johnny's losses came in games in which the Phillies made six errors, seven errors, and errors in two innings that should have ended before their opponents scored a combined seven unearned runs. While on the mound that season, Johnny gave up 40 runs, of which 17 were earned.

In June Lush was moved to first base. He spent the remainder of the season there and in the outfield, batting a very credible .276 with some power. At times he showed his lack of experience. In one game, while playing first base, he made four errors, three in one inning. In another, he decided to cover home plate on a bunted ball, only to see the game lost when the third baseman decided to throw to first, where the only person close to the bag was the opposition's first base coach. He seems to have been better in the outfield, making several outstanding catches. He played well enough to be recognized by a Pittsburgh reporter who commented,

"Johnny Lush, the boy wonder from Williamsport, who signed to pitch for Philadelphia, is rapidly developing into one of the best all around players in the business. He saved the Quakers from defeat at the hands of Brooklyn yesterday by making a difficult catch in the last inning."[52]

After his successful rookie season Lush decided he was worth more money than Philadelphia was prepared to give. He rejected their offer and signed with Williamsport of the outlaw Tri-State League. The Phillies continued to negotiate with him, finally persuading him to return after the independent league's season ended. Johnny got into two games for Philadelphia and won them both, his first victories at the major league level. The second win was against the Giants and Christy Mathewson, in a year when Matty went 31–9 and went on to hurl three straight shutouts in the World Series.[53]

In 1906 Lush started regularly for the Phillies who, while not in the same class with the top three National League clubs, were a notch above the four second-division teams. He also became the Sunday center fielder, filling in for Roy Thomas each Sabbath. In addition, he was regularly called upon to pinch-hit for a couple of the Phillies' weak-hitting pitchers in the late innings of their games. On May 1, he threw a no-hitter against the Brooklyn Superbas, striking out 11 batters and prompting Brooklyn writer Abe Yager to comment, "There wasn't one hit during the game that could leave any iota of doubt—Lush simply mowed our hitsmiths down with a wide outcurve that had them breaking their backs trying to reach." That game came a week after he had stopped Boston with just one hit.[54]

Although already an experienced major leaguer, Johnny was still only 20 years old, and at times displayed a lack of maturity. Once he simply walked off the mound "in disgust" after a wild throw allowed two runs to score. Later, in a game against New York, he became upset after the Giants stole four bases in the fifth inning. After the side was retired he decided he was too ill to pitch the rest of the game. There were also times when he displayed his lack of training in the fine points of the game. He sometimes failed to cover first base on grounders to the first baseman and he did not always exercise good judgment in deciding which base to throw to on bunts. Lush's record in 1906 was 18–15 with a team that finished nine games under .500. His 2.37 earned run average ranked 15th in the league. It is therefore a little puzzling that he told reporters he would give up pitching to become an outfielder the following season.[55]

Despite that announcement, in 1907 Lush's role with the Phillies was unchanged. After a month or so, however, his new manager, Billy Murray, seemed to tire of Lush's attitude. On June 10, Johnny's record was 3–5 when he was traded to St. Louis for Buster Brown, a young pitcher with a fine fastball but few victories to show for it. "The release of Johnny Lush to St. Louis by Philadelphia was due to the disposition of the great pitcher," remarked Brooklyn writer Abe Yager. "When he did not care to pitch he wanted to play the outfield because of his batting, and after playing there a few days he insisted that his proper place was in the box. After keeping this sort of thing up for quite a while the Philadelphia management decided to get rid of him. Hence the deal."[56]

The trade was generally seen as a good one for St. Louis. "Manager McCloskey must be praised for the good exchange when he landed southpaw Lush of Philadelphia for Buster Brown," said one reporter. "Lush had a good year last season and is the best batting pitcher in either league. Should Lush never pitch a game his batting would easily gain him a place in the outfield of the Cardinals, who need another good hitter."[57] With the Cardinals Johnny was used in much the same way as with the Phillies. He was primarily a pitcher, but he played a few games in the outfield. On the mound he went 7–10 with a 2.50 ERA, a pretty good showing considering how bad the Cardinals were in 1907. He hit .280 with two doubles and three triples in 82 at-bats—again, a pretty good performance.

Johnny continued to pitch for the Cardinals through the 1910 season. In 1908 and 1909 he had identical won-lost records of 11–18 with teams that lost 105 and 98 games in those two seasons. He pitched a six-inning no-hitter in 1908, when his earned run average was 2.12. Following that season he apparently announced that he did not want to play with the Cardinals in 1909, though he spent the entire season with them. In 1910 he managed to post a winning record (14–13) with another poor team, the Cardinals struggling to a 63–90 finish under manager Roger Bresnahan. In December of that year Johnny was sold to Toronto in one of a series of moves Bresnahan completed as part of an effort to rid the team of veteran players. Following the sale *The Sporting News* reported, "It is said, on good authority, that Lush and Bresnahan did not pull well together, and several times during the season Bresnahan reprimanded Lush for talking too much." Supposedly, Bresnahan threatened several times to levy a $50 fine if Lush didn't control his tongue.[58]

Although he pitched well for Toronto for the next three years, before going to the Pacific Coast League for another three seasons, Lush never again played at the major league level. He had celebrated his 25th birthday a few days before pitching his last game for the Cardinals.

Eight

1907, American League

Peace and Ginger Fizz: Detroit

Detroit's new manager, Hughie Jennings, knew that his first task was to bring about peace between the team's veteran players and its immensely talented young star, Ty Cobb. Over the winter he visited with Bill Coughlin, the Tiger captain, and with Matty McIntyre, Cobb's chief antagonist. When spring training began he talked to the players about the need for harmony on the team. He set forth three fundamental principles. No dissension. Everything for harmony. Any nine men pulling together and fighting hard are as good as nine stars fighting against each other.[1]

1907 American League Standings

Team	W	L	Pct.	GB
Detroit	92	58	.613	—
Philadelphia	88	57	.607	1.5
Chicago	87	64	.576	5.5
Cleveland	85	67	.559	8
New York	70	78	.473	21
St. Louis	69	83	.454	24
Boston	59	90	.396	32.5
Washington	49	102	.325	43.5

Hughie's "harmony project" received a big setback on March 16. Bungy Davis, the black groundskeeper at the Tigers' spring training site, who was somewhat inebriated at the time, came up to Cobb, gave him a friendly pat on the back, addressed him as "Carrie," and extended his hand for a handshake. The "Georgia Peach" was offended that a black man would seek to put himself on the same social level as a white man. He responded by punching the groundskeeper and the two began to struggle. Breaking free, Davis ran to his house, which was next to the field. Cobb pursued him. There he encountered Davis' wife, who cursed him and tried to intervene.

The Georgian struck her, knocking her down. He jumped on her, grabbing her by the throat. At that point Charlie Schmidt, Detroit's catcher, pulled him off Mrs. Davis and berated him for stooping so low as to strike a woman. Cobb then let loose a tirade against his teammate, telling him where to go. Schmidt retaliated with a punch on the jaw. The two Tigers exchanged a few glancing blows before they were separated by their teammates.[2]

After Cobb's outburst, Jennings made a brief effort to trade him. He offered the young outfielder to Cleveland for Elmer Flick, but received only a counter-offer of cash. New York was willing to give up Frank Delahanty, who had batted almost a hundred points less than Cobb in 1906. But Jennings was not ready to virtually give away a player of Cobb's ability. When Cobb and Schmidt had another fist fight a couple weeks after their first engagement, Hughie sent Cobb back to the hotel to recover from his beating. He called the team together in Cobb's absence. He told the players that Cobb was hot-tempered and easily aroused to anger, but that they had to forget the past and make peace. After the meeting, he called aside several of the team's veterans. He asked them to socialize with Cobb and make him feel like a friend. Later he had a quiet talk with Ty in which he conceded that the other players had not treated the youngster right. He asked Cobb to try to control his temper.[3]

Jennings' tactics succeeded to the extent of persuading the Tigers to be civil toward their prickly young star off the field. On the field the team began displaying the kind of fighting spirit that leads to victories, as opposed to the kind that ends up with broken clubhouse furniture. Two weeks into the season, after a game the Tigers lost when a late-inning rally failed, Joe Jackson of the *Detroit Free Press* remarked, "Jennings certainly has filled his players with pepper of a fiery kind. They didn't know when they were whipped." A Cleveland reporter commented that the Tigers had made a very favorable impression under Jennings. "It is said that the players under him are showing an entirely different spirit than they have heretofore," he said. "Jennings not only is well liked by his players, but they believe in him, and are following his advice. He has teamwork installed, and the Tigers have held their own."[4]

Detroit (92–58)

Name	AVG	OBP	SLG	R	RBI	SB
Davy Jones, lf	.273	.357	.318	101	27	30
Bill Coughlin, 3b	.243	.301	.270	80	46	15
Sam Crawford, cf	.323	.366	.460	102	81	18
Ty Cobb, rf	.350	.380	.473	97	119	49
Claude Rossman, 1b	.277	.318	.342	60	69	20

Name	AVG	OBP	SLG	R	RBI	SB
Red Downs, 2b	.219	.249	.289	28	42	3
or Germany Schaefer, inf	.258	.313	.315	44	32	21
Boss Schmidt, c	.244	.269	.295	32	23	8
or Fred Payne, c	.166	.221	.201	17	14	4
Charley O'Leary, ss	.241	.298	.286	61	34	11

Leading Pitchers	W	L	Pct	IP	H	ERA
George Mullin	20	20	.500	357.3	346	2.59
Ed Killian	25	13	.658	314	286	1.78
Ed Siever	18	11	.621	274.7	256	2.16
Wild Bill Donovan	25	4	.862	271	222	2.19
John Eubank	3	3	.500	81	88	2.67
Ed Willett	1	5	.167	48.7	47	3.70

For a while Jennings attracted almost as much attention for his antics on the coaching lines as his players did for their accomplishments in the games. "Hughie Jennings sure can coach some," said one reporter. "He kept them going all the time and infused a lot of ginger into the contest. Jennings' 'Wee-aa!' and 'Ah-haaa' and his other Indian war cries made a hit with the fans who mimicked him until the eighth inning was over." Another remarked, "Manager Jennings, with his little whistle and endless fund of small talk on the coaching lines, brightened up the rooters even when they were downcast at the way their team was being outplayed. Some of Hughey's lingual effervescence sounds like extracts from a Chinese oration." A third observer added, "Jennings' coaching is somewhat like the yelling of the booster in the circus ring. He and Schaefer gave an exhibition yesterday, using a language that is entirely foreign to the ears of local patrons of the game. It is a mixture of Arabian slang and the Swedish court tongue. The Sorrel-topped manager is a hustler, and does not seem to know what the word quit means."[5]

Early in the season Detroit settled into third place, a few games over .500, and spent most of the first four months there. They didn't take over the lead, but neither did they fall far behind. They were part of a close race that also involved Chicago, Philadelphia and Cleveland. They began the season without one of their top pitchers, Wild Bill Donovan, who was recovering from a sore arm. Jennings gave one of his young pitchers, Ed Willett, a chance to replace Donovan, but Willett was ineffective. George Mullin, the team's workhorse since 1904, took up the slack by pitching well while assuming his normal heavy workload. Mullin's first two starts were three-hit shutouts against the league's perennial slugging leaders, the Cleveland Naps. He won seven of his first nine decisions before leveling off in late May, about the same time Donovan made his season's debut. At season's end

Mullin was second in the league in games pitched, games started, complete games and innings pitched. He did not lead the league in those categories because Ed Walsh shouldered a huge workload for Chicago.

Ed Killian started the season slowly, losing two of his first three decisions, but after that he was very effective. After Ed fought his way to a victory in April, a Cleveland writer observed, "Killian, though hard hit, has a way of sticking out his jaw when it comes to a tight squeeze and pulling through."[6] In May, the left-hander's jaw might have gotten a little bit sore from being thrust out, as he put together a string of 32 consecutive scoreless innings, throwing shutouts against New York and Washington, blanking Philadelphia in two relief innings, and then stopping Cleveland for nine innings before losing 1–0 in a ten-inning game. In addition to starting 34 games in 1906, Killian served as Jennings' left-handed reliever, appearing eight times in relief. He became a "vulture" of sorts, grabbing off five of his victories in that role. In addition to winning 25 games, Killian had a 1.78 ERA in 1907, second only to Walsh among American League pitchers.

Hughie Jennings brought "peace and ginger fizz" to the Tigers after taking over as their manager in 1907 (Library of Congress).

Wild Bill Donovan didn't make his first appearance until May 24, but he made a big impact right away. He won his first five starts and 11 of his first 12 decisions. Although Mullin worked more innings, Donovan was considered the Tigers' ace from the time he came to the team in 1903 until 1906, when a sore arm led to a disappointing 9–15 season. With Brooklyn in 1901, he had replaced Joe McGinnity, who jumped to Baltimore, as the team's staff leader. Although in his first full major league season that year, he turned in a typical "Iron Man" performance, appearing in 45 games, posting a 25–15 record and adding three saves in seven relief appearances.

In 1903, when Connie Mack was asked to name the best pitcher in baseball, he somewhat dodged the question by insisting that the most valuable pitcher was not Cy Young, who was having a great season, but Donovan, who was younger and still retained an outstanding fastball.[7]

By 1907 Donovan had gone through at least three seasons in which he withstood arm and shoulder soreness. He was no longer the fireballer who had overpowered batters in Brooklyn and in his first couple of years with the Tigers. "Bill lost much of his speed, and his arm is no longer as strong as it was," commented one reporter. "As his arm deteriorated his knowledge increased, but there is still enough left in his arm to make the combination a successful one."[8] Donovan saved his most impressive work for September, when his team was locked in a tight three-way battle for first place with the A's and White Sox. On September 12, he finished up a two-hit, 3–2 win over Cleveland with two scoreless innings. The next day he shut out the Naps in a six-inning game. After two days' rest, he shut out Chicago for his third win in five days. His next outing, on September 20, was a two-hit shutout against New York. After resting for a week, he shut out the A's over the first four innings of a 5–4 victory, giving him a streak of 30 scoreless innings pitched when the Tigers most needed it.

On offense, the Tigers led the American League in hitting, their .266 team batting average being 11 points better than the A's .255. They were led by the young man Jennings had been unable to trade—Ty Cobb—and by one of the players Cobb felt was one of his primary tormentors—Sam Crawford. Wahoo Sam led the league in runs scored (102) and finished second in several batting categories—batting average (.323), slugging percentage (.460), total bases (268), doubles (34) and triples (17). By 1907 he had been well established as one of the game's top hitters. His presence among the leaders was not unusual. What was unusual that year, but would become commonplace in the future, was that several of Sam's best numbers were exceeded by one of his teammates. That player was, of course, Cobb, who reached the superstar level in 1907. He led the league in batting average (.350)—the first of a dozen times—slugging percentage (.468), hits (212), runs batted in (119), and stolen bases (53). And he finished among the leaders in just about any other batting category anybody could imagine.

But cold numbers couldn't capture the entirety of the fiery Cobb's game. On opening day, with the psychic wounds of the spring still fresh in everyone's mind, Ty scored both runs in a 2–0 victory over Cleveland. The first run came after he took third base on a short passed ball, just beating the catcher's throw. The second came when he singled, stole second and went to third on the catcher's throwing error. His charge toward third drew a throw from the center fielder that went past the third baseman. The pitcher backed up the play, but Ty kept going, just beating his throw to the plate. A week later Ty let an inside curve nip his abdomen and promptly went from first base to third base on an infield grounder. His play prompted a reporter to comment, "Ty Cobb is hitting and fielding in grand style for the Tigers. The Georgia boy appears to have subdued that nasty temper and jealous disposition of his and is working hard for the success of the club."[9]

As the above comment states, Cobb starred in the field, as well as at bat and on the bases. In June he made several great plays against the A's. "Cobb was again the Detroit star," wrote a reporter. "His greatest catch was made in the fourth, when he jumped against the fence to get Davis's hard drive. Cobb also made a nice catch in the first, on which he doubled Nicholls at third. This is the third play of this sort that he has made in this series."[10] In 1907 Ty led American League outfielders with 30 assists and 12 double plays.

On June 29, Cobb slammed a drive past Cleveland left fielder Joe Birmingham. He had made third base easily, but ran through a stop sign from the third base coach, trying to stretch the hit to a home run. He slipped on his way to the plate, but got up and continued his attempt to score. Ty and the ball arrived at about the same time. Cobb dived toward the plate, crashing into catcher Harry Bemis, knocking him down and the ball out of his hands. Bemis became incensed at the way Cobb came into the plate. He smacked Ty in the jaw. Umpire Silk O'Loughlin immediately stepped between the two players trying to restore order. A couple weeks later Cobb was caught off second base on a pickoff throw. In trying to get back to the base, he slammed into shortstop Kid Elberfeld, hitting him in the stomach and knocking him off his feet. Elberfeld held onto the ball, tagging Cobb out as he went down. He made no effort to retaliate.[11]

While such plays were defended by some baseball people on the grounds that "the basepaths belong to the runner," not everyone accepted that excuse. "In the third Cobb got in one of his dirty slides to the plate, which, from the press box, looked as if he deliberately tried to either jolt the ball out of Powers' hands or else disable him and compel him to leave the game," a Philadelphia writer said, in describing a play similar to the earlier collision between Cobb and Bemis. "Cobb made an effort to score on Rossman's out at first, but was easily doubled up by Davis to Powers. Doc had him at least two yards from the plate, but Cobb never let up in his headlong running and crashed into the Athletics' little catcher full tilt." The writer then commented, "There is no doubt about Cobb's ability as a first-class ballplayer, but such unnecessary actions as that of yesterday were unjustified, and he should be handled in the same way by the opposing side as he tries to do to them." Philadelphia shortstop Simon Nicholls did just that later in the game. Cobb rapped out a double in his next at-bat. As he slid into second base Nicholls took the throw and dropped down on Cobb. When the two got up the game was delayed while Cobb's uniform pants were pinned together. Nicholls had torn them with his spikes.[12]

The 1907 pennant race was so close it's hard to cite any one series as a key to winning the flag. For instance, the Tigers grabbed the lead for the first time on August 2, when they moved ahead of the Chicago by .001, while remaining a half-game behind the White Sox. All four contenders remained in the chase until they gradually ran out of games to play. One game was often cited as showing the grit that won the pennant for Detroit. It was a game that ended in a 17-inning tie. The Tigers had begun a series with Philadelphia on September 27 with a record of 86–56 (.6056), while the A's were 83–54 (.6054). Thus, the Tigers trailed the A's by .0002, putting them in second place, while leading by a half-game in the games-behind column. Detroit took the first game, 5–4, Germany Schaefer driving in three of his team's five runs and scoring the other two. The win gave the Tigers the lead by .007 and 1½ games.

The next game was played on September 30, due to rain on a Saturday and the Sunday blue law in Philadelphia. Donovan, the winning pitcher in Friday's game, pitched on two days' rest. He gave up three runs in the first, two in the third and two more in the fifth, the runs scoring on a combination of infield hits, short fly balls into the crowd ringing the field, and a couple of long drives that would have been good for extra bases had their been no overflow crowd. Going into the seventh inning, the Tigers trailed 7–1 and seemed about to hand the lead back to the A's. In that inning Detroit scored four runs off Rube Waddell with the help of two Philadelphia errors. Sam Crawford smacked a bases-loaded double for two of the runs and the other two scored on difficult infield chances fielded by second baseman Danny Murphy. In the bottom of the inning the A's made the score 8–5, scoring a run on two singles, a sacrifice and a force out. In the eighth Charley O'Leary got that run back with a double, a steal of third and an infield hit. The Tigers still trailed by two with only one inning left. Their two leading batters combined to tie the game. Crawford singled. Then Cobb hit one "a mile over the right field fence."

The game, which for nine innings had been an overflow-crowd slugfest, then became a pitcher's duel between Donovan and Eddie Plank, who had relieved Waddell in the ninth. The two veteran pitchers each gave up one run over the next eight innings. In the 11th Cobb doubled and scored on a hit by Claude Rossman. The A's responded in their half of the inning with a double by Nicholls. He took third on a wild pitch and scored on a long fly ball. After 17 innings the game was called because of darkness, ending in a 9–9 tie. The outcome left Detroit a game and a half ahead of

Philadelphia with seven games remaining.[13] The Tigers won their next five games to clinch the pennant, sweeping Washington and winning the first of a three-game series in St. Louis.

After the season ended Detroit players were discussing the role luck plays in baseball. Cobb insisted that luck played no part. Coughlin thought it was half luck and half ability. Rossman thought luck was the most important factor. They turned to Jennings for his thoughts. "Well," Hughey said, "winning baseball is just about 80 percent 'ginger fizz,' ten percent mechanical play and 10 percent luck." He went on to explain himself. "Translated, 'ginger fizz' means a combination of nerve, energy and determination, with quick thinking and a happy disposition thrown in. Seventy-five percent of the so-called lucky plays are not lucky at all. They are simply the result of superior baseball."[14]

Connie's Veterans Almost Pull It Off: Philadelphia

Philadelphia (88–57)

Name	AVG	OBP	SLG	R	RBI	SB
Topsy Hartsel, lf	.280	.405	.367	93	29	20
Simon Nicholls, ss	.302	.338	.337	75	23	13
or Monte Cross, ss	.206	.316	.282	37	18	17
Socks Seybold, rf	.271	.324	.363	58	92	10
Harry Davis, 1b	.266	.318	.395	84	87	20
Danny Murphy, 2b	.271	.317	.345	51	57	11
Jimmy Collins, 3b*	.278	.332	.333	51	45	8
or Bris Lord, of	.182	.249	.218	12	11	2
Rube Oldring, cf	.286	.305	.390	48	40	29
O. Schrecongost, c	.272	.306	.334	30	38	4
or Mike Powers, c	.182	.217	.201	9	9	1

Leading Pitchers	W	L	Pct	IP	H	ERA
Eddie Plank	24	16	.600	343.7	282	2.20
Rube Waddell	19	13	.594	284.7	234	2.15
Jimmy Dygert	21	8	.724	261.7	200	2.34
Chief Bender	16	8	.667	219.3	185	2.05
Jack Coombs	6	9	.400	132.7	109	3.12

*Includes record with Boston

Connie Mack's rebuilding program took one small step forward in 1907 and two giant steps backwards. A spate of injuries early in the season forced Connie to find out what his young hopefuls could do. The answer wasn't inspiring. Jack Knight, the bright hope of 1905, booted the ball all over the vicinity of third base, while batting poorly. Outfielder Bris Lord didn't get on base often, but when he did, he exhibited some notably boneheaded baserunning. Pitching prospect Rube Vickers displayed a great fastball, which he was unable to control. Jack Coombs pitched well enough in the first couple of months, but then came down with a sore arm. Simon Nicholls, on the other hand, looked like a keeper. He didn't shine in the field, either at shortstop or second base, but he hit well enough to earn a spot in the lineup, putting together a 32-game hitting streak. Mack's attempt to praise his fielding, however, came out more like a mixed review. "Nicholls has been a revelation," Connie said. "He may not be the most brilliant shortstop in the world, but the effectiveness of his inside work more than compensates for anything that he may lack in that direction, although, at that, he gets most anything that any other shortstop would get."[15] Eddie Collins, who joined the team in June, showed some of the talent that eventually earned him a spot in the front row at the Hall of Fame. But the future great played only a few games, Mack preferring to let him learn from the veterans in morning practice and study the game from the bench in the afternoons.[16]

The A's sputtered along through the end of May, winning a few more games than they lost. Then Mack completed a trade that seemed questionable at the time. He traded his exploded phenom, Jack Knight, to Boston for Jimmy Collins. Once considered the game's top third baseman, Collins was still hampered by the knee injury that had limited him to 37 games in 1906. "Jimmy was as clever as ever when he got his hands on anything, but was in some way handicapped in going to the side for a ground ball, and was very weak in coming in for bunts," said a Boston official in explaining the trade. "The other clubs had grown wise to the fact that Collins was not the player of old and won game after game by bunting."[17]

Surprisingly, the gimpy Collins helped to solidify the A's infield. He had been hitting well for Boston, and he continued to drive the ball with Philadelphia. He did not field at his previous outstanding level, but he was steadier than he had been earlier in the season. After he joined the team, the A's began to play at a faster pace. They didn't move much higher in the standings, but they kept up with the other three leaders as they separated themselves from the rest of the league. In mid–July a Philadelphia reporter commented, "No team in the league has an infield that will compare with the Athletics for reliability, while in batting Detroit is about the only one that has anything on the Philadelphia outfit." It took a while, but on August 12, the A's moved past Detroit into first place. They bobbed into and out of first for the next six weeks, exchanging places with the Tigers and White Sox from time to time as the three teams remained basically tied at the top of the standings until late into September. Many baseball men shared the opinion of a Detroit writer when he said, "They said Jimmy Collins was all in. They laughed at Connie

Mack when he took the once king of third sackers at a mighty figure. But Jimmy is far from all in. He is the man who has pulled the Athletics into the lead. They were going badly until he got around third and braced them up."[18]

Third base was not Mack's only worry. His pitching became thin during a couple of periods during the season. Eddie Plank was inconsistent the first month of the season, possibly because of the cold weather that prevailed much of the time. Chief Bender continued to be troubled by gastro-intestinal problems. Rube Waddell, as might be expected, had his own unique set of problems. While Rube had kept himself in good condition over the winter, and reported to spring training in good shape, he had started to go off on drinking binges before the season opened. In his first appearance, Rube pitched seven strong innings in relief of Rube Vickers. The A's led 4–2 entering the ninth. After Rube got the first two men in the ninth, he inexplicably lost track of the plate, walking the next two batters and hitting the third. At that point Mack took him out of the game, sending in Chief Bender, who ended the game by striking out Jimmy Collins on three pitches.

Rube's next outing, against New York, followed a similar scenario, but with a markedly different ending. The A's again led 4–2 in the ninth. This time Rube walked the first batter and allowed a single to the second. Connie waved Bender into the game. The Chief failed to bail out Rube. Instead he gave up two hits sandwiched around a throwing error, resulting in a 5–4 loss. Rube reacted to the disappointing ending by going out on a drinking binge that lasted for a week. When he showed up, Mack announced that the big lefty would be suspended for 30 days. Rube responded with a yarn about being at a "Turkish bath." When Connie saw that Rube was working hard to get into good shape, he decided to suspend the suspension. But he used Waddell only in relief over the next two weeks.

After the A's lost the first three games of a series against the White Sox, Mack decided to start Rube. The big left-hander threw a three-hitter, and seemed to get better as the game progressed. So Connie went with Waddell regularly after that. It turned out to be a somewhat wild ride. Rube celebrated his Chicago victory a bit too long. As a result, the poor-hitting St. Louis Browns found him to be easy pickings. They pounded his pitches for seven runs in four innings. On to Detroit. The good Waddell showed up, blanking the Tigers 3–0 on a five-hitter.

The rest of the summer proceeded along that same path for Rube. Nobody knew what to expect when it was his turn to take the mound. He could be the big guy with the great fastball and sharp-breaking curve. That Rube put together a streak of 23 straight shutout innings during which he fanned 30 batters. Or he could be the prodigal Rube, who took the mound with little on the ball, lasting only a few innings before getting the hook.

By the beginning of July, Mack had tired of Waddell's act. Rumors circulated that Connie was negotiating a trade with New York. "Mack is not sore over the poor pitching of Waddell, but because of its cause, the pitcher having returned to his old course of night training in saloons," a reporter explained. "Within a few minutes of train time last night he was visiting with friends in bar rooms here, and it is understood that this has been his custom elsewhere this season."[19] Connie denied the rumors, but over the winter he sold Waddell to the St. Louis Browns.

One of the ways in which Mack dealt with his pitchers' injuries and illness was to pile a heavy workload on Eddie Plank. Six times he started Plank on two day's rest and another time—in the climactic 17-inning game against Detroit—he asked Eddie to go eight innings in relief on two days' rest. With his staff decimated near the end of the season, he twice started Plank on just one day's rest. Despite the demands Mack placed on him, Plank ranked only third in both games started and innings pitched, trailing Chicago's Ed Walsh and Detroit's George Mullin in both categories. Eddie's eight shutouts led the league, while his 2.20 earned run average was the twelfth-best in the league.

Chief Bender pitched infrequently until mid–June and not at all after September 14. But he won 11 straight games in the middle of the summer. He also seemed to serve as a sort of insurance policy on days when Waddell seemed to be "out of shape" to pitch. He came on as a reliever in five of Rube's games.

Most of Mack's veterans performed at about their normal levels, which were good enough to make the A's perennial pennant contenders. Leadoff man Topsy Hartsel walked 106 times, leading the league for the third season in a row (he led again in 1908). He was also first in on-base percentage (.405) and was fourth in runs scored (93). Rotund Socks Seybold had his last big season at age 36. He drove home 92 runs, trailing only Ty Cobb in that category. His .363 slugging percentage ranked tenth in the league. He had finished among the top ten in that category every season the A's were in existence. Apparently he was still an able fielder. A Cleveland writer remarked, "Socks Seybold also pulled off some fancy stunts in the outfield. Socks carries weight for age, but nevertheless, he can get over the ground as fast as many who do not resemble a freight car in contour."[20]

Danny Murphy was slowing down in the field—he would begin a transition to the outfield in 1908—but he had his normally solid, if unspectacular season at bat. Ossee Schrecongost, Waddell's friend and drinking buddy, was trying something new. He gave up booze. In June, when Mack was separated from the A's while discussing a possible deal for Waddell, he put Schreck in charge of the team. Abstaining from alcohol, however, didn't inhibit Rube's buddy from taking a free-wheeling approach to the game. In June, while he was substituting at first base, an opposing batter smashed a liner towards right field. Schreck saw he couldn't reach the ball with his glove, so he quickly grabbed his cap, threw it at the ball, and knocked it down. He might have gotten a putout if the rules had allowed such a fielding technique. Instead, the umpire gave the batter second base on what would have been a single.[21]

Like Hartsel, Harry Davis's typical season meant leading the league in a couple batting categories. Davis led in home runs for the fourth year in a row, although by modern standards his eight dingers don't seem impressive. He also led in doubles (35), and as usual was among the leaders in slugging percentage (.395) and runs batted in (87).

This was the last season Mack's veterans were able to contend for the pennant. In 1908, with Waddell gone and virtually every seasoned player performing below his former level, the A's finished in sixth place, losing 17 more games than they won.

Baseball's Cinderella Team—The Year After: Chicago

Everyone loves a team that overcomes obstacles to win. The White Sox were the Cinderella team of 1906. The next year everyone seemed to have a soft spot in their hearts for Chicago's defending World Champions. "Managers and players the country over do not hold the same opinions regarding the reasons for the success of the White Sox as they did before the World's Series of games last fall," noted a Cleveland reporter. "Today it is pretty universally agreed that the champions win their games and keep in the lead by always playing ball.... Oh, the team that can beat that aggregation of brains has a walkaway for the pennant."[22]

Chicago (87–64)

Name	AVG	OBP	SLG	R	RBI	SB
Ed Hahn, rf	.255	.359	.294	87	45	17
Fielder Jones, cf	.261	.345	.297	72	47	17
Frank Isbell, 2b	.243	.281	.311	60	41	22
Jiggs Donahue, 1b	.259	.295	.299	75	68	27
George Davis, ss	.238	.313	.288	59	52	15
Patsy Dougherty, lf	.270	.322	.315	69	59	33
George Rohe, 3b-2b	.213	.274	.255	46	51	16
or Lee Quillen, 3b	.192	.256	.225	17	14	8
or Lee Tannehill, 3b	.241	.293	.259	9	11	3
Billy Sullivan, c	.179	.235	.228	30	36	6
or Ed McFarland, c	.283	.340	.362	11	8	3

Leading Pitchers	W	L	Pct	IP	H	ERA
Ed Walsh	24	18	.571	422.3	341	1.60
Frank Smith	23	10	.697	310	280	2.47
Doc White	27	13	.675	291	270	2.26
Nick Altrock	7	13	.350	213.7	210	2.57
Roy Patterson	4	6	.400	96	105	2.62
Frank Owen	2	3	.400	47	43	2.49

Interest in the White Sox was so high that baseball humorist Charley Dryden penned several articles focusing on one of the team's bats. The bat had a name—"Old Betsy"—and belonged to Frank Isbell, one of the stars of the World Series. Betsy had played a central role when Izzy rapped out four doubles in the fifth game of the Series. Like the other members of the team, she had been rewarded with a trip through Mexico during spring training. She spent the last week of the pre-season resting at Isbell's home in Wichita, arriving in Chicago just in time for opening day. The trip must have been tiring, as Izzy went hitless against Harry Howell's spitballs that day.

Betsy's career with the White Sox came to an untimely end before the season was a week old. George Davis borrowed her and shattered her heart while hitting into a double play. Although grieving for his departed favorite, Izzy had no choice but to find a replacement. He chose Evelyn, who helped Izzy pound out two hits in her first game and charitably gifted George Rohe with two more. Rohe was using Evelyn with Izzy's permission. "The real Evelyn had a reputation for breaking hearts," said Isbell, "and for that reason I called my bat after her, for I expect it to break many a pitcher's heart this season."[23]

For much of the season it appeared the White Sox would have an encore year. They grabbed the lead early in the season and held on to it through July, although they never were able to move more than a few games ahead of the next three teams. After the Eastern teams completed their first Western trip, New York manager Clark Griffith was asked which western team looked best. "Well I think that Chicago did," Griff replied, "because the White Sox' pitchers are the best in the league. Those Chicago grounds give them a big advantage because they are slow and it is hard to hit on them. "And last, but not least, Billy Sullivan is a great catcher, and a great catcher always makes a winning team if there is anything to it at all."[24]

As in the previous year, the Sox were constantly praised for playing the game the right way. "There is no individual playing on the team," noted a Washington reporter. "The players work together with one end in view, victory. There is not a throw made which is not backed up and their inside work shows science and judgment. That is why the team wins with few hits.

Watch the in- and outfield change their positions as the different batters come to the plate. The infield watches the catcher's signs and places itself accordingly. It may only be a foot or two, but that cuts a figure very often when the ball is hit on the ground. The team works in a deliberate, yet smooth manner, and everything that is done is done with a purpose in view."[25]

As the season progressed, however, it became apparent that the Sox would have to overcome greater obstacles than those facing the 1906 team. Its star players just couldn't stay healthy. The left side of the infield took a hit early in the season and never recovered. In the team's second game Lee Tannehill incurred a badly spiked ankle that developed blood poisoning. He missed almost all of the first half of the season, and played sparingly in the second half, his year ending early when he suffered a shoulder injury in mid–September.[26] George Rohe, one of the heroes of the World Series triumph, was his principal replacement. Rohe's .213 batting average wasn't that far below Tannehill's normal minuscule level, but he did not even approach Lee's fielding ability.

Shortstop George Davis came down with back miseries in April. He battled through that problem, but in June he wrenched his ankle sliding into the plate. He missed a few games with that injury, but once again returned to the lineup when Frank Isbell came down with "rheumatism" of the back. As would be expected he was not able to play at the top of his game. "Davis is so lame from the strain he received a month ago in Boston, that he cannot cover any ground to speak of and has difficulty in beating out a single to first," said the *Tribune's* Sy Sanborn. "Yet he has been kept in the game by Isbell's sickness and by the fact that there does not seem to be any guiding hand for the infielders when he is off duty."[27] When Isbell was absent (he played only 119 games at second base), the White Sox infield was manned by a second baseman (Rohe) whose fielding average was 40 points below the league average, a gimpy shortstop with little range (Davis), and a third baseman (Lee Quillen) who fielded .871.

The Chicago pitching staff suffered about as much as its infield. Frank Owen, the team's top winner in 1906, came down with malaria over the winter. He recovered fast enough to start three games in April, but then had a relapse and did not pitch again until July. Manager Fielder Jones used him about once a week in relief after that. He appeared in a total of 11 games, starting only once after April, and figuring in only five decisions over the course of the season.[28]

Nick Altrock struggled with arm miseries and bad luck through much of the season. In his first three starts he gave up a total of three runs, but had only a 1–2 mark to show for his efforts. Through May 21 he had given up two runs or less in six of his eight starts, but all he had to show for it was a 4–4 record. Another two-run outing a week later resulted in another loss. At that point the pain in his arm limited him to two appearances over the next seven weeks. After returning in mid–July he pitched sporadically, making a few starts, but appearing more often in relief. He was winless in both roles until September 4, when he pitched seven shutout innings in relief of Frank Smith. He snagged another victory in relief two weeks later and pitched a complete game to beat Boston 2–1 a week before the season ended. Nick's 2.57 ERA was only .03 above the league average, but it yielded only a 7–13 won-lost record.

With Owen out for most of the year, Altrock of little use for weeks at a time, and Roy Patterson not very effective when used, a heavy burden fell to the team's three veteran starters—Frank Smith, Doc White and Ed Walsh. After Altrock dropped out of the rotation at the end of May manager Fielder Jones used these three hurlers in a three-man rotation for about six weeks. With the doubleheaders piling up in July and August Patterson and Altrock were given sporadic starts. After Labor Day, with injuries mounting and the team's pennant chances beginning to fade, Jones once again began to rely heavily on his three favored hurlers.

Fielder's use of a three-man rotation was a throw-back to the 1890s and resulted in a workload distribution similar to that era. The man most affected was Walsh, whose 422⅓ innings pitched was a burden similar to that of Iron Man McGinnity and Jack Chesbro in their top years and at the level of the busiest twirlers of the 90s. Jones seemed to be smitten with Walsh's spitball. In 1906, after Big Ed had won 11 games in a row, Fielder said, "Walsh has mastered a spitball which has no peer. Chesbro's moistened ball never compared with this one of Walsh's. They can't hit it. And what is worse for our opponents, Walsh is able to take the box every other day. He likes work. His physique makes him better qualified to pitch alternative days than Mathewson. Look out for this young man. He is the one best bet in the big league today."[29]

The White Sox manager had great confidence in Walsh's ability to work often. Twice in the early days of the 1907 season reporters commented that Walsh was warming up throughout the game in case he was needed. Jones not only started Big Ed in 46 games, but also brought him in as a reliever 11 times. Eventually the heavy workload caught up with Walsh. In late September, after Washington drove him to the bench after three innings, a *Tribune* reporter commented, "The big spitter's arm is all right, but he seems to have lost the stinger out of it. The Senators waded into him for six swats in a row, which are more than Edward usually allows in an entire game. Perhaps the 50 games Walsh has pitched have soured his good right arm."[30]

In addition to starting the most games in the league, Big Ed also closed out ten games, finishing in a three-way tie for the most saves with four. Despite the burdensome workload he posted the league's lowest earned run average (1.60). Like many spitball pitchers, he gave up more than a normal amount of unearned runs, allowing 45 tainted runs along with 75 legitimate ones. According to *The Sporting News*, his spitball had "extraordinary speed and a sharp outbreak." He induced a large number of ground balls. He set the record for number of assists in a season by a pitcher with 227. Twelve of them came in one game, in which he also recorded three putouts, for a total of 15 chances, also a record.

Given the stellar overall performance, Walsh's won-lost record of 24–18 seems rather disappointing. The explanation was that, too often when he was on the mound, the "Hitless Wonders" played more like the "Runless Hitters," to borrow a phrase from Sy Sanborn. The Sox were shut out in eight of Big Ed's losses. They scored one run in four of his defeats and two in two.[31] Three of the shutout losses came in the second half of July, when the White Sox lost nine out of ten games to begin their slide out of first place. The Tigers passed them the first week of August and shortly thereafter the Athletics pulled ahead of them. The White Sox fought gamely through the end of the season, but they could not overcome the loss of too many of their best players.

Lajoie—Great Player, Yes; Great Manager, Not So Much: Cleveland

We mentioned above that a case can be made for the contention that Honus Wagner was the greatest player in baseball history. During the early Deadball Era, when Wagner was at the height of his career, the debate over Honus's place in baseball's pantheon was about which of the game's two transcendent stars—Wagner or Nap Lajoie—was the greatest player ever to stride onto a diamond.

Both were big men for the era, Wagner standing a bit under six feet tall and Lajoie a shade over and both weighing about 200 pounds. They both exuded strength, but were opposites in their movements. Honus was bow-legged and awkward. "His tread is a cross between that of an elephant and a rhinoceros," said one writer. "In reaching for the leather his arms look like cotton hooks and move about as gracefully as steam cranes." Lajoie, on the other hand, had an almost perfect athletic build and was the definition of grace in motion. "Where Honus hurls himself on the ball as if he expected never to have another chance to make a good play, Larry glides toward it, gathers it in nonchalantly, as if picking fruit, and sends it to first or some other base.... He's a ghost. His mysterious means of locomotion take him from place to place in his position–and frequently in the position of his neighbors–and behold, when the globule gets to that spot he is waiting for it."[32]

Everyone agreed that Wagner was the top batter in the National League and Lajoie in the American. When the 1907 season began, Lajoie had completed his tenth full season in the majors and Wagner his ninth. Lajoie had won batting championships in each of the first four years of the American League's existence, and had finished second in 1906. He had not played enough games to qualify for the 1905 title, but his .329 average was 21 points above Elmer Flick's league-leading mark. And there was the impact of the 1901 season, when his .426 average was 86 points ahead of the Mike Donlin's second-place average, and he led the league in almost every significant batting category. Wagner had also bagged four league batting championships through 1906. (He would win four more, while Lajoie had only one disputed title still to come.) The Dutchman's top mark was .381 in 1900. Career batting averages were not officially tracked at the time, but following the 1905 season, a Cleveland reporter calculated the "grand average" for the top hitters. Lajoie led all players of the preceding ten years with a .361 batting average over that time. Wagner's mark over that period was .347.[33]

Tim Murnane, an ex-ballplayer and the sports editor of the *Boston Globe*, was one of Lajoie's supporters in the debate. "Lajoie is graceful, with no movement for effect, while Wagner will swing his arm and kick up the dust in making the simplest kind of play. To the superficial observer Wagner would take the prize in a cantor; the ballplayer and close observer, however, would pick Lajoie," said Murnane. "Wagner will fumble and make wild throws, while Lajoie is dead onto the mark, and seldom fumbles. He gets a ball away much quicker than Wagner, and, while it may seem the German can run bases better than the Frenchman, the fact is that Lajoie takes chances only when they are called for, and gets there, generally, being fast and a fine slider." In conclusion, Murnane said, "Wagner is the most interesting because of his picturesque style, but Lajoie is the finished ballplayer; the artist without frills, who makes phenomenal plays look easy, and who is without a peer on the ball field."[34]

Abe Yager of the *Brooklyn Daily Eagle* made the case for Wagner. "So far as batting ability is concerned there is little to choose between the men," Yager conceded. "But when it comes to playing the field, running bases and usefulness, Wagner is far superior to Lajoie. The big Frenchman is a great enough second baseman, but he is not in it with Wagner when it comes to running bases, and outside of playing second base, Wagner is much better in any position than Lajoie." Yager went on to mention the factor that was perhaps the most telling difference between the two players. "Another point in which Wagner excels Lajoie is that he is nearly always in the game. Lajoie, on the contrary, seldom goes through a season without losing at least a month's time. One season it is a bad leg and another season it is another ailment. The big Dutchman seldom misses a day. he is always in the game, and can play any position."[35]

Perhaps the last word on the subject should be given to Bob Ganley, who played with Wagner for a season in Pittsburgh before being traded to Washington, where he competed against Lajoie. A Cleveland reporter asked him to compare the two stars. "Why man alive, there's no comparison between 'em," Ganley responded. "All there is to it is that Lajoie is perfection at second base while Wagner is the shortstop supreme. Their methods are wholly different and they are both masters. They're superlatives."

Cleveland (85–67)

Name	AVG	OBP	SLG	R	RBI	SB
Elmer Flick, rf	.302	.386	.412	80	58	41
or Harry Bay, cf	.179	.271	.211	14	7	7
Bill Bradley, 3b	.223	.286	.267	48	34	20
or Pete O'Brien, inf*	.208	.261	.258	15	18	5
Terry Turner, ss	.242	.272	.307	57	46	27
Nap Lajoie, 2b	.301	.347	.395	53	63	24
Nig Clarke, c	.269	.333	.372	44	33	3
or Harry Bemis, c	.250	.283	.291	12	19	5
Bill Hinchman, lf	.228	.311	.305	62	50	15
Joe Birmingham, cf	.235	.265	.300	55	33	23
George Stovall, 1b	.236	.267	.305	38	36	13
Leading Pitchers	W	L	Pct	IP	H	ERA
Addie Joss	27	11	.711	338.7	279	1.83
Glenn Liebhardt	18	14	.563	280.3	254	2.05
Bob Rhoads	15	14	.517	275	258	2.29
Jake Thielman	11	8	.579	166	151	2.33
Otto Hess	6	6	.500	93.3	84	2.89
Walter Clarkson**	5	7	.417	108	96	2.67
Heinie Berger	3	3	.500	87.3	74	2.99

*Includes record with Washington
**Includes record with New York

For five years Lajoie took on a burden Wagner was wise enough to avoid throughout his career. When Bill Armour resigned after the 1905 season, Nap became the manager of the team that bore his name. While Lajoie was a "natural" at playing baseball, he did not find it easy to lead other men. He was almost a direct opposite of men like John McGraw and Armour, who insisted on dictating moves to their players. He felt he knew how to play the game and didn't want to be hampered by instructions from the bench. He wanted to give his players the same freedom. For the Naps, however, that didn't result in a team that was eager to seize every opportunity to pull off a play that would give the team an advantage. One of the team's leaders, Bill Bradley, gave an interview that seemed to represent the prevailing view among Lajoie's players. According to a reporter, Bradley's views could be summed up in one statement: "It's base hits that win games and not teamwork."[36]

During spring training in 1907 Lajoie told reporters he was determined to show the fans that the Naps could play inside baseball. For a while the new emphasis seemed to be working, although it got off to a disappointing start. During spring training the team gave special attention to the squeeze play. On opening day, however, an attempt to pull it off resulted in a double play, as the Naps were shut out, 2–0. Undiscouraged, Lajoie promised to continue working on the play in morning practice. In their next game, the Naps stole six bases and sacrificed four times enroute to a 9–3 spanking of the Tigers.[37]

The team soon started down its well-trod path of hanging just off the lead, threatening to take over first place but never quite doing it. This season, however, they did it differently. The Cleveland "sluggers" weren't slugging. The only two men doing any hitting were Lajoie and Elmer Flick. Amazingly, the Naps—long used as the prime example of a team that couldn't play "scientific baseball"—were winning because they maximized their opportunities. A Cleveland reporter noted, "The style of play has been mixed up skillfully, the hit-and-run and sacrifice being worked with good judgment while the men have run the bases with skill in most instances."

Eventually the inevitable barrage of injuries hit the Naps. Lajoie, Flick, Bradley, center fielder Harry Bay, and pitcher Otto Hess were all out of the lineup in late July, when the Naps dropped four of five games on an Eastern trip. Following a game in Philadelphia Lajoie and first baseman George Stovall got into an argument at the team's hotel. Reportedly Stovall criticized Lajoie for paying attention to advice offered by fans and reporters while refusing to listen to suggestions from the players. He told Lajoie he was the biggest fool in baseball. Nap replied, "Yes, that's what everyone tells me—for keeping you on the team." Stovall continued to argue, and was told he would be fined. Then the first baseman picked up a chair and threw it at his manager. Lajoie ducked but the chair caught him on the back of the head, raising a good-sized lump. Stovall was immediately suspended and sent back to Cleveland, along with Frank Delahanty, who was being punished for getting drunk on the trip.[38]

The Stovall incident, along with the team's failure to meet expectations, increased the call for Lajoie's removal as manager. Cleveland's owners, however, continued to show support for him, asserting that, while he may not be "the best manager ever," he was still above average. Nap continued as Cleveland's manager until August of 1909, when he decided he no longer could take the constant drumbeat of criticism from the Cleveland press and fans. He submitted a letter of resignation effective as soon as the team could hire a replacement. Deacon McGuire served as the Naps' leader during the last six weeks of that season. Lajoie continued to play for Cleveland through the 1914 season.[39]

Unraveling: New York

New York (70–78)

Name	AVG	OBP	SLG	R	RBI	SB
Danny Hoffman, cf	.253	.325	.313	81	46	30
Willie Keeler, rf	.234	.265	.255	50	17	7
Kid Elberfeld, ss	.271	.343	.336	61	51	22
Hal Chase, 1b	.287	.315	.357	72	68	32
Frank LaPorte, 3b-of	.270	.317	.360	56	48	10
or George Moriarty, 3b	.277	.320	.336	51	43	28
Jimmy Williams, 2b	.270	.319	.359	53	63	14
Wid Conroy, lf	.234	.279	.315	58	51	41
or Branch Rickey, ut	.182	.253	.234	16	15	4
Red Kleinow, c	.264	.327	.316	30	26	5
or Ira Thomas, c	.192	.240	.269	20	24	5

Leading Pitchers	W	L	Pct	IP	H	ERA
Al Orth	14	21	.400	248.7	244	2.61
Jack Chesbro	10	10	.500	206	192	2.53
Slow Joe Doyle	11	11	.500	193.7	169	2.65
Bill Hogg	10	8	.556	166.7	173	3.08
Doc Newton	7	10	.412	133	132	3.18
Earl Moore*	3	7	.300	83.3	90	4.10
Frank Kitson**	4	3	.571	93	116	3.39

*Includes record with Cleveland
**Includes record with Washington

The Highlanders' season started coming apart as soon as it became time to get the team together. Two of the team's stars—Hal Chase and Jack Chesbro—missed spring training while holding out for salary increases.

Chase, who had been coaching a college baseball team, showed up for the second game of the season already in shape to play. Chesbro had been tending his farm in Massachusetts. He reported at the beginning of May, but didn't appear in a game until May 18.

Opening day brought a startling development that carried a dark portent for the future. Danny Hoffman was on first base. With two strikes on the batter, Willie Keeler, Hoffman took off for second. Keeler offered at the ball, but missed. The opposing catcher cocked his arm to throw only to find no one covering the bag. The explanation was simple—the batter was Keeler, and everyone expected him to hit the ball. After all, Willie almost never struck out. (The previous year he had fanned five times in 672 plate appearances.) Keeler struck out only eight more times over the course of the season, but he wasn't the hitter he had been before. His batting average plummeted from .304 to .234. Since Willie was the catalyst who ignited the Highlander's attack, the decline in his production was very damaging.[40]

Another seemingly insignificant event also turned out to be an unfavorable sign. On April 15, manager Clark Griffith named Bobby Keefe as his starting pitcher. It wasn't that Keefe was such a bad pitcher—he had won 30 games in the Pacific Coast League in 1905, and Griffith thought he might be another Amos Rusie. But the fact that he was Griff's third starter demonstrated how thin the Highlanders' pitching staff was. Behind veteran Al Orth, Griffith had Bill Hogg, who had compiled a 23-26 record in his two big league seasons; Slow Joe Doyle, who had less than two months of major league experience; Walter Clarkson, who had pitched infrequently for the Highlanders over the last three years; Keefe; and Bill Brockett, another rookie who would start the Highlanders' tenth game. By midseason Keefe and Brockett were back in the minor leagues and Clarkson was in Cleveland. By then Griff had acquired worn-out veterans Earl Moore and Frank Kitson, neither of whom pitched well in New York. Before the season was over the Highlanders had tried 17 different pitchers—about eight or ten more than normal for the era.

Griffith handled Chesbro cautiously the first few weeks after he joined the team. He kept the veteran on the sidelines for over two weeks, then started him about once a week for the next month. In his second start, on May 29, Griff pulled the spitballer with one out in the fourth inning and the game knotted in a scoreless tie. "Jack Chesbro is being handled like a great horse is prepared for a rich stake," remarked a Washington reporter. "He is soft and lacks condition, and Griffith was wise to take him out of the game when he did, or there would have been a different story to tell. Griff will continue to work Chesbro parts of games for a month or so yet, and by that time hopes to have him ready to go the route."[41]

Once he began to work with some regularity, Chesbro exhibited the same pattern he had shown the previous season. He would have one or two pretty good outings, then would last only a few innings before being knocked out of the box. Like some other spitball pitchers, he could be pitching very well for several innings at a time and then completely lose his effectiveness. An example occurred in early August against the Browns. "For six brilliant innings, Jack Chesbro was a perfect puzzle," a reporter wrote. "But in the seventh, Chesbro's arm lost its cunning and his twists were hammered all over the lot. Six successive bingles, including a two-bagger, materialized and when it was all over five St. Louis men had pranced across the rubber, tying the score. Manager Clark Griffith promptly yanked Chesbro and placed Doc Newton on the slab."[42] After the first week in August Chesbro's record was a disappointing 3–7. He rallied after that, however, ending the season with a 10–10 record, which wasn't bad considering the circumstances.

Al Orth began the season as the only pitcher Griffith could count on. In the first week of June his record stood at 8–4, at a time when the team was only a couple games over .500. After that, however, he began to struggle under the heavy workload he was given. He won only six more games during the remainder of the season, while losing 17. As his record faded, so did the Highlanders'. By mid–June the team settled into fifth place, a few games under .500, and stayed there until the end of the season.

By mid–August many of the New York players had lost their zest for the game. "There is no getting away from the fact that the Yankees are in bad shape," said Joe Vila, a *Sporting News* correspondent. "Some of the men appear to be indifferent and are just playing for the salaries. Others, they tell me, are blowing off the broth at night in Harlem joints." Evidently, one of the players who occupied his evenings blowing the bubbles off his brew was second baseman Jimmy Williams.[43]

The Highlanders' second sacker was one of those players who performed at a very respectable level, but received little notice. One reason for that may have been because Nap Lajoie played the same position, so there was no debate over who ranked number one in the league at second base. Williams had made an outstanding major league debut in 1899 with Pittsburgh. He hit .355 and led the National League with 27 triples. He was among the top five in the league in hits, doubles, triples, home runs, RBI's, batting average, and slugging percentage. He was seventh in on-base percentage. The only important offensive category in which he didn't finish among the leaders was stolen bases, and his 26 stolen bases weren't bad. Brooklyn Manager Ned Hanlon said of him, "Williams is a good hitter, base runner, and fielder—in fact, a high-class man. He is scarcely Collins' equal as a third baseman, but for all-around ability there isn't much choice between the two."[44]

Williams jumped to the Baltimore Orioles in 1901. His manager there, John McGraw, was also the team's third baseman. So Jimmy switched to second base. His power output, which had declined in 1900 because of injuries, returned that season. He led the new major league in triples—about the only batting category Nap Lajoie didn't lead—and repeated the next season, both years knocking out 21 three-baggers. He transferred to New York in 1903, along with the other Orioles who didn't follow McGraw to the National League. His power declined somewhat beginning that year, likely because the American League adopted the new foul-strike rule. It declined further as the years passed and he began to put on weight. He remained a pretty good clutch hitter, however, ranking in the top ten in RBIs every season but one while with the Highlanders. Williams was traded to the Browns after the 1907 season ended. At that time Joe Vila remarked, "For a long time, in spite of his steady playing, Jimmy Williams did not please the officials of the New York club. His habits off the ball field were not just what they should have been and his influence upon several of the players was considered not good."[45]

Like Williams and a few other teammates, Kid Elberfeld also became discouraged by the way the season was going. But the "Tobasco Kid" wasn't content to just drown his sorrows in alcohol. He was well known for his temperamental outbursts, which were almost always directed at an umpire. But he had another side to his character. He could exhibit behavior somewhat like a pre-schooler responding to disappointment by screaming and throwing or kicking his toys. He had been traded to New York in 1903 after being charged with "careless and indifferent playing." That season, over a period of about a week, the Kid had made several costly errors and at times seemed to be giving less than full effort. His behavior angered his manager, Ed Barrow, and led to a suspension and an invitation to other clubs to offer whatever they wished for Elberfeld.[46]

In 1907 the Tobasco Kid displayed similar behavior for the Highlanders near the end of July. He made three errors in the opening game of a series against Cleveland. The next day he struck out on three sweeping curves that went far outside the strike zone, offering half-hearted swings for each one. In his game summary a Cleveland writer commented, "Just before the team returned from its recent western tour rumors were rife that Elberfeld was playing for his release. These reports were denied, but today's developments have confirmed the belief of New York baseball followers that the Kid desires a change." The following day Elberfeld again made three errors in the first game of a doubleheader. Frank Farrell, the Highlanders' owner, watched the game and was upset by the Kid's performance. He ordered Griffith to suspend Elberfeld indefinitely, starting with the second game of the doubleheader. Griff was in full agreement with his boss's decision. "I know that Elberfeld wasn't trying," he said. "I don't know what he is sulking about, but he has sulked for several days, and I won't stand for it.... Elberfeld's suspension is indefinite. When he comes around to his senses and shows a desire to go in and help I will put him back at short. Until that time he will be off without pay."[47]

After the 1903 episode the baseball press generally came to Elberfeld's defense. But after this incident the writers were more critical. Still, the Kid was known as a tough competitor and a hard loser. New York writer Sam Crane, an ex-ballplayer, explained why many people were willing to forgive his transgression. Crane explained that, although most players understood that their welfare depended upon their team's success, at times a player would "carry a holdover grouch and become careless and indifferent." Elberfeld wasn't the only player who had been guilty of doing that, Crane said. "But I must say that I never saw one who made his grouchiness so publicly evident. If he wanted to get away from the club he went about it in a most bungling fashion. And still the Kid is a good-hearted fellow; he simply steered himself wrong."[48]

Elberfeld's suspension lasted about two weeks. In his first game after being reinstated he drove in both New York runs in a 2–1 victory over Detroit.[49] Perhaps the most severe punishment he received from Farrell came the following year, when, in June, he replaced Griffith as manager of a hapless New York team that floundered all season, finishing in the cellar, 17 games behind the seventh-place Senators. Under the Kid's leadership that team won 27 games while subjecting their short-fused manager to 71 losses.

As Red John's World Turns: St. Louis

Jack Powell was a fixture on the St. Louis sports scene for almost 15 years. He pitched for St. Louis teams in both the National and American leagues from 1899 to 1912, and was often his team's ace. He was a gregarious fellow, and evidently felt free to share his personal struggles with the city's sportswriters. As a result St. Louis sports pages described not only his pitching feats, but details about his difficulty controlling his weight and his affinity for the wares of "John Barleycorn"—a personification representing intoxicating beverages. When viewed from a broad perspective, the coverage of Powell's career acquired some of the qualities of a long-running soap opera.

St. Louis (69-83)

Name	AVG	OBP	SLG	R	RBI	SB
Harry Niles, 2b	.289	.331	.339	65	35	19
Charlie Hemphill, cf	.259	.319	.322	66	38	14
George Stone, lf	.320	.387	.399	77	59	23
Ollie Pickering, rf	.276	.321	.337	63	60	15
Bobby Wallace, ss	.257	.328	.320	56	70	16
Joe Yeager, 3b	.239	.294	.326	32	44	11
or Roy Hartzell, ut	.236	.285	.295	20	13	7
Tubby Spencer, c	.265	.299	.335	27	25	1
orJim Stephens, c	.202	.270	.272	15	11	3
Tom Jones, 1b	.250	.298	.291	52	34	24

Leading Pitchers	W	L	Pct	IP	H	ERA
Harry Howell	16	15	.516	316.3	258	1.93
Barney Pelty	12	21	.364	273	234	2.57
Jack Powell	13	16	.448	255.7	229	2.68
Fred Glade	13	9	.591	202	187	2.67
Bill Dinneen*	7	14	.333	188	195	2.92
Beany Jacobson*	1	6	.143	59.3	57	3.19

*Includes record with Boston

Powell came to St. Louis in 1899. He was transferred to the Perfectos, as the team was then known, from Cleveland by the teams' ownership. The two clubs had been combined when Frank DeHaas Robison and his brother Frank gained control of the Perfectos while still retaining the Spiders. Powell was one of the stars who were stripped from the Cleveland team, leaving a shell which became known as the "Misfits" while compiling the worst record in major league history. Powell was then in his third year as a major leaguer. He had languished on the bench for almost half a year as a rookie in 1897. He was given a chance to pitch because his manager, Patsy Tebeau, felt Louisville had a jinx over the Spiders which made them unbeatable. He sent "Red John" to the mound as a sacrificial lamb. Powell surprised his manager by pitching a three-hitter to break the jinx. On second thought, make that "to shatter" the jinx—he won by an 18-1 score.[50] He was inserted into the Spider's starting rotation, winning his first four starts and compiling a 15-10 record in his rookie season. He became the Spiders' number two pitcher, behind Cy Young, the following season, going 23-15 and leading the National League in shutouts with six.

It appears that by the time Powell moved to St. Louis he had already developed a drinking problem. During the summer of 1899 several Perfecto players discovered they were being followed by private detectives. Powell became incensed at the invasion of his privacy. He blamed Louis Heilbroner, the team's business manager, who had taken several actions that bothered the players. In August Powell burst into Heilbroner's office, somewhat inebriated. According to one report, he "tried to wreck it and its occupants." He invited Heilbroner to step outside, where Red John promised to demonstrate how John L. Sullivan won his fights. The business manager tried to pacify his hostile ballplayer, but after his initial efforts failed, he quickly disappeared into a back room.[51]

That tantrum didn't seem to stop the surveillance, so Powell decided on a more direct approach. One night in September, while out on the town, Red John and teammate Harry Blake surprised their pursuers and beat them up. The next spring Powell told a reporter he had not taken a drink for two months. "I have cut out practices which I am convinced handicap a player," he said. "My health is all I can ask for and I never felt stronger in my life." That pledge became part of a pattern that would persist for nearly a decade. Red John seems to have wanted to stop drinking, or at least control it. But he was unable to do so. "When Powell is winning he considers it his duty to 'celebrate' his success, and when he's losing he indulges in intoxicants to stop the bad streak," explained one of his teammates.[52]

In the spring of 1902, after jumping to the cross-town Browns, Powell promised he would take "the temperance pledge" and hold to it the entire season. According to his manager, Jimmy McAleer, he lived up to his word. He was McAleer's workhorse, going 22–17 while starting 39 games and relieving in three others. The Browns finished in second place, five games behind the Philadelphia Athletics. They posted the third-highest winning percentage in franchise history, the highest the team would achieve until 1922. It was an accomplishment worth celebrating. While Red John didn't seem to go back to abusing alcohol (for the time being), he seems to have munched his way through the winter. He was overweight when he reported, a bit late, for spring training in 1903. He had to do extra work to take off the excess poundage, and before spring training ended he came down with "rheumatism" in his shoulder and chest. A young man who had always been very healthy, Powell became concerned about the aches and pains. He decided he had appendicitis and, according to *The Sporting News*, "worried about it day and night." Convinced he was in a physical decline, Red John began thinking of ways he could improve his pitching repertoire. He developed a changeup, which he began using about mid-season. He tried it out on Buck Freeman, who was so surprised at the pitch, that he took two of them for strikes before fanning on a fastball. After that Powell began using the "slow ball" regularly.[53]

In 1904, with contracts negotiated during the inter-league war expiring, major league baseball owners began slashing players' salaries. Powell was offered a contract for $3,250, which was $1,250 less than he had earned the previous season. Red John refused to sign at the reduced salary. In March, Clark Griffith offered $5,000 for Powell, who heard of the proposal. Powell told McAleer the Browns should accept the offer. "I want to stay here," he said, "but I'll not put on a uniform for a cent less than $4,500." Red John showed his manager an offer from a brewer to help him get started in the saloon business. If, by the beginning of spring training, he were not signed at his price or traded to a club that would pay it, Powell said, "I'll get a government license and a stock of booze and quit baseball." In short order a deal was arranged in which Powell was sent to New York for $6,000 and Harry Howell, who at the time was considered a throw-in who was included just to give the deal the appearance of being a trade.[54]

Powell seemed to be content his first year in New York, when he and Jack Chesbro shouldered very heavy workloads and almost carried the Highlanders to a championship. In 1905, however, the rains and cold wind that prevailed in April and early May hindered his ability to stay in condition. He developed a sore arm. Although he recovered enough to pitch regularly, he became a victim of the quick hook Griffith exercised beginning that year. He also appeared frequently in relief. Powell rebelled at Griffith's new system. He began drinking again and took on weight. In September he was sent back to St. Louis in a straight deal for cash.

His experience in New York bothered him so much that for over two years Red John continued to complain about the way Griffith handled him. "Griffith certainly adopted wrong tactics with me," he grumbled. "As soon as I would give a base on balls or two or a couple of hits were made off me in an inning, I would be benched. Why, I have always begged to be kept on the firing line when the score was against me. All the managers I worked for except Griffith gave me my way, and many a game have I saved that seemed hopelessly lost. You'll not see McAleer yanking me out as soon as a lit-

Jack Powell's struggles with alcohol and excess weight took on the dimensions of a long-running soap opera over the course of his career (Library of Congress).

tle hitting is done by the visitors." Eventually his criticism went beyond Griffith's approach to using relief pitchers, focusing also on Griffith's relationship with his pitchers. "Every pitcher with Griffith's team is supposed to work according to Griffith's instructions from the bench. I can't stand for that," he said. "I like advice from manager or player and I'll follow general instructions, but when it came to being an automaton for Griffith, why, I lost interest and did not take care of myself. If I am benched for pitching poor ball, I'll wait for a chance to get even with the team that slaughters me, but when I am going well, I can't submit to being yanked out of the box at the beck of any manager."[55]

The drinking and weight problems rekindled by Powell's 1905 troubles carried over into 1906. On opening day, a St. Louis writer commented, "Powell was in uniform, looking fine and fat as a side of bacon." On April 28, he lost a game largely because of his inability to field bunts. "Powell's abdominal protrusiveness prevented him from picking up three bunts in the seventh inning and threw the game into the proverbial sewer," said one game summary. After the game he disappeared, neither club officials nor his wife knowing where he was. "His continued absence is now worrying his friends," reported the *St. Louis Post-Dispatch*. "Powell is a man of impetuous nature, boyish to a degree and generous to a fault. A physical marvel, a giant in stature, he is a very child in disposition, wayward, emotional and reckless of consequences." After an absence of nearly three days, Red John returned, saying he had just taken a little vacation.[56]

The episode seems to have inspired Powell to make a great effort to lose weight. A month later a reporter noted that he had lost about 25 pounds. But by the end of the season the same man complained that Red John was not effective as he could be because his excess poundage hindered his ability to field bunts. Powell's struggle with alcoholic beverages seems to have followed a similar path. In November he was cut when a plate glass window was broken in a saloon brawl.[57]

Powell entered the 1907 season with the best of intentions. In January of that year he asked Browns president Hedges to have a load of coal sent to the team's dressing room at the park. He told Hedges he was going to work out each day and wanted to get down to 165 pounds by April 1, which would have been a huge weight loss. In the spirit of no good deed going unpunished, however, in the preseason city series against the Cardinals, Red John pitched 13 innings in a game, straining his arm and putting himself out of commission for about three weeks. During the first half of the season he tended to lose effectiveness half way through his games, seeming to have lost some of the stamina that previously was a hallmark of his pitching. By the end of the season, though, he was displaying his old form, throwing back-to-back shutouts against the White Sox and Naps in mid-September.[58]

Red John continued to pitch for the Browns through the 1912 season. He seems to have eventually brought his drinking under control. In 1908, however, he learned that he would have to curtail another habit he had been indulging for years. Midway through that season, American League president Ban Johnson sent out a letter directing club owners to curtail the practice of players betting on games. The understanding was that players who gambled on games backed their own teams, but Johnson wanted all betting prohibited. Red John had been one of the players who openly talked about his wagers. He had told reporters that he always bet on himself when he pitched against Cleveland because he always beat the Naps. At the time of Johnson's circular letter, Powell was quoted as boasting that his income from betting on himself to win his games was greater than the salary he received for pitching them.[59]

While the soap opera aspects of Powell's baseball career receded more deeply into the background during his last few years, in his personal life Red John suffered a jarring development suitable for the most sentimental tear-jerker. In September of 1910 St. Louis was hit by a scarlet fever epidemic. At the beginning of that month, Powell's six-year-old son, Joe, succumbed to the disease. Two weeks later he lost Jack, his three-month-old baby.[60]

A Tumultuous Season: Boston

The Boston Americans didn't have a good year in 1907, but they certainly had an eventful one. Managers came and went and so did players. By the time Bostonians gathered on New Year's Eve to bid adieu to 1907 there were few players from the championship years still on the team's roster.

Spring training ended with a tragedy. Chick Stahl, the team's all-star center fielder and new manager, abruptly resigned as the team's leader on March 25. Two days later he swallowed four ounces of carbolic acid, collapsing in front of his friend and roommate, Jimmy Collins, and dying within minutes.

Why Stahl took his own life remains a mystery. At the time, the stress of managing and playing for the Americans was cited as the primary factor. Since then historians have cited other possible reasons. One speculated that a romantic encounter with a woman who became pregnant and threatened to blackmail him might have led to the act. Others have theorized that Stahl suffered from clinical depression, that he had engaged in activities that were counter to the teachings of his Catholic faith, the suicide resulting from his inability to resolve the inner conflict between his religious ideals and his actions.[61]

Boston (59–90)

Name	AVG	OBP	SLG	R	RBI	SB
Jimmy Barrett, lf	.244	.314	.310	52	28	3
Denny Sullivan, cf	.245	.315	.283	73	26	16
or Freddy Parent, of-ss	.276	.321	.355	51	26	12
Bunk Congalton, rf*	.282	.317	.346	46	49	13
Bob Unglaub, 1b	.254	.284	.338	49	62	14
Hobe Ferris, 2b	.241	.254	.314	41	60	11
John Knight, 3b**	.214	.260	.275	37	41	9
or Moose Grimshaw, ut	.204	.273	.265	19	33	6
Heinie Wagner, ss	.213	.275	.275	29	21	20
Lou Criger, c	.181	.251	.199	12	14	2
or Al Shaw, c	.192	.269	.227	10	7	4

Leading Pitchers	W	L	Pct	IP	H	ERA
Cy Young	21	15	.583	343.3	286	1.99
George Winter	12	15	.444	256.7	198	2.07
Ralph Glaze	9	13	.409	182.3	150	2.32
Tex Pruiett	3	11	.214	173.7	166	3.11
Jesse Tannehill	6	7	.462	131	131	2.47
Cy Morgan***	8	11	.421	169.3	154	3.30
Joe Harris	0	7	.000	59	57	3.05

*Includes record with Cleveland
**Includes record with Philadelphia
***Includes record with St. Louis

Cy Young was named as interim manager, remaining at the helm through the first six games, which were split. Young's .500 winning percentage would be the best of the team's four managers in 1907. The Americans' new leader was George Huff, who had been very successful as the baseball coach and Athletic Director at the University of Illinois. He had won seven conference championships while at Illinois and had developed several players who went on to play in the major leagues. For several years he had scouted for the Chicago Cubs. "It is said that he probably knows more good young ballplayers than anyone," said one writer. "this will be a big asset to Huff as manager of the Boston Americans, as there is a great demand for new blood on the team. At present it is a sad relic of the championship aggregation of a few years ago."[62]

Huff lasted about ten days, surprising everybody by announcing his resignation on April 30. It seems he did not receive the respect he thought he deserved from the Americans' veteran ballplayers when he tried to treat them the same way he treated his college players. "I have come to the conclusion that I would not like professional baseball as well as I did college work," Huff said. "I believe that no one can make a success unless his heart is in his work. Furthermore, I doubt whether my temperament is suited for professional baseball. For these reasons, and these reasons only, I am giving up the position."[63] The Americans had played eight games under Huff's direction, losing six of them.

Bob Unglaub, a college-educated man who had served as team captain under Huff, became the next man to try his hand. When he was appointed manager Unglaub had played parts of two seasons with New York and Boston as a utility man, batting just over .200. It was not a resume that would predict great success. He was the manager for about five weeks, the Americans going 9–20 over that time. His replacement was Deacon McGuire, who had been released by the Highlanders so he could accept the job. At the very least, McGuire had a background that would contribute to his success as a manager. He was in his 24th year as a major league catcher. He was highly respected for his knowledge of the game, and had played for well-regarded leaders such as Ned Hanlon and Clark Griffith.

Under the Deacon, Boston began evolving towards a different style of play. "Manager McGuire has introduced several up-to-date plays," a writer noted in mid–June. The Americans were doing more running and bunting under their new manager, although they still weren't doing it all that well. After a 12-inning 4–4 tie with the White Sox, the *Boston Globe* commented, "The Boston men showed the signs of Manager McGuire's handiwork on the bases, and are gradually developing teamwork which should commence to count in winning games." In one respect McGuire was more advanced than the Boston press corps expected. He handled a pitching staff much like his former boss, Griffith. After the Deacon gave a quick hook to Jesse Tannehill, a writer said, "It will ever remain a mystery why Jim McGuire took out Tannehill, who had only been hit for four singles in four innings, and replaced him with Pruiett, the Northwest recruit, who was touched up plenteous and was taken out after the eighth." In an 8–7 loss to Detroit, McGuire used three pitchers, bringing the comment, "Again did McGuire work out enough pitchers to play a game of football and have some left."[64]

For a while McGuire's methods worked pretty well. On August 23, Cy Young beat the Naps 2–1, bringing the Americans' record under their latest manager to 35–33 and prompting a Clevelander to comment, "Talk about a rejuvenation of the ancients, one would hardly recognize the team that played here last July and the one of yesterday representing Boston. McGuire must have found an elixir of life that is certainly doing wonders with a club that was thought to be ready to go to pieces. There is as much difference between the teams of two months ago and now as there is between day and night. The Bostons nowadays are playing the game all the time, pulling off the unexpected and outguessing the other fellow."[65] The team was still the Boston Americans, however, and long losing streaks were a part of its DNA. After September 11, McGuire's rejuvenated ancients won one game, tied three and lost 17.

The most ancient of the Americans seemed to have been rejuvenated before the season began. Cy Young belied his last name by celebrating his 40th birthday on March 29. Old Cy had not had a good season in 1906. Given his age, a further decline could be expected in 1907. But, of course, Cy Young didn't follow the normal career trajectory. He was again one of the top pitchers in the league. He won nearly 60 percent of his decisions on a team that barely won one out of three when he was not on the mound.

In his latter years Cy Young's frame resembled that of a middle-aged businessman, but his arm retained its youthful effectiveness on the mound (Library of Congress).

Only three pitchers in the league threw more innings than Cy, and one them (Eddie Plank) topped his total by one-third of an inning. Despite the impact the heavy workload must have had on a man his age, he still managed to post the fifth-best ERA in the league (1.99). His effectiveness is shown by a modern category. His 0.982 WHIP (walks plus hits per inning) was the lowest of any American League pitcher. Old Cy seems to have resorted to the spitball at times—at least a Cleveland writer thought so—but he still had plenty of speed. On June 1, he shut out the Highlanders 2–0. A Boston writer noted that he had great speed throughout the game. In the fourth inning he had men on second and third with no outs. He induced a weak popup from Wid Conroy, then fanned the next two batters. "It was grand pitching," the writer noted, "the ball shooting over the rubber into Criger's mitt with speed enough to crack a two-inch plank."[66]

At the beginning of the 1907 season the Americans still had nine players who played central roles in winning the 1904 pennant, plus Unglaub, who had played nine games for Boston that season. Buck Freeman was sold to Minneapolis after appearing in only five games in 1907. Bill Dinneen went to St. Louis after four appearances. Jimmy Collins was traded to the A's the first week of June. After the season closed Freddie Parent was dealt to the White Sox and Hobe Ferris to the Browns. Only five players from the 1904 champions remained by the time the winter meetings ended. When the 1908 season ended, the holdovers numbered two–the veteran battery of Cy Young and Lou Criger. Those two went elsewhere before the 1909 season began. Team president John I. Taylor formalized the transition from the old champions to the new rebuilding team in December of 1907 when he announced that his team would henceforth carry an official nickname. Previously baseball writers had referred to the team by several unofficial nicknames, such as Pilgrims, Puritans, Collinsites, and even Yankees, as well as Americans. From now on, Taylor decreed, the team would bear the nickname "Red Sox."[67]

Best Scouting Trip Ever! Washington

Washington (49–102)

Name	AVG	OBP	SLG	R	RBI	SB
Otis Clymer, lf-rf	.316	.382	.403	30	16	18
Bob Ganley, rf-lf	.276	.337	.314	73	35	40
Jim Delahanty, inf*	.279	.350	.361	52	60	24
John Anderson, 1b	.288	.359	.348	33	44	19
or Charlie Hickman, 1b-rf**	.276	.342	.367	21	24	4
Charlie Jones, cf	.265	.304	.343	48	37	26
Dave Altizer, ss	.269	.319	.326	60	42	38
or Tony Smith, ss	.187	.285	.209	12	8	3
or Nig Perrine, 2b-ss	.171	.253	.212	13	15	10
Bill Shipke, 3b	.196	.262	.249	17	9	6
or Lave Cross3b	.199	.246	.248	13	10	3
or Pete O'Brien, 3b	.187	.259	.224	6	12	4
or Rabbitt Nill, 2b-lf***	.229	.289	.283	26	27	8
or Mike Heydon, c	.183	.302	.201	14	9	3
or Cliff Blankenship, c	.225	.248	.245	4	6	3

Leading Pitchers	W	L	Pct	IP	H	ERA
Charlie Smith	10	20	.333	258.7	254	2.61
Casey Patten	12	16	.429	237.3	272	3.56
Cy Falkenberg	6	17	.261	233.7	195	2.35
Long Tom Hughes	7	14	.333	211	206	3.11
Walter Johnson	5	9	.357	110.3	100	1.88
Oscar Graham	4	9	.308	104	116	3.98
Henry Gehring	3	7	.300	87	92	3.31

*Includes record with St. Louis
**Includes record with Chicago
***Includes record with Cleveland

In late June Cliff Blankenship, the Senators' reserve catcher, left the team to go on a scouting trip in the West. Washington's manager, Joe Cantillon, had given Blankenship a list of players to check out. Blankenship was to try to get a commitment from any players he thought might have major league potential. He was gone for about a week. When he returned he announced he had signed a pitcher and an outfielder. In mid–August, Jimmy McAleer, the Browns' manager, while discussing one of the new players remarked, "Blankenship earned his salary for two more seasons." A month later, a Washington reporter said of Blankenship, "Although he has been constantly on the bench, he has more than earned his salary, and should be given a bonus."[68]

Why such praise for Blankenship? A mention of the names of the two players he signed is ample explanation. The pitcher was Walter Johnson, who of course went on to win 417 games in his career, second only to Cy Young. The outfielder—Clyde Milan—is less well-known, but he played 16 years for the Senators, becoming one of the top defensive center fielders in the league. He was a solid hitter, posting a

Reserve catcher Cliff Blankenship more than earned his season's salary when he signed the great Walter Johnson and outfielder Clyde Milan while on a scouting trip for the Senators in 1907 (Library of Congress).

.285 career batting average, and he twice led the American League in steals—not an easy feat for a man whose career paralleled Ty Cobb's. Milan's career stolen base total (495) ranks 40th in major league history.

Johnson's arrival was much anticipated. Only 19 at the time of his debut, his record pitching for Weiser, of the Idaho State League, caught everyone's attention. He was reported to have struck out 166 men in 99 innings, thrown seven shutouts in a row, and pitched 75 innings without giving up a hit. "If this fellow is what they say he is," said Cantillon, with tongue in cheek, "we won't have to use only two men in a game, a catcher and Johnson. He strikes out most of the men, so why have an infield and an outfield. I shall give all the boys but the catchers days off when Johnson pitches."[69]

Walter made his debut on August 2, allowing two runs in a 3–2 loss to Detroit. He allowed only six hits in eight innings, three of the hits coming on bunts. "Walter Johnson is a real phenom," remarked a Washington reporter. "He has some rough edges, but he has more natural ability than any pitcher seen in these parts in many a moon." Wild Bill Donovan, the Tigers' pitcher, was also deeply impressed. "He has remarkable speed and a great shoot on his fastball," said the veteran pitcher. "To tell you the truth, he is the best raw pitcher I have ever seen. If nothing happens to that fellow, he will be a greater pitcher in two years than Mathewson ever dared be. Mark that prediction."[70]

The Idaho phenom's next appearance came against Cleveland and yielded his first major league victory, 7–2. The Naps managed only four hits, but Walter walked three batters, one with the bases full. A Washington reporter thought that Johnson might have trouble pitching to left-handed batters, since only left-handed batters had been able to do anything against him. He was confident, however, that Walter would soon become equally effective against all hitters, "because the quick break on his fastball is sure to fool the southpaw batters." The reporter noted that the Naps were not eager to step into the batter's box against Walter. "Johnson's speed was so terrific that several of the Cleveland players acted as if they did not take particular delight in being at the plate. Once or twice Johnson shot a fast one close to the batter's head and they usually swung at anything that was sent near the plate after that."[71]

Johnson pitched well in all but a couple of his 14 appearances with Washington in 1907, but he soon learned that well-pitched games didn't necessarily mean victories for a Senators pitcher. On August 27 his won-lost record stood at 1–5. Opposing batters had gotten to him in only one of the losses, and even then a couple of infield hits were added to two well-hit balls to beat him. In a September game, the box score showed ten runs on 14 hits, a poor outing on paper. But a reporter saw things a bit differently. "The St. Louis Browns are credited with making 14 safe drives off the Idaho Wonder's delivery," he said. "About half of these were of the fluke variety, a fourth the result of poor field work and the other fourth were clean drives. Johnson was given miserable and discouraging support. For six innings he held the visitors down to two scratch hits and not a run. In the seventh, a scratch single, a clean drive, a little fly to center, which Milan lost in the sun, caused the visitors to score their first brace of tallies." The Browns added four runs in each of the last two innings, aided greatly by Washington misplays.[72]

The Senators' two veteran catchers, Mike Kahoe and Jack Warner, both gushed over Johnson's ability. "I can hold my glove wherever I want to and Johnson can put the ball in the center of it at full speed," said Kahoe. "He has more speed on his ball than any pitcher I have ever caught, and while he is not finished, because he lacks experience, I make the prediction now that he will develop into a wonder." Warner insisted that Walter was better than Christy Mathewson was at the same stage of his career. "Matty was not steady, and he did not have near the stuff that Johnson has," Warner said.[73]

Despite the praise, everyone seemed to agree that Johnson's raw talent would improve with experience. Near the end of the season, Cantillon revealed that his young star had added a changeup to his repertoire. "Johnson," remarked Cantillon, "is the most apt youngster that ever broke into the game. He learns quicker than any player I have ever come across. He mastered the slow ball [changeup] in less than half an hour."[74]

Clyde Milan, the other player Blankenship recruited on his scouting trip, received considerably less attention than Johnson. But his performance alone would have made Blankenship's sojourn well worth the time and cost. "Milan is beyond doubt the fastest man I have ever encountered," said Bob Ganley, the Senators' captain. "He is a left-handed hitter, and talk about speed—well, I have never seen anything to beat it. He is a flash to first, and when it comes to covering ground in the outfield, even Charley Jones has nothing on him." (Jones, the Senators' center fielder, was widely considered a terrific fielder, with great range.)[75]

"It seems that Cantillon has picked up another star in the rough in young Milan," a *Washington Post* reporter observed in late August. "All pitchers seem to look alike to Milan. Ever since he joined the club he has hit them all.... In Detroit, he even hit Siever, a left-hander, usually most effective against left-handed batters, with the same ease that that he drives out singles against right-handers.... Milan looks like a fixture in the outfield. A youngster of his ability cannot be kept on the bench."[76]

Milan's career was, of course, not nearly as outstanding as Johnson's—only a handful of players came close to that level—but he was a very good ballplayer. He received a smattering of votes for admission to the Hall of Fame, starting with one vote in 1938 and topping out with six votes in 1955.

Cubs Kling to Victory: 1907 World Series

Yeah, that's a bad pun.

In the early Deadball Era games were often decided by the rival catchers' ability to stop opposing baserunners. To some extent the 1907 World Series tilted towards the Cubs because Johnny Kling was able to contain Detroit baserunners, while the Tigers' catchers didn't have much success stopping the Cubs' running game.

A key play in the series occurred in the ninth inning of the opening game. The Tigers had scored three runs in the top of the eighth to take a 3–1 lead. In the Cubs' last chance to get back in the game, Chance led off the bottom of the ninth with a single. Steinfeldt walked. After Kling popped out, Evers reached first on a fumble by third baseman Bill Coughlin, loading the bases. One run scored and the other runners moved up on a bounder to first by Schulte. Wild Bill Donovan got two strikes on Del Howard. Then he sent in a low curve ball over the inside corner for strike three. The ball hit Charlie Schmidt's glove and bounced away, allowing Steinfeldt to score the tying run, while Howard raced to first.[77]

Schmidt's error didn't lose the game, which was still tied at 3–3 when the umpires called the game after 12 innings because of darkness. But the play seemed to bring a sharp shift in momentum. The Tigers didn't do much in the remaining four games of the series, while the Cubs played at pretty much their normal pennant-winning pace. A significant part of the difference lay in the play of the teams' catchers. In his game summary, Joe Jackson, the sports editor of the *Detroit Free Press*, noted the importance of baserunning in the series. "The Cubs showed much the better in their work on the bases," he observed. "It was here that the battle was expected to come. It had been admitted that both teams can hit the ball, and that both can field. There was a chance for argument on which would be able to make the greater going on the sacks, both in stealing bases and in running out extra bases on hits by batsmen following. There was plenty of base stealing with the Cubs doing most of it."[78] Over the next four games—all won by the Cubs—Kling held Detroit's baserunners in check. In the opening game, for instance, he caught two Tiger runners off third base. The Tigers, on the other hand, used three different catchers without much success.

Chicago's great catcher, Johnny Kling, held the Tigers' baserunners in check during the 1907 series, while the Cubs were taking liberties on the basepaths against Detroit's catchers (Library of Congress).

The Cubs moved ahead in the Series by winning game two. The Tigers sent backup catcher Fred Payne behind the plate, but he didn't fare much better than Schmidt had in game one. The Cubs, who had stolen seven bases off Schmidt, pilfered five off Payne, including two in the fourth inning, when the Bruins scored two runs to grab a 3–1 lead that held up through the remainder of the game. Tinker led off that inning with an infield hit off pitcher George Mullin's leg. He was sacrificed to second. Third baseman Coughlin moved in to guard against an expected bunt from Jimmy Slagle. Tinker stole third, aided by the time it took Coughlin to get back to the bag for Payne's throw. He scored as Slagle was beating out a bouncer to shortstop. The Cubs' center fielder immediately stole second and scored when Jimmy Sheckard doubled to right field. Once again, the *Free Press's* Jackson credited Kling with being the key to victory. Kling "did some throwing that was deadly in its accuracy," Jackson said, "and cut short all efforts of the Tigers to show speed on the sacks. As on the previous day, he was the works of his team, and his individual play was enough to decide the result."[79]

Chicago won game three, 5–1. Once again Kling came in for praise, this time from Sy Sanborn of the *Chicago Tribune*. "Kling was a fearsome object to the enemy all day long and not a man of them made even a bluff to take any liberties on the bases," said Sanborn. "He handled Reulbach's sharp, tricky curve with as much ease and elegance as if he was sitting in a Morris chair at home in the parlor counting his share of the winner's end of the coin."[80]

Reulbach held the Tigers down to six hits in that game. Orval Overall, who had pitched the opening game, topped that by one hit in game four, limiting Detroit to five hits in a 6–1 victory. Donovan was again Overall's opponent, and once more ran into ill luck. He had given up only two harmless singles over the first four innings. Leading off in the fifth, Evers reached first on an error. At that point the game was delayed by rain. When it resumed, Wild Bill's arm had tightened up. His fastball had lost speed and his curve lacked the bite it had previously shown. Donovan walked Schulte, moving Evers to second. Tinker sacrificed, putting runners on second and third with one out. Overall lined a single to center, scoring Evers and putting Schulte on third, from where he scored on Slagle's fly to left field.

In the seventh the Cubs worked the "buntation" attack. Schulte led off by beating out a slow bounder that Donovan fielded, too late to get the batter. Tinker bunted, with Schulte beating Donovan's throw to second. Overall sacrificed. Slagle grounded to shortstop O'Leary, whose throw to the plate was high, allowing Schulte to score, Tinker taking third on the play. Sheckard followed with another bunt, directed toward first baseman Claude Rossman, who fielded the ball, but found no one at first base to receive a throw. Tinker, of course, scored on the squeeze play. Chance hit into a force out at second. Slagle moved to third on the play. While Steinfeldt was batting, Chance started to steal second, drawing a throw. Slagle scored while Chance was being run down.[81]

With Three-Finger Brown on the mound and pitching at his best, the Cubs clinched the series in game five, 2–0. Jimmy Archer, the Tigers' third-string catcher, tried his hand in this game, with the usual results. Stolen bases played a part in both Chicago runs. Slagle opened the game by drawing a walk. After the next two batters went out, he stole second base, sliding in safely when Archer's throw went wide of the bag. Harry Steinfeldt followed with a single to center field plating Slagle with the first run. In the second inning Evers was safe at first on a low throw by Coughlin. After Schulte fouled out, Tinker singled, putting runners at first and second. The Cubs middle infielders then pulled off a double steal, Evers making third when Archer's low throw bounded away from Coughlin. Brown walked, filling the bases, and Evers scored when Slagle grounded out to second base.[82]

In celebrating the victory, the *Tribune's* Sanborn commented that the championship was the first for the Chicago National League team in its four "Worlds Series."[83] Sanborn was counting the two series between Cap Anson's White Stockings and Charlie Comiskey's St. Louis Browns, who represented the American Association. The 1885 meeting between those two teams ended in a tie, each team winning three games and one game ending in a tie. In 1886, the Browns beat the White Stockings four games to two. In 1906, of course, the Cubs were trounced four games to two by their crosstown rivals, the White Sox. The Cubs won a second straight championship in 1908, again beating the Tigers four games to one. Then came a pause of 108 years before the Cubs won another World Series, going into the tenth inning of the seventh game before beating the Cleveland Indians in 2016.

Chapter Notes

Introduction

1. David Nemec, *The Great Encyclopedia of 19th Century Major League Baseball* (New York: Donald I Fine Books, 1997), pp. 629–36; Burt Solomon, *Where They Ain't: The Fabled Life and Untimely Death of the Original Baltimore Orioles, the Team That gave Birth to Modern Baseball* (New York: The Free Press, 1999), pp. 137–157.
2. *Sporting News*, Nov. 11, 1899, p. 3; Dec. 16, 1899, pp. 1, 3.
3. *Sporting News*, Dec. 23. 1899, p. 3; Jan. 13, 1900, p. 1; Mar. 17, 1900, pp. 5–6, 8.
4. *Chicago Tribune*, Apr. 1, 1900, p. 17; Apr. 15, 1900, p. 17.
5. *Sporting News*, Apr. 14, 1900, p. 2.
6. Eugene Murdock, *Ban Johnson: Czar of Baseball* (Westport, CT: Greenwood Press, 1982), pp. 42–49.
7. *Sporting News*, Jun 22, 1901, p. 6.
8. *Sporting News*, Aug. 3, 1901, p. 4; *Pittsburgh Dispatch*, Aug. 12, 1901, p. 9; *Boston Globe*, Sep. 11, 1901, p. 2.
9. *Sporting News*, Apr. 19, 1902, p. 5; Apr. 26, 1902, p. 5; *Boston Globe*, Apr. 20, 1902, p. 44.
10. *Boston Globe*, Apr. 6, 1902, p. 6; May 12, 1902, p. 4; *Philadelphia Public Ledger*, May 5, p. 16; *Philadelphia Enquirer*, Apr. 22, 1902, p. 5; *Cleveland Plain Dealer*, May 31, 1902, p. 8; *Baltimore Sun*, Jul. 1, 1902, p. 6; Jul. 8, 1902, p. 6; Jul 9, 1902, p. 6; Jul. 18, 1902, p. 6; *New York Press*, Jul. 17, 1902, p. 5.
11. Murdock, *Ban Johnson*, pp. 60–3; *Sporting News*, Dec. 20, 1902, pp. 1–2; Jan. 17, 1903, pp. 4–6; *Sporting Life*, Jan. 17, 1903, pp. 4–5.
12. *Sporting News*, Jan. 17, 1903, p. 6.
13. *New York Times*, Jan. 17, 1903, p. 11; *Sporting News*, Jan. 24, 1903, p. 6.
14. Jerold Casway, *Ed Delahanty in the Emerald Age of Baseball* (Notre Dame: University of Notre Dame Press, 2004), pp.244–52; *St. Louis Globe-Democrat*, Mar. 29, 1903, p. 14; *Sporting News*, May 9, 1903, p. 1; *Chicago Tribune*, Jun. 26, 1903, p. 8; Jun. 27, 1903, p. 6; Jul. 4, 1903, p. 6.
15. *Chicago Tribune*, Jun. 30, 1903, p. 13.
16. *Boston Globe*, Jul. 5, 1903, p. 30.
17. *St. Louis Globe-Democrat*, Jul. 26, Ed. Sec. p. 9; *Chicago Tribune*, Jun. 30, 1903, p. 13; *New York Times*, Jul. 21, 1903, p. 7.

Chapter One

1. *Chicago Tribune*, Apr. 1, 1901, p. 8.
2. David Fleitz, "Frank Selee,"in http//sabr.org/bioproj.
3. *Sporting News*, Apr. 9, p. 1.
4. *Sporting News*, Mar. 22, p. 1; Aug. 23, 1902, p. 1.
5. *Sporting News*, Aug. 8, 1903, p. 4; Nov. 28, 1903, p. 4.
6. *Sporting News*, Apr. 26, 1902, p. 5.
7. *Sporting News*, Sep. 10, 1904, p. 6.
8. *Sporting News*, May 21, 1904, p. 4; *Cincinnati Commercial Tribune*, Sep. 1, 1904, p. 7.
9. *Cincinnati Commercial Tribune*, Jul. 16, 1904, p. 7; Sep. 1, 1904, p. 7; *St. Louis Globe-Democrat*, May 18, 1904, p. 15.
10. Ejections are from individual player records at //retrosheet.org/; *New York Times*, Aug. 18, 1904, p. 5.
11. *St. Louis Globe-Democrat*, May 8, 1904, p. 15.
12. *Sporting News*, Jan. 9, 1904, p. 3.
13. *Cincinnati Commercial Tribune*, Sep. 3, 1903, p. 7; Sep. 18, 1903, p. 7.
14. *Sporting News*, Apr. 9, 1904, p. 1.
15. *Cleveland Plain Dealer*, Sep. 4, 1904, Sec. 3, p. 9.
16. *Baltimore Sun*, Sep. 30, 1899, p. 6; *Brooklyn Daily Eagle*, Sep. 7, 1900, p. 13.
17. Don Doxsie, *Iron Man McGinnity: A Baseball Biography* (Jefferson, NC: McFarland, 2009), p. 35.
18. Charles C. Alexander, *John McGraw* (Lincoln: University of Nebraska Press, 1995) p. 108.

19. *Sporting News*, Feb. 13, 1904, p. 5; Mar. 26, 1904, p. 2.
20. *Sporting Life*, May 2, 1903, p. 16.
21. *Sporting Life*, May 2, 1903, p. 14.
22. *Chicago Tribune*, Jul. 17, 1904, Sec. 2, p.2; *Sporting Life*, Sep. 10, 1904, p. 9.
23. *Sporting News*, Dec. 19, 1903, p. 4.
24. *Chicago Tribune*, Sep. 8, 1904, p. 6; Brian Marshall, "Mordecai Peter Centennial 'Three-Fingered' Brown," in Tom Simon, ed., *Deadball Stars of the National League* (Dulles, VA: Brassey's Inc., 2004), p. 103; Cindy Thomson and Scott Brown, *Three Finger: The Mordecai Brown Story* (Lincoln: University of Nebraska Press, 2006), pp. 11–12, 213–5.
25. *Sporting Life*, Apr. 16, 1904, p. 11; *Cincinnati Commercial Tribune*, Sep. 16, 1903, p. 7; *Boston Globe*, Aug. 22, 1904, p. 3.
26. *Chicago Tribune*, May 16, 1904, p. 8; Jun. 12, 1904, p. 9; Jun. 14, 1904, p. 8; *Brooklyn Daily Eagle*, May 19, 1904, p. 15.
27. *Cincinnati Commercial Tribune*, Jun. 20, 1904, p. 7.
28. *Pittsburgh Dispatch*, Jul. 5, 1904, p. 10.
29. *Sporting News*, Nov. 19, 1904, p. 7.
30. *Sporting News*, May, 7, 1904, p. 4; May 28, 1904, p. 4; *Cincinnati Commercial Tribune*, Jul. 7, 1904, p. 7; *Sporting Life*, Aug. 20, 1904, p. 5.
31. *Cincinnati Commercial Tribune*, Apr. 19, 1904, p. 8; Jul. 17, 1904, p. 10; Lawrence S. Ritter, *The Glory of Their Times: The Story of the Early Days of Baseball Told by the Men Who Played It*, Quill Edition (New York: William Morrow and Company), p.71.
32. *Cincinnati Commercial Tribune*, Aug. 30, 1903, p. 12; May 3, 1904, p. 8; Jul. 17, 1904, p. 10; Jul. 25, 1904, p. 7; *Cleveland Plain Dealer*, Jul. 19, 1904, p. 8.
33. *Cincinnati Enquirer*, Apr. 10, 1904, p. 10; *Cincinnati Commercial Tribune*, Jun. 26, 1904, p. 9; *Sporting Life*, Dec. 24, 1904, p. 9; Feb. 4, 1905, p. 5.
34. *Cincinnati Commercial Tribune*,; May 14, 1904, p. 8; Jun. 22, 1904, p. 8.
35. *Cincinnati Commercial Tribune*, Apr. 12, 1904; *Pittsburgh Dispatch*, May 21, 1904, p. 12; Jun. 24, 1904, p. 14; Jun. 30, 1904, p. 14; Jul. 2, 1904, p. 14; Jul. 9, 1904, p. 14; Jul. 12, 1904, p. 14; Aug. 2, 1904, p. 12; Aug. 16, 1904, p. 12; Aug. 21, 1904, p. 8.
36. *Sporting Life*, Aug. 3, 1904, p. 3; *Pittsburgh Dispatch*, Aug. 3, 1904, p. 12.
37. *Pittsburgh Dispatch*, May 28, 1904, p. 12; Jun. 19, 1904, Sec. 3, p. 6; *Philadelphia North American*, Jun. 13, 1904, p. 12; *Cincinnati Commercial Tribune*, May 28, 1904, p. 8; *Sporting Life*, Jul. 2, 1904, p. 7; *Sporting News*, Dec. 24, 1904, p. 3.
38. *Sporting News*, Apr. 5, 1902, p. 2.

39. *Sporting News*, Apr. 22, 1899, p. 6; Apr. 29, 1899, p. 4; Apr. 12, 1902, p. 6.
40. *Chicago Tribune*, Oct. 6, 1900, p. 6; *St. Louis Globe-Democrat*, May 22, 1904, Ed. Sec., p. 13.
41. David Fleitz, *Ghosts in the Gallery at Cooperstown* (Jefferson, NC: McFarland, 2004), p. 89.
42. *Sporting News*, Oct. 16, 1897, p. 2; *Cincinnati Commercial Tribune*, Sep. 11, 1904, p. 10.
43. *St. Louis Globe-Democrat*, Aug. 12, 1904, p. 12; *Cincinnati Commercial Tribune*; Sep. 12, 1904, p. 9; *Sporting Life*, May 20, 1905, p. 10.
44. *Brooklyn Daily Eagle*, Oct. 17, 1900, p. 17; May 7, 1904, p. 3; *Sporting News*, Feb. 3, 1900, p. 5; *Baltimore Sun*, Oct. 12, 1899, p. 6.
45. *Brooklyn Daily Eagle*, May 3, 1901, p. 13; Jul. 19, 1901, p. 9.
46. *Brooklyn Daily Eagle*, Jun. 20, 1902, p. 19.
47. *Sporting News*, May 28, 1904, p. 4.
48. *Brooklyn Daily Eagle*, May 11, 1904, p. 14; Jun. 23, 1904, p. 20.
49. *Sporting Life*, Jan. 21, 1905, p. 7; Apr. 15, 1905, p. 4.
50. J. M. Murphy, "Napoleon Lajoie: Modern Baseball's First Superstar," in *The National Pastime*, Spring, 1988, pp. 14–5.
51. *Boston Globe*, May 28, 1904, Ev. Ed., p.11.
52. *Sporting News*, Mar. 19, 1904, p. 2; *Brooklyn Daily Eagle*, p. 13.
53. *Boston Globe*, May 23, 1904, p. 3.
54. *Philadelphia North American*, May 30, 1904, p. 6.
55. *Philadelphia North American*, Jun. 16, 1904, p. 6; Jun. 18, 1904, p. 11.
56. *Sporting Life*, Jul. 23, 1904, p. 4.
57. *Cincinnati Commercial Tribune*, Jul. 10, 1904, p. 10.
58. *Philadelphia North American*, Jun. 30, 1904, p. 12; *Sporting Life*, Sep. 3, 1904, p 2; Tom Simon, "Sherwood Robert Magee," in *Deadball Stars of the National League*, p. 193.
59. Bill James, *The New Bill James Historical Baseball Abstract* (New York: The Free Press, 2001), p.79; *Cincinnati Commercial Tribune*, May 31, 1900, p. 5.
60. *Cincinnati Commercial Tribune*, Apr. 30, 1900, p. 5; John J. Evers and Hugh S. Fullerton, *Touching Second: The Science of Baseball* (Chicago: The Reilly and Britton Company, 1910), pp. 108–9.
61. *Cleveland Plain Dealer*, Jul. 9, 1902, p. 6; *Brooklyn Daily Eagle*, Jul. 25, 1900, p. 6.
62. *Brooklyn Daily Eagle*, Jun. 11, 1904, p. 3; *Pittsburgh Chronicle-Telegraph*, Sep. 27, 1900, p. 2.
63. *Chicago Tribune*, Aug. 3, 1901, p. 7; *Detroit Free Press*, Oct. 5, 1901, p. 3.

64. *Chicago Tribune*, Aug. 29, 1902, p. 2; *Pittsburgh Post*, Aug. 31, 1902, Sec. 2, p. 2; *Boston Globe*, Aug. 31, 1902, p. 4.
65. *Sporting News*, May 14, 1904, p. 4; Sep. 10, 1904, p. 7.
66. *Sporting Life*, Jun. 27, 1908, p. 2.
67. *Sporting News*, Nov. 20, 1897, p. 2.
68. Noah Liberman, *Glove Affairs* (Chicago: Triumph Books, 2003), pp. 15–17.
69. *Cincinnati Commercial Tribune*, May 18, 1904, p. 8; May 1, 1904, p 10; May 3, 1904, p. 9; *Boston Globe*, Jul. 11, 1904, Eve Ed., p. 2; *Sporting News*, Aug. 6, 1904, p. 1; Dec. 16, 1905, p. 1;
70. *Sporting News*, Jun. 22, 1895, p. 4. *Spalding's Official Baseball Guide, 1905 (*New York: American Sports Publishing Company, 1905), Appendix, Figures BX, BXS, Pc, 2 X.
71. *Sporting News*, Mar. 20, 1897, p. 5.
72. *Detroit Free Press*, Apr. 30, 1905, Pt. I, p. 12.
73. *Pittsburgh Post*, Apr. 23, 1904, p. 6.
74. *Pittsburgh Dispatch*, May 21, 1904, p. 12.
75. *Pittsburgh Dispatch*, Jun. 6, 1904, p. 6.
76. *Chicago Tribune*, Aug. 14, 1904, Sec. 2, p. 1.
77. *Cleveland Plain Dealer*, Aug. 12, 1904, p. 8.
78. *Philadelphia North American*, May 12, 1904, p. 12.
79. *Chicago Tribune*, Jun. 5, 1905, p. 8.
80. *Washington Post*, May 3, 1902, p. 9; *Cleveland Plain Dealer*, Jun. 10, 1902, p. 6; *Boston Globe*, Aug. 2, 1900, p. 5; *Pittsburgh Chronicle-Telegraph*, Jul. 21, 1900, p. 2; *Pittsburgh Post*, Jul. 17, 1902, p. 8; *Chicago Tribune*, May 18, 1904.
81. *Boston Globe*, Jun. 11, 1904, p. 8.
82. *Chicago Tribune*, Jul. 26, 1905, p. 4.
83. *Chicago Tribune*, May 22, 1906, p. 6.
84. *Cincinnati Commercial Tribune*, May 18, 1904, p. 8; *Boston Globe* Sep. 1, 1901, p. 5.
85. *Cincinnati Commercial Tribune*, May 1, 1904, p. 10; *Boston Globe*, May 15, 1903, p. 5; *Sporting News*, Aug. 22, 1903, p. 1.
86. *Pittsburgh Post*, Jun. 29, 1907, p. 6; *Chicago Tribune*, Jun 29, 1907.
87. *Detroit Free Press*, Jun. 28, 1905, p. 9.
88. *Philadelphia Record*, Jun. 29, 1905, p. 9.
89. *Cincinnati Enquirer*, Jul. 15, 1905, p. 8.
90. *St. Louis Post-Dispatch*, Jun. 16, 1906, p. 4.
91. *Brooklyn Eagle*, Sep. 6, 1907, Sec. 2, p. 2

Chapter Two

1. *Cleveland Plain Dealer*, Apr. 17, 1904, Sec. 4, p. 6; *Boston Globe*, Aug. 1, 1903, p. 5.
2. *Sporting News*, Jun. 4, 1904, p. 1; *Boston Globe*, Jun. 18, 1904, p. 9; Jun. 19, 1904, p. 6; Jun. 22, 1904, p. 2.
3. *Washington Post*, May 11, 1904, p. 8; Jun. 24, 1904, p. 8; *Boston Globe*, Jul. 3, 1904, p. 5; Jul. 11, 1904, Eve. Ed., p. 2; Sep. 12, 1904, p. 8;.
4. *Boston Globe*, May 12, 1904, Eve. Ed., p. 2; May 20, 1904, Eve. Ed., p. 2.
5. *Boston Globe*, May 27, 1904, p. 3; Jun. 28, 1904, p. 5; Aug. 18, 1904, p. 2;
6. *Boston Globe*, Sep. 13, 1904, p. 5; Sep. 28, 1904, p. 3.
7. *Boston Globe*, Oct. 8, 1904, pp. 1, 4; Oct. 9, 1904, pp. 1, 5; Oct. 11, 1904, pp. 1, 4; *Sporting News*, Dec. 31, 1904, p. 3.
8. *Sporting News*, Apr. 16, 1904, p. 4.
9. *Boston Globe*, Jul. 17, 1904, p. 27.
10. *Brooklyn Daily Eagle*, Apr. 22, 1904, p. 18.
11. *Sporting News*, Oct. 29, 1904, p. 2.
12. *Sporting News*, Jan. 28, 1905, p. 1.
13. *Washington Post*, Jan. 28, 1938, p. 23.
14. *Sporting News*, Jul. 9, 1904, p. 6.
15. *New York American*, Oct. 8, 1904, p. 8.
16. *Chicago Tribune*, Aug. 16, 1903, p. 15.
17. *Chicago Tribune*, Apr. 29, 1904, p. 8.
18. *Chicago Tribune*, Mar. 20, 1904, p. 11.
19. *Chicago Tribune*, Jun. 24, 1904, p. 10.
20. Jack Smiles, *Big Ed Walsh* (Jefferson, NC: McFarland, 2008), pp. 15–28.
21. *Chicago Tribune*, Aug. 28, 1904, Sec. 2, p. 1; Sep. 7, 1904, p. 6.
22. *Chicago Tribune*, Aug. 7, 1904, Sec. 2, p. 2.
23. *Sporting News*, Apr. 9, 1904, p. 5; Apr. 23, 1904, p. 3; May 14, 1904, p. 4; Scott Longert, *Addie Joss: King of the Pitchers* (Birmingham, AL: EBCO Media, 1998), pp. 66–8.
24. *Cleveland Plain Dealer*, May 20, 1904, p. 8; May 23, 1904, p. 6.
25. *Sporting News*, Jun. 25, 1904, p. 1.
26. *Detroit Free Press*, Jul. 3, 1904, p. 6; *Cleveland Plain Dealer*, Aug. 13, 1904, p. 6.
27. *Boston Globe*, May 24, 1904, p. 3; *Sporting News*, Jun. 4, 1904, p. 1; *Cleveland Plain Dealer*, Jun. 16, 1904, p. 6; Jul. 31, 1904, Sec. 3, p. 9; Sep. 5, 1904, p. 6.
28. Alan H. Levy, *Rube Waddell: The Zany, Brilliant Life of a Strikeout Artist* (Jefferson, NC: McFarland, 2000), p. 161.
29. *Philadelphia North American*, May 3, 1904, p. 12.
30. *Philadelphia North American*, Jun. 6, 1904, p. 12.
31. *Philadelphia North American*, Jun 8, 1904, p. 6; Jun. 9, 1904, p. 12.
32. *Philadelphia North American*, May 21, 1904, p. 6.
33. *Philadelphia North American*, Jul. 2, 1904, p. 11; Jul. 12, 1904, p. 6; Norman Macht, *Connie Mack and the Early Years of Baseball* (Lincoln: University of Nebraska Press, 2007), pp. 329, 331.

34. *Sporting News*, Sep. 1, 1900, p. 4.
35. *Sporting News*, Jun. 27, 1896, p. 4.
36. *Sporting New*, Oct. 12, 1901, p. 4.
37. *St. Louis Globe-Democrat*, Jun. 7, 1901, p. 11.
38. *Sporting News*, Jul. 1, 1899, p. 4.
39. *Cincinnati Commercial Tribune*, Jun. 24, 1900, p. 14.
40. *Sporting News*, Feb. 4, 1905, p. 7.
41. *Sporting News*, Nov. 15, 1902, p. 2.
42. *Sporting News*, Sep. 3, 1892, p. 3; Jul. 29, 1893, p. 5.
43. *Sporting News*, Jun. 12, 1897, p. 4.
44. Fleitz, *Ghosts in the Gallery*, p. 66.
45. *Sporting News*, Aug. 27, 1904, p. 4
46. *St. Louis Globe-Democrat*, May 15, 1904, p. 15.
47. Fleitz, *Ghosts in the Gallery*, pp. 75–6.
48. Fleitz, *Ghosts in the Gallery*, pp. 64–5; *New York Times*, Dec. 24, 1935, p. 20.
49. Ed Barrow with James M. Kahn, *My Fifty Years in Baseball* (New York, NY: Coward-McCann, Inc., 1951), pp. 58–9.
50. Sam Crawford, "What I Think About Baseball," *Baseball Magazine*, Feb., 1916, pp. 42–3.
51. *Sporting News*, Apr. 2, 1904, p. 7; Apr. 9, 1904, p. 7.
52. *Sporting News*, Apr. 16, 1904, p. 7; *Washington Post*, Apr. 11, 1904, p. 8.
53. *Washington Post*, Apr. 15, 1904, p. 9.
54. *Washington Post*, May 11, 1904, p. 8; May 13, 1904, p. 8.
55. *Washington Post*, Sep. 11, 1904, Sp. Sec. p. 1.
56. *Washington Post*, Jul. 21, 1904, p. 8; Jul. 23, 1904, p. 8; Jul. 30, 1904, p. 8.
57. *Detroit Free Press*, Jun. 19, 1904, p. 12.
58. *Washington Post*, Oct. 11, 1904, p. 8.
59. *Sporting News*, Oct. 10, 1903, p. 2; Oct. 17, 1903, p. 2;
60. *Sporting Life*, Jul. 30, 1904, p. 4.
61. *Cleveland Plain Dealer*, Sep. 20, 1904, p. 8; *Brooklyn Daily Eagle*, Oct. 3, 1904, p. 7.
62. *Sporting Life*, Oct. 1, 1904, p. 5.
63. *Sporting Life*, Sep.24, 1904, p. 4.
64. *Sporting News*, Apr. 9, 1904, p. 2; Apr. 16, 1904, p. 2.
65. *Chicago Tribune*, May 31, 1904, p. 10.
66. *Pittsburgh Dispatch*, Jun. 14, 1904, p. 14; Jun. 15, 1904, p. 14.
67. *St. Louis Globe-Democrat*, Jun. 18, 1904, p. 11.
68. *Philadelphia North American*, Jul. 2, 1904, p. 11.
69. *Pittsburgh Dispatch*, Jul. 12, 1904, p. 14; Sep. 4, 1904, Sec. 3, p. 8; *Sporting Life*, Oct. 29, 1904, p. 8.
70. *Washington Post*, Jul. 16, 1904, p. 8; Jul. 17, 1904, Sp. Sec., p. 1.
71. *Philadelphia North American*, Jul. 23, 1904, p. 6.
72. *Cincinnati Commercial Tribune*, Jul. 29, 1904, p. 7.
73. *Washington Post*, Jul. 30, 1904, p. 8.
74. *St. Louis Globe-Democrat*, Jul. 31, 1904, p. 15.
75. *St. Louis Globe-Democrat*, Aug. 3, 1904, p. 7; Aug. 4, 1904, p. 5; Aug. 19, 1904, p. 11; *Sporting Life*, Oct. 1, 1904, p. 11.
76. *Sporting News*, Aug. 13, 1904, p. 6.
77. *Washington Post*, Aug. 12, 1904, p. 8.
78. *Cleveland Plain Dealer*, Sep. 15, 1904, p. 8.
79. *Sporting News*, Oct. 29, 1904, p. 2; *Sporting Life*, Oct. 15, 1904, p. 12.
80. *Sporting News*, Oct. 29, 1904, p. 2; Nov. 25, 1904, pp. 3,4; Dec. 24, 1904, p. 4; *Sporting Life*, Oct. 15, 1904, p. 12.
81. *Sporting News*, Jun. 17, 1905, p. 4.
82. *Sporting Life*, Oct. 15, 1904, p. 12; *Sporting News*, Mar. 4, 1905, p. 3.
83. *Sporting News*, Nov. 26, 1904, p. 5; Jan. 21, 1905, p. 4; *Sporting Life*, Oct. 15, 1904, p. 12; Oct. 29, 1904, p. 8.
84. *Sporting News*, Oct. 15, 1904, p. 4; *Sporting Life*, Oct. 15, 1904, p. 12.

Chapter Three

1. *Pittsburgh Chronicle-Telegraph*, May 17, 1900, p. 2.
2. *Philadelphia Public Ledger*, Aug. 18, 1900, p. 16; Sep. 20, 1900, p. 16.
3. *Sporting News*, Oct. 25, 1902, p. 2.
4. *Boston Globe*, Jul. 23, 1904, p. 5
5. *Philadelphia North American*, Sep. 28, 1902, p. 11; *Washington Post*, May 5, 1903, p. A10.
6. Evers and Fullerton, *Touching Second*, p. 171.
7. Ty Cobb, with Al Stump, *My Life in Baseball: The True Record*, Bison Books (Lincoln: University of Nebraska Press, 1993), pp. 164–5.
8. *Washington Post*, Aug. 25, p. 9.
9. *Cincinnati Enquirer*, Jul. 9, 1905, p. 8.
10. *Sporting News*, Apr. 14, 1900, p. 2.
11. *Sporting News*, Apr. 4, 1903, p. 1.
12. *Pittsburgh Press*, Sep. 15, 1907, p. 18.
13. Ritter, *The Glory of Their Times*, pp. 52,98.
14. John J. McGraw, *My Thirty Years in Baseball*, Bison Books (Lincoln: University of Nebraska Press, 1995), p. 159.
15. James, *New Bill James Historical Baseball Abstract*, p. 82.
16. *Cincinnati Commercial Tribune*, Jul. 8, 1903, p. 7; Aug. 4, 1903, p. 7; Aug. 5, 1903, p. 7.

17. *Sporting News*, Jun. 30, 1900, pp. 1, 4; Michael Betzold, "Michael Joseph Donlin," in *Deadball Stars of the National League*, pp. 55–6.
18. *Pittsburgh Post*, Sep. 26, 1905, p. 6; Sep. 27, 1905, p. 8; Sep. 28, 1905, p. 8.
19. *Chicago Tribune*, Jun. 14, 1905, p.6; *Sporting News*, Oct. 21, 1905, p. 3.
20. *New York Evening World*, Jun. 10, p. 1.
21. *Philadelphia Inquirer*, Apr. 23, 1905, p. 15.
22. *Pittsburgh Post*, May 19, p. 9; May 20, p. 8; May 21, Part II, p. 2.
23. *Sporting Life*, Jun. 3, 1905, p. 3; Jun. 10, 1905, p. 3; Charles C. Alexander, *John McGraw*, Bison Books (Lincoln: University of Nebraska Press, 1995), pp. 113–4.
24. *Pittsburgh Post*, Aug. 6, Part I, p. 1.
25. *Pittsburgh Post*, Aug. 22, p. 6.
26. *St. Louis Republic*, Jun. 19, p. 5.
27. *Detroit Free Press*, Aug. 28, 1904, p. 12.
28. *New York Evening World*, Mar. 10, 1905, p. 10; *Brooklyn Daily Eagle*, Jun. 30, 1905, p. 9; Jimmy Keenan, "Moonlight Graham," in http//sabr.org/bioproj.
29. *Sporting News*, Jul. 14, 1894, p. 1.
30. *Sporting News*, May 18, 1901, p. 7.
31. *Sporting News*, Jul. 24, 1897, p. 5; Aug. 21, 1897, p. 6.
32. *Pittsburgh Chronicle-Telegraph*, May 7, 1900, p. 2.
33. *Boston Globe*, May 12, 1900; *Sporting News*, Jul. 28, 1900, p. 5.
34. *Pittsburgh Post*, May 16, 1902, p. 8; *Brooklyn Daily Eagle*, May 19, 1902, p. 6.
35. *Sporting News*, Mar. 3, 1900, p. 2.
36. *Sporting News*, Jan. 17, 1946, p. 13.
37. *Sporting News*, Mar. 14, 1951, p. 16.
38. *Sporting News*, Oct. 16, 1897, p. 2.
39. *Pittsburgh Post*, Jul. 6, 1903; *Pittsburgh Press*, Jul. 2, 1906, p. 4..
40. *Sporting News*, May 5, 1900, p. 1.
41. *Sporting News*, Jun. 1, 1901, p. 6; *Cincinnati Commercial-Tribune*, Apr. 23, 1904, p. 8.
42. Ronald T. Waldo, *Fred Clarke: A Biography of the Baseball Hall of Fame Player-Manager* (Jefferson, NC: McFarland, 2011), pp. 101–2.
43. *Sporting News*, Jul. 8, 1905, p. 2.
44. *Sporting News*, May 6, 1905, p. 4.
45. *Sporting News*, May 13, 1905, p. 1.
46. *Cincinnati Enquirer*, May 14, 1905, Sec. 4, p. 1
47. *Cincinnati Enquirer*, May 7, 1905 p. 34.
48. *Chicago Tribune*, Jun. 8, 1905, p. 8; Aug. 20, Pt. 2, p. 1; Jun. 12, p. 8.
49. *Chicago Tribune*, Apr. 27, 1905, p. 6.
50. *Chicago Tribune*, Jun. 25, 1905, Part 2, p. 1; Aug. 25, p.8.
51. Thomson and Brown, *Three Finger*, p. 33.

52. *Sporting News*, Apr. 1, 1905, p. 1; Aug. 5, 1905, p. 1; Aug. 19, 1905, p. 1.
53. *St. Louis Republic*, Aug. 6, 1905, Part III, p. 6.
54. Bill Lambert, "Roy A. Thomas," *Deadball Stars of the National League*, p.187.
55. James, *New Bill James Historical Baseball Abstract*, p. 685.
56. *Pittsburgh Post*, Jul. 21, 1905, p. 6.
57. Frederick G. Lieb, "Sherwood R. Magee," *Baseball Magazine*, Dec., 1910, p. 35; *Sporting News*, Mar. 25, 1905, p. 5.
58. *Pittsburgh Dispatch*, Aug. 25, 1904, p. 12; *Philadelphia Record*, May 18, 1906, p. 9; *Chicago Tribune*, Jun. 10, 1907, p. 11.
59. Allan Wood, "John Franklin Titus," *Deadball Stars of the National League*, pp. 191–2.
60. Bill Kirwin, "Cy Seymour: Baseball's Second Most Versatile Player," *Baseball Research Journal*, No. 29, pp. 3–13.
61. *Sporting News*, Jan. 21, 1899, p. 6.
62. *Sporting News*, Mar. 11, 1905, p. 6.
63. *Sporting News*, May 29, 1899, p. 1; Jan. 25, 1902, p. 1.
64. *Cincinnati Enquirer*, Jul. 14, 1906, Sec. 4, p. 2.
65. Norman Macht, *Connie Mack*, pp. 131, 144; *Sporting News*, Oct. 29, 1898, p. 5; Apr. 15, 1899, p. 2.
66. *Sporting News*, Jan. 21, 1905, p. 4.
67. *Chicago Tribune*, Jul. 3, 1900, p. 7; Jul. 6, 1900, p. 10.
68. *Chicago Tribune*, Jul. 27, 1901, p. 7; Aug. 4, 1901, p. 18.
69. Dan Ginsburg, "John W. Taylor," *Deadball Stars of the National League*, p. 93.
70. *St. Louis Globe-Democrat*, May 29, 1902, p. 15.
71. *Washington Post*, Aug. 14, 1906, p. 8.
72. *Sporting News*, Feb. 11, 1905, p. 4.
73. Ginsburg, "John W. Taylor," p. 94; Lowell L. Blaisdell, "Trouble and Jack Taylor," *The National Pastime*, No. 16, 1996, pp. 132–6; *Sporting News*, Oct. 22, 1904, p. 5; Jan. 21, 1905, pp. 1, 3–4; Feb. 11, 1905, p. 1; Feb. 25, 1905, pp. 4, 7.
74. *St. Louis Republic*, May 4, 1905, p. 9; Aug. 5, 1905, p. 8; Aug. 11, 1905, p. 8.
75. *Sporting News*, Oct. 28, 1905, p. 4.
76. Harold Kaese, *The Boston Braves* (New York: G. P. Putnam's Sons, 1948), pp. 110–1.
77. *Sporting News*, May 6, 1905, p. 6.
78. *Cincinnati Enquirer*, Jul. 12, p. 4.
79. https://en.wikipedia.org
80. *Boston Globe*, Apr. 26, 1903, p. 44; Aug. 18, 1905, p. 5.
81. *Boston Globe*, Jul. 25, 1906, p. 5.
82. *Sporting News*, Sep. 17, 1904, p. 1.
83. *Sporting News*, Nov. 23, 1901, p. 6.

84. *Sporting News*, Feb. 22, 1902, p. 3; Jul. 14, 1900, p. 5.
85. *Brooklyn Daily Eagle*, May 11, 1905, p. 13.
86. *Brooklyn Daily Eagle*, May 30, 1905, p. 5.
87. *Brooklyn Daily Eagle*, Jun. 30, 1905, p. 15.
88. *Brooklyn Daily Eagle*, Jun. 3, 1905, p. 9; Jun. 13, 1905, p. 19.
89. *Brooklyn Daily Eagle*, Jun. 13, p. 9; *Sporting News*, Mar. 25, p. 1.
90. *Brooklyn Daily Eagle*, Jun. 14, p. 17.
91. *Sporting News*, Apr. 29, 1905, p. 1; Dec. 23, 1905, p. 4.

Chapter Four

1. *Sporting News*, Apr. 29, 1905, p. 4.
2. *Chicago Tribune*, Apr. 13, p. 6.
3. *New York Times*, Apr. 19, 1905, p. 12; *Pittsburgh Post*, Apr. 19, 1905, p. 9; *Chicago Tribune*, Apr. 26, 1905, p. 6; Apr. 30, 1905, Pt. 2, p. 1; *Boston Globe*, Apr. 27, 1905, p. 5; *Washington Post*, May 3, 1905, p. 8; *Cleveland Plain Dealer*, May 26, 1906, p. 8.
4. *Philadelphia Record*, Jul. 14, 1905, p. 9; *Detroit Free Press*, May 9, 1905, p. 8.
5. *Chicago Tribune*, May 22, 1905, p. 8; May 30, 1905, p. 10; *Cincinnati Enquirer*, Aug. 14, 1905, p. 3; *Cleveland Plain Dealer*, Jul. 5, 1905, p. 11; *St. Louis Republic*, May 9, 1905, p. 9, *Boston Globe*, May 25, p. 9.
6. *Cleveland Plain Dealer*, May 7, 1905, Sp. Sec., p. 1; *Philadelphia Record*, Jun. 29, 1905, p. 9; *Washington Post*, Sep. 18, 1905, p. 8; *New York Evening World*, Jun. 20, 1905, p. 2; *Boston Globe*, Jun. 16, 1906, p. 5.
7. *Washington Post*, Aug. 10, 1907, p. 8.
8. *Philadelphia Record*, Apr. 15, 1905, p. 11; *Sporting Life*, May 6, 1905, p. 7; Jul. 29, 1905, p. 7; Bill Knowlin, "John Knight," sabr.org.bioproj.
9. *Philadelphia Record*, Aug. 31, 1905, p. 9
10. Norman Macht, *Connie Mack*, p. 342.
11. *Philadelphia Record*, Jun. 26, 1905, p. 9.
12. *Chicago Tribune*, Jun. 10, 1905, p. 10; *Philadelphia Record*, Jun 14, 1905, p. 10.
13. *Philadelphia Record*, Jul. 5, 1905, p. 10.
14. *Boston Globe*, Sep. 6, 1905, pp. 1, 3.
15. Macht, *Connie Mack*, pp. 347–8.
16. *Chicago Tribune*, Sep. 29, 1905, p. 6.
17. *Philadelphia Record*, Oct. 6, 1905, p. 12; Oct. 7, 1905, p. 11; Oct. 8, 1905, p. 11.
18. *Chicago Tribune*, Apr. 28, 1905, p. 10.
19. *Chicago Tribune*, Apr. 26, 1905, p. 6; May 10, 1905, p. 8; Aug. 3, 1907, p. 4; *Cleveland Plain Dealer*, May 7, 1905, Sp. Sec., p. 1.
20. James D. Szalontai, *Small Ball in the Big Leagues: A History of stealing, Bunting, Walking and Otherwise Scratching for Runs* (Jefferson, NC: McFarland, 2010), p. 7.

21. *Pittsburgh Dispatch*, Sep. 6, 1901, p. 9; *Sporting News*, Apr. 5, 1902, p.3. Bill Lamb, "A Question of Character: George Davis and the Flora Campbell Affair," *Baseball Research Journal*, Vol. 45, Issue 2, pp. 81–2.
22. *Boston Globe*, Aug. 17, 1901, p. 4; *Chicago Tribune*, May 16, 1903, p. 7.
23. *Washington Post*, May 18, 1902, p. 9; *Sporting Life*, Aug. 27, 1904, p. 4.
24. *Sporting News*, Nov. 24, 1906, p. 6.
25. *Boston Globe*, Jun. 17, 1905, p. 8.
26. *Sporting News*, Mar. 18, 1905, p. 3; Apr.8, 1905, p. 6; *Cleveland Plain Dealer*, Apr. 28, 1905, p. 10.
27. *Detroit Free Press*, Apr. 17, 1905, p. 8; May 4, 1905, p. 10.
28. *Detroit Free Press*, Apr. 27, 1905, p. 10; *Philadelphia Inquirer*, Jul. 16, 1905, Sec. 1, p. 18.
29. *Detroit Free Press*, May 8, 1906, p. 8; Jun. 25, 1906, p. 8; *Chicago Tribune*, Jun. 25, 1906, p. 8.
30. Ritter, *Glory of Their Times*, pp. 35–6; *Detroit Free Press*, Jun. 25, 1906, p. 8.
31. *Cleveland Plain Dealer*, Jul. 4, 1906, p. 6.
32. *Detroit Free Press*, Apr. 28, 1905, p. 8; Aug. 12, 1905, p. 9; Jul. 2, 1905, Pt. 1, p. 11.
33. *Sporting News*, Oct. 14, 1905, p. 4.
34. *Sporting News*, Jun. 3, 1905, p. 2; Jul. 29, 1905, p. 2.
35. *Detroit Free Press*, Jun. 17, 1905, p. 10; Jun. 18, 1905, Pt. 1, p. 11.
36. *Washington Post*, May 21, 1905, Sp. Sec., p.1; *Boston Globe*, Apr. 30, 1905, p. 4; Jul. 2, 1905, p. 6; Sep. 25, 1905, p. 8.
37. *Boston Globe*, May 27, 1905, p. 5; Sep. 18, 1905, p. 8; Sep. 24, 1905, p. 1.
38. *Sporting Life*, Dec. 31, 1904, p. 3; *Sporting News*, Sep. 20, 1902, p. 6.
39. *Sporting News*, Mar. 11, 1899, p. 2.
40. *Chicago Tribune*, Jun. 21, 1900, p. 7.
41. *Detroit Free Press*, May 12, 1903, p. 10; *Pittsburgh Chronicle-Telegraph*, Jul. 3, 1900, p. 2.
42. http//baseball-reference.com. (As of August, 2017.)
43. David L. Fleitz, *Napoleon Lajoie: King of Ballplayers* (Jefferson, NC: McFarland, 2013) pp. 128-31.
44. *Cleveland Plain Dealer*, Aug. 18, 1905, p. 8.
45. *Sporting News*, Jan. 23, 1971, p. 45; Feb. 9, 1963, p. 6; *Sporting Life*, Oct. 20, 1900, p. 6.
46. *Sporting News*, Apr. 9, 1904, p. 2.
47. *Sporting News*, Jul. 6, 1898, p. 7; Sep. 10, 1898, p. 5.
48. *Cincinnati Commercial-Tribune*, May 12, 1900, p. 5.
49. Angelo Luisa, "Elmer Harrison Flick," in David Jones, ed. *Deadball Stars of the Amer-*

ican League (Dulles, VA: Potomac Books, Inc, 2006) p. 650; *Sporting Life*, Sep. 23, 1905, p. 9.
 50. Luisa, "Elmer Harrison Flick," pp. 650-1; *Sporting News*, Feb. 9, 1963, p. 5.
 51. *Sporting News*, Feb. 9, 1963, p. 10.
 52. James, *New Bill James Historical Baseball Abstract*, pp. 843-5.
 53. *Sporting News*, Aug. 17, 1963, p. 13; Jan. 23, 1971, p. 45; *New York Times*, Aug. 6, 1963, p. 37.
 54. *Cincinnati Enquirer*, Apr. 9, 1905, Sec. 4, p. 2; *Boston Globe*, May 4, 1905, p. 2; *Chicago Tribune*, May 14, 1905, Pt. 2, p. 1.
 55. *Washington Evening Star*, Apr. 22, 1905, p. 8.
 56. *Sporting News*, May 20, p. 6; *Philadelphia Inquirer*, Apr. 27, p. 10; *Cleveland Plain Dealer*, Apr. 29, p. 10.
 57. *New York Times*, May 7, 1905, p. 11.
 58. *Sporting News*, May 27, 1905, p. 4; *New York Times*, May 6, 1905, p. 6.
 59. *Sporting News*, Feb. 10, 1906, p. 4.
 60. *Sporting News*, Feb. 4, 1905, p. 3; Apr. 8, 1905, p. 2; *Cleveland Plain Dealer*, Apr. 17, 1905, p. 8.
 61. *Washington Post*, May 14, 1905, Sp. Sec., p. 1.
 62. *Washington Post*, May 2, 1905, p. 8; May 3, 1905, p. 8; May 4, 1905, p. 9.
 63. *Washington Post*, Jul. 22, 1905, p. 8.
 64. *Sporting Life*, Oct. 28, 1905, p. 4.
 65. *Sporting News*, Mar. 10, 1900, p. 2.
 66. *Sporting News*, Mar. 11, 1899, p. 2.
 67. *Sporting News*, Aug. 19, 1899, p. 5.
 68. *Sporting News*, Oct. 29, 1904, p. 2.
 69. *Sporting News*, Mar. 12, 1904, p. 4.
 70. *Sporting News*, May 28, 1904, p. 4.
 71. *St. Louis Republic*, Apr. 26, 1905, p. 9.
 72. *St. Louis Republic*, May 1, 1905, p. 4; May 7, Pt. III, p. 4.
 73. Eric Sallee and David Jones, "Harry Taylor Howell," *Deadball Stars of the American League*, p. 780.
 74. *St. Louis Republic*, May 17, 1905, p. 8.
 75. Sallee and Jones, "Harry Taylor Howell," p. 781.
 76. Alexander, *John McGraw*, p. 116.
 77. *New York Times*, Oct. 10, 1905, p. 4.
 78. *New York Times*, Oct. 11, 1905, p. 8; Oct. 13, 1905, p. 6; Oct. 14, 1905, p. 10; Oct. 15, 1905, pp. 1, 7.

Chapter Five

 1. *Sporting News*, Nov. 4, 1905, p. 4.
 2. *Sporting News*, Dec. 23, 1905, p. 4.
 3. *Cincinnati Commercial Tribune*, Jul. 8, 1900, p. 14; *Sporting News*, Mar. 19, 1898, p. 5.
 4. *Sporting News*, Apr. 5, 1902, p. 7.
 5. *Sporting News*, Nov. 26, 1898, p. 2; Feb. 14, 1903, p. 1; *Cincinnati Commercial Tribune*, Aug. 5, 1900, p. 14; May 25, 1903, p. 7.
 6. *Sporting News*, Oct. 7, 1905, p. 6.
 7. *Sporting News*, Feb. 3, 1906, p. 4; Jan. 20, 1906, p. 8.
 8. *Chicago Tribune*, May 7, 1906, p. 10.
 9. *Chicago Tribune*, May 15, 1906, p. 6.
 10. *Chicago Tribune*, May 8, 1906, p. 6.
 11. *Chicago Tribune*, Aug. 7, 1906, p. 6.
 12. *Chicago Tribune*, Aug. 12, 1906, Pt. 2, p. 1; Aug. 23, 1906, p. 6; Sep. 16, 1906, Pt. 2, p. 1.
 13. *Chicago Tribune*, Aug. 1, 1906, p. 6; Aug. 2, 1906, p. 6.
 14. *Sporting News*, Nov. 10, 1906, p. 3.
 15. *Chicago Tribune*, Jun. 8, p. 10; *New York Sun*, Jun. 8, p. 8.
 16. *Sporting News*, Jun. 16, p. 1.
 17. *Chicago Tribune*, Jul. 5, 1906, p. 10.
 18. *Chicago Tribune*, Aug. 7, 1906, p. 6; Aug. 8, 1906, p. 8.
 19. *Sporting Life*, Oct. 28, 1905, p. 5.
 20. *Sporting News*, Feb. 17, 1906, pp. 1, 6; Mar. 24, 1906, p. 2; *New York Sun*, May 16, 1906, p. 10.
 21. *Washington Post*, Apr. 13, 1906, p. 9; *New York Sun*, May 6, 1906, p. 12; *Sporting News*, May 26, p. 4.
 22. *St. Louis Post-Dispatch*, Jul. 15, 1906, Pt. 2, p. 12.
 23. *Sporting News*, Jul. 21, 1906, pp. 3-4.
 24. *Brooklyn Daily Eagle*, Apr. 18, 1906, p. 14; *Chicago Tribune*, Jul. 18, 1906, p. 10; *New York Sun*, Jul. 25, 1906, p. 8; *Sporting News*, Aug. 4, p. 1.
 25. *Chicago Tribune*, Aug. 7, 1906, p. 6; Aug. 8, 1906, p. 8; Alexander, *John McGraw*, p. 122.
 26. *Sporting News*, Aug. 4, 1906, p. 2; Nov. 10, 1906, p. 7.
 27. *Sporting News*, Aug. 4., 1906, p. 2; May 19, 1906, p. 4.
 28. *Sporting News*, Mar. 17, 1906, p. 7.
 29. *Chicago Tribune*, Jul. 5, 1906, p. 10; *Pittsburgh Post*, Sep. 27, 1906, p. 10.
 30. Craig R. Wright and Tom House, *The Diamond Appraised* (New York: Simon and Shuster, 1989), pp. 366-409.
 31. *Sporting News*, Jan. 12, 1933, p. 8.
 32. *Sporting News*, Apr. 18, 1896, p. 3.
 33. Dan Lindner, "William J. Gleason (Kid)" *Baseball's First Stars*, Frederick Ivor-Campbell, Robert L. Tiemann, and Mark Rucker, eds. (Cleveland: Society for American Baseball Research, 1996), p. 68.
 34. *Sporting News*, Oct. 8, 1892, p. 1; Jun. 30, 1894, p. 1; Feb. 2, 1895, p. 4.
 35. *Sporting News*, Aug. 6, 1892, p. 1; Sep. 23, 1893, p. 1; Jul. 6, 1895, p. 5.
 36. *Sporting News*, Nov. 30, 1895, p. 3.
 37. *Sporting News*, Apr. 10, 1897, p. 3; Feb. 4, 1897, p. 7.

38. *Sporting News*, Dec. 8, 1900, p. 6.
39. *Sporting News*, Oct. 9, 1897, p. 5; Jul. 29, 1899, p. 4.
40. *Washington Star*, May 6, 1901, p. 9.
41. *Philadelphia North American*, May 20, 1903, p. 6.
42. *Sporting News*, Jan. 12, 1933, p. 2.
43. *Chicago Tribune*, Jun. 10, 1907, p. 11.
44. https://en.wikipedia.org/wiki/Dave_Kingman; http://www.sportsonearth.com.
45. *St. Louis Globe-Democrat*, Apr. 24, 1902, p. 2.
46. *Milwaukee Sentinel*, Jul. 24, 1901, p. 4; Sep. 6, 1901, p. 4; *Washington Post*, Sep. 22, 1901, p. 8.
47. *St. Louis Globe-Democrat*, Jun. 19, 1902, p. 13; *Cleveland Plain Dealer*, Apr. 26, 1902, p. 6; *Cincinnati Enquirer*, Sep. 3, 1902, p. 4; *Detroit Free Press*, Sep. 16, 1902, p. 10.
48. *Cincinnati Commercial-Tribune*, Sep. 9, 1902, p. 7.
49. *Cleveland Plain Dealer*, Aug. 5, 1904, p. 6.
50. *Cincinnati Enquirer*, Jun. 27, 1905, p. 4; *New York Times*, Aug. 10, 1905, p. 5.
51. *Brooklyn Daily Eagle*, Sep. 21, 1906, p. 12.
52. *Brooklyn Daily Eagle*, Apr. 29, 1907, Sec. 2, p. 2.
53. *Sporting News*, Dec. 23, 1905, p. 4; Mar. 3, 1906, p. 5.
54. *Sporting News*, Apr. 18, 1906, p. 1; *Cincinnati Enquirer*, May 5, 1906, p. 3.
55. *Cincinnati Enquirer*, Oct. 7, 1906, Sec. 4, p. 2.
56. *Cincinnati Enquirer*, Jul. 14, 1906, Sec. 4, p. 2.
57. *Sporting Life*, Jan. 30, 1915, p. 11.
58. Peter Golenbock, *Wrigleyville: A Magical History Tour of the Chicago Cubs* (New York: St. Martin's Press, 1996), p. 104; Donald Dewey and Nicholas Acocella, *The Biographical History of Baseball* (New York: Carroll &Graf Publishers, Inc., 1995), p. 194.
59. *Sporting News*, Apr. 28, 1900, p. 1; Aug. 30, 1961, p. 7.
60. *Cleveland Plain Dealer*, Oct. 16, 1904, Sec. 3, p. 3.
61. *Baltimore Sun*, Jun. 3, 1902, p. 6.
62. *St. Louis Globe-Democrat*, Sep. 9, 1902, p. 13; *Cleveland Plain Dealer*, Aug. 21, 1902, p. 6.
63. *Cleveland Plain Dealer*, Sep. 13, 1902, p. 6.
64. *Sporting News*, Mar. 7, 1903, p. 2; *Cincinnati Commercial Tribune*, Aug. 11, 1903, p. 7; Oct. 4, 1903, p. 9.
65. *Cincinnati Commercial Tribune*, Apr. 10, 1904, p. 10.
66. *Cincinnati Commercial Tribune*, May 31, 1904, p. 8.
67. *Sporting Life*, Apr. 29, 1905, p. 2; Aug. 5, 1905, p. 5; Sep. 9, 1905, p. 5; Oct. 28, 1905, p. 6.
68. *Sporting Life*, Sep. 22, 1906, p. 5; Oct. 13, p. 8; Dec. 1, 1906, p. 4.
69. *Sporting Life*, Jun. 1, 1907, pp. 13, 17; *Sporting News*, Apr. 6, 1907, p. 4.
70. http://sabr.org/bioproj; *Sporting Life*, Jun. 15, 1907, p. 18.
71. *Sporting News*, Aug. 30, 1961, p. 7.
72. *Sporting News*, Jul. 30, 1892, p. 3; Oct. 8, 1892, p. 5.
73. *Sporting News*, Jan. 19, 1901, p. 2; Fleitz, *Ghosts in the Gallery*, p. 155.
74. *Cincinnati Commercial-Tribune*, May 11, 1900, p. 5; May 12, 1900, p. 5.
75. *Sporting News*, Nov. 28, 1903, p. 2.
76. *St. Louis Republic*, Jun. 4, 1905, Sec. III, p. 7; *St. Louis Post-Dispatch*, May 26, 1906, p. 6.
77. *Cincinnati Commercial-Tribune*, May 20, 1903, p. 10; May 25, 1903, p. 7.
78. *St. Louis Post-Dispatch*, Jul. 5, 1906, p. 14.
79. Fleitz, *Ghosts in the Gallery*, p. 162.
80. *Cincinnati Enquirer*, Jun. 4, 1905, Sec. 4, p. 1.
81. *Boston Globe*, Apr. 13, 1906, p. 1; Jun. 19, 1906, p. 7; Jul. 3, 1906, p. 5; Aug. 4, 1906, p. 7.

Chapter Six

1. *Chicago Tribune*, Apr. 8, 1906, Pt. Two, p. 3; *Sporting News*, May 5, 1906, p. 1.
2. *Chicago Tribune*, May 11, 1906, p. 6; Jul. 7, 1906, p. 10.
3. Smiles, *Big Ed Walsh*, pp. 57–9.
4. *St. Louis Post-Dispatch*, Apr. 29, 1906, Pt. 3, p. 12.
5. *Chicago Tribune*, Jun. 11, 1906, p. 10; *Washington Post*, Jun. 15, 1906, p. 9.
6. *Washington Evening Star*, Jun. 12, 1906, p. 9; *Cleveland Plain Dealer*, Jul. 1, 1906, Sp. Sec., p. 1.
7. *Chicago Tribune*, Aug. 26, 1906, Pt. 2, p. 1.
8. *Detroit Free Press*, Sep. 8, 1906, p. 9.
9. *Sporting News*, Jun. 2, p. 1.
10. *Sporting News*, Jul. 14, 1906, p. 2; *Cleveland Plain Dealer*, Jun. 17, 1906, Sp. Sec., pp. 1, 2.
11. *Detroit Free Press*, Jun. 17, 1906, p. 17.
12. *Sporting News*, Mar. 13, 1897, p. 1; Jan. 1, 1898, p. 4.
13. *Chicago Tribune*, Sep. 8, 1900, p. 8.
14. *Boston Globe*, Jun. 5, 1906, p. 9.
15. Chris Hauser, "Albert Lewis Orth," *Deadball Stars of the American League*, p. 711.
16. Rod Caborn and Dave Larson, "1906 Cleveland Naps: Deadball Era Underachiever,"

Baseball Research Journal, Spring 2012, pp. 78–85; *Cleveland Plain Dealer*, Jul. 30, 1906, Sp. Sec., p. 1; Aug. 2, 1906, p. 6; Sep. 6, 1906, p. 8.

17. *Cleveland Plain Dealer*, Jul. 19, 1906, p. 6; Jul. 24, p. 6; Aug. 12, Sp. Sec., p. 1.

18. Scott Turner, "Terrence Lamont Turner," *Deadball Stars of the American League*, pp. 666-7.

19. Ward Mason, "The Last of an All-Star Team," *Baseball Magazine*, Feb., 1916, p.34.

20. *Sporting News*, Jan. 13, 1906, p. 5.

21. Levy, *Rube Waddell*, pp. 187–9.

22. *Philadelphia Record*, May 24, 1906, p. 11.

23. Levy, *Rube Waddell*, pp. 193–4.

24. *Philadelphia Record*, Jul. 27, 1906, p. 9.

25. *Philadelphia Inquirer*, Aug. 14, 1906, p. 13.

26. *Washington Post*, Aug. 21, 1906, p. 6; *Philadelphia Record*, Sep. 5, 1906, p. 8.

27. *St. Louis Post-Dispatch*, Feb. 24, 1906, p. 14.

28. *Sporting News*, Nov. 3, 1906, p. 7; *St. Louis Post-Dispatch*, Sep. 28, 1906, p. 14.

29. *St. Louis Republic*, Jun. 18, 1905, Pt. III, p. 6; Jul. 22, 1905, p. 8.

30. *St. Louis Post-Dispatch*, Jun. 11, 1906, p. 12.

31. *St. Louis Post-Dispatch*, Jun. 24, 1906, Pt. 3, p. 14; Jul. 29, 1906, Pt. 3, p. 9.

32. Murray Polner, *Branch Rickey: A Biography* (New York: Atheneum, 1982), pp. 37–43.

33. *Detroit Free Press*, May 5, 1906, p. 10; *Boston Globe*, May 13, 1906, p. 11; *Washington Post*, May 22, 1906, p. 9; *St. Louis Post-Dispatch*, May 15, 1906, p.8.

34. *St. Louis Post-Dispatch*, Jun. 2, 1906, p. 6.

35. *St. Louis Post-Dispatch*, Jun. 8, 1906, p. 14; Sep. 23, 1906, Pt. 3, p. 12; *Chicago Tribune*, Sep. 16, 1906, Pt. 2, p. 1.

36. Tony Bunting, "Wesley Branch Rickey," *Deadball Stars of the American League*, pp. 784–5.

37. Charles C. Alexander, *Ty Cobb* (New York: Oxford University Press, 1984), pp. 39–41.

38. Lawrence S. Ritter, *Glory of Their Times*, pp. 41, 62.

39. *Sporting News*, May 12, 1906, p. 3; *Detroit Free Press*, May 8, 1906, p. 91 May 9, 1906, p. 9: Sep. 3, 1906, p. 10.

40. *Detroit Free Press*, Jun. 24, 1906, p. 13; Jun. 27, 1906, p. 9; Jul. 1, 1906, p. 13; *Sporting News*, Jul. 7, 1906, p. 4.

41. *Pittsburgh Press*, Jun. 26, 1906, p. 14.

42. *Detroit Free Press*, Aug. 10, 1906, p. 10: Aug. 12, 1906, p. 11; Aug. 27, 1906, p. 8.

43. *Detroit Free Press*, Aug. 10, 1906, p. 10; *Cleveland Plain Dealer*, Aug. 10, 1906, p. 6.

44. *Detroit Free Press*, Oct. 7, 1906, p. 11; Oct. 8, 1906, p. 8.

45. *Detroit Free Press*, May 22, 1906, p. 9; Jun. 1, 1906, p. 10.

46. *Boston Globe*, Sep. 20, 1902, p. 5; *Cleveland Plain Dealer*, May 20, 1903, p. 8.

47. *Detroit Free Press*, Jul. 2, 1905, p. 11.

48. *New York Press*, Apr. 28, 1901, p. 5.

49. *Washington Post*, Jul. 10, 1905, p. 8.

50. *Chicago Tribune*, Jul. 16, 1905, Sec. 2, p. 1.

51. *Washington Post*, Jul. 27, 1905, p. 8; Jul. 29, 1905, p. 8; *St. Louis Republic*, Sep. 30, 1905, Sec. II, p. 2.

52. *Washington Post*, May 1, 1906, p. 10.

53. *Washington Post*, May 28, 1906, p. 8.

54. *Washington Post*, Apr. 26, 1906, p. 8; May 25, 1906, p. 9; Jun. 10, 1906, Sp. Sec., p. 1; Jul. 10, 1906, p. 8; Sep. 27, 1906, p. 8.

55. *Boston Globe*, Apr. 18, 1907, p. 6; *Chicago Tribune*, Aug. 9, 1907, p. 6; *Sporting News*, Dec. 26, 1907, p. 7.

56. *Sporting News*, Mar. 31, 1906, p. 5; *Boston Globe*, Apr. 29, 1906, p. 13; Aug. 18, 1906, p. 7.

57. *Boston Globe*, Sep. 9, 1906, p. 12.

58. *Boston Globe*, May 19, 1906, p. 11; May 24, 1906, p. 6; *St. Louis Post-Dispatch*, Jun. 15, 1906, p. 14.

59. *Detroit Free Press*, Jul. 27, p. 10.

60. *Boston Globe*, Jul. 13, 1906, p. 4; Aug. 16, 1906, p. 7; Sep. 21, 1906, p. 8.

61. *Cleveland Plain Dealer*, Aug. 7, 1906, p. 6.

62. *Boston Globe*, Jun. 21, 1906, p. 9.

63. *Boston Globe*, May 11, 1906, p. 6; Jul. 31, 1906, p. 5; Aug. 9, 1906, p. 5; Sep. 2, 1906, pp. 1,2.

64. *Sporting News*, May 19, 1906, pp. 1, 4; *Boston Globe*, Jul. 20, 1906, p. 4.

65. *Detroit Free Press*, Jul. 17, 1906, p. 9; *Sporting News*, Jul. 28, 1906, p. 1; Sep. 1, 1906, p. 1; Sep. 8, 1906, p. 4.

66. *Chicago Tribune*, Oct. 10, 1906, pp. 1, 2.

67. *Chicago Tribune*, Oct. 11, 1906, pp. 1, 2.

68. *Chicago Tribune*, Oct. 12, 1906, pp. 1, 2.

69. *Chicago Tribune*, Oct. 13, 1906, pp. 1, 2.

70. *Chicago Tribune*, Oct. 14, 1906, pp. 1, 2.

71. *Chicago Tribune*, Oct. 15, 1906, pp. 1, 2.

Chapter Seven

1. *Sporting News*, Apr. 6, 1907, p. 4.

2. *Chicago Tribune*, Apr. 9, 1905, Pt. 2, p. 3.

3. *Chicago Tribune*, Aug. 6, 1905, Pt. 2, p. 1; *Sporting Life*, Aug. 25, 1905, p. 9.

4. *Sporting News*, Nov. 10, 1906, p. 3.

5. *Pittsburgh Press*, Jun. 17, 1907, p. 12; *Chicago Tribune*, Jul. 2, 1907, p. 7.

6. *Sporting News*, Aug. 29, 1907, p. 1.
7. *Chicago Tribune*, Jul. 27, 1907, p. 6; Sep. 19, 1907, p. 6.
8. *Sporting News*, Nov. 14, 1907, p. 4.
9. *Sporting News*, Mar. 9, 1907, p. 4.
10. *Sporting News*, Jan. 5, 1907, p. 5; Mar. 9, 1907, p. 6.
11. *Pittsburgh Post*, Apr. 22, 1907, p. 5; *Boston Globe*, May 15, 1907, p. 8; *Pittsburgh Press*, Jun. 23, 1907, p. 8; *Chicago Tribune*, Jul. 1, 1907, p. 6.
12. *Pittsburgh Post*, Jun. 9, 1907, Sp. Sec., p. 1; Jul. 28, 1907, Sp. Sec., p. 1; Sep. 12, 1907, p. 9; *Boston Globe*, Jul. 21, 1907, p. 6; *Brooklyn Daily Eagle*, Aug. 16, 1907, Sec. 2, p. 2.
13. *Sporting News*, Sep. 26, 1907, p. 4.
14. Bill Lamb, "Frank Corridon," in http://sabr.org/bioproj/.
15. *Chicago Tribune*, May 11, 1904, p. 13.
16. *Sporting News*, May 6, 1905, p. 1.
17. *Sporting Life*, Apr. 7, 1906, p. 13.
18. *Sporting Life*, Jul. 13, 1907, p. 1.
19. Lamb, "Frank Corridon."
20. *Sporting News*, Aug. 6, 1898, p. 5; Sep. 17, 1898, p. 7.
21. *Brooklyn Daily Eagle*, Apr. 27, 1902, p. 6.
22. *Pittsburgh Press*, May 12, 1906, p.10.
23. *Cincinnati Enquirer*, Aug. 14, 1906, p. 4.
24. Evers and Fullerton, *Touching Second*, p. 106.
25. *Sporting News*, May 25, 1907, pp. 1, 2.
26. *Pittsburgh Press*, Jun. 21, 1907, p. 26.
27. *Pittsburgh Press*, Jun. 18, 1907, p. 14.
28. *Cincinnati Enquirer*, Jun. 29, 1907, p. 4; *Sporting News*, Jul. 25, 1907, p. 1; *Boston Globe*, Sep. 19, 1907, p. 5; *Pittsburgh Press*, Sep. 24, 1907, p. 14.
29. *New York Times*, Apr. 17, 1907, p. 7; *Sporting News*, Jun. 8, 1907, p. 4; *Cincinnati Enquirer*, Jul 16, 1907, p. 4.
30. *Sporting News*, Aug. 22, 1907, p. 1; Sep. 19, 1907, p. 1.
31. *Brooklyn Daily Eagle*, Jul. 26, 1907, Sec. 2, p. 2.
32. *Brooklyn Daily Eagle*, Oct. 4, 1907, Sec. 2, p. 2.
33. *Brooklyn Daily Eagle*, Sep. 20, 1907, Sec. 2, p.2.
34. *Brooklyn Daily Eagle*, Apr. 7, 1904, p. 3; Apr. 14, 1904, p. 13; Apr. 20, 1904, News/Cable Sec., p. 15.
35. *Sporting News*, Nov. 5, 1904, p. 5; Sep. 23, 1905, p. 3; Sep. 29, 1906, p. 4.
36. Tom Simon, "Harry G. Lumley," in Simon, ed., *Deadball Stars of the National League*, p. 280.
37. *Sporting News*, Feb. 9, 1907, p. 5.
38. *Sporting News*, Oct. 7, 1905, p. 2; *Chicago Tribune*, Apr. 12, 1906, p. 8.

39. *Sporting News*, Jul. 28, 1906, p. 2.
40. *Sporting News*, Mar. 23, 1907, p. 4.
41. *Sporting News*, Jun. 22, 1907, p. 5.
42. *Cincinnati Enquirer*, Jul. 14, 1907, p. 10; *Sporting News*, Jul. 18, 1907, p. 4.
43. *Cincinnati Enquirer*, Jul. 22, 1907, p. 4; Jul. 28, 1907, Sec. 4, p. 2; *Sporting News*, Aug. 1, 1907, p. 4; *Pittsburgh Press*, Jul. 24, 1907, p. 8.
44. *Sporting News*, Apr. 22, 1937, p. 12.
45. *Sporting News*, Mar. 9, 1907, p.4; Mar. 30, 1907, p.5.
46. Dennis DeValeria and Jean Burke DeValeria, *Honus Wagner: A Biography* (New York: Henry Holt and Company, Inc., 1995), p. 83; *Sporting News*, Aug. 5, 1899, p. 5.
47. *Sporting News*, Jul. 29, 1899, p. 4; Aug. 19, 1899, p. 5.
48. *Sporting News*, May 4, 1907, p. 3; *Boston Globe*, Sep. 27, 1907, p. 5.
49. Dennis Auger, "Dave Brain," in http://sabr.org/bioproj.
50. Terry Bohn, "Patsy Flaherty," in http://sabr.org/bioproj; *Boston Globe*, May 25, 1907, p. 2; Jul. 17, 1907, p. 4; Aug. 20, 1907, p. 4.
51. *Sporting News*, Jul. 11, 1907, p. 2.
52. *Philadelphia North American*, Jun. 12, 1904, p. 11; Aug. 13, 1904, p. 6; Jun. 30, 1904, p. 12; Jul. 22, 1904, p. 12; *Pittsburgh Dispatch*, Jun. 22, 1904, p. 14.
53. *Sporting News*, Oct. 7, 1905, p.6; *Philadelphia Record*, Oct. 6, 1905, p. 12.
54. *Boston Globe*, Apr. 24, 1906, p. 10; *Sporting News*, May12, 1906, p. 4.
55. *Pittsburgh Post*, May 15, 1906, p.8; *New York Sun*, Apr. 28, 1906, p. 11; Jun. 5, 1906, p. 9; *Philadelphia Record*, Apr. 17, 1906, p. 11; *Cincinnati Enquirer*, Sep. 25, 1906, p. 4.
56. *Brooklyn Daily Eagle*, Jul. 3, 1907, p. 16.
57. *St. Louis Post-Dispatch*, Jun. 11, p. 14.
58. *Sporting Life*, Mar. 20, 1909, p. 2; *Sporting News*, Dec. 15, 1910, p. 1.

Chapter Eight

1. *Sporting News*, Jan. 12, 1907, p. 3; Mar. 2, 1907, p. 8.
2. *Detroit Free Press*, Mar. 17, 1907, Pt. 1, p. 17; Jack Smiles, *"Ee-Yah" The Life and Times of Hughie Jennings, Baseball Hall of Famer* (Jefferson, NC: McFarland, 2005), p. 116.
3. Smiles, *"Ee-Yah,"* pp. 120–1.
4. *Detroit Free Press*, Apr. 29, 1907, p. 6; *Cleveland Plain Dealer*, Apr. 30, p. 8.
5. *Cleveland Plain Dealer*, Apr. 19, 1907, p. 8; *Detroit Free Press*, Jun. 9, 1907, p. 13; *Washington Post*, Jun. 16, 1907, Sp. Sec., p. 1.
6. *Cleveland Plain Dealer*, Apr. 23, 1907, p. 8.

Notes—Chapter Eight 351

7. *Detroit Free Press*, Aug. 7, 1903, p. 10.
8. *Washington Post*, Sep. 29, 1907, Sp. Sec., p.3.
9. *Pittsburgh Press*, May 9, 1907, p. 15.
10. *Detroit Free Press*, Jun. 21, 1907, p. 7.
11. *Cleveland Plain Dealer*, Jun. 30, 1907, Sp. Sec., p. 1; *Detroit Free Press*, Jul. 11, p. 6.
12. *Philadelphia Inquirer*, Aug. 9, p. 6.
13. *Detroit Free Press*, Oct. 1, 1907, pp. 1, 6.
14. *Sporting News*, Oct. 10, p. 6.
15. *Philadelphia Inquirer*, Jul. 24, p. 6.
16. Norman Macht, *Connie Mack*, p. 388.
17. *Boston Globe*, Jun. 8, 1907, p. 6.
18. *Sporting News*, Aug, 29, 1907, p. 6.
19. Levy, *Rube Waddell*, pp. 211–13; *Philadelphia Inquirer*, Jul. 7, 1907, p. 12.
20. *Cleveland Plain Dealer*, May 26, 1907, Sp. Sec., p. 1.
21. *Philadelphia Inquirer*, Jun. 29, 1907, p. 10.
22. *Cleveland Plain Dealer*, Jun. 15, 1907, p. 6.
23. *Chicago Tribune*, Apr. 12, 1907, p. 11; Apr. 16, 1907, p. 6; Apr. 18, 1907, p. 6; *Cleveland Plain Dealer*, Apr. 26, 1907, p. 6.
24. *Washington Post*, May 29, 1907, p. 8.
25. *Washington Post*, Jun. 11, 1907, p. 8.
26. *Sporting News*, May 4, 1907, p. 1; Aug. 15, 1907, p. 1; *Chicago Tribune*, Sep. 17, 1907, p. 5.
27. *Chicago Tribune*, Apr. 23, 1907, p. 6; Jul. 13, 1907, p. 6; *Sporting News*, Jul. 25, 1907, p. 1.
28. *Sporting News*, Jul. 4, 1907, p. 1.
29. *Chicago Tribune*, Aug. 25, 1906, p. 8.
30. *Boston Globe*, May 1, 1907, p. 8; *Detroit Free Press*, May 2, 1907, p. 7; *Chicago Tribune*, Sep. 23, 1907, p. 10.
31. Smiles, *Big Ed Walsh*, p.99.
32. *Sporting News*, Mar. 3, 1906, p. 7.
33. *Sporting News*, Jan. 6, 1906, p. 7.
34. *Boston Globe*, Apr. 30, 1906, p. 8.
35. *Brooklyn Daily Eagle*, Apr. 22, 1906, News/Cable, p. 8.
36. Fleitz, *Napoleon Lajoie*, pp. 113–4; *Sporting News*, May 23, 1907, p. 6.
37. *Sporting News*, Apr. 13, 1907, p. 4; Apr. 20, 1907, p. 5; *Cleveland Plain Dealer*, Apr. 12, p. 8; Apr. 14, Sp. Sec., p. 1.
38. *Sporting News*, Aug. 1, 1907, p. 4; *Cleveland Plain Dealer*, Aug. 5, 1907, p. 6.
39. *Sporting News*, Nov. 14, 1907, p. 5. Fleitz, *Napoleon Lajoie*, pp. 168–70.
40. *Sporting News*, Apr. 20, 1907, p. 4.
41. *Washington Post*, May 30, 1907, p. 8.
42. *New York Times*, Aug. 9, 1907, p. 8.
43. *Sporting News*, Aug. 15, 1907, p. 1; November 14, 1907, p. 1.
44. *Sporting News*, Sep. 30, 1899, p. 5.
45. *Sporting News*, Nov. 14, 1907, p. 1.
46. *Detroit Free Press*, Jun. 3, 1903, p. 10.

47. *Cleveland Plain Dealer*, Jul. 26, 1907, p. 6; Jul. 27, 1907, p. 8; *St. Louis Post-Dispatch*, Jul. 30, 1907, p 12.
48. *Pittsburgh Press*, Jul. 31, 1907, p. 8.
49. *Detroit Free Press*, Aug. 16, 1907, p. 6.
50. *Sporting News*, Jul. 17, 1897, p. 6.
51. *St. Louis Globe-Democrat*, Aug. 2, 1901, p. 11.
52. *Sporting News*, Sep. 16, 1899, p. 4; Mar. 17, 1900, p. 4; Dec. 4, 1901, p. 4.
53. *Sporting News*, Oct. 4, 1902, p. 4; Apr. 4, 1903, p. 4; Nov. 14, 1903, p. 4; Feb. 6, 1904, p. 4.
54. *Sporting News*, Mar. 12, 1904, p. 4; Apr. 30, 1904 p. 6.
55. *Sporting News*, Feb. 10, 1906, p. 4; Feb. 16, 1907, p. 4.
56. *St. Louis Post-Dispatch*, Apr. 18, 1906, p. 15; Apr. 29, 1906, Pt. 3,p. 12; Apr. 30, 1906, p. 8; May 2, 1906, p. 9.
57. *St. Louis Post-Dispatch*, Jun. 2, 1906, p. 6; Sep. 24, 1906, p. 8; *Sporting News*, Nov. 24, 1906, p. 4.
58. *Sporting News*, Apr. 13, 1907, p. 4; Jul. 11, 1907, p. 4; Sep. 26, 1907, p. 4.
59. *Sporting Life*, Jun. 27, 1908, p. 1; *Cleveland Plain Dealer*, Aug. 6, 1904, p. 6.
60. *Sporting Life*, Sep. 3, 1910, p. 11; Sep. 17, 1910, p. 19.
61. Dennis Auger, "Chick Stahl" in http://sabr.org. bioproject.
62. *Pittsburgh Press*, Apr. 22, 1907, p. 24.
63. *Boston Globe*, May 1, 1907, p. 8.
64. *Boston Globe*, Jun. 19, 1907, p. 5; Jun. 22, 1907, p. 7; Jul. 9, 1907, p. 5; Aug. 23, 1907, p. 9.
65. *Boston Globe*, Aug. 24, 1907, p. 4.
66. *Cleveland Plain Dealer*, May 16, 1907, p. 8; *Boston Globe*, Jun. 2, 1907, p. 12.
67. *Sporting News*, Dec. 26, 1907, p. 7.
68. *Sporting News*, Aug. 22, 1907, p. 4; Sep. 19, 1907, p. 6.
69. *Sporting News*, Aug. 22, 1907, p. 4; *Washington Post*, Jun. 30, 1907, Sp. Sec., p. 1.
70. *Washington Post*, Aug. 3, 1907, p. 8.
71. *Washington Post*, Aug. 8, 1907, p. 8.
72. *Detroit Free Press*, Aug. 27, 1907, p. 6; *Washington Post*, Sep. 25, p. 8.
73. *Washington Post*, Aug. 29, 1907, p. 8; Sep. 8, 1907, Sp. Sec., p. 1.
74. *Washington Post*, Sep. 29, 1907, Sp. Sec., p. 1.
75. *Washington Post*, Aug. 29, 1907, p. 8.
76. *Washington Post*, Aug. 31, 1907, p. 8.
77. *Chicago Tribune*, Oct. 9, 1907, pp. 1, 2; *Sporting News*, Nov. 7, p. 4.
78. *Detroit Free Press*, Oct. 9, 1907, p. 2.
79. *Detroit Free Press*, Oct. 10, 1907, p. 1.
80. *Chicago Tribune*, Oct. 11, 1907, p. 1.
81. *Chicago Tribune*, Oct. 12, 1907, p. 2.
82. *Chicago Tribune*, Oct. 13, 1907, pp. 1, 2.
83. *Chicago Tribune*, Oct. 13, 1907, p. 1.

Bibliography

Newspapers and Periodicals

Boston Globe
Brooklyn Daily Eagle
Chicago Tribune
Cincinnati Commercial Tribune
Cincinnati Enquirer
Cleveland Plain Dealer
Detroit Free Press
New York American
New York Evening World
New York Sun
New York Times
Philadelphia Inquirer
Philadelphia North American
Philadelphia Record
Pittsburgh Dispatch
Pittsburgh Post
Pittsburgh Press
St. Louis Globe-Democrat
St. Louis Post-Dispatch
St. Louis Republic
Sporting Life
The Sporting News
Washington Evening Star
Washington Post

Books

Alexander, Charles C. *John McGraw*. Lincoln: University of Nebraska Press, 1995.
_____. *Ty Cobb*. New York: Oxford University Press, 1984.
Barrow, Ed, with Kahn, James M. *My Fifty Years in Baseball*. New York: Coward-McCann, Inc., 1951.
Casway, Jerold. *Ed Delahanty in the Emerald Age of Baseball*. Notre Dame: University of Notre Dame Press, 2004.
Cobb, Ty, with Stump, Al. *My Life in Baseball: The True Record*. Bison Books. Lincoln: University of Nebraska Press, 1993.
DeValeria, Dennis, and DeValeria, Jean Burke. *Honus Wagner: A Biography*. New York: Henry Holt and Company, Inc., 1995.
Dewey, Donald, and Acocella, Nicholas. *The Biographical History of Baseball*. New York: Carroll & Graf Publishers, Inc., 1995.
Doxsie, Don. *Iron Man McGinnity: A Baseball Biography*. Jefferson, NC: McFarland, 2009.
Evers, John J., and Fullerton, Hugh S. *Touching Second: The Science of Baseball*. Chicago: The Reilly and Britton Company, 1910.
Fleitz, David. *Ghosts in the Gallery at Cooperstown*. Jefferson, NC: McFarland, 2004.
_____. *Napoleon Lajoie: King of Ballplayers*. Jefferson, NC: McFarland, 2013.
Golenbock, Peter. *Wrigleyville: A Magical History Tour of the Chicago Cubs*. New York: St. Martin's Press, 1996.
Ivor-Campbell, Frederick, Tiemann, Robert L., and Rucker, Mark, eds. *Baseball's First Stars*. Cleveland: Society for American Baseball Research, 1996.
James, Bill. *The New Bill James Historical Baseball Abstract*. New York: The Free Press, 2001.
Kaese, Harold. *The Boston Braves*. New York: G.P. Putnam's Sons, 1948.
Levy, Alan H. *Rube Waddell: The Zany, Brilliant Life of a Strikeout Artist*. Jefferson, NC: McFarland, 2000.
Liberman, Noah. *Glove Affairs*. Chicago: Triumph Books, 2003.
Longert, Scott. *Addie Joss: King of the Pitchers*. Birmingham, AL: EBCO Media, 1998.

McGraw, John J. *My Thirty Years in Baseball*. Bison Books. Lincoln: University of Nebraska Press, 1995.

Macht, Norman. *Connie Mack and the Early Years of Baseball*. Lincoln: University of Nebraska Press, 2007.

Murdock, Eugene. *Ban Johnson: Czar of Baseball*. Westport, CT: Greenwood Press, 1982.

Nemec, David. *The Great Encyclopedia of 19th Century Major League Baseball*. New York: Donald I. Fine Books, 1997.

Polner, Murray. *Branch Rickey: A Biography*. New York: Atheneum, 1982.

Ritter, Lawrence S. *The Glory of Their Times: The Story of the Early Days of Baseball Told by the Men Who Played it*. Quill ed. New York: William Morrow and Company, 1985.

Simon, Tom, ed. *Deadball Stars of the National League*. Dulles, VA: Brassey's Inc., 2004.

Smiles, Jack. *Big Ed Walsh*. Jefferson, NC: McFarland, 2008.

_____. *"Ee-Yah" The Life and Times of Hughie Jennings, Baseball Hall of Famer*. Jefferson, NC: McFarland, 2005.

Solomon, Burt. *Where They Ain't: The Fabled Life and Untimely Death of the Original Baltimore Orioles, the Team That gave Birth to Modern Baseball*. New York: The Free Press, 1999.

Szalontai, James D. *Small Ball in the Big Leagues: A History of Stealing, Bunting, Walking and Otherwise Scratching for Runs*. Jefferson, NC: McFarland, 2010.

Thomson, Cindy, and Brown, Scott. *Three Finger: The Mordecai Brown Story*. Lincoln: University of Nebraska Press, 2006.

Waldo, Ronald T. *Fred Clarke: A Biography of the Baseball Hall of Fame Player-Manager*. Jefferson, NC: McFarland, 2011.

Wright, Craig R., and House, Tom. *The Diamond Appraised*. New York: Simon and Shuster, 1989.

Articles

Blaisdell, Lowell L. "Trouble and Jack Taylor." *The National Pastime*, No. 16, 1996, pp. 132–6.

Caborn, Rod, and Larson, Dave. "1906 Cleveland Naps: Deadball Era Underachiever." *Baseball Research Journal*, Vol. 41, No. 1 (2012), pp. 78–85.

Crawford, Sam. "What I Think About Baseball." *Baseball Magazine*, Feb. 1916, pp. 39–43.

Kirwin, Bill. "Cy Seymour: Baseball's Second Most Versatile Player." *Baseball Research Journal*, Vol. 29 (2000), pp. 3–13.

Lamb, Bill. "A Question of Character: George Davis and the Flora Campbell Affair." *Baseball Research Journal*, Vol. 45, No. 2, pp. 81–2.

Lieb, Frederick G. "Sherwood R. Magee." *Baseball Magazine*, Dec. 1910, pp. 33–36.

Mason, Ward. "The Last of an All-Star Team." *Baseball Magazine*, Feb. 1916, pp. 33–38.

Murphy, J. M. "Napoleon Lajoie: Modern Baseball's First Superstar." *The National Pastime*, Spring 1988.

Internet Sites

http://www.baseball-reference.com
http://www.la84.org
http://www.retrosheet.org
http://www/sabr.org/bioproject

Index

Abbaticchio, Ed 47, 142, 144–5, 273–4, 276, 293
Abbott, Fred 79, 80, 115, 130
Alexander, Grover Cleveland 41–2, 132
Alperman, Whitey 213, 286–7
Altrock, Nick 76, 102–3, 157, 159, 233–4, 265, 312–4
Ames, Leon (Red) 17, 19, 111–4, 202, 282
Anderson, Edward (Goat) 273–5
Anson, Cap 339
Archer, Jimmie 338
Armour, Bill 151, 165–6, 255, 257, 317–8
Arndt, Harry 136, 225, 227

Babb, Charlie 19, 43, 147
Bancroft, Frank 33
Barbeau, Jap 242–3
Barrett, Jimmy 4, 91–2, 165, 219, 270, 329
Barrow, Ed 90–1, 322
Barry, Jack (Shad) 25, 52, 133, 218–9, 278, 296
Batch, Emil 127, 147–8, 213, 287
Bates, Johnny 229–31, 293
Bausewine, George 116
Bay, Harry 78, 171, 175, 242–3, 317–8
Beaumont, Ginger 34, 118, 127–8, 206, 274–5, 293–5
Beckley, Jake 15, 17, 37, 136, 141, 225–8, 296
Beebe, Fred 199, 225, 297
Bell, George 286–7
Bemis, Harry 79, 80, 171, 242, 305, 317
Bender, Charles (Chief) 63, 82, 152, 154–5, 157–8, 189–90, 246–8, 307, 309–10
Bennett, Charlie 40, 102
Bennett, Pug 225, 296
Bergen, Bill 43, 147, 213, 287
Bergen, Martin 252
Bernhard, Bill 6, 63, 79, 80, 171, 242
Beville, Monte 70, 91
Birmingham, Joe 305, 317
Blake, Harry 325
Blankenship, Cliff 332–3, 335
Bonds, Barry 177, 208
Bowerman, Frank 8, 16, 17, 19, 111, 117, 202, 282
Bradley, Bill 59, 63, 78, 99, 171–2, 242–5, 258, 317–8
Brain, Dave 37, 119, 124, 141, 229, 293, 295
Bransfield, Kitty 29, 35–7, 61, 124, 130, 205–6, 209, 277, 279
Bresnahan, Roger 16–9, 111–3, 127, 188–90, 201, 204, 217, 282–5, 299
Bridwell, Al 133, 208, 216, 229, 293, 295
Briggs, Herbert (Buttons) 25, 126, 192
Brockett, Bill 320
Brouthers, Art 246
Brouthers, Dan 225
Brown, Charles (Buster) 136, 277, 298–9
Brown, Mordecai (Three-Finger) 25–7, 38, 114, 126, 128, 193, 198–200, 207, 224–5, 265–7, 271–2, 281, 285, 338
Brown, Sam 229, 293
Browne, George 16–7, 111, 117, 148, 188, 190, 201, 282–3
Brush, John T. 1, 4, 7, 9–11, 63, 96–7, 116, 188, 283
Buckenberger, Al 143
Buelow, Fritz 79, 100, 171
Burke, Frank 293
Burke, Jimmy 37, 136, 141–2
Burkett, Jesse 85–90, 167, 250

Caborn, Rod 243
Caffyn, Ben 243
Callahan, Jimmy 75–7, 81, 159, 232–3
Camnitz, Howie 274, 276–7
Cannell, Rip 48, 142, 270
Cantillon, Joe 333–5
Carney, Pat (Doc) 48
Carr, Charlie 91–2, 98, 171, 219, 260
Carrigan, Bill 261, 264,
Case, Charlie 35, 119, 125
Casey, Jimmy (Doc) 24, 27, 49, 59, 126, 192, 213, 287
Cassidy, Joe 93–5, 181, 183, 258
Chadwick, Henry 39
Chance, Frank 1, 14, 24, 27–9, 58, 98, 125–7, 129, 191–3, 195–7, 199–201, 205, 213, 216, 218, 221, 223–4, 265–7, 268, 270–2, 336, 338
Chapman, Jack 185
Chapman, Ray 97
Chase, Hal 178, 238–40, 319–20
Chech, Charlie 133, 219
Chesbro, Jack 1, 13, 23, 63, 67–9, 70, 72–4, 100–2, 150, 178–80, 184, 186–7,

355

Index

207, 236, 238, 240–1, 278–9, 314, 319–21, 326
Childs, Cupid 88, 119–20
Clancy, Bill 119, 124, 128
Clarke, Bill (Boileryard) 93
Clarke, Fred 33–6, 90, 118–25, 169–70, 181, 206–7, 273–6, 283, 294
Clarke, Josh 109, 136
Clarke, Nig 171, 174, 242, 253, 317
Clarkson, John 174
Clarkson, Walter 239, 317, 320
Clymer, Otis 118, 124, 206, 332
Coakley, Andy 152, 155–8, 246, 284, 289, 292
Cobb, Ty 89, 107, 111, 126, 162, 174, 208, 247, 253–6, 300–1, 304–7, 310, 334
Collins, Eddie 308
Collins, Jimmy 39, 59, 62–5, 68, 106, 156, 166–7, 187, 250, 261–4, 307–9, 321, 328, 332
Comerford, Dan 286
Comiskey, Charlie 10, 63, 74–6, 78, 140–1, 158–62, 212, 233, 239, 339
Congalton, Bunk 242–3, 329
Connolly, Tom 245
Connor, Roger 225
Conroy, Wid 13, 70, 178, 238, 319
Cooley, Richard (Duff) 47, 59, 162, 164
Coombs, Jack 246, 248, 264, 307–8
Corcoran, Tom 30, 58, 133, 193, 218–9, 282–3
Corridon, Frank 51–2, 101–2, 130, 277–9
Coughlin, Bill 61, 64, 90, 93, 95, 100, 162, 254, 300–1, 307, 336–8
Courtney, Ernie 129–30, 210, 277
Crandall, Doc 117
Crane, Sam 109, 323
Cravath, Gavvy 135
Crawford, Forrest 225
Crawford, Sam 4, 8, 63, 91–2, 110–1, 162, 166, 252, 254, 256, 301, 304, 306
Criger, Lou 62, 64–5, 69, 167, 261, 329, 332

Cronin, Jack 19, 43
Cross, Lave 5, 45, 53, 59, 63, 82, 147, 152, 154, 188, 245, 257, 259, 332
Cross, Monte 59, 82, 152–4, 158, 188–90, 246, 259, 307
Cuppy, George 38, 88

Dahlen, Bill 17, 19–20, 43–4, 111, 113–4, 189–90, 199–200, 202, 208, 227, 282–3
Daily, Con 118
Daly, Tom 43, 192
Davis, Alfonzo (Lefty) 13, 70, 288
Davis, Bungy 300
Davis, George 7–11, 13, 63, 75–6, 119, 158, 160–1, 212, 234, 236, 258, 265, 267, 311–3
Davis, Harry 59, 63, 71, 81–2, 152–4, 156–7, 164, 188, 245–6, 305, 307, 311
Davis, Ralph 124
Delahanty, Ed 5, 7–9, 13, 89, 107, 131–2, 134, 175–6, 257
Delahanty, Frank 238, 301, 319
Delahanty, Jim 48, 61, 142, 218–9, 332
DeMontreville, Gene 122
Devlin, Art 16–17, 19, 28, 59, 111, 113–4, 189–90, 199–200, 202, 282
Dillon, Frank (Pop) 42, 44
Dinneen, Bill 40, 62, 65–9, 167, 261, 263, 324, 332
Doheny, Ed 35
Dolan, Pat (Cozy) 30–1, 142, 229
Donahue, John (Jiggs) 49, 59, 60, 75–6, 159, 161, 234, 311
Donahue, Red 79–80, 103, 171, 174, 254
Donahue, She 50, 58
Donlin, Mike 15, 19, 30–1, 111–3, 148, 188, 201–3, 316
Donovan, Jerry 210
Donovan, Patsy 40, 66, 93–5, 103, 182, 222, 291
Donovan, Wild Bill 64, 91–2, 101, 156, 163, 254, 302–4, 306, 334, 336, 338

Dooin, Charles (Red) 16, 50, 59, 61, 130, 210, 277, 279
Doolin, Mickey 61, 130, 210, 277
Doran, Tom 164
Dorner, Gus 219, 228–9, 293
Dougherty, Patsy 62, 65–6, 69–71, 83, 178, 233–6, 265, 267, 311
Dovey, George 292
Dovey, John 292
Doyle, Jack 43–4, 50–2
Doyle, Larry 282–3
Doyle, Slow Joe 319–20
Dreyfuss, Barney 4, 36, 96, 115–6, 123, 274–5, 294
Drill, Lew 91, 94–5, 162
Druhot, Carl 219, 225
Dryden, Charley 83–4, 183, 186, 312
Duffy, Hugh 51–2, 90, 130, 132, 278, 281
Duggleby, Bill 6, 51–2, 130, 210
Dundon, Gus 75–6, 159, 232, 234
Dunkle, Dave 93–5
Dunlap, Fred 55
Dunn, Jack 17, 289
Dygert, Jimmy 246–8, 307

Ebbets, Charles 146, 149, 287
Eells, Harry 150, 242
Elberfeld, Norman (Kid) 4, 8, 10, 70, 91, 178, 212, 238–9, 305, 319, 322–3
Elliott, Claude 111, 117, 204
Ely, Fred 5
Emslie, Bob 116, 205
Eubank, John 240, 254, 302
Evans, Billy 165
Evans, Dwight 176
Evers, Johnny 14, 24–5, 27–8, 59, 107, 126, 193, 196, 199, 265–6, 269–70, 272–3, 281, 296, 336, 338
Ewing, Bob 30, 100–1, 133, 218, 289, 292
Ewing, William (Buck) 193, 212, 226

Falkenberg, Cy 182–3, 257, 333
Farrell, Duke 43, 46, 65
Farrell, Frank 322–3
Farrell, John 37

Index

Feller, Bob 82
Ferguson, Cecil 202, 204, 282
Ferris, Hobe 62, 64–5, 68–9, 167, 260, 329, 332
Flaherty, Patsy 35, 77, 119, 124, 128, 274, 293, 295
Fleitz, Dave 228
Flick, Elmer 6, 58, 63, 78, 99, 163, 170–7, 242–3, 250, 258–9, 301, 316–8
Fogarty, Jim 173
Fraser, Charles (Chick) 6, 51, 130, 142, 218–9, 271
Freedman, Andrew 7, 212
Freeman, Buck 62, 65, 167, 261–2, 325, 332
Frick, Ford 177
Fullerton, Hugh 107, 126, 138, 170, 220–1, 223, 281
Fultz, Dave 8, 13, 70–1, 178

Galvin, Pud 39, 42
Ganley, Bob 206, 317, 332, 335
Garvin, Ned 43, 53–5
Gear, Dale 37
Geier, Phil 47–8
Gessler, Doc 42, 49, 147–8, 193
Gibson, George 119, 206, 273, 283
Gibson, Norwood 39, 65–8, 101, 151, 167
Gilbert, Billy 17, 111, 189–90, 202, 283
Glade, Fred 85, 99, 184, 249, 324
Gleason, Harry 85, 99–100, 184
Gleason, Kid 50, 58, 91, 129, 132, 209–13, 277, 292
Gochnaur, John 80
Grady, Mike 37–8, 109, 136, 142, 225
Graham, Archie (Moonlight) 111, 117–8
Graham, Oscar 333
Green, Danny 76, 159–60, 232
Greminger, Ed 60
Griffin, Mike 44
Griffith, Clark 33, 38–9, 63–4, 70–4, 94, 108, 170, 177–81, 215, 238–40, 312, 320–1, 323, 326–7, 330

Grillo, Ed 32, 123, 154, 194
Guerrero, Pedro 176
Hahn, Ed 164, 178, 233–4, 265–7, 311
Hahn, Frank (Noodles) 30, 49, 133
Hall, Bob 50, 52, 147
Hall, Charley 218, 289
Hamilton, Billy 86, 173, 176, 288
Hanlon, Ned 15, 31, 45, 47, 123, 146–9, 160, 185, 195, 203, 211, 218–20, 287–92, 297, 321, 330
Harper, Jack 30, 32, 98, 133, 218–24
Harris, Joe 261, 263–4, 329
Harrison, James 54
Hart, Bill 102
Hart, Jim 116, 137, 139–41, 195
Hartsel, Topsy 62, 82, 152–3, 155, 157–8, 246, 307, 310–1
Hartzell, Roy 249, 324
Hedges, Robert 84, 186, 222, 253, 327
Heilbroner, Louis 324–5
Hemphill, Charlie 85, 249, 324
Hemphill, Frank 233
Henley, Weldon 82, 152, 155, 157
Herrmann, Garry 8, 32, 144, 149, 188, 218–9
Hess, Otto 79, 171, 242, 317–8
Hickman, Charlie 78, 80, 92, 165–6, 181, 183, 256–60, 332
Hill, Hunter 60, 93, 181, 183
Hillebrand, Homer 119, 125, 206
Hinchman, Bill 219, 317
Hoey, Jack 261–2
Hoffman, Danny 82–4, 98, 152–4, 238, 319–20
Hoffman, Harry 94
Hofman, Art (Solly) 126–7, 193, 265, 268–72
Hogg, Bill 178, 180–1, 238, 319–20
Holmes, Ducky 59, 75–6, 158, 160, 232–3, 258
Hornsby, Rogers 89
House, Tom 208

Howard, Del 119, 124, 229, 293, 296, 336
Howell, Harry 70, 85, 100–1, 184–7, 249, 312, 324, 326
Huelsman, Frank 93, 99, 181, 183
Huff, George 329–30
Huggins, Miller 30–1, 60–1, 99, 133, 216, 218, 288, 291
Hughes, Tom 64, 70–2, 93, 182–4, 257, 333
Hulswitt, Rudy 45, 50, 52

Irwin, Arthur 55–6, 61, 211
Irwin, Charlie 193
Isbell, Frank 59, 75–6, 158, 161–2, 232, 234–5, 265–7, 311–3

Jackson, Jim 59, 171, 242–3
Jackson, Joe 164, 301, 336–7
Jackson, Shoeless Joe 118
Jacobson, Albert (Beany) 93, 182–3, 249, 324
James, Bill 53, 111, 131, 176–7
Jennings, Hughie 43, 86, 289, 292, 300–4, 307
Johnson, Ban 6–7, 10, 15, 63, 65, 93, 96, 150–1, 182, 186, 279, 328
Johnson, Walter 41–2, 333–6
Johnstone, Jim 115–6, 205
Jones, Charlie 181, 257, 332, 335
Jones, Davey 24, 27, 165, 254, 301
Jones, Fielder 59, 75–8, 103, 158, 160, 187, 232, 234–5, 237, 265–6, 311, 313–4
Jones, Oscar 16, 40, 43, 147
Jones, Tom 85, 184, 249, 324
Jordan, Dutch 43
Jordan, Tim 213, 286–7
Joss, Addie 63, 79, 150, 171, 242–4, 248, 317
Joyce, Bill 119
Jude, Frank 218, 220, 231

Kahoe, Mike 85, 284, 335
Keefe, Bobby 320
Keeler, Willie 43, 63, 68, 70–1, 81, 85–6, 90, 147, 160, 178, 206, 238, 275, 319–20

Kelley, Joe 15, 18, 26, 30–2, 40, 43, 109, 111–2, 133, 140, 194, 197, 218–20, 222, 227, 251, 292
Kellum, Win 30–2, 136, 223
Kennedy, Roaring Bill 35, 38
Killian, Ed 64, 91, 163, 254–5, 302–3
Killilea, Henry 7, 96
Kingman, Dave 213–4, 217
Kinsella, W.P. 118
Kirwin, Dan 134
Kitson, Frank 91, 163, 257, 319
Kittridge, Malachi 71, 93–5, 181
Kleinow, Red 69–70, 178, 238, 319
Kling, Johnny 14, 24–5, 27–8, 126, 192–3, 196, 265, 270, 272, 284, 336–8
Knabe, Otto 213, 277
Knight, Jack 152–4, 246, 307–8, 329
Knoll, Punch 181, 183
Koufax, Sandy 82
Krueger, Otto (Oom Paul) 35, 61, 98, 124, 130

Lachance, Candy 64–5, 68–9
Lajoie, Napoleon (Larry) 6, 15, 27, 29, 48, 59, 61, 63, 71, 78–81, 99, 107, 163, 171, 174–5, 194, 242–3, 245, 257–8, 315–9, 321–2
Lancaster, Burt 118
Lanigan, Ernest 38, 41
Larson, Dave 243
Lauder, Billy 18–9
Leach, Tommy 18, 34–5, 118, 124, 128, 197, 205–6, 273–6
Leever, Sam 33–5, 119, 124, 170, 205–6, 272, 274, 276, 279
Leifield, Lefty 119, 125, 200, 206–7, 274, 276
Lennox, Eddie 246
Leonard, Hub (Dutch) 198
Lewis, Phil 147–9, 208, 213, 287
Lindaman, Vive 229, 293, 296
Lindsay, Chris 162, 166, 254

Lobert, Hans 218, 220, 288, 291
Loftus, Tom 93–4, 170
Long, Herman 172
Lord, Bris 152–3, 157, 189, 246, 307–8
Lowe, Bobby 91–2, 120, 162, 254
Lumley, Harry 42, 147, 213, 286–8
Lundgren, Carl 14, 25, 126, 193, 198, 200, 224, 271–2
Lush, Johnny 50, 52, 78, 99, 210, 297–9
Lynch, Mike 35, 114–5, 119, 124, 206, 282

Mack, Connie 5–6, 83–4, 107, 113, 137, 152–8, 160, 181, 215, 245–6, 248, 264, 304–11
Maddox, Nick 274, 277
Magee, Sherry 50, 52, 129–32, 135, 210, 231, 272, 277, 295
Malay, Charlie 127, 147
Maloney, Billy 61, 125–6, 192, 213–7, 287
Manning, Jimmy 93
Mantle, Mickey 16
Maris, Roger 16
Marshall, William (Doc) 17, 49, 203, 225, 296
Mason, Del 94, 289
Mathews, Bobby 102
Mathewson, Christy 1, 8, 14, 16–7, 20–3, 26, 28, 41–2, 53, 59, 97, 111, 114–6, 128, 188–90, 198–203, 229, 241, 282, 285, 298, 314, 334–5
Mays, Willie 208
McAleer, Jimmy 63, 84–5, 89, 215, 222, 250, 252, 256, 325–6, 333
McBride, George 136, 225, 227
McCarthy, Jack 24, 27, 125, 127–8, 192, 213
McCloskey, John 297, 299
McCormick, Barry 84, 93
McCormick, Harry (Moose) 17, 19, 34, 124
McCormick, Mike 43
McFarland, Charles (Chappie) 37, 98, 136

McFarland, Ed 75–6, 159, 241, 311
McGann, Dan 16–7, 60, 111, 113–5, 188, 197, 201, 282–3
McGinnity, Joe 13–4, 16–7, 20–4, 26–8, 41, 77, 97, 111, 114, 189, 198–9, 202–5, 223, 282–3, 285–6, 303, 314
McGraw, John 1, 3, 6–8, 10, 13, 15–21, 23, 25, 39, 43, 45, 63, 72, 86, 88, 90, 96–7, 107, 110–7, 124, 134, 145, 151, 160, 181, 185–6, 190, 194, 199–205, 220, 226, 280, 282–3, 285–6, 289, 292, 318, 322
McGuire, Deacon 43, 69–70, 178, 238, 319, 330–1
McIntire, Harry 147, 149, 214, 230, 286–7
McIntyre, Matty 91, 162, 254–6, 300
McJames, Doc 49
McKean, Ed 88
McLean, Larry 288, 292
McNichol, Ed 48
McPhee, Bid 55–7, 193
Merkle, Fred 273, 283
Mertes, Sam 8, 17, 63, 111, 113–4, 188–90, 201, 203, 227
Milan, Clyde 333–6
Miller, Roscoe 19, 35, 99
Mitchell, Fred 51, 147
Mitchell, Mike 288, 291
Moore, Earl 63, 79, 171, 319–20
Moran, Charles 85
Moran, Pat 48, 142–3, 192–3, 200, 270, 272
Morgan, Cy 185, 329
Morgan, James (Red) 261–2
Mowrey, Mike 219–20, 291
Mulford, Ren 109
Mullin, George 64, 91–2, 101, 163, 254, 302–3, 310, 337
Mullin, Jim 93, 181
Murnane, Tim 5–6, 10, 60, 120, 125, 145, 151, 161, 167, 178, 252, 261, 263, 294, 316
Murphy, Charles 191, 221
Murphy, Danny 82, 152, 154, 164, 188–90, 246, 306–7, 310

Index

Murray, Billy 213, 298
Murray, Red 225, 296

Nabors, Jack 264
Nash, Billy 48
Navin, Frank 255
Nealon, Joe 195, 205–6, 273
Needham, Tom 48, 142, 144, 228–9, 293
Newton, Doc 181, 239, 319, 321
Nicholls, Simon 305–8
Nichols, Charles (Kid) 37–42, 130, 141–2
Nill, Rabbitt 181, 183, 257, 332

O'Brien, Jack 64
O'Brien, Pete 249, 317, 332
O'Connor, Jack 13, 70, 249, 252
Odwell, Fred 30–1, 46, 133, 218–9, 288
Oldring, Rube 246–7, 307
O'Leary, Charley 64, 90–1, 162–4, 171, 254, 302, 306, 338
Oliva, Tony 176
O'Loughlin, Silk 305
O'Neill, Bill 64–6, 93, 99, 233–4, 266
O'Neill, Jack 24–5, 126, 192, 229
O'Neill, Mike 37
Orth, Al 64, 68, 70–2, 94, 100, 178, 180, 234, 236, 238, 240–1, 256, 319–21
Overall, Orval 133, 193, 199, 219, 224, 271–2, 338
Owen, Frank 76, 159, 233–4, 236–7, 266, 312–4
Owens, Reddy 148

Parent, Fred 62, 64–5, 69, 166–7, 260, 285, 329, 332
Paskert, Dode 291
Patten, Casey 4, 64, 93–5, 101, 151, 158, 182–3, 257, 333
Patterson, Frank 185
Patterson, Roy 76–8, 100, 159, 234–7, 312, 314
Payne, Fred 254, 302, 337
Peitz, Heinie 30–1, 58, 119, 124, 204, 206
Peterson, Bob 261, 263
Pfeffer, Jeff 192, 229, 293

Pfiester, Jack 193, 199, 224, 266, 269, 271–2
Phelon, W.A. 27
Phelps, Ed 35, 98, 124, 133, 205–6, 216, 219, 273–5
Phillippe, Charles (Deacon) 35, 113–4, 119, 124, 131, 169, 205–6, 274, 276, 279
Phillips, Bill 105
Pickering, Ollie 82, 324
Pittinger, Togie 15, 47–8, 50, 130, 210, 277
Plank, Eddie 63, 82, 152, 154–5, 157, 168, 178, 188–9, 246–8, 306–7, 309–10, 331
Pond, Arlie (Doc) 49
Powell, Jack 68, 70, 72, 101, 178–81, 186, 249, 323–8
Powers, Mike (Doc) 49, 82, 152, 246, 305, 307
Pruiett, Tex 329–30
Pulliam, Harry 10, 17, 115–6, 150, 204–5, 283
Puttmann, Ambrose 178, 181

Quillen, Lee 311, 313
Quinn, Joe 87

Radbourne, Charles (Old Hoss) 33
Rankin, Wil 289
Raymer, Fred 48, 118, 142
Reese, Bonesetter 34
Reisling, Doc 48, 148
Reitz, Heinie 211
Reulbach, Ed 126, 128, 193, 198–9, 224, 230, 265, 271–2, 338
Rhoads, Bob (Dusty) 79, 101, 171, 242, 317
Rice, Sam 174
Rickey, Branch 249, 251–3, 319
Ritchey, Claude 35, 59, 116, 119, 206, 274–5, 292–3, 295
Ritter, Lawrence 110
Ritter, Lew 43, 147, 213, 287
Rixey, Eppa 174
Robinson, Clyde (Rabbit) 91, 100
Robinson, Jackie 253
Robinson, Wilbert 3, 186, 292
Robison, Frank DeHaas 3, 7, 41, 324

Robison, Stanley 3, 41, 142
Robitaille, Chick 125
Rogers, John I. 9
Rohe, George 159, 234, 265–7, 311–3
Rose, Pete 131, 177
Rossman, Claude 242–4, 301, 305–7, 338
Roth, Frank 50, 184, 237
Rusie, Amos 72, 320
Ruth, Babe 134, 177, 208
Ryan, Nolan 82
Ryder, Jack 109, 126, 135, 220, 291

Sanborn, Ira (Sy) 20, 74, 76–8, 125, 129, 141, 198, 200, 216, 278, 313, 315, 338–9
Scanlan, Doc 43, 49, 147, 214, 287
Schaefer, Herman (Germany) 90, 162–5, 254, 302, 306
Schlei, Admiral 30–2, 133, 288, 291
Schmidt, Charlie (Boss) 254, 301, 302, 336–7
Schmidt, Henry 15
Schrecongost, Ossee 82, 152, 154, 157, 188, 246, 252, 307, 310–1
Schulte, Frank (Wildfire) 125, 192–3, 196–7, 199, 270, 272, 336, 338
Schwartz, Bill 80
Scott, Ed 105
Sebring, Jimmy 35–6, 108–9, 133, 191–2, 205
Selbach, Kip 61, 65–6, 69, 71, 95, 166–7, 261–2
Selee, Frank 1, 14, 24–6, 28–9, 125–6, 128–9, 139, 194
Seybold, Ralph (Socks) 4, 63, 82, 152, 154, 246, 307, 310
Seymour, Cy 15, 30–1, 58, 133–5, 203, 218–20, 282, 290
Shannon, Mike (Spike) 37, 99, 136, 201, 203, 225, 282
Sharpe, Bud 143–4
Shay, Danny 29, 37–8, 136, 142
Sheckard, Jimmy 6, 42–7, 49, 147, 192–3, 195–7, 199–201, 217, 270, 337–8

360 Index

Sheehan, Tom C. 264
Sheehan, Tommy 206, 273–4
Siegle, Johnny 219
Siever, Ed 85, 254, 256, 302, 335
Singleton, Ken 177
Slagle, Jimmy 24, 27–8, 125, 193, 195–6, 199–200, 216–7, 265, 270, 337–8
Slattery, Jack 75
Smith, Aleck 202
Smith, Charlie 257, 333
Smith, Ed 249
Smith, Frank 76–7, 159, 233–4, 236, 312, 314
Smith, Fred 289
Smith, Harry 35
Smith, Tony 332
Snodgrass, Fred 110
Soden, Arthur H. 116
Spahn, Warren 41–2
Sparks, Frank (Tully) 51–2, 128, 130, 210, 277, 279–81
Spencer, Tubby 184, 249, 252, 324
Stahl, Chick 62, 65, 166–7, 251, 260, 328
Stahl, Jake 93, 95, 100, 181–3, 236, 245, 257, 259–60, 264
Stallings, George 76, 241
Staub, Rusty 176
Steinfeldt, Harry 15, 29–30, 32, 133, 191–7, 199–200, 265–6, 270, 336, 338
Stone, George 61, 89, 184, 239, 249–51, 256, 264, 324
Stovall, George 59, 79, 99, 171, 242–3, 317–9
Stovall, Jesse 91
Strang, Sammy 43, 111–3, 202, 205, 216–7, 282
Street, Gabby 144
Stricklett, Elmer 72, 102, 147, 149, 214, 278, 286–7
Sugden, Joe 85, 215
Sullivan, Billy 75–6, 159, 234, 237, 266, 311–2
Sullivan, Denny 329
Sullivan, John 164
Sutthoff, Jack 51–2, 130
Sweeney, Bill 293, 296

Tannehill, Jesse 13, 63–8, 70, 167–70, 261, 263, 279, 329–30

Tannehill, Lee 59, 75–6, 159, 161, 232, 234, 237, 265–6, 311, 313
Taylor, Brewery Jack 137
Taylor, Jack 14, 25, 37–8, 128, 136–42, 193, 199, 224, 271–2
Taylor, John I. 65, 332
Taylor, Luther (Dummy) 17, 20–2, 111, 197, 199, 202, 282
Tebeau, George 87
Tebeau, Patsy 87, 221, 324
Tenney, Fred 15, 29, 36, 47, 49–50, 58–61, 120, 142–4, 229, 293, 295–6
Thomas, Ira 238, 319
Thomas, Roy 50, 105, 129, 130–2, 209, 277, 298
Thompson, Gus 225
Thompson, Sam 172–3, 225
Thoney, Jack 70, 94
Tinker, Joe 14, 24–7, 125, 127, 193, 196–7, 199, 208, 265–6, 269–73, 337–8
Titus, John 50, 52, 129–32, 210, 277
Townsend, Jack 93, 101, 103, 182–3, 242
Triumvirs 142–3, 292
Tucker, Tom 252
Turner, Terry 79–80, 165, 171, 242–5, 317

Unglaub, Bob 65–6, 167, 329–30, 332

Van der Ahe, Chris 210
Van Haltren, George 18–9
Veil, Bucky 35
Vickers, Rube 308–9
Vila, Joe 239, 321–2
Vinson, Rube 233

Waddell, Rube 63, 82, 95, 99, 138, 152, 154–8, 161, 168, 186, 246–8, 279, 306–7, 309–11
Wagner, Heinie 329
Wagner, Honus 18–9, 29, 34–6, 52, 58–9, 107, 113, 118, 135, 195, 197, 206–8, 220, 273–6, 294–5, 315–7
Walker, Tom 30–1, 33, 101, 133
Wallace, Bobby 85, 184, 187, 249, 324

Walsh, Ed 72, 76–7, 151, 157, 159, 233–7, 248, 265–7, 303, 310, 312, 314–5
Ward, Joe 209
Ward, John Montgomery 55
Warner, John 8, 17, 136, 162, 166, 254–6, 335
Watkins, W.T. 216
Weimer, Jake 14, 25–6, 39, 126, 128, 191, 218, 289, 292
Welch, Curt 173
White, Guy Harris (Doc) 49, 76, 151, 155, 159, 164, 233–7, 265–7, 281, 312, 314
Wicker, Bob 14, 22, 25–6, 58, 126, 139, 199, 216, 218, 231
Wilhelm, Kaiser 48, 50, 142, 144
Willett, Ed 302
Williams, Jimmy 69–71, 178, 238, 319, 321–2
Williams, Otto 25
Williams, Phil 224
Willis, Vic 15, 47–8, 138, 142, 144, 206–7, 274, 276, 295–6
Wilson, Highball 94
Wiltse, George (Hooks) 17, 19–20, 22, 111, 114, 202, 282
Winter, George 65–7, 167, 261, 329
Wolfe, Barney 70–1, 93, 99, 182
Wolverton, Harry 50, 52, 142
Woodruff, Sam 30–2
Wright, Craig 208
Wright, Harry 210

Yager, Abe 28, 44–6, 148–9, 204, 217, 280, 288, 298–9, 316–7
Yastrzemski, Carl 172–3
Yeager, Joe 178, 238, 324
Young, Cy 26, 38, 41–2, 62, 65–9, 72, 88, 153, 156, 167–8, 261–3, 304, 324, 329–33
Young, Irv (Young Cy) 142, 144, 229–30, 293

Zimmer, Charles (Chief) 13, 21, 123
Zuber, Charley 192

www.ingramcontent.com/pod-product-compliance
Lightning Source LLC
Chambersburg PA
CBHW051205300426
44116CB00006B/450